GROWTH AND DISTRIBUTION

GROWTH
AND
DISTRIBUTION

W. A. Eltis

Fellow and Lecturer in Economics
Exeter College, Oxford

Macmillan

First published 1973 by
THE MACMILLAN PRESS LTD
London and Basingstoke
Associated companies in New York Dublin
Melbourne Johannesburg and Madras

SBN 333 14610 7

Printed in Great Britain by
T. AND A. CONSTABLE LTD
Edinburgh

‹ C

0- 333- 14610- 7

Contents

Preface

GROWTH theory has several objectives. At the practical level it is concerned with the explanation of the growth of the world's economies, and explanation can lead to prescription once the reasons for slow growth are understood. At the theoretical level growth theory must play a crucial role in any general theory of the working of economies. This must be dynamic if it is to be wholly satisfactory, which means that the relationships between investment, the potential for technical advance and growth must be fully taken into account. These relationships have a pervasive influence, and they will certainly have important effects on capital intensity, the profitability of firms and the distribution of the National Income. Ideally, growth theory will provide a plausible explanation of both historical growth rates and interconnections between the major economic variables.

The potential gain to economics from a satisfactory account of the growth process would obviously be very great, but economists are very far from this. Recent work on capital theory has undermined or at any rate questioned the theoretical foundations of neoclassical growth theory (and most modern econometric work on growth rests on this), while an alternative theoretical framework that is capable of producing a testable account of the growth process has not yet emerged.

There are several possible starting points for the work on growth theory which is now needed, for there are a number of elementary propositions about growth that are well known and understood – it is their relevance to the growth of real economies that is in doubt. For instance, if it is assumed that an economy produces a single good in conditions of perfect competition and constant returns to scale, then the fundamental neoclassical results that are outlined in Chapters 1 and 2 of the present book follow. The results of Chapter 3 follow with the further assumption that modern plant is technically superior to old plant, the efficiency of plant depending on the year of its construction or 'vintage'. Some fundamental Keynesian propositions about growth are outlined in Chapter 4 and these must play a part in a complete theory of growth, but they do not by themselves take the argument very far.

The unreal assumptions in the simple accounts of growth in these chapters cannot all be relaxed at the same time, for a theory that accurately reflects all the chaos of the real world must be as chaotic as the real world, but some of the unreal assumptions can be relaxed. Unfortunately, where particular assumptions are relaxed, others cannot be, so what will turn out to be the best way of making growth theory more realistic is very much an open question. Some of the effects of relaxing the assumption that an economy produces a single good are outlined in Chapter 5. This is the assumption in elementary neoclassical theory that has aroused most current controversy (it is not needed for the Keynesian theory of Chapter 4), and it is shown in Chapter 5 that certain basic neoclassical propositions will not necessarily follow (though they mostly will) once it is assumed that output is produced by a series of capital goods which are themselves manufactured in specified ways. While this may lead to reswitching in particular circumstances, 'orthodox' results should still follow in most cases. The assumption of heterogeneous capital and consumer goods greatly increases the complexity of the argument and especially its mathematical complexity, and this means that almost the entire scope for greater realism that is available from the relaxation of the assumptions of the early chapters must be devoted to the relaxation of the one-good assumption. A great deal of work is now being done on sophisticated models with heterogeneous capital goods, and much is likely to be achieved in this direction in the next decade. Testable propositions will need to emerge from such models if they are to be of real value, and it is to be hoped that these will be found.

It is obviously desirable to relax the one-good assumption, but this is not the only way in which growth theory can proceed. A possible alternative approach to a more realistic theory of growth is outlined in Part II of the present book where two of the unsatisfactory assumptions in elementary growth theory are relaxed, and the consequences of alternative assumptions worked through in a vintage model. The assumptions that are questioned are those that relate to the determination of the economy's rate of technical progress and its share of investment, which are both assumed to be exogenously given in elementary neoclassical theory. It is argued in the present book that an economy's rate of technical progress will vary with its share of investment in the National Income with the result that an economy with a higher share of investment will have a higher equilibrium rate of growth.[1] It is also argued that an economy's equilibrium rate of capital accumulation will depend on its rate of profit and the preferences of its entrepreneurs and wealth owners between capital accumulation and current consumption. In consequence, the economy's rate of technical progress and its share of investment in the National Income will both become variables and not exogenously given constants. The central feature of the growth model that follows with these new functions is that the economy's equilibrium rate of profit and its equilibrium rate of growth are simultaneously determined by the investment function and an investment opportunity function that is derived from the technical progress function and other relationships. It is shown that an economy with greater technical opportunities for growth than another will (*cet. par.*) have a higher equilibrium rate of growth and a higher rate of profit, while an economy with a stronger investment function will have a faster rate of growth and a lower rate of profit. Higher profits are associated with higher investment and faster growth, and there is a strong inter-relationship between profits, investment and growth. The model makes use of both neoclassical and neo-Keynesian propositions, but these are really classical results, and it is shown in Chapter 9 that Malthus's view of the growth process was very similar.

The model outlined in Part II is an equilibrium growth model, and it can only be used to make comparisons between economies in steady growth with different parameters. In Part III the model is extended to take account of problems in disequilibrium growth. The effects of increasing returns to scale are analysed in Chapter 11, and it is shown that these will apply a multiplier to growth from any other source, and they will also generally lead to a falling share of profits and a falling capital–output ratio. After this, the relationship between actual and equilibrium growth is analysed and it is argued that actual growth paths will often correspond quite closely to equilibrium growth paths. The various propositions about income distribution are brought together in Chapter 13 to produce a theory which owes much to both neoclassical and Keynesian theory. In this, distribution is influenced by technical factors, the market power of labour and capital, and Keynesian effective demand. The book concludes with

---

[1] In his review of R. M. Solow, *Growth Theory: An Exposition* (Oxford U. P., 1970), M. Inagaki suggests that precisely this change should be made to make neoclassical theory more realistic. (*Journal of Economic Literature*, vol. x, June 1972, p. 469.)

A*

an account of some of the policy implications of the argument, which include some new propositions about the taxation of profits and wealth which follow from the analysis of wealth owners' preferences and their influence on the investment function in Part II.

Whether the model's principal innovations, the technical progress function, the investment function and the analysis of increasing returns to scale, are useful is something that only rigorous testing can show. Certainly the model passes the crude test of 'stylised' facts which Kaldor has suggested that all growth models should pass.[1] In Kaldor's version of the stylised facts, all models should produce constant capital–output ratios, constant shares of profit and constant rates of profit, but the share of profits has fallen fairly continuously in the U.S.A. and the U.K. since 1900, and the capital–output ratio has fallen fairly continuously in the U.S.A.[2] To keep in line with these stylised facts, a model should ideally produce a falling capital–output ratio and a falling share of profits, and in addition, it should be capable of explaining the well-known evidence that fast-growing economies have higher shares of investment, higher shares of profit and lower capital–output ratios than slow-growing economies.[3] These results all follow from the model that is outlined in this book.

A problem which all authors of books on growth theory must face is how much mathematics to use. In this book I have avoided the use of anything more difficult than partial differentiation in most of the chapters in the hope that this will make the book widely accessible, and many of the main propositions are established diagrammatically. There are, however, a few problems, especially those associated with vintage growth theory and reswitching, where the use of more difficult (or more tedious) mathematics is inevitable. The passages in question (in Chapters 3, 5, 7, 10 and 11) are preceded by an asterisk, and some readers may prefer to omit them. They will only lose a small fraction of the argument if they do this. An equally difficult problem is how much basic knowledge of growth theory to take for granted. I have decided to provide an exposition of very basic neoclassical and neo-Keynesian growth theory in the early chapters, which should be particularly useful to those who are not already thoroughly familiar with growth theory. Those who are will

[1] See N. Kaldor, 'Capital accumulation and economic growth', in F. A. Lutz and D. C. Hague (eds.), *The Theory of Capital* (Macmillan, 1961) pp. 178-9.
[2] See p. 266 below.
[3] See Kaldor, op. cit., who cites some of these further relationships, and p. 215 below.

gain little from Chapters 1, 2, the early part of 3 and 4, but the remaining chapters all contain new lines of argument.

This book has taken a long time to evolve. I first used the technical progress and investment functions which play a central role in the book in articles which appeared in 1963 and 1968, but I became convinced that the full effects of these functions could only be worked through in a book. I owe the time I needed to write much of this one to Professor R. T. Appleyard of the University of Western Australia, where I spent a sabbatical year in 1970. He asked me to do negligible teaching, and he gave me secretarial assistance on a scale which is almost unknown in Oxford. The chapters that I wrote in Australia were read by Professor G. C. Harcourt, Professor I. I. Bowen, Dr R. Gabbay and Mr R. W. Peters, and I benefited greatly from their comments, and from the comments I received when I read papers based on some of the chapters in the Universities of Adelaide, Melbourne, Monash, New South Wales and Newcastle. I completed the book in Oxford on my return where I received invaluable help from Mr J. S. Flemming and Mr M. FG. Scott, who read early drafts of all the chapters and made innumerable helpful suggestions. I owe the title of the book, the titles of the parts and much else besides to Mr Scott. At a very late stage, Professor J. A. Mirrlees read the vintage growth chapter and pointed out a vital mistake in the mathematics. I am also grateful to Mr R. Van Noorden, Mr C. A. B. Peacocke and Mr C. R. Smallwood for helpful comments on various chapters. The responsibility for the errors that remain is entirely mine.

Chapter 6 appeared in a slightly different version in the *Economic Journal* in September 1971, and I am grateful to the Editors for permission to reprint the article, and I am also grateful to the Editors of *Oxford Economic Papers* for permission to reproduce passages from articles which appeared there.

September 1972 W. A. ELTIS

PART I

Neoclassical and Neo-Keynesian Growth Theory

1

Marginal Productivity and Growth

MARGINAL PRODUCTIVITY theory plays a central role in neo-classical growth theory. It has also been much used in empirical work to identify the factors responsible for growth, for if marginal productivity theory is accepted in its entirety, the contribution of particular factors of production to growth can be derived quite straightforwardly from published statistics.[1] With no other theory can it be claimed that the contribution of, for instance, engineers to the growth rate can be measured. However, according to *simpliste* marginal productivity theory where perfect competition in factor and product markets is assumed, their contribution will be precisely the rate of increase in an economy's 'stock' of engineers, times the share of the National Income which engineers receive. Much skill and ingenuity may be needed to estimate these, because this information may not be published in precisely the form needed for the calculation. However, this kind of calculation is relatively straightforward.

In this chapter the basis of the relationship between marginal productivity theory and growth, and the assumptions on which it is based, will be outlined, and two of the mathematical production functions based on the theory, the Cobb–Douglas and the 'Constant Elasticity of Substitution' or CES production functions, will be explained together with some of the results which follow from them.

The Relationship between Marginal Productivity and Growth

In this part of the chapter a number of elementary neoclassical propositions will be outlined, and the basic proposition that the contribution

[1] Perhaps the most notable uses of marginal productivity theory to explain past growth are *Why Growth Rates Differ: Postwar Experience in Nine Western Countries*, by Edward F. Denison, assisted by Jean-Pierre Poullier (Washington, D.C.: Brookings Institution, 1967); and D. W. Jorgensen and Z. Griliches, 'The explanation of productivity change', *Review of Economic Studies*, vol. XXXIV (July 1967).

each factor of production makes to growth will equal its own rate of growth times the share of the National Income it receives will be explained first. It will be assumed throughout the chapter that capital and what it produces can be measured in the same units. The problems that arise when this assumption is relaxed will be discussed in Chapter 5.

The marginal product of a factor of production is the increase in total production, i.e. the growth in production, which is due to the use of an extra unit of it. If, for initial simplicity, it is first assumed that labour and capital are the only factors of production, and that growth is entirely due to increases in the quantity of these, the growth in output, ΔY, over a *very short* period will be the increase in the labour force in that period, ΔL, times the marginal product of labour, $\partial Y/\partial L$, plus the increase in the capital stock, ΔK, times the marginal product of capital, $\partial Y/\partial K$, i.e.

$$\Delta Y = \Delta L \cdot \frac{\partial Y}{\partial L} + \Delta K \cdot \frac{\partial Y}{\partial K}. \qquad (1.1)$$

If there are n factors of production, $a_1 \ldots a_n$, the growth in output will be the sum of the increase in the quantity of each factor times its marginal product, i.e.

$$\Delta Y = \Delta a_1 \cdot \frac{\partial Y}{\partial a_1} + \Delta a_2 \cdot \frac{\partial Y}{\partial a_2} + \ldots + \Delta a_n \cdot \frac{\partial Y}{\partial a_n}. \qquad (1.2)$$

$\Delta a_1 \ldots \Delta a_n$ can be measured fairly straightforwardly, but there is no simple and direct way of measuring $\partial Y/\partial a_1 \ldots \partial Y/\partial a_n$, the marginal products of factors $a_1 \ldots a_n$. The simplest approach to the measurement of $\partial Y/\partial a_1 \ldots \partial Y/\partial a_n$ follows from the assumption that factors of production are paid their marginal products, for ample statistics are generally available on what factors of production are paid. They will be paid their marginal products provided that there is perfect competition in factor and product markets, and that entrepreneurs push their use of factors to the point of profit maximisation. With these assumptions, $\partial Y/\partial a_1$ will equal w_1 where w_1 is the rate of remuneration of factor a_1, $\partial Y/\partial a_2$ will equal w_2, and so on. Substituting in (1.2):

$$\Delta Y = \Delta a_1 \cdot w_1 + \Delta a_2 \cdot w_2 + \ldots + \Delta a_n \cdot w_n. \qquad (1.3)$$

Every term in (1.3) can be measured quite straightforwardly, but (1.3) (unlike (1.2)) is based on the arbitrary assumptions of entrepreneurial rationality and perfect competition in factor and product markets. From (1.3) it follows that:

$$\frac{\Delta Y}{Y} = \frac{\Delta a_1 . w_1}{Y} + \frac{\Delta a_2 . w_2}{Y} + ... + \frac{\Delta a_n . w_n}{Y} \qquad (1.4)$$

i.e.

$$\frac{\Delta Y}{Y} = \frac{\Delta a_1}{A_1} . \frac{w_1 . A_1}{Y} + \frac{\Delta a_2}{A_2} . \frac{w_2 . A_2}{Y} + ... + \frac{\Delta a_n}{A_n} . \frac{w_n . A_n}{Y} \qquad (1.5)$$

where $A_1 ... A_n$ are the quantities of $a_1 ... a_n$. $(\Delta Y/Y)$ is g, the rate of growth of the National Product, while $\Delta a_1/A_1 ... \Delta a_n/A_n$ are the rates of growth of $a_1 ... a_n$, and these can be written as $g_1 ... g_n$. Moreover, $(w_1 . A_1)/Y ... (w_n . A_n)/Y$ are the shares of the National Income received by $a_1 ... a_n$, and these can be written as $X_1 ... X_n$. Then:

$$g = g_1 . X_1 + g_2 . X_2 + ... + g_n . X_n. \qquad (1.6)$$

Thus the contribution to the growth rate which is made by each factor of production is its own rate of growth times the share of the National Income it receives.

One question about the marginal productivity theory of distribution on which this result is based is whether it is in fact possible for each factor to be paid its marginal product. There might be too little total product to pay each factor its marginal product, or there might be produce left over. It can be shown quite simply that the payment of its marginal product to each factor of production will just exhaust total output where returns to scale are constant.

Suppose, for simplicity, that labour and machines are the only factors of production, and that 100 workers plus 100 machines produce 1,000. Suppose now that one extra worker and one extra machine is used, and that this raises total output from 1,000 to 1,010, i.e. by 10. Then the marginal product of a *worker and machine* is 10. There are now 101 workers and 101 machines, and if each *worker and machine* receives its marginal product, workers and machines will receive 101 × 10 or 1,010 altogether. This works out right since total output is 1,010.

But what if the addition of one worker and one machine raises total output from 1,000 to 1,009 or to 1,011? Then the marginal product of a *worker and machine* will be 9 or 11, and if workers and machines receive their marginal products, they will receive 101 × 9 = 909, or 101 × 11 = 1,111, which is too little or too much.

The case which worked out right was the constant returns to scale case where a 1 per cent increase in workers and machines raised output 1 per cent from 1,000 to 1,010.[1] Where it raised output 0·9 or 1·1 per cent, there would be too much or too little total output to pay both factors their marginal products. Thus the assumption of constant returns to scale (as well as the assumptions of perfect competition in product and factor markets) is implicit in an equation like (1.6) which states that the growth rate will be the sum of the rate of growth of each factor times its share of the National Income. With increasing returns to scale and/or imperfect competition, factors may be paid much less than their marginal products, so the effect on the growth rate of, for instance, increased employment of engineers may much exceed the actual increase in the incomes of engineers.

Until quite recently it was assumed by most marginal productivity theorists that increases in factor supplies were entirely responsible for growth. Thus there could be no growth in an economy where the quantities of labour, capital and other factors of production were constant. This assumption is implicit in (1.6). Solow's empirical study which suggested that only $12\frac{1}{2}$ per cent of U.S. growth in labour productivity from 1909 to 1949 was due to increases in capital per worker, while $87\frac{1}{2}$ per cent was due to shifts in the production function quite independent of increases in labour and capital, did much to shatter this position.[2]

It is now customary to assume that there will be technical progress in an economy permitting growth which may be independent of any increase in labour, capital or other factors of production. Technical progress may raise the marginal products of some or all factors of production. Where it raises the marginal products of all factors in the same proportion it may be described as 'Hicks-neutral'.[3] If m is the rate of Hicks-neutral technical progress, the growth rate will be

[1] This is simply a special case of Euler's theorem which shows that total product is exhausted when all factors receive their marginal products with all production functions which are homogeneous to the first degree. See, for instance, Joan Robinson, 'Euler's theorem and the problem of distribution', *Economic Journal*, vol. XLIV (Sep 1934).

[2] R. M. Solow, 'Technical change and the aggregate production function', *Review of Economics and Statistics*, vol. XXXIX (Aug 1957).

[3] J. R. Hicks, *The Theory of Wages* (Macmillan, 1932) p. 121. Here he defined technical progress as neutral where it raised the marginal products of labour and capital, the two factors he was considering, in the same proportion. The equivalent assumption with more than two factors is that the marginal product of each factor is increased in the same proportion.

the sum of m and the growth made possible by increases in factor supplies, i.e.

$$g = m + g_1 . X_1 + g_2 . X_2 + ... + g_n . X_n. \qquad (1.7)$$

This equation attempts to show the effect of technical progress and increased factor supplies on the growth rate, so it will explain growth in so far as this is the *consequence* of the growth of the various factors of production, but it does not attempt to explain the ultimate causes of growth, namely what causes the supply of factors to grow, i.e. what determines $g_1...g_n$ and m. Complete theories of the working of an economy and the determination of its growth rate have naturally attempted to take the argument further. For instance, what follows is an approach which will be developed considerably in Part II of this book.

A Malthusian argument, starting from (1.7), might go as follows. Technical progress raises the marginal products of labour and capital (and presumably of other factors), and it will therefore raise the wage, the rate of return on capital, the rent of land, etc. If wages rise as a result of technical progress, population will grow more quickly because people will marry younger, have more children, and a higher proportion of these children will survive. With faster population growth, there will be faster growth of the labour force, and this, taken by itself, will tend to reduce the marginal product of labour and the wage. In the long run, a Malthusian would expect the favourable effects of technical progress on the marginal product of labour, and the unfavourable effects of population growth, more or less to cancel out, with the result that wages would remain at a kind of subsistence level, while population would always rise at the rate needed to keep wages at that level. Thus while technical progress would raise the marginal products of both labour and capital *ab initio*, it would appear *ex post* as if only the marginal product of capital had risen. Wages would then be roughly constant from generation to generation, and the rate of return on capital would rise continuously. Population would grow *pari passu* with output, and increased employment would then be immediately responsible for a good deal of the growth that took place, but the ultimate cause of growth would be the technical progress which made increased population growth possible.

An argument of this kind might have appeared quite plausible early in the nineteenth century, but a prediction that population growth would keep pace with increased production, preventing any rise in the marginal product of labour, would have been poor. It might now be argued that for developed economies, at any rate, there is no clear functional relationship between the real wage and the rate of population growth. However, a reversal of the Malthusian argument so that Malthus's theory of population applies to capital instead of to labour might explain much that has happened. Malthus was aware of this possibility, for he wrote in 1820:

> The laws which regulate the rate of profits and the progress of capital, bear a very striking and singular resemblance to the laws which regulate the rate of wages and the progress of population . . . a further proof of [this] is to be found in the rapidity with which the loss of capital is recovered during a war which does not interrupt commerce. The loans to government convert capital into revenue, and increase demand at the same time that they at first diminish the means of supply. The necessary consequence must be an increase of profits. This naturally increases both the power and the reward of accumulation; and if only the same habits of saving prevail among the capitalists as before, the recovery of the lost stock must be rapid, just for the same kind of reason that the recovery of population is so rapid when, by some cause or other, it has been suddenly destroyed.[1]

It may well be that capital accumulates at a rate depending upon the rate of profit, for the reasons that Malthus suggests. Where the rate of profit is high, firms will plough back a great deal of this profit which will rapidly increase the capital stock, and they will have strong motives to do so. In a sense, capital 'breeds' rapidly where the rate of profit is high. Where it is low, there will be little profit to plough back, and the motive to reinvest profits will be slight, so the rate of capital accumulation will be low. Initially, technical progress will raise the marginal products of labour and capital, but the rising marginal product of capital will result in a rising rate of profit which will lead to increased capital accumulation which will depress the marginal product of capital again. In the long run, the tendency of technical progress to raise the marginal product of capital, and of consequent capital accumulation to depress it, may more or less cancel out (for reasons which will be discussed in detail in Part II of this book). Then capital will receive a rate of return that does not persistently

[1] T. R. Malthus, *Principles of Political Economy* (London, 1820) pp. 370, 373-4.

rise or fall, but the wage will rise continuously, for technical progress will raise the marginal product of labour and therefore the wage, and the capital accumulation consequent upon technical progress will raise it further. With a Malthusian relationship of this kind between the rate of profit and the rate of capital accumulation, output and capital will grow at about the same rate in the very long run. Technical progress will be the ultimate cause of this growth, and the capital accumulation consequent upon it will reinforce the growth due to technical progress.

If technical progress is as important as this, the causes of growth are hardly explained if what determines technical progress is left unexplained. Much attention has been devoted to this problem. One approach, and this has been the approach of marginal productivity theorists, has been to attempt to reduce the unexplained element in technical progress by attributing as much of it as possible to factor inputs. If, for instance, technical progress is largely the result of education or industrial research and development, the benefits from these, or their marginal products, might be thought to depend upon what is spent. Jorgensen and Griliches have managed to eliminate residual technical progress altogether from their statistical estimates of what determined growth in the U.S. economy from 1945 to 1965 by allowing for the effect of education, and for a number of other effects.[1]

There are other approaches to the determination of the rate of technical progress which will be discussed in detail in the second part of this book. It may be that there is a strong interconnection between capital accumulation and technical progress, with the causation coming from capital accumulation.[2] Alternatively, much of the observed increase in productivity that appears to be due to technical progress may really be due to economies of scale.[3] What determines the rate of technical progress is clearly one of the central questions in growth theory, and it is very much an open question.

It needs to be remembered that the principal marginal productivity

[1] Jorgensen and Griliches, op. cit.
[2] See, for instance, N. Kaldor, 'A model of economic growth', *Economic Journal*, vol. LXVII (Dec 1957); Joan Robinson, *Essays in the Theory of Economic Growth* (Macmillan, 1962) II, 'A model of accumulation'; and K. J. Arrow, 'The economic implications of learning by doing', *Review of Economic Studies*, vol. XXIX (June 1962).
[3] J. R. Hicks, 'Thoughts on the theory of capital – the Corfu Conference', *Oxford Economic Papers*, vol. XII (June 1960).

growth equation (1.7) depends upon the particular assumptions which have been made. These are that competition is perfect in factor and product markets, that returns to scale are constant, and that entrepreneurs push their use of factors to the point of profit maximisation. (1.7) will give an imperfect account of what determines growth, to a greater or lesser extent, where these assumptions are unrealistic. There is no doubt that imperfections in competition are widespread in factor and product markets. There is much evidence of increasing returns to scale in industry.[1] There are many areas in an economy which are not run by profit-maximising entrepreneurs. Given this, it would be most surprising if statistical work based on (1.7) was particularly accurate unless these complications were allowed for in some way or other. Econometricians have shown great ingenuity in their attempts to allow for these effects, but it is to be questioned whether it will ever be possible to derive satisfactory results which explain, for instance, the economic rate of return from education from statistics on what the educated are paid when many of them are employed by non-profit-maximising government departments, armed services, publicly owned industries and local education authorities. In addition, the markets for teachers and doctors are highly imperfect, and the employment of scientists and engineers in industry may be intimately associated with the ability to exploit technical progress.

On the other hand, it must always be remembered that almost all propositions in elementary economic theory rest on unreal assumptions. Most simple accounts of a problem will be inaccurate for this reason, and the question is how close a simple account comes to what happens in actual economies, and how readily unreal assumptions can be corrected for. Many have found marginal productivity theory a useful starting-point for the analysis of real economies.

The Cobb–Douglas Production Function

The simplest mathematical function which can be used to produce some of the results of marginal productivity theory is the Cobb–Douglas production function[2]:

$$Y_t = \beta . e^{mt} . K_t^{\alpha} . L_t^{1-\alpha} \tag{1.8}$$

[1] See, for instance, P. J. D. Wiles, *Price, Cost and Output*, 2nd ed. (Blackwell, 1961) appendix to chap. 12; and A. A. Walters, 'Production and cost functions', *Econometrica*, vol. XXXI (Jan–Apr 1963).

[2] The Cobb–Douglas production function was first formulated independently by Knut Wicksell, *Lectures on Political Economy* (Routledge & Kegan Paul, 1934;

where Y_t, K_t and L_t are output, the capital stock and the labour force at time t; β is a constant, and m is the rate of Hicks-neutral technical progress. α, the capital exponential, is the Cobb–Douglas production function's principal parameter.

The marginal products of labour and capital which equal the rate of profit (r) and the wage (w) where factors receive their marginal products, are obtained by differentiating (1.8) with respect to K and L. Thus:

$$r = \frac{\partial Y}{\partial K} = \alpha . \frac{Y}{K} \tag{1.9}$$

$$w = \frac{\partial Y}{\partial L} = (1-\alpha) . \frac{Y}{L}. \tag{1.10}$$

It is to be noted that the rate of profit is always α times the output–capital ratio (or α/V where V is the capital–output ratio), and that the wage is always $(1-\alpha)$ times output per worker.

Where factors receive their marginal products, the K units of capital in the economy will each earn a rate of return of $\alpha . (Y/K)$, so aggregate profits will be $\alpha . Y$ which means that the share of profits in the National Income will always be α. Thus:

$$X_p = \alpha. \tag{1.11}$$

Similarly, if L workers each receive a wage of $(1-\alpha) . (Y/L)$, aggregate wages will be $(1-\alpha) . Y$, and the share of wages will be $(1-\alpha)$. Then:

$$X_w = 1-\alpha. \tag{1.12}$$

It will be noted that $(X_p + X_w) = 1$, so the National Income is entirely accounted for by the sum of wages and profits. This result is arrived at because returns to scale are constant in (1.8), for a z times increase in labour and capital will raise output z times.[1] Returns to scale are constant because the sum of the capital and labour exponentials, α and $(1-\alpha)$, is unity. There will be increasing returns if the sum of these exceeds 1 (the effects of this will be analysed

---

the Lectures were published in Sweden in 1901) vol. I, pp. 128, 286; and C. W. Cobb and Paul H. Douglas, 'A theory of production', *American Economic Review*, supplement, vol. XVIII (Mar 1928). The e^{mt} term to take account of the possibility of technical progress is a more recent addition to the original Wicksell and Cobb–Douglas production function.

[1] A z times increase in labour and capital will raise output from

$$\beta . e^{mt} . K^\alpha . L^{1-\alpha} \text{ to } \beta . e^{mt} . (zK)^\alpha . (zL)^{1-\alpha} = \beta . e^{mt} . K^\alpha . L^{1-\alpha} . (z^{\alpha+1-\alpha}) =$$
$$(\beta . e^{mt} . K^\alpha . L^{1-\alpha}) . z.$$

in Chapter 11), and there will then be insufficient total output to pay both factors their marginal products. Conversely, there will be diminishing returns if the sum of the exponentials is less than 1, and there will then be produce left over after factors have received their marginal products. The simple case is of course the constant returns one where the exponentials are α and $(1-\alpha)$, and factors can then receive their marginal products, the share of profits in the National Income always being α, and the share of wages $(1-\alpha)$.

The property that X_p always equals the constant, α, and $X_w (1-\alpha)$ follows from the assumption implicit in the Cobb–Douglas production function that σ, the elasticity of substitution between labour and capital, is unity.[1] This means that a proportional increase in capital relatively to labour will lead to an equi-proportional fall in the marginal product of capital relatively to the marginal product of labour. The fact that the relative prices of the two factors of production always change in exactly the same proportion (and in the opposite direction) to their relative quantities means that their shares of the National Income, α and $(1-\alpha)$, can never change. Nothing that happens to a Cobb–Douglas economy can change α and the shares of profits and wages, and this result follows from the arbitrary assumption (which makes (1.8) much simpler than it otherwise would be) that σ is unity.

The rate of growth of the economy is found by differentiating (1.8) with respect to t:

$$\frac{1}{Y} \cdot \frac{dY}{dt} = m + \alpha \cdot \frac{1}{K} \cdot \frac{dK}{dt} + (1-\alpha) \cdot \frac{1}{L} \cdot \frac{dL}{dt}$$

or, writing g for $(1/Y) \cdot (dY/dt)$, the rate of growth of output, k for the rate of growth of capital and n for the rate of growth of the labour force:

$$g = m + \alpha \cdot k + (1-\alpha) \cdot n. \tag{1.13}$$

This result is a special case of (1.7) for just two factors, labour and capital.

These are some of the properties of the Cobb–Douglas production

[1] The concept of the 'elasticity of substitution between labour and capital' was first formulated independently by Hicks, in his *Theory of Wages*, and Joan Robinson, *The Economics of Imperfect Competition* (Macmillan, 1933) pp. vii, 330. By Joan Robinson's definition, σ is 'the proportionate change in the ratio of the amounts of the factors divided by the proportionate change in the ratio of their marginal physical productivities'. The mathematical derivation of a formula for σ is to be found in Hicks, *Theory of Wages*, pp. 242-5.

function. Its weaknesses result from the arbitrary nature of the assumptions on which it is based. For instance, there is no reason to expect σ to be unity in the real world, and the Cobb–Douglas will give inaccurate results to the extent that it is less than or greater than unity.

The other weaknesses of the Cobb–Douglas are mainly those which follow from the assumptions on which marginal productivity theory is based, and these have already been referred to. The weakness that there are only two factors of production can readily be removed with a multi-factor Cobb–Douglas: suppose that factors $a_1 \ldots a_n$ are available in quantities $A_1 \ldots A_n$; then:

$$Y = \beta . e^{mt} . A_1^{x_1} . A_2^{x_2} \ldots A_n^{x_n} \qquad (1.14)$$

where $(x_1 + x_2 + \ldots + x_n) = 1$. This will produce essentially the same results as (1.8) to (1.13).

The weakness of an elasticity of substitution between labour and capital of unity is overcome in a more complex production function – the Constant Elasticity of Substitution or CES production function which is discussed below.

The CES Production Function

In the early 1960s a production function began to be used which had most of the properties of the Cobb–Douglas and which, in addition, allowed for an elasticity of substitution between labour and capital (σ) which differed from unity.[1] This function, the CES production function, is restricted to the extent that (as its name suggests) σ must take the same value for all combinations of labour and capital, but σ can take any value. (1.15) is a CES production function with Hicks-neutral technical progress and constant returns to scale.

$$Y_t = \lambda . e^{mt} (h . K_t^{-u} + (1-h) . L_t^{-u})^{-1/u}. \qquad (1.15)$$

λ is a constant, and Y_t, K_t, L_t and m are defined as in previous equations. The new parameters are h and u, where h indicates the degree to which the technology is capital-intensive, and

$$u = \frac{1}{\sigma} - 1.$$

[1] Kenneth J. Arrow, H. B. Chenery, B. Minhas and R. M. Solow, 'Capital–labour substitution and economic efficiency', *Review of Economics and Statistics*, vol. XLIII (Aug 1961); and Murray Brown and J. S. de Cani, 'Technological change and the distribution of income', *International Economic Review*, Vol. IV (Sep 1963).

The marginal products of capital and labour which equal the rate of profit and the wage where factors receive their marginal products, are found by differentiating (1.15) with respect to K and L. Thus:

$$r = \frac{\partial Y}{\partial K} = \frac{Y}{K} \cdot \frac{1}{1 + \left(\frac{1-h}{h}\right) \cdot \left(\frac{K}{L}\right)^{(1/\sigma - 1)}} \qquad (1.16)$$

$$w = \frac{\partial Y}{\partial L} = \frac{Y}{L} \cdot \frac{1}{1 + \left(\frac{h}{1-h}\right)\left(\frac{K}{L}\right)^{(1 - 1/\sigma)}}. \qquad (1.17)$$

If the rate of profit equals the marginal product of capital, total profits will be K times this, and the share of profits in the National Income (X_p) will be K/Y times the marginal product of capital. Then, from (1.16):

$$X_p = \frac{1}{1 + \left(\frac{1-h}{h}\right) \cdot \left(\frac{K}{L}\right)^{(1/\sigma - 1)}}. \qquad (1.18)$$

Similarly, if the wage equals the marginal product of labour, total wages will be L times this, and the share of wages in the National Income (X_w) will be L/Y times the marginal product of labour. Then, from (1.17):

$$X_w = \frac{1}{1 + \left(\frac{h}{1-h}\right) \cdot \left(\frac{K}{L}\right)^{(1 - 1/\sigma)}}. \qquad (1.19)$$

$(X_p + X_w) = 1$, so the National Product is exactly accounted for by the sum of wages and profits where each factor receives its marginal product. This is to be expected with a constant returns to scale production function.

It is to be noted that X_p and X_w will only be constant if either K/L is constant, or $\sigma = 1$. If σ is less than 1, and K/L grows with the passage of time as a result of economic growth, X_p will fall, and X_w will rise. Conversely, if σ exceeds 1 and K/L grows, X_p will increase and X_w decline. These results are to be expected.

The rate of growth of the economy is found by differentiating (1.15) with respect to t. When X_p and X_w are substituted for the expressions in (1.18) and (1.19), the following standard marginal productivity result is again arrived at:

$$g = m + X_p.k + X_w.n. \tag{1.20}$$

These are some of the properties of the CES production function. It can take account of everything the Cobb–Douglas takes account of, and in addition it can allow for a σ which differs from unity. Its weaknesses will be those which follow from the assumptions on which marginal productivity theory is based, and in addition it is, of course, quite arbitrary to assume that σ will be the same for all combinations of labour and capital; though this is preferable to assuming that σ is always one.

Production with Fixed Coefficients

The elasticity of substitution between factors of production which the CES production function takes account of may sometimes be of great importance, and an economy with very low factor substitutability will differ in many of its fundamentals from an economy with high factor substitutability. If the elasticity of substitution between factors is reasonably high, growth will not be much inhibited by shortages of one of the factors of production. It will always be possible to substitute other factors for the scarce factor. It will also follow that no one factor is likely to be responsible for a high proportion of growth. Each factor will play a part which will depend upon its own rate of growth and its share of the National Income. This may sometimes give an unreal account of the contribution of the various factors of production to growth, for it may be necessary to combine certain (or all) factors in given proportions. If this is the case, a lack of just one of these factors will prevent the full utilisation of the others. An increase in the supply of the scarce factor will then have a disproportionate effect on the growth rate, for it will permit increased supplies of the other factors to be used.

An extreme and very simple case of non-substitutability of factors of production is the case of fixed coefficients. It could be assumed that the elasticity of substitution between the various factors of production is zero. Then production would require a precise combination of factors, and the supply of any factors in excess of the amounts needed to combine with the others would make no contribution whatsoever to growth. The marginal product of such factors would be zero, and in a perfectly competitive world their share of the

National Income would become zero, and their contribution to growth would be zero in terms of the standard marginal productivity equations.

Suppose that there are three factors of production, labour, machines and engineers, and that one worker is needed to work each machine, and that one engineer is needed for every hundred machines. If there are 12 million workers, 11 million machines and 120,000 engineers, it is evident that 1 million workers and 10,000 engineers will be unemployed, for given that there are only 11 million machines, work can only be found for 11 million workers and 110,000 engineers. The effective constraint (or bottleneck) on production will be machines, and the other factors will not be fully usable until more machines are produced.

So far as growth is concerned, the slowest-growing factor will set the ultimate limit to the rate of growth. Suppose there are initially 10 million workers, 10 million machines and 100,000 engineers so that their combination is just right for full employment. Suppose also that the supply of workers and machines increases by 2 per cent per annum, while the supply of engineers increases by only 1 per cent per annum. Then, after a year, there will be 10,200,000 workers and machines, and only 101,000 engineers. Given the assumed factor proportions, only 10,100,000 workers and machines will be able to produce if there are only 101,000 engineers, so the growth rate of output and employment will be 1 per cent, the rate of growth of the slowest-growing factor, engineers. Any growth of workers and machines in excess of 1 per cent simply results in unemployment and underutilisation. If a way was found of increasing the supply of engineers by 2 per cent instead of 1 per cent per annum, the country's growth rate would double, and looked at from a certain point of view, the contribution to growth made by 1 per cent growth in engineers would be a full 1 per cent. The three factors together contribute this 1 per cent, but without engineers the contributions of the others would be useless.

According to the basic marginal productivity growth equation (1.7), if engineers receive only $\frac{1}{2}$ per cent of the National Income (and they might receive as little as this in conditions of imperfect competition), 1 per cent growth in the number of engineers will only contribute 0·005 per cent to the growth of the National Product. This brings out how enormously the assumption of fixed coefficients can increase the possible importance of individual factors of production.

A factor which receives a very small share of the National Income may act as a bottleneck which prevents the full utilisation of other factors which receive higher income shares, and slow growth of the bottleneck factor will keep the economy's growth rate low. An increase in its rate of growth would then permit an equivalent increase in the rate of growth of total production, which might mean that an economy could raise its growth quite cheaply if it could identify such bottleneck factors and increase their supply.

It will be seen that whether there are fixed coefficients or whether there is reasonable substitutability between factors will have a considerable influence upon growth theory (and policy). The assumption of fixed coefficients leads to input–output analysis and linear programming, and a great deal of work has been done on models which follow from such assumptions. The case for detailed national planning and state intervention may also be strengthened in a world where the supply of factors of production amounting to quite a small proportion of a nation's resources has a considerable effect on the wealth of all.

Of course, the real question in any situation is whether there are indeed only slight possibilities for factor substitution, but it will be clear that this is an important question, and that the absence of substitutability between factors will have far-reaching effects.

Embodied and Disembodied Technical Progress

It was argued in the last section that marginal productivity theory would give a misleading account of the growth process if factors of production were not substitutable for each other, i.e. if there was strong complementarity between factors of production. Another equally important possibility is that there might be complementarity between technical progress and various factors of production, and particularly between technical progress and investment.

It has been assumed up to this point in the argument that technical progress will raise output at a rate of m whatever the rate of increase in the supply of other factors. It may be, however, that technical progress is often due to better designed plant, or a revolutionary change in production processes requiring an entirely different kind of plant which might frequently produce entirely new products. It would be impossible to exploit the potential for growth which is due to technical progress in such cases without investment, for the technical advances need to be *embodied* in new plant. Then capital accumulation and technical progress would be complementary, and the growth which was due to investment would include some of the benefits which followed from technical progress, in addition to those which were simply due to capital accumulation.

This is important because the contribution which investment makes to growth may be much understated until this is understood. According to the theory presented up to this point in the argument, the growth which is due to investment will be $k . X_p$, the rate of growth of capital times the share of profits in the National Income. If k is 4 per cent in a typical developed economy, and X_p is 0·25, the growth due to investment will be something like 1 per cent per annum. According to E. F. Denison, from 1950 to 1962 investment contributed 0·51 per cent to the U.K.'s growth rate of 2·29 per cent per annum, 0·83 per cent to the U.S.A.'s growth rate of 3·32 per cent, 1·41 per cent to West Germany's growth rate of 7·26 per cent, and 0·70 per cent to Italy's growth rate of 5·96 per cent.[1] It is unlikely that many would argue that West Germany's and Italy's growth rates would have been 5·85 and 5·26 per cent per annum respectively if their net investment had been zero, but that is the implication of Denison's analysis. Part of this West German and Italian growth would arguably not have occurred if these economies had invested less and therefore had less opportunity to take advantage of technical advances, and indeed to exploit economies of large-scale production which also require investment.

This is not to say that all technical advances need to be embodied in new plant. Some will be exploitable without investment, and such technical progress is usually referred to as disembodied technical progress. This will have the effect on the economy that has already been analysed, for the m of equation (1.7) is disembodied technical progress. The part of technical progress which needs to be embodied in new plant requires a different kind of analysis which makes the benefits from investment depend upon the year in which the investment is made. Technical progress causes the benefits from new investment to rise through time, and investment and technical progress are thus complementary.

This type of analysis of the growth process has been called 'vintage' growth theory, because the benefits from investment depend upon

1 Denison, *Why Growth Rates Differ*, chap. 21.

its 'vintage', i.e. the year in which the investment is made. Some of the main features of 'vintage' growth theory will be outlined in Chapter 3, and considerable use will be made of 'vintage' models in the remainder of this book.

Conclusion

It will be clear that much can be made of marginal productivity theory if its assumptions are accepted; or if the inaccuracies which are due to its unreal assumptions can be removed in some way.

Such inaccuracies will mainly follow from the assumptions of perfect competition and constant returns to scale, and the absence of these in real economies will vitiate some of the results of *simpliste* marginal productivity studies. Moreover, alternative theories which arrive at results which contradict marginal productivity results may sometimes be correct, for factors may receive much less than their marginal products in a world of imperfect competition and increasing returns to scale. This means that where Keynesian growth theory (which will be discussed in Chapter 4) and marginal productivity theory arrive at contradictory results, it is very much an open question which will come nearest to describing the behaviour of real economies.

The weakness of marginal productivity theory where there are fixed production coefficients matters less, for it would be widely recognised that input–output analysis is what is appropriate in such cases. The inadequate analysis of embodied technical progress in *simpliste* marginal productivity theory is also not particularly damaging, because 'vintage' growth theory has been developed to take account of this, and it will be seen in Chapter 3 that this is very much an extension of marginal productivity theory.

The crucial weaknesses follow from the assumptions of perfect competition and constant returns to scale, and these are problems which other growth theory has not entirely come to terms with.

There is a further weakness which is now receiving much attention. Given the complexity and the many stages of production processes, it is not clear that the value of capital can be clearly defined in relation to the value of what it produces. It may be that concepts like *more* capital, *less* capital, a higher and a lower capital–labour ratio, and particularly the marginal product of capital, do not have clear meanings in real situations. The very serious problems due to this will be discussed in Chapter 5.

2

Steady Growth

A DEVICE which is much used in growth theory is the comparison of steady-state growth paths. This is the equivalent for dynamic theory of static comparisons between firms or industries in long-run equilibrium. Where a firm or an industry is in long-run static equilibrium, it is possible to specify its inputs and outputs precisely, and to use these results to compare firms or industries in differing conditions to ascertain the long-term effects of a variety of influences. Many of the conclusions of microeconomics depend on this kind of analysis, but it suffers from two major weaknesses.

The first and obvious weakness is that, apart from a fluke, actual firms and industries will not be in long-period equilibrium. This means that equilibrium diagrams and equations will correspond to situations which will never be reached, and comparisons between firms will be comparisons between hypothetical firms in unreal situations. However, the alternative, a comparison between actual firms, cannot provide general results, though it obviously has a most important place in economics. Reality is so complex, and the immediate consequences of new events like wage increases or changes in taxation so various, that the examination of actual firms in real situations will rapidly disintegrate into a wide range of immediate consequences; and if further events are allowed to intrude (as they do in the real world) before the full consequences of initial events have had time to work themselves through, results can be so various that nothing clear and simple can be said. Given this, there is room for long-term equilibrium analysis which should provide a clear picture (if it is well done) of the direction in which a particular event will take a firm or industry in the long run, and the precise long-term influences it can be expected to have when these are isolated from the consequences of other events. There is naturally also room for empirical and historical analyses of the behaviour of actual firms and industries, and economists' accounts of the world are likely to take both information derived from facts and information derived from hypothetical equilibrium comparisons into account.

A further weakness in long-period static equilibrium comparisons can be removed by making theory dynamic. If a firm is in long-period *static* equilibrium, its methods of production, its capital stock and its outputs will necessarily be stagnant, for it will already be producing in the optimum way. An economy where all firms are in long-period static equilibrium will then be one where there is no net investment, no technical progress and no growth. This is completely out of line with Keynesian analyses of the economy at large, and an economy with all firms in static equilibrium could not find macroeconomic equilibrium at full employment if there was any saving in the economy. Moreover, it is obviously unrealistic that the investment process should play no part in the long-period analysis of the firm, and that no account should be taken of technical change. A result of the latter defect is that almost all microeconomic textbooks have to ignore research and development expenditures because these are likely to produce continuing improvements to a firm's technology (for research departments would be closed down once optimum technology was achieved) and thus make a long-period static equilibrium unachievable. These defects in static analyses of the firm can be remedied if dynamic equilibrium paths are also studied. Then a moving or dynamic equilibrium can be envisaged where the firm or economy expands output at a certain annual rate, invests at a certain rate, advances its technology at a certain rate, and so on. The theory of the firm will then be able to take a wider range of factors into account, and the important Keynesian variables, investment, technical progress, etc., will emerge as 'outputs' from microeconomic analysis.

It became clear in the 1930s that the Keynesian revolution created a need for dynamic theory to analyse the long-term consequences of continuous net investment and produce a theory of the firm which was in line with the new theory of employment. Harrod took the first step towards this new dynamic economics. He postulated that in equilibrium, entrepreneurs would expand at a certain rate per annum, and that they would be in equilibrium if the future turned out as they expected. At the same time he assumed that labour productivity and the labour force would expand at constant and given annual rates, and he showed that if a constant fraction of the National Income was saved, there would be only *one* possible steady-state

B

growth path for the economy.[1] Harrod's was the first steady-state growth path to be discovered, and it was the counterpart of long-period equilibrium in static theory.

Perhaps the simplest definition of the kind of steady-state growth path which Harrod discovered is 'A growth path where all ratios between economic variables are constant, and all quantities increase at a constant rate'. Ratios may be pure ratios or fractions which are independent of a time dimension, like S, the share of saving in the National Income, and X_p, the share of profits in the National Income, and these must certainly be constant in steady growth. Other ratios, for instance r, the rate of profit on capital, and V, the capital–output ratio, have a time dimension, for the rate of profit is the ratio of profits over a particular time period, usually a year, to a stock of capital, and changing the period to a month would reduce profits by 11/12 without reducing the stock of capital, and so reduce r by 11/12. Similarly, the capital–output ratio is the ratio of a stock (capital) to a flow (output). For steady growth, these ratios with time dimensions must be constant with any specified time unit, as well as the pure ratios. At the same time, all quantities, output, labour, capital, etc., must each expand steadily at a constant rate. It is as if an economy in static equilibrium (and the constancy of ratios will ensure that it is always, in a certain sense, the same economy) were now to be imagined to expand at a constant rate. Then there would be most of the relationships entailed by static equilibrium and, in addition, the further relationships such as continuous net investment entailed by growth.

A steady-state equilibrium growth path of this kind will naturally suffer from the first disadvantage of equilibrium theory, that it describes a set of relationships which will hardly be found in any real situation, for real economies are no more in long-run equilibrium than firms. The dilemma is the same as with static equilibrium theory, and the answer must surely be the same; that there is room for both a multifarious analysis of the growth of real economies, and also for the analysis of unique equilibrium relationships.

In the main, since Harrod's original work, growth theory has been concerned with the analysis of equilibrium growth paths. The effect that the savings ratio and the other principal economic variables will have on the growth rate has been analysed by comparing the steady

[1] R. F. Harrod, 'An essay in dynamic theory', *Economic Journal*, vol. XLIX (Mar 1939).

growth paths of economies which are similar in every respect except that they have different savings ratios, or different rates of population growth or technical progress. This analysis can be divided into two parts, for two entirely different types of problem need to be solved.

First, it is necessary that the assumptions which are made to arrive at dynamic steady growth paths should take the major decisions which play a part in the determination of an economy's growth rate into account. This means that the factors which influence industrial investment decisions and research and development will need to play a significant part in growth theory. Then, where an economy follows an equilibrium growth path, entrepreneurs will be investing at equilibrium rates which depend on plausible assumptions about how investment decisions are taken, and technology will be advancing at rates depending upon the resources devoted to research and development where decisions to spend on this also rest on plausible assumptions. A surprising proportion of growth theory (and principally neoclassical growth theory) ignores factors of this kind, even though they must play a significant role in the determination of an economy's equilibrium growth rate. The factors which influence investment decisions and decisions to devote resources to research and development will play a considerable part in the growth model that is developed in Part II of this book.

The second type of problem which must be solved is the purely technical one of deriving steady growth paths where all consumers and producers are in equilibrium from the supposedly plausible assumptions which have been fed into the analysis. The technicalities of growth theory consist very largely of this. In general, where more realistic assumptions are made about microeconomic behaviour, and more factors are allowed to influence the growth rate of an economy, the derivation of steady-state growth paths from the assumptions will become more difficult, and more mathematical intricacy will be required.

The best starting-point for the technical task of deriving steady-state growth paths from postulated assumptions is to show how this can be done with very simple assumptions. It is then possible to go on to more realistic cases, and this will be done in Part II of this book.

One of the simplest cases to start with is the basic neoclassical model which is the steady growth counterpart of the analysis of Chapter 1 of this book. The analysis starts from the marginal productivity theory of Chapter 1, for it is assumed that the two factors in the model, labour and capital, are paid their marginal products. It is assumed that there is a constant savings ratio, S, and that *ex-ante* full-employment saving is automatically invested. It is also assumed that the labour force grows at a constant rate, n, and that there is a constant rate of technical progress of a. A further crucial assumption is that the economy in question produces a single good which can be used either as a capital good or a consumer good – and this good does not depreciate with use. The steady growth relationships between the major economic variables in these conditions will be outlined to show the simplest possible set of interrelationships. The analysis will then be extended to show the major characteristics of steady growth in economies where the above assumptions are made, and where, in addition, the production function is either of the Cobb–Douglas or the CES form.

In later chapters, further assumptions will be made, and models will be derived where a wider range of factors will influence steady growth paths. The more limited neoclassical analysis of this chapter will serve as an introduction to the more realistic analysis of later chapters, but it will be more than this. The results which are obtained in later chapters are bound to follow in part from some of the basic neoclassical results obtained here, for the share of investment and the rate of technical progress must always be constant in steady growth. The manner in which the constant investment ratio and rate of technical progress are arrived at will differ in later chapters (and it should be more realistic), but the principal effects of a constant S will be much the same, whatever determines S. Then the neoclassical model may provide part of a nucleus for more complicated growth models. It will certainly act as an example to show how steady growth paths can be derived from particular assumptions.

Neoclassical Steady Growth

A very simple diagram has been used by Solow and developed by Johnson to explain the principal characteristics of steady growth with neoclassical assumptions, and this diagram and the results that follow from it will now be outlined and explained.[1] Fig. 2.1 shows a production function, OX, which relates net output per worker,

[1] See R. M. Solow, 'A contribution to the theory of economic growth', *Quarterly Journal of Economics*, vol. LXX (Feb 1956); and H. G. Johnson, 'The neo-classical one-sector growth model: a geometrical exposition and extension to a monetary economy', *Economica*, vol. XXXIII (Aug 1966).

Y/L, to net capital per worker, K/L, and OX is drawn on the assumption of diminishing returns to each factor of production. To assume a fixed production function which shows that given outputs per worker will result from each capital–labour ratio is apparently to assume that there is no technical progress. It will emerge that technical progress can be brought into the analysis very simply, but for initial simplicity it will be assumed that the output per worker with each capital–labour ratio is constant.

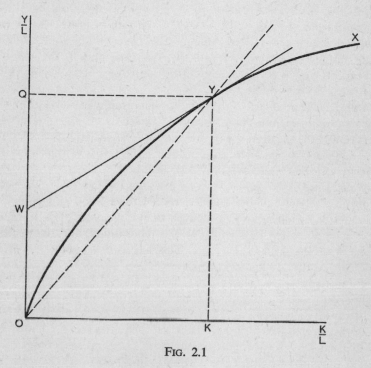

FIG. 2.1

If the wage is OW, a profit-maximising entrepreneur will choose the technique of production at Y which is found by drawing a tangent from W to OX. Profit per worker at Y is WQ (i.e. output per worker OQ less the wage OW), and capital per worker is OK which equals QY, so the rate of profit (which is profit per worker/capital per worker) is WQ/QY, the slope of WY. The tangent, WY, is the steepest line which can be drawn from W to OX, so the highest possible rate of profit is earned by using the technique shown by Y. Alternatively, if it is merely known that entrepreneurs choose Y, it can be deduced that if they are profit maximisers, the wage must be OW, the point where the tangent at Y intersects the Y/L axis.

The capital–output ratio, V, is also shown in Fig. 2.1, for capital per worker is OK, output per worker OQ, and the capital–output ratio, OK/OQ, is the inverse of the slope of OY. Then V will be the inverse of the slope of a straight line from the origin to the point on the production function at which the economy is producing.

Then three of the economy's principal variables can be deduced from the production function, given the assumption of profit maximisation. At any point on this, r, the rate of profit will be the slope of the tangent to that point; w, the wage, will be shown by the intersection of that tangent with the Y/L axis; and V, the capital–output ratio, will be the inverse of the slope of a straight line from the origin to that point.

But that is not all, for X_w and X_p, the shares of wages and profits in the National Income, can also be deduced from the production function if the point at which the economy is working is known. If the wage is OW and output per worker is OQ, it is evident that X_w will be OW/OQ, and that X_p will be WQ/OQ.

Thus, once Y is known, r, w, X_p, X_w and V can all be deduced from it, and none of these will change if there is no change in the production function and no change in the position of Y upon it. It is now necessary to show how Y is determined, and this will be done with the help of Fig. 2.2. This has two schedules on it in addition to the production function, OX.

First, there is the schedule OS_y which shows saving per worker. This is drawn on the assumption that a constant proportion of income, S, is saved. Saving per worker will then always be $S.(Y/L)$, and OS_y is drawn so that for every K/L its height is S times the Y/L shown by OX. Then OS_y rises proportionately with OX, and each point on it has S times the height of the corresponding point on OX.

The other new schedule is OK_n which shows the amount of investment per worker that is needed to keep capital per worker constant. If the size of the labour force was constant, any investment at all would raise capital per worker, so OK_n would then have to coincide with the K/L axis, and show zero investment for all K/L's. If the labour force is growing, OK_n will be above the K/L axis. If the rate of growth of the labour force is 3 per cent per annum, and capital per worker is 100, investment per worker will need to be 3 if the new workers are to be equipped with as much capital, 100, as existing

workers are equipped with. If capital per worker is 200, investment
per worker will need to be 6 if new workers are to be equipped with
200. More generally, if the rate of growth of the labour force is n, and
capital per worker is K/L, investment per worker will need to be
$n.(K/L)$ if new workers are to be equipped with the same capital per
worker as existing workers. Then OK_n, the line showing the investment per worker that is needed to keep capital per worker constant,
will have a height of $n.(K/L)$ for all values of K/L. This is shown by a
straight line through the origin with a slope of n, as in Fig. 2.2.

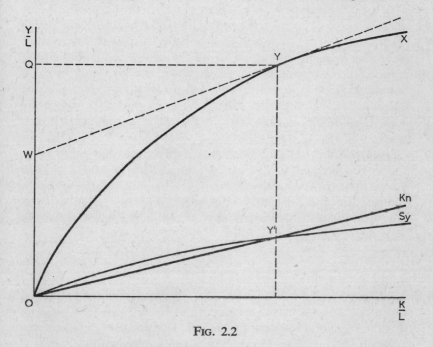

FIG. 2.2

OS_y and OK_n intersect at Y', and it can be shown that this will give
the capital–labour ratio and the consequent output per worker
which the economy will tend towards. If the economy is initially to
the left of Y', OS_y will be above OK_n, which means that saving per
worker and therefore investment per worker (for it is assumed that
saving is automatically invested) will exceed the investment per
worker that is needed to keep K/L constant. Then with more-than
sufficient investment to keep K/L constant, K/L will rise, which means
that the economy will move to the right towards Y'. Similarly, to the

right of Y', saving (and therefore investment) per worker will be insufficient to keep K/L constant, so K/L will fall, which means that the economy will move to the left towards Y'. At Y', saving (and investment) per worker will be just sufficient to keep K/L constant, so the economy will remain at Y'. Then Y' will be a point of stable equilibrium, and it will show the K/L and Y which the economy will tend towards.

Indeed, the economy will tend towards and then remain at Y, the point on the production function which is vertically above Y', and a number of conclusions follow from this. It was shown above that where Y is a fixed point on the production function, and this remains unchanged, r, w, V, X_p and X_w can be deduced from this point, and they will all remain constant. Then where there is continuous equilibrium at Y, the rate of profit, the capital–output ratio and the share of profits will all be constant, so a number of the conditions which are needed for steady growth will be fulfilled. It can be shown that the other conditions, constant rates of growth of output, capital and labour, will also be fulfilled.

Since OS_y and OK_n intersect at Y', the height of OS_y which is $S.(Y/L)$ will equal the height of OK_n which is $n.(K/L)$. Then $S.(Y/L) = n.(K/L)$, so that $n = S.(Y/K) = S/V$. Moreover, with V constant at Y, capital and output will grow at the same rate so that $g = k$, and with K/L constant, capital and labour will grow at the same rate so that $k = n$. It follows from this that at Y':

$$g = k = n = \frac{S}{V}. \tag{2.1}$$

Then output, capital and labour all grow at rate n, so the economy will be on a steady-state growth path. A central neoclassical result that the share of investment has no influence on the equilibrium rate of growth follows from (2.1), where if two economies have the same n, they must have the same g and the same k, even if the S of one economy is twice that of the other. The effect of the higher S will then simply be a proportionately higher V.

These results have been arrived at with the assumption that there is no technical progress, but technical progress can be brought into the argument very simply. Suppose technical progress takes the form of a continuous increase in the effectiveness of labour, so that while the actual physical labour force remains constant, what labour can perform (because of the continuous advance of technology which is occurring) increases at an annual rate of a, so that one man can do what $(1+a)$ men were needed for the year before. Analytically, the effect of this will be the same as the effect of no technical progress and growth in the labour force at a rate of a. In both cases, the rate of growth of the labour force, measured in *efficiency* units, will be a. If growth in the physical labour force, and in the efficiency units of labour provided by a worker, have the same mathematical effect, growth in the effective labour force will be the sum of these, or $(a+n)$. It turns out that the type of technical progress which is represented by a, and this is sometimes referred to as 'labour-augmenting technical progress' for obvious reasons, is Harrod-neutral. Harrod defined neutral technical progress as technical progress which will not disturb the capital coefficient where the rate of interest is constant.[1] Here there is an annual rise in labour productivity in the ratio $(1+a):1$, and no other change, i.e. no change in the capital–output ratio or the rate of interest (or, what is more relevant in this context, in the rate of profit).

The earlier argument will be almost completely unaltered if labour-augmenting or Harrod-neutral technical progress at a constant rate of a is brought into it. Then the effective labour force will grow at a constant rate of $(a+n)$ instead of just n, the slope of OK_n will be $(a+n)$, and at Y', $S.(Y/L)$ will equal $(a+n).(K/L)$ so that $(a+n) = S/V$. Then the steady-state growth path of an economy in the conditions assumed earlier, with, in addition, Harrod-neutral technical progress at rate a, will be defined by the following equation:

$$g = k = (a+n) = \frac{S}{V}. \qquad (2.2)$$

Once again, a higher S will leave the equilibrium rate of growth unaltered. It follows from (2.2) that:

$$V = \frac{S}{a+n}. \qquad (2.3)$$

(2.2) and (2.3) describe the principal characteristics of the steady-state growth path that has been found; and it is possible to use these to show the principal effects of differences in the savings ratio, and in the rates of technical progress or labour growth between two economies in steady growth.

[1] R. F. Harrod, *Towards a Dynamic Economics* (Macmillan, 1948) pp. 22-3.

B*

Consider first the situation where one economy has a higher savings ratio than another, and the same rates of technical progress and labour growth. It is evident from (2.2) that g (which equals $(a+n)$) will be the same in both economies, so the economy with a higher savings ratio will not have a faster steady growth rate. However, it is evident from (2.3) that it will have a higher capital–output ratio,

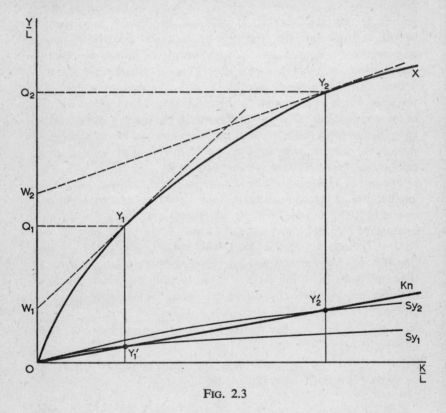

FIG. 2.3

and therefore higher output per worker if both economies produce on the same production function.

This, and a number of further results, can be arrived at diagrammatically. In Fig. 2.3, the different savings ratios are shown by OS_{y1} and OS_{y2}, and these produce equilibrium positions on OX at Y_1 and Y_2. It is clear that output per worker is higher at Y_2, and it is also clear that the economy with a higher savings ratio will have a lower rate of profit (for a tangent to OX must be less steep at Y_2 then at Y_1)

and a higher wage (for the tangent at Y_2 must cut the vertical axis at a higher point). However, nothing can be said about the relative distribution of income in the two economies, for it is not clear whether OW_2/OQ_2 will be higher or lower than OW_1/OQ_1.

A further proposition which has recently received much attention can be derived from Fig. 2.3. It is not immediately clear whether the economy with a higher savings ratio, which must have a higher wage and higher output per worker, will also enjoy higher consumption per worker. Consumption per worker is the excess of output per worker over investment per worker, and this is shown by $Y_1 Y_1'$ and $Y_2 Y_2'$ for the two economies. It is evident that the vertical distance between OK_n and the production function, which $Y_1 Y_1'$ and $Y_2 Y_2'$ show, will be maximised where the slope of the production function equals the slope of OK_n; and consumption per worker will therefore be higher in the economy which produces nearest to the point on OX where this condition is fulfilled. The slope of OK_n is $(a+n)$ which equals g (from (2.2)), and the slope of OX is r, so consumption per worker will be maximised where the rate of profit equals the rate of growth.[1] Then the economy with the higher savings ratio (which is bound to have the lower rate of profit) will have higher consumption per worker provided that its rate of profit exceeds its rate of growth.

These are the various results which follow from the assumption that the two economies have different savings ratios. Suppose now that they have the same savings ratio, but that their labour forces grow at different rates. It follows from (2.2) that the economy with a higher n will enjoy a faster rate of growth, and it is evident from (2.3) that it will have a lower capital–output ratio, and therefore lower output per worker if both economies produce on the same production function. From Fig. 2.4 it is evident that the economy with a higher n, and therefore the higher OK_{n2}, will have a higher rate of profit and a lower wage than the other economy.

Analytically, a faster rate of technical progress should produce exactly the same results as a faster rate of growth of the labour force, for these will both make OK_n steeper. It is, however, a little more difficult to interpret the results. At first sight, it could even be

---

[1] See Alvin L. Marty, 'The neoclassical theorem', *American Economic Review*, vol. LIV (Dec 1964), and Johnson, op. cit., for diagrammatic demonstrations of this proposition. See also Joan Robinson, 'A neo-classical theorem', *Review of Economic Studies*, vol. XXIX (June 1962), and the articles by J. E. Meade, D. G. Champernowne and J. Black in the same issue.

supposed that a faster rate of technical progress, like faster growth of the labour force, would be associated with a lower wage. Naturally this is not the case, and what happens here is that an *efficiency unit of labour* will receive a lower wage, but with technical progress an individual worker represents a growing number of efficiency units, so his wage will rise at the same rate as technical progress. Then,

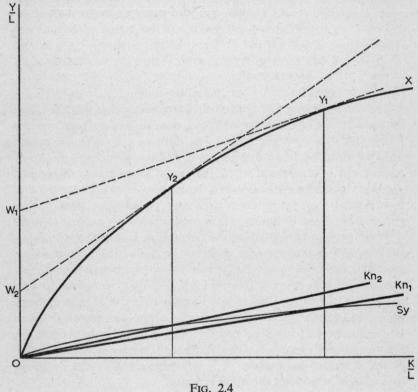

FIG. 2.4

with faster technical progress, his wage will rise more quickly than the wage of a worker in another economy where technical progress is slower, and it must then overtake the other worker's wage, however much lower its starting-point.

It will be clear that comparisons between steady growth paths allow firm conclusions about the effects of differences in S, a and n to be arrived at. However, nothing has yet been assumed about the precise mathematical form of the production function, for results up to this point have simply depended on the assumption that there are diminishing returns to each factor of production. More precise results can be arrived at if a precise production function is assumed, and the characteristics of steady growth paths where the production function is Cobb–Douglas and CES will now be outlined. The results arrived at in (2.2) and (2.3) will hold in steady growth with any diminishing returns production function, so they will hold if the production function is Cobb–Douglas or CES. What will now be shown is that certain additional propositions can be arrived at in these cases.

Steady Growth with the Cobb–Douglas Production Function

It was shown in Chapter 1 that where the production function has the form $Y_t = \beta . e^{mt} . K_t^\alpha . L_t^{1-\alpha}$, an economy's rate of growth will be $m + \alpha . k + (1-\alpha) . n$ (1.13). Where $g = k$, i.e. where output and capital grow at the same rate so that V is constant, the economy's rate of growth will then be $(m/(1-\alpha) + n)$, and it is possible to show that this will be a steady-state equilibrium rate of growth. If the economy grows at this rate, V will be constant, and the share of profits will be the constant, α, as it always is with the Cobb–Douglas. In addition, if V is constant, the rate of profit which equals $\alpha . (Y/K)$ or α/V (from (1.9)) must also be constant. Then $(m/(1-\alpha) + n)$ will be a steady growth rate.

But the Cobb–Douglas economy's steady growth rate must also be $(a + n)$, for (2.2) must hold. This means that Hicks-neutral technical progress at a rate of $m/(1-\alpha)$ and Harrod-neutral technical progress at a rate of a are equivalent, and the Cobb–Douglas is, in fact, the only production function where this is so. If $m/(1-\alpha) = a$, the rate of Hicks-neutral technical progress must be multiplied by $1/(1-\alpha)$ to arrive at the rate of Harrod-neutral technical progress. The reason for this is that Hicks-neutral technical progress simply shows the immediate increase in labour productivity which is due to technical progress, while Harrod-neutral technical progress shows the increase in productivity *at a constant capital–output ratio*. Hicks's m, taken by itself, raises output relatively to capital and thus lowers the capital–output ratio. The restoration of the original capital–output ratio will require capital accumulation, and this will raise productivity further so that Harrod's a – the increase in productivity at a constant capital–output ratio – will exceed m by a factor of $1/(1-\alpha)$ where this is a kind of capital accumulation multiplier. Then the Cobb–Douglas economy's steady growth rate can be regarded as $(m/(1-\alpha)+n)$ or $(a+n)$, and these will be two ways of describing *the same growth process*. $(a+n)$ is perhaps the more straightforward of these, and this is what will be referred to subsequently as the Cobb–Douglas economy's steady growth rate. With this Harrod-neutral formulation, the Cobb–Douglas production function will simply be $Y_t = \beta \cdot K_t^{\alpha} \cdot L_t^{1-\alpha}$, and whatever technical progress there is augments L_t, which grows at an exponential rate of $(a+n)$.

The steady growth characteristics of a Cobb–Douglas economy can now be outlined, i.e. the steady growth values of the economy's principal variables can be expressed in terms of the parameters, a, n, S and α. Most of these have already been shown, but it will be convenient to list them together here:

$$g = a + n$$

$$V = \frac{S}{a+n}$$

$$X_p = \alpha$$

$$r = \frac{\alpha(a+n)}{S} \quad \text{(from (1.9) and (2.3))}. \tag{2.4}$$

The only new equation here is (2.4), which shows the relationship between r and S. The effect of the rate of profit on investment decisions and therefore on S will be analysed in some detail in later chapters. (2.4) shows that in a Cobb–Douglas economy, r will vary proportionately with $(a+n)$ and in inverse proportion with S. Then doubling $(a+n)$ will double the rate of profit, while doubling S will halve it. This result follows from the assumption that σ is unity which is implicit in the Cobb–Douglas production function. It will now be seen that there is a rather different relationship between r and S with the CES production function where σ can take any value.

Steady Growth with a CES Production Function

It was shown in Chapter 1 that where the production function has the form $Y_t = \lambda \cdot e^{mt} \cdot (h \cdot K_t^{-u} + (1-h) \cdot L_t^{-u})^{-1/u}$, the shares of wages and profits in the National Income will be functions of the constants h and u, and (apart from the Cobb–Douglas case where $u = 0$ so that $\sigma = 1$) also of K/L ((1.18 and (1.19)). This means that where σ differs from one, steady growth will only be possible if K/L is constant, i.e. if the rate of growth of the labour force (n) equals the rate of growth of capital (k). In steady growth, k must also equal g, and this means that steady growth will only be possible if $g = k = n$. It was shown in Chapter 1 that $g = m + X_p . k + X_w . n$ with a CES production function (1.20), and if $g = k = n$, the only possible value for m is zero. This means that the rate of Hicks-neutral technical progress must be zero if there is to be steady growth with a CES production function. Technical progress will therefore need to be Harrod-neutral, and the function will then be written:

$$Y_t = \lambda . (h . K_t^{-u} + (1 - h) . L_t^{-u})^{-1/u} \tag{2.5}$$

and technical progress will augment L_t which will grow at an exponential rate of $(a + n)$.

The steady growth characteristics of a CES economy can now be outlined. The argument represented by the Solow–Johnson diagrams showed that there could be steady growth with any diminishing returns production function (including the CES) where technical progress is Harrod-neutral, and (2.2) and (2.3) will therefore show the rate of growth and the capital–output ratio of a CES economy in steady growth.[1] However, the steady growth values of the share of profits (X_p) and the rate of profit (r), expressed in terms of the parameters a, n, S, h, λ and σ (which equals $1/(1 + u)$), still need to be found. They can be found if (2.5) is differentiated with respect to K.[2]

Then the steady growth characteristics of a CES economy will be:

$$g = a + n$$

$$V = \frac{S}{a + n}$$

$$X_p = J . \left(\frac{a + n}{S}\right)^{\left(\frac{1}{\sigma} - 1\right)} \tag{2.6}$$

[1] In Fig. 2.2, the production function was drawn so that it passed through the origin. A CES production function will not pass through the origin, for (2.5) shows that Y_t will be positive where $K_t = 0$. However, with diminishing returns assumptions, an S_y line which shows positive saving where $K/L = 0$ must eventually intersect a rising straight line, OK_n, from above, as in Fig. 2.2, thus producing an equivalent equilibrium.

[2] r will be $\partial Y/\partial K$, and X_p, which equals $V.r$, will be $V.(\partial Y/\partial K)$. In steady growth, $V = S/(a + n)$, so this can be substituted for V and K/Y in the expressions.

$$r = J \cdot \left(\frac{a+n}{S}\right)^{\frac{1}{\sigma}} \tag{2.7}$$

where the constant, J, has been substituted for $h \cdot \lambda^{\left(1-\frac{1}{\sigma}\right)}$.

These relationships show that the effects of S and $(a+n)$ on the equilibrium value of V are the same with CES and Cobb–Douglas assumptions, but their effect on the equilibrium values of the share of profits and the rate of profit are rather more complex with CES assumptions.

The elasticity of the share of profits with respect to the share of investment and the equilibrium rate of growth $(a+n)$ can be found from (2.6).[1] Thus:

Elasticity of X_p with respect to S

$$= 1 - \frac{1}{\sigma} \text{ which is } \gtrless 0 \text{ where } \sigma \gtrless 1 \quad (2.8)$$

Elasticity of X_p with respect to $(a+n)$

$$= \frac{1}{\sigma} - 1 \text{ which is } \gtrless 0 \text{ where } \sigma \lessgtr 1. \quad (2.9)$$

Then, where σ is less than 1, and this is usually thought to be the case,[2] a higher share of investment will be associated with a lower share of profits (which is well known), and a higher equilibrium growth rate will be associated with a higher share of profits (which is less generally appreciated).

The elasticity of the rate of profit with respect to the share of investment and the equilibrium rate of growth can be found from (2.7). Thus:

$$\text{Elasticity of } r \text{ with respect to } S = -\frac{1}{\sigma} \tag{2.10}$$

---

[1] The elasticity of X_p with respect to S is $\partial X_p / X_p$ divided by $\partial S/S$ which equals $(S/X_p) \cdot (\partial X_p / \partial S)$, and this can be found if (2.6) is differentiated with respect to S. The elasticity of $(a+n)$ with respect to X_p is found similarly.

[2] Values of σ in the range 0·5–0·7 have been found in a number of econometric studies. The evidence is summarised by R. Sato in 'The estimation of biased technical progress and the production function', *International Economic Review*, vol. XI (June 1970), who quotes estimates by Chenery, Arrow, Minhas and Solow of 0·569, by Kendrick and Sato of 0·58, and by Kravis of 0·64. Sato's own estimate is 0·525. These estimates are derived from U.S. data.

$$\text{Elasticity of } r \text{ with respect to } (a+n) = \frac{1}{\sigma}. \qquad (2.11)$$

Then, not unexpectedly, where σ is less than 1, a higher share of investment will reduce the rate of profit more sharply than with Cobb–Douglas assumptions, and a higher equilibrium growth rate will raise the rate of profit more sharply. (2.11) gives a very simple account of the relationship between the rate of profit and the share of investment, and this is a relationship which will play a considerable role in Part II of this book.

It will be seen that the steady growth characteristics of a CES economy are much less complex than a first impression of the function might suggest. This means that the neoclassical parts of the argument that follows can accommodate the possibility of a σ which differs from unity with only a slight cost in terms of extra complexity.

Conclusion

The analysis of the steady growth implications of particular assumptions is bound to play an important part in growth theory. It provides one of the techniques which is used for the analysis of the growth process, and it may well be the sharpest technique of all. The argument of this chapter has been confined to neoclassical theory, but this does not mean that steady growth comparisons are only used by neoclassical theorists. Steady growth theory was originated by Harrod,[1] and steady growth comparisons play an indispensable part in the growth theory of Joan Robinson,[2] and a considerable part in some of Kaldor's work.[3] Indeed, it is difficult to see how firm *theoretical* conclusions about the effects the various economic variables will have on the growth process can be arrived at without an analysis of the full equilibrium effects of those variables. Anything short of this will show partial and speculative effects which can only apply to a particular situation in a particular period of time. It may be that such partial analysis can often throw light on actual current or historical situations, but it will also be desirable to delve deeper than this.

In later chapters, attempts will be made to derive steady growth

[1] Harrod, 'An essay in dynamic theory'.
[2] See, for instance, Joan Robinson, *The Accumulation of Capital* (Macmillan, 1956).
[3] See, for instance, Kaldor, 'A model of economic growth'.

paths which are more realistic than those which were analysed in this chapter, for more attention will be paid to the decisions which are likely to influence the investment and technical change of economies. It will be seen that some of the basic results arrived at in this chapter, for instance the result that $V = S/g$ in steady growth, are so fundamental that no change of assumptions will disturb them. Other results depend much more critically on the precise nature of the assumptions made, and here more realistic assumptions should produce better theory. But even if this is achieved, it may be questioned whether steady growth theory can ever have much relevance to growth in actual economies which will scarcely ever be in equilibrium. However, it is possible that growth theory could come closer to predicting what is likely to happen in real situations than is sometimes supposed. If equilibrium paths are stable rather than unstable, there will often be forces moving real economies towards equilibrium growth paths. It is one of the ultimate objectives of economics to be able to analyse and predict those forces; and if theory is well done, the time may come when that objective can be realised. From this point of view, it is a matter of prime importance whether steady growth paths are stable or unstable, for few would expect growth in a real economy to follow an unstable growth path at all closely. This is a problem which will receive some attention in Chapter 12 of this book.

There is one final reservation about steady growth theory which may have some importance. There may be a presumption that certain rates of change will not be constant. For instance, the possibility will emerge in Part II of this book that there may be factors tending to produce an *increasing* rate of technical progress. To the extent that there are such forces, steady growth theory will miss out essential elements in the historical growth process. But if theory is to cope with such problems, the easier steady growth theory must be mastered first. As Harrod wrote in 1939: 'In dynamics, I suggest, we should postulate first a constant rate of change, and then, when our theory becomes strong enough to stand it, a changing rate of change, in the fundamental determinants.'[1] Thus steady growth theory is a necessary foundation for a more ambitious theory of growth.

[1] Harrod, in *Economic Journal* (June 1939) p. 299.

3

Vintage Growth Theory

THE purpose of vintage growth theory is to take account of the fact that new plant will generally be much more effective than old. In Chapters 1 and 2, capital was regarded as a homogeneous factor of production with a quantity of K, a rate of growth of k, and a marginal product of $\partial Y/\partial K$. This failed to distinguish new plant from old – for both were simply regarded as part of the same capital stock, with the same marginal products, etc. If new plant is really much more effective than old, partly because it embodies a proportion of the technical advances which are made, and partly because it has had less time to deteriorate with use, it will be worth complicating the theory of the productive process to take this into account. It is taken into account by regarding plant produced in separate years as separate parts of the capital stock with different costs, productivities, etc. The effectiveness of plant will then depend upon the year in which it was produced, i.e. upon its 'vintage'.

There are three broad types of vintage theory. First, there is theory where it is assumed that there is only one kind of machine which can be bought in a particular year, and no change can be made to it after it is bought. This type of theory is called 'clay-clay': for something made of clay must be used as it is, or broken up. The second kind of theory is based on the assumption that there is a wide spectrum of techniques of production from which new machines can be chosen by entrepreneurs, on the basis of present and expected costs of labour and capital, but once entrepreneurs have chosen which machine to order, they are committed to it for its whole life, and they can make no modification which will alter the amount of labour which is needed to operate it. This type of theory is called 'putty-clay', for capital is malleable (like putty) at the time entrepreneurs place their orders for equipment, but once they have placed their orders they have a machine which (like clay) is not malleable.

The third possibility, 'putty-putty', is choice by entrepreneurs when they purchase machinery, plus the subsequent possibility of altering the machinery, including the amount of labour which is needed to operate it. The account of vintage theory in this chapter will concentrate on 'putty-clay' models. 'Clay-clay' is a special case of 'putty-clay' for it simplifies the argument of 'putty-clay' by obliging entrepreneurs to choose one particular kind of new capital. Thus an account of 'clay-clay' models can be derived quite simply from what is said below. 'Putty-putty' models will not be discussed at all, for the reason that to assume that significant modifications can generally be made to machinery after it is bought to take account of changing conditions loses one of the main features of vintage growth theory: that irrevocable decisions in a world of changing technology are often forced upon industrialists, and that the way those decisions are taken affects the future development of the economy in question.

Some of the principal characteristics of vintage growth theory will now be outlined. After this, certain mathematical relationships in vintage theory will be shown.

Investment, Growth, Income Distribution and the Rate of Profit

Suppose there is an economy with a constant labour force, where a constant number of workers is equipped with new plant each year. With embodied technical progress, the new capital with which workers are equipped will be superior each year to the new capital of the previous year. The nature of its superiority must now be defined. It will be assumed that technical progress is Harrod-neutral, and that each year output per worker with new capital with any given capital–output ratio will be higher in the ratio $(1 + a) : 1$ than output per worker with new capital (with the same capital–output ratio) in the previous year. With this assumption, it is possible to raise the economy's output in two ways. First, new capital can be substituted for older capital which has benefited less from embodied technical progress, and second, capital with a higher capital–output ratio can be substituted for capital with a lower capital–output ratio.[1] To simplify the argument and focus attention on the effect of embodied technical

---

[1] Raising the capital–output ratio must raise output per worker, for it would be unprofitable to raise the capital–output ratio which would raise capital costs per unit of output unless output per worker could be increased as a result of this. In consequence, any technique of production which raised the capital–output ratio without also raising output per worker would not be considered seriously by rational entrepreneurs.

progress, it will be assumed initially that the second effect is absent, so that each year entrepreneurs invest in new capital which has the same gross capital–output ratio, C, that new capital has had in all previous years. Then, with the capital–output ratio constant, growth will be entirely due to the substitution of modern plant for old plant. It will now be shown that the basic neoclassical result that higher investment has no influence on the equilibrium rate of growth will hold with these vintage assumptions.

If the total labour force is L, the life of plant is T years, and workers are equipped at a constant rate, L/T workers will work the plant of each vintage. If output per worker with new plant is Q at time 0, total output with new plant will be $(L/T).Q$. It will be assumed that this plant will continue to produce Q per worker for as long as it is used. The total output with one-year-old plant will be less than $(L/T).Q$, for it will have benefited less from embodied technical progress, and labour productivity with one-year-old plant will be $(1+a)^{-1}$ times labour productivity with new plant as a result of this. Then the aggregate output of one-year-old plant will be $(L/T).Q.(1+a)^{-1}$, and similarly, the aggregate output of b-year-old plant will be $(L/T).Q.(1+a)^{-b}$. Total output at time 0, Y_0, will be the sum of output with plant of each vintage in use, so it will be the sum of output with new plant, one-year-old plant, two-year-old plant, and so on, up to $(T-1)$-year-old plant, i.e.

$$Y_0 = \frac{L}{T}.Q + \frac{L}{T}.Q.(1+a)^{-1} + \frac{L}{T}.Q.(1+a)^{-2}$$
$$+ \ldots + \frac{L}{T}.Q(1+a)^{-(T-1)}. \quad (3.1)$$

In the following year, which will be time 1, L/T workers will be equipped with new plant, and labour productivity with this will be $Q(1+a)$, so total output with this will be $(L/T).Q(1+a)$. The workers to work this new plant will be taken from the oldest plant in use, plant which was $(T-1)$ years old in the previous year, and is now T years old, so the output of this plant will now be lost to the economy. All the other capital will continue to be used as before. Output at time 1, Y_1, will therefore be:

$$Y_1 = \frac{L}{T}.Q(1+a) + \frac{L}{T}.Q + \frac{L}{T}.Q(1+a)^{-1}$$
$$+ \ldots + \frac{L}{T}.Q(1+a)^{T-2}. \quad (3.2)$$

It can be seen that Y_1 is $(1+a)$ times Y_0, for each term on the right-hand side of (3.2) is $(1+a)$ times the corresponding term in (3.1). Then, as output grows $(1+a)$ times in a year, its rate of growth is a, the rate of embodied Harrod-neutral technical progress. Then, so long as the life of capital is constant, the rate of growth depends only on the rate of technical progress.[1]

The interesting consequence of this result is that the rate of growth is apparently independent of the rate of investment. Twice as much investment would be needed to equip twice as many workers with new capital each year, and this would halve the life of capital,[2] but the rate of growth would still be a, for the long-term rate of growth is independent of T, the life of plant. Thus the assumption that technical advances need to be embodied in new plant apparently has no effect on the basic result arrived at in Chapter 2 that $g = a$ where the capital–output ratio is constant, and, as in this case, $n = 0$.

However, this result is only true in the very long run where the same number of workers is equipped with new plant for at least T years. If several such economies with different lives of plant and therefore different shares of investment are compared, it will be found that they will all have a rate of growth of a, for (3.1) and (3.2) will apply to all of them. However, if T is shorter in one such economy than in another, because it has a higher share of investment in output, its average labour productivity will be higher because a greater proportion of its labour force will be equipped with modern plant. The situation is illustrated in Fig. 3.1, where $G_1 G_1$ is the growth path of an economy with a shorter life of plant. The slopes of these GG lines show what the rates of growth of these economies will be if these lives of

---

1 This result has been arrived at with the assumption that the size of the labour force is constant. It will be shown in the mathematical section at the end of the chapter, where continuous exponential series will be used, that where the labour force grows at a constant exponential rate of n, the rate of growth is $(a+n)$ with all lives of capital.

2 The formula for the relationship between T and S, the share of gross investment in the National Product, can be arrived at quite simply. Investment at time 0 is C times gross output with new plant at time 0 or $C . Q . (L/T)$. S will be $C . Q . (L/T)$ divided by Y_0. Then, from (3.1) using the formula for the sum of a geometric progression to sum the right-hand side of (3.1):

$$S = \frac{C\left(\frac{a}{1+a}\right)}{1-(1+a)^{-T}}. \tag{3.3}$$

With a and C constant, a higher S will be associated with a lower T. C will vary proportionately with S where a and T are constant.

plant are maintained, and this will be *a* in each case. The heights of the lines show output per worker, and G_1G_1 is drawn above G_2G_2 because, with a shorter life of plant, output per worker will always be higher.

Suppose that, at time t_1, economy 2 started to equip as many workers per annum as economy 1. Then its life of plant would gradually fall to that of economy 1, and after a very long period of time (at t_2), economy 2 would be identical with economy 1. On Fig. 3.1 it would move from *A* to *B* between t_1 and t_2, and it is evident

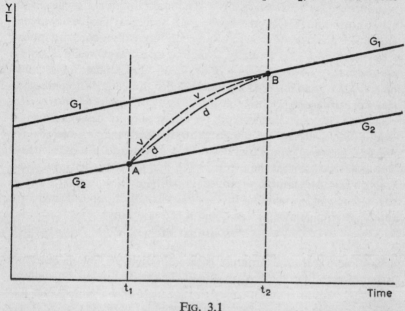

FIG. 3.1

that its rate of growth along *AB* must exceed *a* for the slope of a line from *A* to *B* must be steeper than G_1G_1 and G_2G_2 which both have a slope of *a*. Then an economy's rate of growth will exceed *a* while its life of capital is actually becoming shorter, so investment will influence the rate of growth in a transitional period such as that between t_1 and t_2, when the life of capital is actually changing. On the other hand, when the life of capital is constant, the rate of growth is always *a*.

This does not involve any departure from the results of Chapter 2, for there too output per worker was higher in an economy with a higher share of investment, for this was associated with a higher capital–output ratio (where $(a+n)$ was the same in the two economies) and therefore higher output per worker. Thus, with disembodied technical progress, G_1G_1 could represent the growth path of an economy with a higher S than an economy which moved up G_2G_2, and the second economy might follow a path like AB if it raised its S to that of the first economy at time t_1.

Up to this point there has been no clear difference between vintage growth and the account of growth in Chapters 1 and 2, where technical progress was disembodied, except that average output per worker is influenced by T as well as by V. The main difference comes in the very short run. In Chapter 1 where all technical progress was disembodied, the rate of growth of an economy with a constant labour force was $(m+k.X_p)$. Initially, doubling investment would double k and raise the growth rate $(m+2k.X_p)/(m+k.X_p)$ times, i.e. it would be much less than doubled if m was at all significant. With embodied technical progress, doubling gross investment would mean transferring twice as many workers from the oldest plant to new plant, which would practically double the growth rate. With the passage of time, the gap between productivity with new plant and the oldest plant would narrow, so that the extra growth due to the higher investment would diminish (until it disappeared altogether at time t_2), but in the first instance, doubling investment virtually doubles the growth rate with vintage assumptions, and it raises it only

$$(m+2k.X_p)/(m+k.X_p)$$

times where technical progress is disembodied. A vintage economy might then follow a path from A to B like the dotted line vv, while an economy with an equal increase in the share of investment and disembodied technical progress might follow a line like that shown by the dotted line dd. The difference between the adjustment paths, vv and dd, shows the only essential difference between the effect of investment on the growth rate in vintage models, and in models where technical progress is assumed to be disembodied.

With vintage assumptions, it is possible to make a precise analysis of the distribution of income between wages and profits. If perfect competition in factor and product markets is assumed, and if it is also assumed that there is no working capital, it will pay entrepreneurs to use equipment so long as the output it produces exceeds the wages they have to pay to operate it. Then, in equilibrium, the wage will equal output per worker with the least productive equipment in use. It cannot exceed this, for if it did, some entrepreneurs would be paying some workers more than the extra output they obtained as a result of their employment, and this would not be rational. If, on the other hand, the wage was less than output per worker with the least productive equipment in use, extra workers could be employed and extra profits earned from their employment, so the labour market would not be in equilibrium.

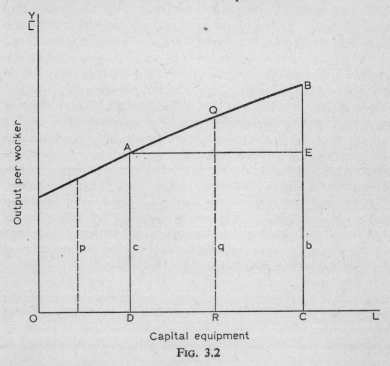

Fig. 3.2

The situation is illustrated in Fig. 3.2, where items of capital equipment, each worked by one worker, are listed along *OL* (a capital good worked by 10 workers being represented by 10 units along *OL*), and labour productivity with this equipment is shown on the vertical axis. The equipment is listed along *OL* in ascending order of labour productivity, the equipment, *b*, with the highest labour productivity being to the right of the diagram. Labour productivity with *b* is *BC*. If *CD* workers are available, only the capital equipment between *C* and *D* can be worked. In equilibrium at full employment, with *CD* workers employed, the wage must be *AD*, output per worker with equipment *c* which is the least productive equipment that needs to be used if CD workers are to be employed. If the wage was higher than AD, capital equipment c could not be worked profitably, so it would not be profitable to employ as many as CD workers. If the wage was less than AD, it would be profitable to work capital equipment less productive than c, for instance equipment p, which would mean that some entrepreneurs owning equipment more productive than c, for instance q, could not get labour to work all their capital. It would pay an entrepreneur in this situation to offer to pay a wage higher than AD (the entrepreneur owning q would offer to pay up to QR) to draw workers away from capital equipment less productive than c rather than see their capital stand idle and produce no output. There would be 'wage drift' for this reason at any wage less than AD, so the labour market would only be in equilibrium at full employment if the wage was AD.

If the wage is AD, and it is assumed that all CD workers are paid the same wage, it is evident that total wages will be AD times CD, which is represented by the rectangle $AECD$. Total output will be represented by $ABCD$, which is the sum of the output of each worker. Then the share of wages in the National Income, with the labour market in equilibrium at full employment, will be represented by $AECD/ABCD$. If wages are $AECD$, and output $ABCD$, profits which are the surplus of output over wages will be ABE, and the share of profits in the National Income will be $ABE/ABCD$.

In this theory, profits per worker with any item of equipment are the excess of output per worker with this equipment over output per worker with the least productive equipment in use. Thus the theory has obvious parallels with Ricardo's theory of rent (where no rent is paid for the use of marginal land, and rent is paid for the use of intra-marginal land at a rate depending upon the extent to which its fertility exceeds that of marginal land).[1] Here, c is the marginal item of equipment which earns no profit, and profits with items of equipment to the right of c will be the excess of their output per worker over AD – the most productive item of equipment producing a profit of BE. Because of the similarity of this theory to the theory of rent, ABE, the total gross profits of the economy in full-employment equilibrium, are sometimes referred to as the economy's total quasi-rent, and $ABE/ABCD$ will be the economy's 'equilibrium share of quasi-rent'.

[1] David Ricardo, *The Principles of Political Economy and Taxation* (London, 1817); reprinted P. Sraffa (ed.), *Works* (Cambridge U.P. 1951) vol. I, chap. 2.

It is clear that the economy's share of profits, or its share of quasi-rent, will depend quite substantially upon the ratio of BC to AD. If, to give a very simple arithmetical approximation, AB is a straight line, the area of ABE (which represents profits) is $\frac{1}{2}BE.AE$, while the area of $ABCD$ (which represents output) is $\frac{1}{2}(AD+BC).AE$, so that $ABE/ABCD$, the share of profits in the National Income, is

$$\frac{BE}{AD+BC} = \frac{BC-AD}{BC+AD} = \frac{(BC/AD)-1}{(BC/AD)+1}.$$

Then the share of profits will be solely a function of BC/AD. It will be one-half if $BC/AD = 3$, one-third if $BC/AD = 2$, and one-fifth if $BC/AD = 1\frac{1}{2}$. These are, of course, approximations which depend on the assumption that AB is a straight line, and a fuller mathematical account of the relationship between BC/AD and the share of profits will be given in the mathematical section at the end of the chapter, where much the same result is arrived at. It will be clear that an increase in the ratio of productivity with new plant to productivity with the oldest plant will be associated with a considerable increase in the share of gross profits in the National Income.

The ratio of productivity with new plant to productivity with the oldest plant will depend substantially on the life of capital and the rate of technical progress. In (3.1), where productivity with new plant was Q, productivity with the oldest plant was $Q.(1+a)^{-(T-1)}$, making the ratio of productivity with new plant to productivity with the oldest plant $(1+a)^{T-1}$. Then faster technical progress or a longer life of plant will be associated with a higher share of gross profits in the National Income. If higher investment led to a shorter life of plant, and no change in the rate of technical progress, it would then lead to a lower share of profits.

This analysis of the distribution of income, where the wage equals output per worker with the least productive plant in use, is clearly close to the marginal productivity theory of distribution (where the wage equals the marginal product of labour) as well as the theory of rent. It will suffer from much the same weaknesses as the marginal productivity theory, for the assumptions – perfect competition in factor and product markets, etc. – are equally restrictive. There is indeed a further restriction with vintage theory, for the attribution of productivity to the date of the plant with which labour works removes the possibility that differences in the quality of labour may influence productivity, while with marginal productivity theory, workers with

different skills will have different marginal products, receive different
rates of pay and make different contributions to growth. The main
point of difference between vintage theory and the marginal productivity theory of Chapter 1 is that the distribution of income depends
substantially upon the life of plant with vintage theory, a variable
which does not appear in ordinary marginal productivity analysis.

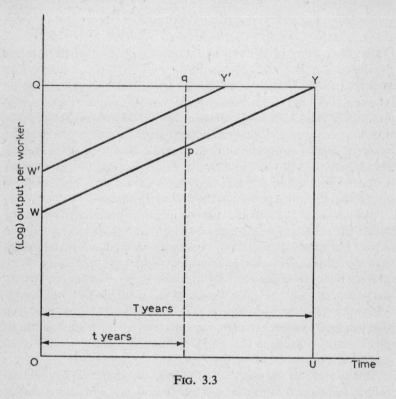

FIG. 3.3

However, in marginal productivity analysis, the distribution of
income is influenced by σ, the elasticity of substitution between labour
and capital, and it will be shown below that an equivalent parameter
will influence the life of capital and therefore the distribution of
income in vintage models.

The next economic variable which will be considered is r, the rate
of profit, which will be analysed with the help of Fig. 3.3. Here, the
quasi-rents earned with a machine worked by one worker are shown
for its full working life. It produces an annual gross output of OQ

throughout its life of T years, and this is shown by the horizontal line, QY. The wage is OW when the machine is new, and it gradually rises to UY, so the wage through time is shown by WY. The wage will be output per worker with the least productive plant in use, and if the life of capital is constant, this will rise at the same rate as productivity with the most productive plant, i.e. at rate a, the rate of technical progress. Then it might be envisaged that the wage will rise at rate a through time, and the slope of WY would then be a. The annual gross quasi-rent which is earned with the machine is the excess of its output over the wage, and this will be WQ when the machine is new, pq when it is t years old, and zero at Y when it is T years old, after which it is scrapped. The upward slope of WY which is due to technical progress causes the falling quasi-rent as the machine ages, and it does this because, through the labour market, it causes a continuous rise in the wage relatively to the static output of any particular machine. The quasi-rents which are earned throughout the machine's life are represented by the triangle QWY, and r, the rate of profit, is the rate of discount which equates QWY to the cost of the machine, which will be its gross capital–output ratio when new, C, times its annual output, OQ, i.e. $C.OQ$. Then r will be the discount rate which equates the quasi-rents represented by QWY to $C.OQ$.[1] There is no simple approximation for r, and the rather complex relationship between r and C, T and a is a reason why those parts of the argument of this book which make use of r require a certain amount of mathematics.

However, something can be said about the relationship between r and the other variables from Fig. 3.3. Suppose there is another economy which is similar in every respect except that its life of capital is shorter. In that economy the machine would be scrapped at Y' instead of at Y. Moreover, with a shorter life of plant, and the same rate of technical progress, the wage (which is $(1+a)^{-(T-1)}$ times output per worker with new plant) would be closer to output per

---

[1] This diagram is used by Sir Robert Shone in his 1966 Stamp Memorial Lecture, *Investment and Economic Growth*. The quasi-rent earned in the tth year is pq, and the discounted present value of this at the time the machine is new is $pq.e^{-rt}$. The total 'present value' of discounted quasi-rents at the time the machine is new is

$$\int_0^T (\text{output}_t - \text{wage}_t)e^{-tr}dt$$

and this must equal C times OQ. r is the solution of this equation.

worker with new plant, so it would be W' instead of W. Then the quasi-rents earned with the machine during its lifetime would be represented by $QW'Y'$ instead of QWY, and the r which discounted this to equality with the same $C.OQ$ would obviously be much lower. Thus a shorter life of capital will be associated with a lower rate of return on capital, and vice versa. This means that in vintage models, the rate of profit as well as the share of profits varies strongly with the life of capital.

Suppose now that C is higher in the other economy, but that T is the same in both economies. In this case, QWY will be discounted to equal the higher C times OQ, and the rate of discount which equates QWY to the higher C times OQ will have to be lower. Then a higher C will be associated with a lower r.

It is then evident that both a shorter life of plant and a higher capital–output ratio with new plant will be associated with a lower rate of profit. This means that a higher S will be associated with a lower r, both if it reduces the life of plant, and if it raises the capital–output ratio. The precise mathematical relationships between r, T, C and S are complex, and they will be shown in the mathematical part of the argument which follows.

It is now time to say something about the determination of C, the capital–output ratio of new plant, in vintage models. It is an essential feature of 'putty-clay' models that entrepreneurs are free to choose any technique of production from a wide spectrum of possible techniques, but once they have chosen, they must continue to use that equipment until it is scrapped without any further possibility of substituting capital for labour, or vice versa. The choice of technique with disembodied technical progress depended upon the wage and the production function. In Chapter 2, for instance, a tangent was drawn from W (representing the current wage) to the production function in Fig. 2.1 to arrive at the technique of production which would maximise the rate of return on capital. With vintage models, entrepreneurs can be expected to anticipate that the profits they earn with any particular item of equipment will fall as the equipment ages (as in Fig. 3.3) as a result of the rising wage in relation to output from any given equipment. It is to be expected that their decisions will be influenced by the profile of expected earnings throughout the anticipated life of their plant, and not simply by the wage, capital costs and output per worker when the equipment is new. One way in which this could be taken into account would be for entrepreneurs to equate the capital cost of saving a worker (as a result of the purchase of plant with a higher capital–labour ratio and consequently lower labour requirements to produce a particular output) with the discounted cost of that worker throughout the lifetime of the plant.[1] If the capital cost of saving a worker was less than the discounted cost of a worker, it would pay entrepreneurs to increase capital intensity, and vice versa if the capital cost of saving a worker was greater. With rational enterpreneurs and perfect foresight, the discounted cost of a worker throughout the life of plant will equal the capital cost of saving a worker.

This means that all the various factors which influence the discounted cost of a worker throughout the lifetime of plant, T, r, X_p and a, and the technical factors which determine the capital cost of saving a worker, will influence C. In turn, r and T and therefore X_p will be influenced by C. It was possible to arrive at a number of simple propositions in the earlier part of the argument of this chapter by assuming that C was given, but clearly a certain amount of mathematics is needed to disentangle the situation once it is admitted that C is a variable depending on other variables.

The necessary mathematics is worked out in the next section, 'The Mathematics of Vintage Growth', and this can be regarded as a mathematical appendix to the chapter. It is shown there that the principal relationships come out clearly where the *ex-ante* production function with new plant takes the algebraic CES form. The principal difficulty with vintage theory (once C is admitted to be a variable) is that it is not clear whether particular differences in parameters (for instance, in the savings ratio or the rate of technical progress) between economies will produce differences in the capital–output ratio with new plant or differences in the life of plant, and these will produce very different effects on the other major variables like the rate of profit and the share of profits in the National Income. With non-vintage CES theory, a higher share of investment must raise V, the *net* capital–output ratio, *pari passu*, and it will reduce or raise the share of profits depending on whether $\sigma \lessgtr 1$ (from (2.8)). With vintage theory, a higher share of investment may raise the capital–output ratio *pari passu* as with non-vintage theory (in which case it will leave the life of capital unaltered), but it may also have its entire effect on the life of plant (as in Fig. 3.3), leaving the capital–output

[1] See R. C. O. Matthews, 'The new view of investment: Comment', *Quarterly Journal of Economics*, vol. LXXVIII (Feb 1964).

ratio unaltered (which is impossible with non-vintage theory), and it is in fact likely to influence both the life of plant and the capital–output ratio. Its exact influence can be disentangled, for there is a *critical* value of θ, the parameter equivalent to σ in the CES production function with new plant, of around 0·70–0·83, and where θ is at the critical value, θ^*, higher investment leaves the life of plant unaltered and raises the capital–output ratio proportionately. Where θ is less than θ^*, higher investment will shorten the life of plant and raise the capital–output ratio less than proportionately, while where θ exceeds θ^*, a higher share of investment will be associated with a lengthening of the life of plant and a more than proportionate increase in the capital–output ratio.[1] The crucial propositions can be written as:

Elasticity of T with respect to $S \gtreqless 0$ where $\theta \gtreqless \theta^*$

(from (3.42) and (3.44))   (3.4)

Elasticity of C with respect to $S \gtreqless 1$ where $\theta \gtreqless \theta^*$

(from (3.42) and (3.46))   (3.5)

$$\text{where } \theta^* = \frac{2}{3} + \frac{a.T}{18} + \frac{T^2}{135}(r^2 + \tfrac{1}{4}ra - \tfrac{1}{2}a^2)....$$

Moreover, it was shown earlier in the chapter that the share of profits in the National Income, X_p, depends on the life of plant and the rate of technical progress (and this is confirmed by (3.20)), and a higher share of investment will leave this unchanged where it leaves the life of plant unaltered, and will raise the share of profits where it raises the life of plant. Hence:

Elasticity of X_p with respect to $S \gtreqless 0$ where $\theta \gtreqless \theta^*$

(from (3.42) and (3.47)).   (3.6)

If this is contrasted with non-vintage CES theory where the elasticity of X_p with respect to S is greater or less than 0 where σ is greater or less than 1 (from (2.8)), it is evident that a principal difference between vintage and non-vintage theory is that with non-vintage

[1] These results are less complex than those of C. J. Bliss, 'On putty-clay', *Review of Economic Studies*, vol. xxxv (Apr 1968), and Pranab Bardhan, 'Equilibrium growth in a model with economic obsolescence of machines', *Quarterly Journal of Economics*, vol. LXXXIII (May 1969), largely because it is assumed that the production function with new plant takes the algebraic CES form, while they use a more general form of the production function.

theory the *critical* value of the elasticity of substitution is 1, while it is rather less than 1 with putty-clay vintage theory. However, with both vintage and non-vintage assumptions, whether higher investment will raise or lower the share of profits depends on σ or θ, and the only difference is that the critical value of this is somewhat lower with vintage theory. The principal reason for this is the influence of entrepreneurs' expectations of a rising wage which will influence the choice of technique with vintage theory. This makes vintage entrepreneurs somewhat keener to substitute capital for labour where the share of investment is higher,[1] so that a CES parameter of 0·70–0·83 leads to the same degree of substitution as a parameter of 1 in a non-vintage world.

Curiously, there is no parallel to this where the rate of technical progress differs between two economies. Here:

Elasticity of X_p with respect to $a \gtrless 0$ where $\theta \lessgtr 1$

$$\text{(from (3.54))} \quad (3.7)$$

which is similar to the result with non-vintage theory where the elasticity of X_p with respect to a is greater or less than 0 where σ is less or greater than 1 (from (2.9)). There is then an interesting difference between the results of vintage and non-vintage theory. With non-vintage theory there are two basic situations, namely those where σ is greater and those where it is less than 1. Where σ is less than 1, higher investment reduces the share of profits, but faster technical progress raises it; and where σ exceeds 1, higher investment raises the share of profits and faster technical progress reduces it. The corresponding situations with vintage theory are a θ of less than θ^* (where higher investment reduces and faster technical progress raises the share of profits) and a θ of more than 1. There is, however, a third possible situation where $1 > \theta > \theta^*$, and here higher investment and faster technical progress will *both* raise the share of profits. There is no corresponding range of values of σ in non-vintage theory.

What emerges from this analysis is that there is no particular presumption that a higher share of investment will be associated with a shorter life of capital in putty-clay vintage models. This will only be the case where θ is less than θ^*. There is also no presumption that a higher S will have any particular effect on the share of profits

---

[1] See Matthews, op. cit.

C

in the National Income, for this too will depend on θ. The position will be perfectly clear with 'clay-clay' models (which are putty-clay models with $\theta = 0$), and there a higher S will be associated with a shorter life of plant and therefore a lower share of gross profits in the National Income, etc., but putty-clay assumptions which involve a choice of technique with new plant have the effect of making what happens depend substantially on the value of θ.

In Part II of this book, considerable use will be made of a technical progress function which leads to certain modifications to the argument. It will be argued in Chapter 6 that an economy's rate of technical progress is likely to vary with S, for weaknesses in the design and performance of new machinery will be removed more quickly if more new machines of particular kinds are sold (through 'learning by doing'), and the development of technically superior machinery will be more profitable to machinery manufacturers where markets are larger. An interconnection between S and a will obviously influence the relationships between S, C, T, r and X_p in important ways, and the effect of this on the basic vintage results will be analysed in Chapter 7.

In this chapter where S and a have been regarded as parameters and not variables, few significant differences have been found between the long-term results which follow from vintage assumptions, and the results in Chapters 1 and 2 where all technical progress was assumed to be disembodied. The main differences between vintage growth and growth with disembodied technical progress have come in the very short run. This might suggest that vintage assumptions complicate growth models unnecessarily. It is certainly realistic to assume that some technical advances need to be embodied in new plant, and it is an advantage that vintage models allow for this, but there are so many unreal features in all growth models that it could well be thought that priority should be given to the removal of unreal features which seriously influence the conclusions of a model; for such amendments, if managed successfully, will bring the analysis substantially closer to the real world.

This view of vintage growth models would be unjustified, for there are a number of arguments in their favour. First, if the relationship between investment and the rate of technical progress is a close one, and the view will be taken in Part II that it is, vintage theory provides the ideal tools to analyse this relationship and its consequences. Second, vintage theory permits a much more precise analysis of the relationship between investment, depreciation and the rate of return on capital than models where the profit profile of items of equipment cannot be specified. These relationships play an important role in the argument of Part II of this book, where the rate of profit is assumed to have a considerable influence over investment decisions, and vintage theory is a necessary tool for this. Third, vintage theory has clear advantages for the analysis of short-run situations, where there clearly are differences between the results arrived at in this chapter, and those arrived at in Chapters 1 and 2, which means that it will be useful in Part III which is concerned with growth and distribution in situations where there is not steady growth. And there is a further point in favour of vintage analysis. Econometric studies are generally concerned with growth rates in rather short periods, and vintage theory may well provide a better basis for this than models where all technical progress is assumed to be disembodied.

*The Mathematics of Vintage Growth

Some of the principal mathematical relationships in vintage growth theory will be outlined in this section. Some of the results arrived at earlier in the chapter will now be arrived at with less limiting assumptions, and the mathematical relationships between the various parameters and variables of the model will be outlined.

It will emerge that the central mathematical feature of putty-clay vintage models is that there are three equations to determine the equilibrium values of the three variables which need to be determined (where S and a are regarded as parameters): r the rate of profit, C the gross capital–output ratio with new plant, and T the life of plant.

First, there will always be a technical equation showing the share of investment that is needed for particular combinations of C and T. With T, a and n given, a particular increase in C will require a particular increase in S (and vice versa), while a shorter T will also entail a higher S with C, a and n given. There will be a particular relationship between these in given technical conditions, and the equation describing the relationship can be written in the general form:

$$S = f(C, T, a, n). \qquad (3.8)$$

(3.3) showed the form this equation would take in particular limiting conditions, but a more useful form of this equation will be found below.

A second equation which must be satisfied in putty-clay vintage models shows the relationship between the quasi-rents earned with a particular item of plant throughout its life and its initial cost. In equilibrium the cost of plant will equal the 'present value' of the quasi-rents earned with it when these are discounted at rate r, which will produce an equation of the form:

$$C = f(T, r, a). \qquad (3.9)$$

A particular form of this relationship was illustrated in Fig. 3.3, but a more general equation must now be found.

The third equation is derived from the proposition that entrepreneurs equate the capital cost of saving a worker with new plant to the discounted cost of the wages they expect to have to pay to a worker throughout the lifetime of plant. This, together with the *ex-ante* production function with new plant, produces an equation of the general form:

$$C = f(T, r, a, \theta). \qquad (3.10)$$

(3.8), (3.9) and (3.10) are sufficient to determine the equilibrium values of r, C and T if S, a, n and θ are given. These equations must therefore be found and solved, and in addition to this, various other important relationships like the share of profits and the rate of depreciation which depend on these variables and parameters must be found.

(3.8) will be found first, and for this, expressions for total output and gross investment at time t are needed. Let the number of workers available to work new plant at time t be $p \cdot e^{nt}$. Then the number of workers available to work new plant at time $(t-b)$ was $p \cdot e^{n(t-b)}$. If the workers available to work new plant are always equipped with it, and plant is worked until it is T years old, the total labour force at time t, L_t, will be $\int_0^T p \cdot e^{n(t-b)} db$. Then:

$$L_t = p \cdot e^{nt} \left(\frac{1 - e^{-nT}}{n} \right). \qquad (3.11)$$

L_t grows at an exponential rate of n where T and n are constant.

Let the unit of output be so chosen that labour productivity with new plant at time 0 is at an annual rate of q. Labour productivity at time t will then be at an annual rate of $q \cdot e^{at}$, and labour productivity with plant produced at time $(t-b)$ is $q \cdot e^{a(t-b)}$. The aggregate output of plant produced at time $(t-b)$ will be this times the $p \cdot e^{n(t-b)}$

workers equipped with it, or $p.q.e^{(a+n)(t-b)}$, and this is the aggregate output of plant that is b years old at time t. Then total output at time t, Y_t, is $\int_0^T p.q.e^{(a+n)(t-b)}db$, if capital is scrapped when it is T years old. Then:

$$Y_t = p.q.e^{(a+n)t}\left(\frac{1-e^{-(a+n)T}}{a+n}\right). \tag{3.12}$$

Y_t grows at an exponential rate of $(a+n)$ where a, n and T are constant.

S_t, the share of gross investment in gross output at time t, will now be worked out. The cost of the capital needed to equip a worker is C times annual output per worker with that capital, for C is the gross capital–output ratio with new plant. Then gross investment at time t, I_t, will be C times the annual rate of output with new plant at time t, so that:

$$I_t = p.q.C.e^{(a+n)t}. \tag{3.13}$$

S_t will be I_t divided by Y_t, so (from (3.12) and (3.13)):

$$S_t = \frac{(a+n)C}{1-e^{-(a+n)T}}. \tag{3.14}$$

S will be constant where C, T, a and n are constant. (3.14) is a form of (3.8) which can be used to help determine the equilibrium values of r, C and T.

Formulae for the ICOR and the shares of wages and profits in the National Income will be found at this point before the argument turns to the derivation of appropriate forms for (3.9) and (3.10).

The incremental capital–output ratio, or ICOR, is the economy's gross investment ratio divided by its growth rate, so it will be S_t divided by $(a+n)$. Then, from (3.14):

$$\text{ICOR} = \frac{C}{1-e^{-(a+n)T}}. \tag{3.15}$$

The formulae for X_w and X_p, the shares of wages and gross profits in gross output, will now be outlined. The wage is output per worker with the least productive equipment in use, and this is $q.e^{at}.e^{-aT}$ at time t. Total wages at time t, W_t, will be the wage times L_t, i.e. from (3.11):

$$W_t = p.q.e^{(a+n)t}.e^{-aT}.\left(\frac{1-e^{-nT}}{n}\right). \tag{3.16}$$

X_w is W_t divided by Y_t, so from (3.12) and (3.16):

$$X_w = e^{-aT} \cdot \left(\frac{1-e^{-nT}}{n} \right) \left(\frac{a+n}{1-e^{-(a+n)T}} \right). \tag{3.17}$$

X_p is $(1-X_w)$, so that:

$$X_p = \frac{n(e^{aT}-1)-a(1-e^{-nT})}{n(e^{aT}-e^{-nT})}. \tag{3.18}$$

If the labour force is constant so that $n = 0$, then, from (3.17)[1]:

$$X_w = \frac{a \cdot T}{e^{aT}-1} \tag{3.19}$$

$$X_p = \frac{e^{aT}-a \cdot T-1}{e^{aT}-1}. \tag{3.20}$$

It will be seen that X_w and X_p are functions of a, n and T, and that they are independent of C. These are rather involved expressions, but by Taylor expansion of (3.18):

$$X_p = \frac{a \cdot T}{2} \left(\frac{1+\frac{1}{3}(a-n)T+\frac{1}{12}(a^2-an+n^2)T^2 +\frac{1}{60}(a^3-a^2n+an^2-n^3)T^3 \ldots}{1+\frac{1}{2}(a-n)T+\frac{1}{6}(a^2-an+n^2)T^2 +\frac{1}{24}(a^3-a^2n+an^2-n^3)T^3 \ldots} \right)$$

$$X_p \simeq \frac{aT}{2}(1-\frac{1}{6}(a-n)T). \tag{3.21}$$

The ratio of productivity with new plant to labour productivity with the oldest plant is e^{aT}, and this approximation for X_p is predominantly a function of $a \cdot T$. The accuracy of the approximation can be judged by the following example. If T is 25 years, a is 0·03 and n is 0·01, the approximation for X_p (from (3.21)) is 0·344, while the accurate value (from (3·18)) is 0·339. The approximation will be less accurate than this where $a \cdot T$ exceeds the 0·75 assumed in this example, and more accurate where $a \cdot T$ is less than 0·75.

A general form for (3.9) will now be found. Plant worked by one worker which is new at time t costs $q \cdot C \cdot e^{at}$, and its gross output is at an annual rate of $q \cdot e^{at}$. Since the wage is $q \cdot e^{a(t-T)}$ at time t, gross quasi-rent with new plant at time t is at an annual rate of $q \cdot e^{at}(1-e^{-aT})$. When the plant is b years old at time $(t+b)$ its output will still be $q \cdot e^{at}$, but the wage will have risen to $q \cdot e^{a(t+b)} \cdot e^{-aT}$, and

---

[1] It is to be noted that $(1-e^{-nt})/n$ tends to T as n tends to 0.

the gross quasi-rent with plant will then be at an annual rate of $q.e^{at}.(1-e^{-aT}.e^{ab})$, and the 'present value' of this at time t will be e^{-rb} times the quasi-rent, or $q.e^{at}(e^{-rb}-e^{-(r-a)b}.e^{-aT})$. The 'present value' of the total quasi-rents which will be earned during the full life of the machine will be $q.e^{at}.\displaystyle\int_0^T (e^{-rb}-e^{-(r-a)b}.e^{-aT})db$, and this must equal the cost of the machine, $q.C.e^{at}$. Hence:

$$C = \frac{r(1-e^{-aT})-a(1-e^{-rT})}{r(r-a)}. \tag{3.22}$$

There are circumstances where the Taylor expansion of (3.22) will give a more useful expression of this relationship. i.e.

$$C = \tfrac{1}{2}.a.T^2(1-\tfrac{1}{3}(r+a).T + \frac{T^2}{12}(r^2+ra+a^2)$$

$$-\frac{T^3}{60}(r^3+r^2a+ra^2+a^3) + \frac{T^4}{360}(r^4+r^3a+r^2a^2+ra^3+a^4)...) \tag{3.23}$$

(3.22) and (3.23) provide alternative forms for (3.9), but the complexity of this mathematical relationship has led some to seek a simpler connection between these variables. This can be achieved with the assumption of 'radiation depreciation'. With this assumption, the annual rate of depreciation with plant of any age is the constant, d_r, times the value of the plant, so the ratio depreciation/capital with new plant is simply d_r. r, the net rate of return on capital is R, the gross rate of return (i.e. gross profits per worker with new plant/capital per worker with new plant) minus depreciation/capital with new plant. Gross profit per worker with new plant at time t is output per worker with new plant at time t, $q.e^{at}$, minus the wage at time t, $q.e^{at}.e^{-aT}$; while the cost of equipping a worker at time t is $q.C.e^{at}$. Then:

$$R = \frac{1-e^{-aT}}{C} \tag{3.24}$$

and

$$r = \frac{1-e^{-aT}}{C} - d_r. \tag{3.25}$$

Clearly, (3.25) is very much simpler than (3.22) and (3.23), and it will be desirable to use it if the assumption of 'radiation depreciation' is a good one. There is no doubt that (3.22) and (3.23) give the correct value of r i.e. the true yield of an investment, but the relative simplicity of (3.25) would make this a useful alternative equation if the answer it provided was much the same. It will be seen below that 'radiation depreciation' is a reasonable approximation for 'correct depreciation' where T is a constant. There is, however, as is to be expected, a strong inverse relationship between depreciation/capital and T, the life of plant, and the assumption that depreciation/capital is a constant, d_r, ignores this important aspect of the economic world.

The 'correct' rate of depreciation with new plant, D_0, is the difference between the gross rate of return with new plant, R, and the true net rate of return, r, that is derived from (3.22) or (3.23). Then, from (3.22) and (3.24):

$$D_0 = \frac{r.a(e^{-aT} - e^{-rT})}{r(1 - e^{-aT}) - a(1 - e^{-rT})} \tag{3.26}[1]$$

and by Taylor expansion:

$$D_0 = \frac{2}{T}\left(1 - \frac{T}{6}(r+a) + \frac{T^2}{36}(r^2 - ra + a^2)\right.$$
$$\left. - \frac{T^3}{540}(r^3 - 1\tfrac{1}{2}r^2a - 1\tfrac{1}{2}ra^2 + a^3)...\right) \tag{3.27}$$

The correct rate of depreciation with new plant which is shown by (3.27) will be fairly stable if T is constant (and r varies within a plausible range of, say 0·07 to 0·20). In that case the assumption of 'radiation depreciation' would lead to little inaccuracy. It is evident, however, that the correct rate of depreciation will vary in more than inverse proportion with T, so that halving T would more than double D_0. This means that the assumption of 'radiation depreciation' is ludicrous where T is variable. In consequence, the results which follow from the use of (3.25) will be seriously inaccurate wherever there is considerable variation in T, which means that (3.22) and (3.23) must be preferred to (3.25), in spite of their complexity, if important aspects of the relationship between the rate of investment, C, T and r are not to be missed, or indeed confused.

A useful equation of the general form $r = R - D_0$ can be obtained

[1] $D_0 = R - r = \dfrac{(1 - e^{-aT})}{C} - r$ (from (3.24)). Substitute from (3.22).

from (3.24) and (3.27) by making use of an interesting feature of (3.24). If (3.24) is compared with (3.15), it will be evident that:

$$R = \frac{1}{\text{ICOR}} = \frac{g}{S} \text{ where } n = 0. \tag{3.28}$$

Then, using (3.28) and (3.27) to substitute in $r = R - D_0$:

$$r = \frac{g}{S} - \frac{2}{T}\left(1 - \frac{T}{6}(r+a) + \frac{T^2}{36}(r^2 - ra + a^2)..., \text{etc.}\right) \tag{3.29}$$

Some use will be made of this equation for r in Part II of this book.

It is now time to turn to the derivation of a precise form for (3.10), the third equation that is needed to determine the equilibrium values of r, C and T. (3.10) equates the capital cost of saving a worker to the expected cost of a worker throughout the lifetime of plant.

A constant returns to scale production function for new plant of the algebraic CES form can be written as:

$$Y^{-u} = \lambda.[h.K^{-u} + (1-h).L^{-u}] \tag{3.30}$$

where Y is gross output, K is capital and L is labour, all with new plant, while λ and h are constants, and $u = (1/\theta) - 1$. Technical progress must be Harrod-neutral or labour-augmenting if there is to be steady growth with a CES production function, and this means that L must measure labour in efficiency units.[1] The other putty-clay vintage relationships of the model clearly require that labour be measured in natural units. Let an efficiency unit of labour equal a natural unit at time 0. Then (3.30) will measure labour in the same units as the other equations at time 0, but a correction factor will need to be applied at other dates. This raises no special problems.

The capital cost of saving a worker with new plant, K^*, is found through the partial differentiation of (3.30) with respect to L and K. The partial differentiation of (3.30) with respect to L will show the output that is lost through the employment of one worker fewer with new plant. This will reduce gross output by $(1-h).\lambda(Y/L)^{u+1}$. This must be made good through the use of extra capital, and (3.30) can be partially differentiated with respect to K to find the increase in output that will result from the use of an extra unit of capital. Each extra unit of capital will raise gross output by $h.\lambda.(Y/K)^{u+1}$. The

---

[1] See pp. 34-5 above.

B*

number of units of capital that will be needed to leave output unchanged where one worker fewer is used will then be

$$(1-h).\lambda.(Y/L)^{u+1}$$

divided by

$$h.\lambda.\left(\frac{Y}{K}\right)^{u+1} = \left(\frac{1-h}{h}\right).\left(\frac{K}{L}\right)^{u+1},$$

and this can be written as

$$\left(\frac{1-h}{h}\right).\left(\frac{K}{Y}\right)^{u+1}.\left(\frac{Y}{L}\right)^{u+1},$$

and since C can be written for (K/Y), the capital–output ratio with new plant, then the following expression can be written for K^*, the capital cost of saving a worker with new plant at time 0:

$$K^* = \left(\frac{1-h}{h}\right).C^{u+1}.\left(\frac{Y}{L}\right)^{u+1}. \tag{3.31}$$

A worker thus saved at time 0 will be paid a wage that is initially $q.e^{-aT}$, and this rises at rate a over the following T years to q. W^*, the discounted present value of the wages of a worker saved over the T years $(0...T)$, will then be

$$\int_0^T q.e^{-aT}.e^{(a-r)b}db = q\left(\frac{e^{-aT}-e^{-rT}}{r-a}\right).$$

Now (Y/L) can be written for q at time 0, and

$$\left(\frac{e^{-aT}-e^{-rT}}{r-a}\right) = \left(\frac{1-e^{-rT}}{r}-C\right) \quad \text{(from (3.22))}.$$

Then:

$$W^* = \left(\frac{Y}{L}\right).\left(\frac{1-e^{-rT}}{r}-C\right) \tag{3.32}$$

in equilibrium, $W^* = K^*$, i.e.

$$\left(\frac{1-h}{h}\right).C^{u+1}.\left(\frac{Y}{L}\right)^{u} = \frac{1-e^{-rT}}{r}-C. \tag{3.33}[1]$$

---

[1] This equation also shows the relationship between these variables at time t, for the change from time 0 to time t raises both W^* and K^* e^{aT} times. W^* is raised because the wage is e^{aT} times as high at time t as at time 0, while K^* is raised because this is the capital cost of saving an efficiency unit of labour, and e^{at} efficiency units of labour equal one natural unit at time t.

Now

$$\left(\frac{Y}{L}\right)^u = \frac{1}{\lambda.(1-h)} - \left(\frac{h}{1-h}\right).\left(\frac{K}{Y}\right)^{-u} = \frac{1}{\lambda.(1-h)} - \left(\frac{h}{1-h}\right).C^{-u}$$

(from (3.30)).

Then, substituting for $(Y/L)^u$ in (3.33), and writing $1/\theta$ for $(u+1)$:

$$\left(\frac{1}{h.\lambda}\right).C^{\frac{1}{\theta}} = \frac{1-e^{-rT}}{r} \qquad (3.34)$$

and by Taylor expansion:

$$\left(\frac{1}{h.\lambda}\right).C^{\frac{1}{\theta}} = T.\left(1 - \frac{r.T}{2} + \frac{r^2T^2}{6} - \frac{r^3T^3}{24} + \frac{r^4T^4}{120} ..., \text{etc.}\right) (3.35)$$

(3.34) and (3.35) provide alternative forms for (3.10).

(3.14), and (3.22) or (3.23), and (3.34) or (3.35) provide the three equations that are needed to determine the equilibrium values of r, C and T, but there is obviously no straightforward way of solving them to find expressions for the equilibrium values of r, C and T in terms of parameters alone. It is, however, relatively simple to find the *elasticities* of the variables with respect to the parameters, and this is the information that is actually of most interest. The three equations can be differentiated with respect to S to produce three equations that are linear in terms of $(S/r).(\partial r/\partial S)$, $(S/T).(\partial T/\partial S)$ and $(S/C).(\partial C/\partial S)$, the elasticities of r, T and C with respect to S. These can then be solved to produce the equilibrium values of these three elasticities. The elasticities of r, C and T with respect to a can be found similarly.

In Part II of this book an investment function and a technical progress function will be brought into the argument with the result that S and a will become variables instead of parameters, with the investment and technical progress functions providing the two further equations which will then be needed. S and a are parameters in thi chapter, and they will be differentiated as such in the main text. Some of the chapter's equations will be outlined in an appendix to the chapter, with S and a differentiated as variables, and these will be useful in later chapters.

It will slightly simplify the rather complex mathematics that follows if the labour force is assumed constant so that $n = 0$. This will not significantly alter the results because two of the fundamental equations are independent of n, while in the third, (3.14), n has exactly the same effect as a so it is immaterial whether labour growth is measured in natural units or efficiency units. Then so far as the model's fundamental equations are concerned, a can stand for both labour growth and technical progress. n and a do, however, have slightly different effects on income distribution, as (3.21) shows.

How a difference in S between two otherwise similar economies will influence their relative rates of profit, lives of plant and capital–output ratios with new plant is found by differentiating (3.14), (3.23) and (3.35) with respect to S. Then:

$$\frac{S}{C}\cdot\frac{\partial C}{\partial S} = 1 + \left(\frac{aT}{e^{aT}-1}\right)\cdot\frac{S}{T}\cdot\frac{\partial T}{\partial S} = 1 + X_w\cdot\frac{S}{T}\cdot\frac{\partial T}{\partial S} \quad \text{(from (3.19))} \quad (3.36)$$

$$\frac{S}{r}\cdot\frac{\partial r}{\partial S} = \frac{S}{T}\cdot\frac{\partial T}{\partial S}\cdot\frac{6}{r.T}\left(1 - \frac{aT}{4} + \frac{T^2}{60}(r^2 - 3\tfrac{1}{2}ra + 3\tfrac{1}{4}a^2)\right.$$

$$\left. - \frac{T^3}{240}(r^2a - 3ra^2 + 1\tfrac{3}{4}a^3)...\right) - \frac{S}{C}\cdot\frac{\partial C}{\partial S}\cdot\frac{3}{r.T}\left(1 + \frac{T}{6}(r - \tfrac{1}{2}a)\right.$$

$$\left. + \frac{T^2}{60}(r^2 - ra + \tfrac{3}{4}a^2) + \frac{T^3}{480}(a^2r - \tfrac{1}{2}a^3)...\right) \quad (3.37)$$

$$\frac{S}{r}\cdot\frac{\partial r}{\partial S} = \frac{S}{T}\cdot\frac{\partial T}{\partial S}\cdot\frac{2}{r.T}\left(1 - \frac{rT}{3} + \frac{r^2T^2}{36} + \frac{r^3T^3}{540}...\right)$$

$$- \frac{S}{C}\cdot\frac{\partial C}{\partial S}\cdot\frac{2}{\theta.r.T}\left(1 + \frac{rT}{6} + \frac{r^2T^2}{36} + \frac{r^3T^3}{540}...\right). \quad (3.38)$$

(3.36), (3.37) and (3.38) provide three equations that are linear in terms of $(S/T).(\partial T/\partial S)$, $(S/C).(\partial C/\partial S)$ and $(S/r).(\partial r/\partial S)$, the elasticities of T, C and r with respect to S, and these can be solved very simply. Eliminate $(S/r).(\partial r/\partial S)$ from (3.37) and (3.38):

$$\frac{S}{T}\cdot\frac{\partial T}{\partial S} = \frac{S}{C}\cdot\frac{\partial C}{\partial S}\left[\left(\tfrac{3}{4} + \tfrac{7}{32}aT + \frac{T^2}{240}(r^2 + 4ra + 7\tfrac{5}{16}a^2)\right.\right.$$

$$\left. + \frac{T^3}{960}(r^2a + 7\tfrac{1}{2}ra^2 + \tfrac{3}{32}a^3)...\right)$$

$$- \frac{1}{2\theta}\left(1 + \tfrac{3}{8}aT + \frac{T^2}{60}(r^2 + \tfrac{3}{2}ra + 3\tfrac{9}{16}a^2)\right.$$

$$\left.\left. + \frac{T^3}{240}(r^2a + 3\tfrac{1}{4}ra^2 + \tfrac{21}{32}a^3)...\right)\right] \quad (3.39)$$

then $\dfrac{S}{T} \cdot \dfrac{\partial T}{\partial S} = 0$ where

$$\theta = \frac{2}{3} + \frac{aT}{18} + \frac{T^2}{135}(r^2 + \tfrac{1}{4}ra - \tfrac{1}{2}a^2)$$
$$- \frac{T^3}{1620}(r^2a - \tfrac{1}{2}ra^2 + \tfrac{1}{2}a^3)... \quad (3.40)$$

Let

$$\frac{2}{3} + \frac{aT}{18} + \frac{T^2}{135}(r^2 + \tfrac{1}{4}ra - \tfrac{1}{2}a^2)... = \theta^*.$$

θ^* is an important expression, and it is useful to know something about its probable range of values. It is clear from (3.40) that it will slightly exceed two-thirds with ordinary values of $a.T$ and $r.T$. The value of $a.T$ can be inferred from the economy's share of profits (from (3.20)), and $a.T$ will have lower and upper limits of 0·55 and 1·26 if the share of profits has plausible lower and upper limits of 0·25 and 0·50. $r.T$ is r/g times $a.T$ (where $n = 0$), and this will be 3·78 if the share of profits is 0·50 and the rate of profit is three times the rate of growth, perhaps as favourable a situation for profits as can be imagined. $r.T$ will be 1·10 if the rate of profit is twice the rate of growth and the share of profits is only 0·25 – perhaps the most unfavourable situation. The first four terms of the above Taylor expansion suggest that θ^* will be 0·835 at the upper limit where $X_p = 0·50$ and $r/g = 3$, and 0·706 at the lower limit where $X_p = 0·25$ and $r/g = 2$. These calculations can be checked against the complete non-Taylor formula for θ^* which is:

$$\theta^* = \left(\frac{e^{rT}-1}{e^{rT}-rT-1}\right) \cdot \left(1 - \frac{\left(\dfrac{a.r}{r-a}\right)(e^{-aT}-e^{-rT}) - arT.e^{-rT}}{r(1-e^{-aT}) - a(1-e^{-rT})}\right).$$

$$(3.41)[1]$$

This comes to 0·812 where $r.T = 3·78$, $a.T = 1·26$, $r = 0·15$ and $a = 0·05$ against the 0·835 obtained from the Taylor expansion; and where $r.T = 1·10$, $a.T = 0·55$, $r = 0·06$ and $a = 0·03$, the correct value of θ^* is 0·709 while the value obtained from the Taylor expansion is 0·706. It will be noted that the Taylor expansion is only slightly

[1] This is derived from the non-Taylor version of (3.39) which is obtained by partially differentiating (3.22) and (3.34) with respect to S, and eliminating $(S/r).(\partial r/\partial S)$ from the resulting expressions.

inaccurate, especially where $r.T$ has moderate values, and that the value of θ^* is likely to lie in the range 0·70–0·83.

It will simplify the subsequent exposition if the following substitution is made in the expressions:

$$U = \tfrac{3}{4}\left(\frac{\theta^*-\theta}{\theta}\right) \cdot \left(1+\tfrac{7}{24}aT+ \frac{T^2}{180}\,(r^2+4ra+7\tfrac{5}{16}a^2)\right.$$

$$\left. + \frac{T^3}{720}\,(r^2a+7\tfrac{1}{2}ra^2+\tfrac{33}{32}a^3)...\right). \quad (3.42)$$

The value of U depends on the degree to which θ differs from θ^*. It will be zero where $\theta = \theta^*$, positive where $\theta^*>\theta$, and negative where $\theta>\theta^*$.

Substituting U in (3.39), this can be rewritten as:

$$\frac{S}{T}\cdot\frac{\partial T}{\partial S} = -U\cdot\frac{S}{C}\cdot\frac{\partial C}{\partial S}. \quad (3.43)$$

Then, from (3.36) and (3.43):

$$\frac{S}{T}\cdot\frac{\partial T}{\partial S} = -\frac{U}{1+U.X_w}. \quad (3.44)$$

As $(1+U.X_w)$ must be positive,[1] $(S/T).(\partial T/\partial S)$ will be >0 where $U<0$, i.e. where $\theta>\theta^*$, and vice versa.

$(S/C).(\partial C/\partial S)$ is also derived from (3.36) and (3.43):

$$\frac{S}{C}\cdot\frac{\partial C}{\partial S} = \frac{1}{1+U.X_w}. \quad (3.46)$$

It will be evident that $(S/C).(\partial C/\partial S)$ must be positive, and that it will exceed 1 where U is negative, i.e. where $\theta>\theta^*$, and be less then 1 where $\theta^*>\theta$ when U will be positive.

---

[1] $(1+U.X_w)$ can be written as

$$\left(\tfrac{1}{4}+\tfrac{5}{32}aT-\frac{T^2}{240}(r^2+4ra-3\tfrac{15}{16}a^2)+\frac{T^3}{960}(r^2a+\tfrac{1}{2}ra^2-3\tfrac{29}{32}a^3)...\right)$$

$$+\frac{1}{2\theta}\left(1-\frac{aT}{8}+\frac{T^2}{60}(r^2+\tfrac{3}{2}ra-2\tfrac{11}{16}a^2)...\right) \quad (3.45)$$

and this must be positive. This expression is obtained by substituting for θ^* in (3.42), and using the Taylor expansion of (3.19) to substitute for X_w.

$\dfrac{S}{X_p} \cdot \dfrac{\partial X_p}{\partial S}$ is derived from (3.20)[1] and (3.44):

$$\frac{S}{X_p} \cdot \frac{\partial X_p}{\partial S} = -\frac{U\left(1 - \dfrac{aT}{6} - \dfrac{a^2 T^2}{36} + \dfrac{a^3 T^3}{270} \ldots\right)}{1 + U \cdot X_w}. \qquad (3.47)$$

Then $(S/X_p) \cdot (\partial X_p / \partial S)$ will be >0 where $U<0$, i.e. where $\theta > \theta^*$, and vice versa.

$(S/r) \cdot (\partial r / \partial S)$ is derived from (3.37), (3.44) and (3.46):

$$\frac{S}{r} \cdot \frac{\partial r}{\partial S} = -\frac{3}{r \cdot T}\left(1 + \frac{T}{6}(r - \tfrac{1}{2}a) + \frac{T^2}{60}(r^2 - ra + \tfrac{3}{4}a^2)\ldots\right)$$

$$- \frac{3}{r \cdot T}\left(\frac{U \cdot X_w}{1 + U \cdot X_w}\right) \cdot \left(1 - \frac{T}{6}(r - 3\tfrac{1}{2}a) + \frac{T^2}{60}(r^2 - 6ra + 10\tfrac{3}{4}a^2)\ldots\right)$$

$$(3.48)$$

(3.48) is usefully approximated by the expression which results if it is assumed that each Taylor series is the exponential series with the same first two terms, i.e.

$$\frac{S}{r} \cdot \frac{\partial r}{\partial S} \simeq -\frac{3}{r \cdot T}\left(e^{\frac{T}{6}(r - \frac{1}{2}a)} + \left(\frac{U \cdot X_w}{1 + U \cdot X_w}\right) \cdot e^{-\frac{T}{6}(r - 3\frac{1}{2}a)}\right). \qquad (3.49)$$

The approximate values of $(S/r) \cdot (\partial r / \partial S)$ that are provided by (3.49) can easily be checked against the correct values for two cases where an expression for the correct values can be obtained without difficulty. These cases occur where, first, $(S/T) \cdot (\partial T / \partial S)$ is zero so that higher investment has its entire effect on C, and second where $(S/C) \cdot (\partial C / \partial S)$ is zero so that higher investment has its entire effect on T. In the first case U is zero (from (3.44)), so the approximate value of $(S/r) \cdot (\partial r / \partial S)$ (from 3.49)) is

$$- \frac{3}{r \cdot T} \cdot e^{\frac{T}{6}(r - \frac{1}{2}a)}.$$

This comes to $-1 \cdot 71$ where $r = 0 \cdot 10$, $T = 25$ years and $a = 0 \cdot 03$, when the correct value of $(S/r) \cdot (\partial r / \partial S)$ is $-1 \cdot 72$.[2] Where

[1] Differentiate (3.20) with respect to S:

$$\frac{S}{X_p} \cdot \frac{\partial X_p}{\partial S} = \frac{S}{T} \cdot \frac{\partial T}{\partial S}\left(\frac{aT \cdot (aT \cdot e^{aT} - e^{aT} + 1)}{(e^{aT} - aT - 1) \cdot (e^{aT} - 1)}\right) = \frac{S}{T} \cdot \frac{\partial T}{\partial S}\left(1 - \frac{aT}{6} - \frac{a^2 T^2}{36} + \frac{a^3 T^3}{270}\ldots\right). \quad (3.50)$$

[2] The complete equations for $\dfrac{S}{r} \cdot \dfrac{\partial r}{\partial S}$ for the conditions assumed in this paragraph are derived and checked against the approximations in W. A. Eltis, 'Technical progress, profits, and growth', *Oxford Economic Papers*, vol. xx (July 1968) pp. 191-3.

$(S/C).(\partial C/\partial S)$ is zero, $\theta = 0$, when $U.X_w/(1+UX_w) = 1$, and the approximate value of $(S/r).(\partial r/\partial S)$ from (3.49) is

$$-\frac{3}{r.T}\left(e^{\frac{T}{6}(r-\frac{1}{4}a)}+e^{-\frac{T}{6}(r-3\frac{1}{4}a)}\right) \simeq -\frac{6}{r.T}.e^{\frac{aT}{4}}.$$

This comes to $-2\cdot90$ with the above values of r, T and a, while the correct value is $-2\cdot97$. These are the only cases where (3·49) can easily be checked against a complete formula, but they do suggest that (3.49) may be quite an accurate approximation. Accuracy will be reduced where $r.T$ exceeds the $2\cdot50$ assumed in these examples.

The elasticities of T, C, r and X_p with respect to a can be found in exactly the same way as the elasticities of these variables with respect to S. Differentiate (3.14), (3.23) and (3.35) with respect to a, and solve the resulting three equations to obtain expressions for $(a/T).(\partial T/\partial a)$, $(a/C).(\partial C/\partial a)$ and $(a/r).(\partial r/\partial a)$:

$$\frac{a}{T}.\frac{\partial T}{\partial a} = -1+\frac{1}{2}\left(\frac{1-\theta}{\theta}\right).\left(\frac{1+\frac{3}{8}aT+\dfrac{T^2}{60}(r^2+\frac{3}{2}ra+3\frac{9}{16}a^2)...}{1+U.X_w}\right) \quad (3.51)$$

$$\frac{a}{C}.\frac{\partial C}{\partial a} = -1+\frac{1}{2}\left(\frac{1-\theta}{\theta}\right).X_w\left(\frac{1+\frac{3}{8}aT+\dfrac{T^2}{60}(r^2+\frac{3}{2}ra+3\frac{9}{16}a^2)...}{1+U.X_w}\right)$$

$$(3.52)$$

$$\frac{a}{r}.\frac{\partial r}{\partial a} = 1+\frac{1\frac{1}{2}}{r.T}\left(\frac{1-\theta}{\theta}\right)\left(\frac{1-\dfrac{T}{6}(r-2\frac{3}{4}a)+\dfrac{T^2}{30}(r^2-1\frac{5}{8}ra+\frac{59}{32}a^2)...}{1+U.X_w}\right).$$

$$(3.53)$$

The elasticity of X_p with respect to a can be obtained from (3.20) and (3.51):

$$\frac{a}{X_p}.\frac{\partial X_p}{\partial a} = \frac{1}{2}\left(\frac{1-\theta}{\theta}\right).\left(\frac{1+\frac{5}{24}aT+\dfrac{T^2}{60}(r^2+\frac{3}{2}ra-\frac{89}{48}a^2...)}{1+U.X_w}\right). \quad (3.54)$$

Much can be deduced about further relationships between r, T, C, a, S and θ, and the other major economic variables. This will be analysed further in Part II of this book. The vintage growth equations in this chapter will provide some of the tools which are needed for this further analysis.

APPENDIX

In the main text of the chapter, a and S were differentiated as constants, but they will be variables in Part II of this book. The important equations that are used in Part II of this book are given below with a and S differentiated as variables. They are derived in exactly the same way as the equations in the main text, and they are numbered similarly with the letter A added. Thus equation (3.44) in the main text is (3.44A) in its complete form which is given below.

$$\frac{S}{T}.\frac{\partial T}{\partial S} = \left[1 - \frac{S}{a}.\frac{\partial a}{\partial S}\right].\left[-\frac{U}{1+U.X_w}\right]$$

$$+ \left[\frac{S}{a}.\frac{\partial a}{\partial S}\right].\left[-\frac{\left(\frac{3}{4} - \frac{aT}{32} + \frac{T^2}{240}(r^2 - ra - \frac{3}{16}a^2)...\right) + U.X_w}{1+U.X_w}\right].$$

$$(3.44\text{A})$$

$$\frac{S}{C}.\frac{\partial C}{\partial S} = \left[1 - \frac{S}{a}.\frac{\partial a}{\partial S}\right].\left[\frac{1}{1+U.X_w}\right]$$

$$+ \left[\frac{S}{a}.\frac{\partial a}{\partial S}\right].\left[\frac{X_w\left(\frac{1}{4} + \frac{aT}{32} - \frac{T^2}{240}(r^2 - ra - \frac{3}{16}a^2)...\right)}{1+U.X_w}\right]. \quad (3.46\text{A})$$

$$\frac{S}{X_p}.\frac{\partial X_p}{\partial S} = \left[1 - \frac{S}{a}.\frac{\partial a}{\partial S}\right].\left[-\frac{U.\left(1 - \frac{a.T}{6} - \frac{a^2T^2}{36} + \frac{a^3T^3}{270}...\right)}{1+U.X_w}\right]$$

$$+ \left[\frac{S}{a}.\frac{\partial a}{\partial S}\right].\left[\frac{\frac{1}{4} - \frac{aT}{96} - \frac{T^2}{240}(r^2 - ra + \frac{131}{48}a^2)...}{1+U.X_w}\right]. \quad (3.47\text{A})$$

$$\frac{S}{r}.\frac{\partial r}{\partial S} = \left[1 - \frac{S}{a}.\frac{\partial a}{\partial S}\right].\left[-\frac{3}{r.T}\left(1 + \frac{T}{6}(r - \frac{1}{2}a) + \frac{T^2}{60}(r^2 - ra + \frac{3}{4}a^2)...\right)\right.$$

$$\left. - \frac{3}{r.T}\left(\frac{U.X_w}{1+U.X_w}\right)\left(1 - \frac{T}{6}(r - 3\frac{1}{2}a) + \frac{T^2}{60}(r^2 - 6ra + 10\frac{3}{4}a^2)...\right)\right]$$

$$+ \left[\frac{S}{a}.\frac{\partial a}{\partial S}\right].\left[-\frac{2\frac{1}{4}}{r.T}\left(1-\frac{T}{6}(r+1\frac{3}{12}a)+\frac{T^2}{45}(r^2-1\frac{1}{16}ra+\frac{63}{64}a^2)...\right)\right.$$

$$\left.-\frac{\frac{3}{4}}{r.T}\left(\frac{U.X_w}{1+U.X_w}\right).\left(1-\frac{T}{6}(r-\frac{5}{4}a)-\frac{T^2}{48}(ra+\frac{3}{4}a^2)...\right)\right].$$

$$(3.48\text{A})$$

$$\frac{S}{r}.\frac{\partial r}{\partial S}\simeq\left[1-\frac{S}{a}.\frac{\partial a}{\partial S}\right].\left[-\frac{3}{r.T}\left(e^{\frac{T}{6}(r-\frac{1}{2}a)}+\left(\frac{U.X_w}{1+U.X_w}\right).e^{-\frac{T}{6}(r-3\frac{1}{2}a)}\right)\right]$$

$$+\left[\frac{S}{a}.\frac{\partial a}{\partial S}\right].\left[-\frac{2\cdot25}{r.T}\left(e^{-\frac{T}{6}(r+1\frac{3}{4}a)}+\frac{1}{3}\left(\frac{U.X_w}{1+U.X_w}\right).e^{-\frac{T}{6}(r-\frac{5}{4}a)}\right)\right].$$

$$(3.49\text{A})$$

$$\frac{S}{X_p}.\frac{\partial X_p}{\partial S}=\left[\frac{S}{T}.\frac{\partial T}{\partial S}+\frac{S}{a}.\frac{\partial a}{\partial S}\right]\left[1-\frac{aT}{6}-\frac{a^2T^2}{36}+\frac{a^3T^3}{270}...\right].$$

$$(3.50\text{A})$$

$$\frac{a}{T}.\frac{\partial T}{\partial a}=-1+\frac{1}{2}\left(\frac{1-\theta}{\theta}\right).\left(\frac{1+\frac{3}{8}aT+\frac{T^2}{60}(r^2+\frac{3}{2}ra+3\frac{9}{16}a^2)...}{1+U.X_w}\right)$$

$$+\left[\frac{a}{S}.\frac{\partial S}{\partial a}\right].\left[-\frac{U}{1+U.X_w}\right]. \quad (3.51\text{A})$$

$$\frac{a}{C}.\frac{\partial C}{\partial a}=-1+\frac{1}{2}\left(\frac{1-\theta}{\theta}\right).X_w.\left(\frac{1+\frac{3}{8}aT+\frac{T^2}{60}(r^2+\frac{3}{2}ra+3\frac{9}{16}a^2)...}{1+U.X_w}\right)$$

$$+\left[\frac{a}{S}.\frac{\partial S}{\partial a}\right].\left[\frac{1}{1+U.X_w}\right]. \quad (3.52\text{A})$$

$$\frac{a}{r}.\frac{\partial r}{\partial a}=1+\frac{1\cdot5}{r.T}\left(\frac{1-\theta}{\theta}\right).\left(\frac{1-\frac{T}{6}(r-2\frac{3}{4}a)+\frac{T^2}{30}(r^2-1\frac{5}{8}ra+\frac{59}{32}a^2)...}{1+U.X_w}\right)$$

$$+\left[\frac{a}{S}.\frac{\partial S}{\partial a}\right].\left[-\frac{3}{r.T}\left(1+\frac{T}{6}(r-\frac{1}{2}a)+\frac{T^2}{60}(r^2-ra+\frac{3}{4}a^2)...\right)\right.$$

$$\left.-\frac{3}{r.T}\left(\frac{U.X_w}{1+U.X_w}\right).\left(1-\frac{T}{6}(r-3\frac{1}{2}a)+\frac{T^2}{60}(r^2-6ra+10\frac{3}{4}a^2)...\right)\right].$$

$$(3.53\text{A})$$

$$\frac{a}{X_p} \cdot \frac{\partial X_p}{\partial a} = \tfrac{1}{2} \left(\frac{1-\theta}{\theta}\right) \cdot \left(\frac{1 + \tfrac{5}{24} aT + \dfrac{T^2}{60}(r^2 + \tfrac{3}{2} ra - \tfrac{89}{48} a^2)\ldots}{1 + U \cdot X_w}\right)$$

$$+ \left[\frac{a}{S} \cdot \frac{\partial S}{\partial a}\right] \cdot \left[-\frac{U\left(1 - \dfrac{aT}{6} - \dfrac{a^2 T^2}{36} + \dfrac{a^3 T^3}{270} \ldots\right)}{1 + U \cdot X_w}\right]. \quad (3.54\text{A})$$

4

Keynesian Growth Theory

A CENTRAL feature of Keynesian theory is the importance which is attached to entrepreneurial investment decisions. These are assumed to be independent of saving decisions, and to have a dominant influence on the economy. In Keynes's own work, they played a major role in the determination of effective demand and employment in the short run,[1] and their influence on this will be analysed in Chapter 12 of the present book. It can be argued that investment decisions will also play a major role in the determination of the share of profits in the National Income, the rate of profit on capital, the rate of technical progress and the rate of growth. These possibilities will be outlined in turn in this chapter.

Keynesian Theories of Income Distribution

National Income accounting identities play a part in the clarification of Keynesian theory, and this is the case with the theory of distribution as it is with the theory of employment. Kalecki[2] and Kaldor[3] have derived illuminating results from them, and since Kalecki's theory is the simpler of the two, it will be explained first.

For simplicity, it will be assumed that profits (P) and wages (W) account for the entire National Income (Y), so that $Y \equiv P + W$. A closed economy will be assumed, and the effect of taxation and government expenditure will be neglected at the start of the argument. With consistent definitions and the avoidance of double counting, Y equals both $(P + W)$ and *investment* (I) plus *consumption* (C) which is the sum of *consumption by entrepreneurs and rentiers* (C_P) and *consumption by workers* (C_w), with the result that:

$$Y \equiv P + W \equiv I + C_P + C_w$$

[1] J. M. Keynes, *The General Theory of Employment, Interest and Money* (Macmillan, 1936).

[2] M. Kalecki, *Theory of Economic Dynamics* (Allen & Unwin, 1954).

[3] N. Kaldor, 'Alternative theories of distribution', *Review of Economic Studies*, vol. XXIII (2) (1955-56).

i.e.

$$P \equiv I + C_P + (C_w - W)$$

where workers' saving which equals $(W - C_w)$ is W_s:

$$P \equiv I + C_p - W_s. \tag{4.1}$$

The importance of this identity, and its relevance to the theory of distribution, will be explained in the next few pages.

The identity shows that total profits will be the sum of investment and the consumption of entrepreneurs and rentiers if workers do not save. If workers save, profits will be less than this by the amount of workers' saving. The identity shows that there can be no profits in an economy where there is no investment and no use of profit incomes (dividends, interest, etc.) for consumption, however efficiently production is carried on, and whatever the relative scarcities of labour and capital may be. The reason why this must be so can be seen quite simply.

With no investment, and no use of profit incomes for consumption, the only goods sold will be goods bought by workers, so total business revenues will equal workers' expenditures on goods. However, the wages from which those expenditures are made are themselves direct business costs. If wages are entirely spent on consumption, total business revenues will equal total direct business costs, and profits will be zero. If a proportion of wages is saved, what businesses pay out in the form of wages will be less than their receipts from the expenditure of wages, and there will then be aggregate business losses equalling the amount of workers' saving. Hence, business in the aggregate cannot earn profits by selling to workers. Businesses merely receive back sums of money which cannot exceed the wage costs they have previously incurred. In the short run, a firm which had judged what workers will wish to buy with exceptional skill may earn a profit, but there must be corresponding losses by businesses which have judged the market less well. There can only be profits in the aggregate if money which has not already been entered in business accounts as a direct cost of production is spent on goods.

Suppose now that wages are entirely spent on consumption, and that in addition £1 million of the money received from dividends is spent on consumption. Businesses in the aggregate will now sell goods to the public for an amount equal to *total wages* plus *£1 million*, while total direct costs of production equal *total wages*. Hence, businesses will earn aggregate profits of £1 million.

If businesses spend £1 million on capital investment, while all consumption comes from wages (out of which there is no saving), businesses will receive back the total wages they have paid out through their sales of consumer goods, *plus* £1 million from sales of investment goods, while total direct costs of production will equal total wages. Hence, aggregate profits will be £1 million as in the situation where consumption from dividends was £1 million. Hence, expenditure on investment, and on consumption out of profit incomes, leads to profits equal to such expenditures. The spending of wages does not contribute to aggregate profits, and saving out of wages actually reduces profits. That Keynes was aware of this relationship is evident from the following passage (which Kaldor quotes):

> If entrepreneurs choose to spend a portion of their profits on consumption (and there is, of course, nothing to prevent them from doing this) the effect is to *increase* the profit on the sale of liquid consumption-goods by an amount exactly equal to the amount of profits which have been thus expended. . . . Thus, however much of their profits entrepreneurs spend on consumption, the increment of wealth belonging to entrepreneurs remains the same as before. Thus profits, as a source of capital increment for entrepreneurs, are a widow's cruse which remains undepleted however much of them may be devoted to riotous living.[1]

(4.1) merely states that aggregate profits must be identical to aggregate spending by entrepreneurs and rentiers, minus workers' saving. It is an identity which says nothing about causation. Profits may be high because investment and the consumption of entrepreneurs and rentiers are high, or alternatively, high profits may be the cause of high investment and consumption out of profits. The passage quoted from Keynes transforms the identity into a Keynesian equation with the statement 'If entrepreneurs choose to spend a portion of their profits on consumption (and there is, of course, nothing to prevent them from doing this) . . .' which makes entrepreneurial spending decisions an independent variable.

To arrive at the Keynesian theory which uses (4.1), it is thus necessary to make the characteristic Keynesian assumption that investment decisions are independent of *ex-ante* saving. Then, if entrepreneurs decide to undertake a great deal of investment, the

[1] J. M. Keynes, *A Treatise on Money* (Macmillan, 1930) vol. I, p. 139.

economy's investment will be high, and a consequence of this will be high *ex-post* profits as well as high *ex-post* saving. Similarly, it can be supposed that the financial circumstances of entrepreneurs and rentiers are such that their decisions to spend on consumption are largely independent of current incomes (through their individual power to borrow or to sell capital). These spending decisions will then generate equivalent profit incomes, and while these will not accrue directly to the actual entrepreneurs who take the spending decisions, equivalent profits will be earned somewhere in the economy. Hence, with the assumption that entrepreneurs and rentiers are so financially circumstanced that they can take spending decisions which are independent of current incomes, it follows that these decisions determine the amount of aggregate profits, and the identity (4.1) shows the precise connection between profits and entrepreneurial and rentier spending.

The argument that aggregate profits are *determined* by the aggregate spending decisions of entrepreneurs and rentiers is sufficient to explain the size of aggregate profits, but it says nothing about aggregate wages or the distribution of the National Income between profits and wages. A further relationship is needed to arrive at these. Kalecki and Kaldor use different relationships to carry the argument to the point of explaining the distribution of the National Income between wages and profits. Kalecki's will be explained first.

Kalecki argues that competitive conditions in a particular country at a particular time will determine the ratio of prices to average direct costs of production in the economy as a whole. The fundamental principle involved can be seen most clearly if the simplifying assumptions are made that wages are the sole direct cost of production, and that competitive conditions are such that the ratio of prices to average direct costs of production is $1:U$. Then, since wages are the sole direct cost of production, the ratio of prices to average wage costs per unit of output will be $1:U$, and wage costs per unit of output will be U times price per unit. Aggregate sales equal the National Income, and aggregate wage costs equal aggregate wages, so if wage costs are U times price per unit, the share of wages in the National Income, X_w, will be U,

i.e. $$X_w = U. \tag{4.2}$$

Then $$X_p = (1 - U). \tag{4.3}$$

Thus the shares of wages and profits in the National Income will depend simply on competitive conditions, which determine the ratio of prices to average direct costs of production. Weaker competition (Kalecki would say 'a higher degree of monopoly'), which allows entrepreneurs to raise prices in relation to direct costs of production, will mean a lower U, a lower X_w and a higher X_p. Stronger competition will raise U and X_w. Thus the relative shares of wages and profits in the National Income apparently depend entirely on competitive conditions in industry, while the aggregate spending of entrepreneurs and rentiers appears to be irrelevant to their determination. It will become evident that this is not the case.

From (4.1), profits are investment *plus* consumption by entrepreneurs and rentiers *minus* workers' saving. Combining this with (4.3), it is evident that profits must be $(1 - U)$ times the National Income (Y), i.e.

$$Y = \frac{I + C_p - W_s}{1 - U}. \tag{4.4}$$

(4.4) will hold if it is possible for the National Income to be as large as this. If Y_f is the National Income at full employment, (4.4) will hold if $Y_f > Y$. In this case X_p will always equal $(1 - U)$ so it will be independent of entrepreneurial spending. A change in investment will have no influence on the *share* of profits, but, through (4.4), it will influence Y, the actual National Income. An increase in investment (or in consumption by entrepreneurs and rentiers) of ∂I will raise Y by $\partial I/(1 - U)$ from (4.4) so the investment multiplier will be $1/(1 - U)$. Hence U determines the distribution of income and the size of the multiplier, while spending decisions by entrepreneurs and rentiers determine what is multiplied, so these determine the actual size of the National Income, the level of employment, etc.

This is what will happen if $Y_f > Y$. What of the situation where Y (from 4.4) exceeds Y_f? Clearly, the National Income cannot exceed Y_f, but effective demand can exceed the economy's full-employment output. Where this occurs, there will be excess demand with a consequent lengthening of delivery dates, the diversion of demand to overseas suppliers (if the assumption of a closed economy is momentarily relaxed), and, what is of most importance in this context, a rise in prices in relation to costs. A cause of the excess of Y over Y_f is a U that is too high, i.e. prices which are too low in relation to average direct costs of production. In Kalecki's terminology, the 'degree of monopoly' is so low that demand exceeds an economy's full-employment output. This is not plausibly a state of affairs which will last, for while it is clear that restricted competition may set a *lower* limit to the ratio of prices to average direct costs of production which will last, it is far less clear that it will set an *upper* limit. With excess demand, entrepreneurs have clear incentives to raise prices in relation to direct costs of production, and the 'degree of monopoly' need not prevent this. Then, at full employemt, U should adjust to equate the right-hand side of (4.4) to Y_f.

In this case:

$$U = \frac{Y_f - I - C_p + W_s}{Y_f} \qquad (4.5)$$

and, substituting in (4.3):

$$X_p = \frac{I + C_p - W_s}{Y_f}. \qquad (4.6)$$

(4.6) shows that the share of profits will be the total profits given by (4.1) divided by Y_f, the full-employment National Income. What this means is that in a full-employment situation, entrepreneurs and rentiers will obtain the resources they demand (because they supposedly have sufficient financial resources to pay what is necessary to obtain them) and workers will simply obtain what remains. The share of wages will then depend on what entrepreneurs and rentiers leave to workers, and the share of profits will amount essentially to the ratio of entrepreneurial and rentier spending to the full-employment National Product. This will be the position at full employment. At less than full employment, the share of profits will be $(1-U)$ or, alternatively, it could be stated that X_p will be whichever is *higher* of $(1-U)$ and the right-hand side of (4.6). Where the budget surplus (B) and the trade balance (F) are allowed for, (4.1) will be modified so that[1]:

$$P \equiv I + C_p - W_s - B + F. \qquad (4.7)$$

A budget deficit always increases profits by an equivalent amount, and at less than full employment it will increase Y by the deficit times the Kalecki multiplier of $1/(1-U)$. Thus full employment can always be maintained by traditional Keynesian budgetary methods, provided that a budget deficit does not produce an equivalent deficit in the balance of payments.

[1] Kalecki, *Theory of Economic Dynamics*, pp. 48-9.

The important equation from the point of view of what follows is (4.6), the equation for the share of profits at full employment, for growth theory is largely concerned with full-employment situations. It will be shown below that Kaldor has arrived at what is essentially the same equation in a slightly different way.

His approach is as follows.[1] Suppose that entrepreneurs decide to invest I, and those who receive profits save a fraction, S_p, of their incomes, while those who receive wages save a fraction, S_w, of their incomes. Then total saving will be $P.S_p + W.S_w$, and since $W \equiv (Y-P)$, total saving is $P.S_p + (Y-P).S_w$.

Since saving must equal investment:

$$I \equiv P(S_p - S_w) + Y.S_w \qquad (4.8)$$

and since $Y = Y_f$ at full employment, then at full employment

$$X_p = \frac{P}{Y_f} = \frac{I}{Y_f} \cdot \frac{1}{S_p - S_w} - \frac{S_w}{S_p - S_w}. \qquad (4.9)$$

(4.9) comes to the same answer as (4.6), as can be seen if $P(1 - S_p)$ is substituted for C_p in (4.6), and $(Y_f - P).S_w$ for W_s.

Thus the formulations of Kalecki and Kaldor are very similar at full employment. At less than full employment, Kalecki's share of profits is $(1 - U)$, and there is an equivalent relationship in Kaldor's theory, for there are a number of constraints which may prevent the share of profits from being that shown by (4.9). The one which corresponds to Kalecki's formulation is '. . . there may be a certain minimum rate of profit on turnover – due to imperfections of competition, collusive agreements between traders, etc., and which we call m, the "degree of monopoly" rate. Hence the restriction: $P/Y > m$.'

This is identical to the Kalecki formulation where $m = (1 - U)$. As with his theory, full employment cannot be maintained where the right-hand side of (4.9) is less than m, for prices cannot then become low enough in relation to direct costs of production to give the low share of profits shown by (4.9).

Kaldor's other constraints may also be of importance. In particular, the share of wages cannot be so low that the real wage falls below 'a subsistence minimum'. This does not appear to be relevant to present-day developed economies at first sight, for the real wage must be well above a classical subsistence minimum in all developed

[1] Kaldor, 'Alternative theories of distribution'.

economies, and no change in the distribution of income could plausibly bring it below a subsistence minimum defined in the classical sense. However, the modern variant of the 'subsistence minimum' is Joan Robinson's 'inflation barrier':

> But there is a limit to the possible maximum proportion of quasi-rent to wages, which is set by what we may call the *inflation barrier*. Higher prices of consumption goods relatively to money-wage rates involve a lower real consumption by workers. There is a limit to the level to which real-wage rates can fall without setting up a pressure to raise money-wage rates. But a rise in money-wage rates increases money expenditure, so that the vicious spiral of money wages chasing prices sets in. There is then a head-on conflict between the desire of entrepreneurs to invest and the refusal of the system to accept the level of real wages which the investment entails; something must give way. Either the system explodes in a hyper-inflation, or some check operates to curtail investment.[1]

If an attempt to reduce the share of wages below W_u (where W_u is less than U) results in an intolerable wage–price spiral, the share of profits cannot exceed $(1 - W_u)$. If the right-hand side of (4.9) exceeds $(1 - W_u)$, the government is bound to intervene to reduce it which will involve government measures to reduce I, or to raise S_p or S_w (or to reduce the budget deficit or increase the budget surplus). In one of these ways, the share of profits will need to fall to $(1 - W_u)$, and the strength of a country's trades unions (which will be a major factor influencing W_u) will thus influence the share of profits in the National Income.

If W_u exceeds U, there will be a straight conflict between the share of the National Income which the trades unions seek for labour, and the share which entrepreneurs seek for capital through their pricing policies. The conflict will produce inflation, and the government will need to have W_u reduced or U increased to control this. Whichever group is more susceptible to control is likely to have its share reduced below that initially sought.

The end result of this is that in the Kalecki–Kaldor theory of distribution the share of profits will be that shown by (4.9) and (4.6) at full employment, subject to two constraints. First, industrial pricing policies must permit the share of profits to be as low as this.

[1] Robinson, *The Accumulation of Capital*, p. 48.

Second, trades unions must allow it to be as high as this. Between outer limits set by industrial pricing policies and trades unions, the share of profits will depend on investment and the saving propensities of entrepreneurs and workers in the manner shown by (4.6) and (4.9). This result ignores what was said about the relationship between the share of profits and marginal products, elasticities of substitution, the life of capital, etc., in Chapters 1, 2 and 3. The argument of these chapters was conducted with the assumptions of perfect competition in product and factor markets, and constant returns to scale. With imperfect competition and increasing returns to scale, the account of income distribution in this chapter may come closer to the forces which determine distribution in the real world.[1] A resolution of some of the contradictions between the marginal productivity and vintage theories of distribution on the one hand, and the Kalecki–Kaldor Keynesian theory of distribution on the other, will be attempted in Chapter 13.

The Rate of Profit

An equation similar to (4.9) can be arrived at which makes the rate of profit on capital a function of investment and saving propensities. Divide both sides of (4.8) by K (where K is the value of the capital stock):

$$\frac{P}{K} \equiv \frac{I}{K} \cdot \frac{1}{S_p - S_w} - \frac{Y}{K} \cdot \frac{S_w}{S_p - S_w}.$$

P/K is r, the rate of profit; I/K is k, the rate of growth of capital; and Y/K is $1/V$ where V is the capital–output ratio. Then:

$$r \equiv \frac{k}{S_p - S_w} - \frac{S_w}{V(S_p - S_w)}. \tag{4.10}$$

In equilibrium growth, where $g = k$, this formula takes a particularly simple form where $S_w = 0$, i.e. $r = g/S_p$. Pasinetti has shown that this is the relevant formula, even where S_w exceeds zero (though it must obviously be less than I/Y) in the longest of long runs.[2]

[1] See N. Kaldor, 'Marginal productivity and the macro-economic theories of distribution', *Review of Economic Studies*, vol. xxxiii (Oct 1966).

[2] L. L. Pasinetti, 'Rate of profit and income distribution in relation to the rate of economic growth', *Review of Economic Studies*, vol. xxix (Oct 1962). See G. C. Harcourt, *Some Cambridge Controversies in the Theory of Capital* (Cambridge U.P., 1972) chap. 5, for an account of the subsequent literature.

Pasinetti's argument is based on the proposition that in the very long run the proportion of aggregate profits that each class receives will equal the proportion of the capital stock that it owns, and this in turn will equal the proportion of aggregate savings that it contributes. Thus, on a steady-state growth path (where this exists), workers will necessarily receive one-quarter of aggregate profits and own one-quarter of the capital stock if they provide one-quarter of the economy's savings. Now it turns out that the rate of profit will then be determined by S_c, the savings propensity of the 'pure capitalists' who receive no earned incomes. If they provide a fraction, ϕ, of aggregate saving, they will receive a fraction, ϕ, of aggregate profits, and their total saving can then be written as $\phi.I$ (since aggregate saving equals I, the economy's aggregate investment), and the profits they receive as $\phi.P$. Since they save a fraction, S_c, of their incomes which consist exclusively of profits, $\phi.I = S_c.\phi.P$, so that $I/K = S_c.P/K$, i.e. $k = S_c.r$. Then in steady growth:

$$r = \frac{g}{S_c}. \tag{4.11}$$

Thus, in steady growth, the rate of profit will be solely a function of the economy's equilibrium rate of growth and the savings propensity of 'pure capitalists'. It is to be noted that S_c will normally differ from S_p, for S_c is the savings propensity of 'pure capitalists' while S_p is the propensity to save from profits of all classes, so it will be some kind of weighted average of S_c and the proportion of the profits they receive that workers and salary earners save.

It is clear (from (4.10) and (4.11)) that the rate of growth will have a considerable influence on the rate of profit, whether this depends on just S_c or on both S_p and S_w. An economy with a high rate of growth will (cet. par.) have a high rate of profit, and vice versa. In Chapters 1 and 2 the rate of growth influenced the rate of profit, but this also depended on the coefficients of the relevant production functions, etc., while the Keynesian rate of profit is, of course, independent of the production function. An attempt will be made in later chapters to resolve this contradiction between the Keynesian and neoclassical theories of how the rate of profit is determined.

Technical Progress

Up to this point in the argument, it has been suggested that high entrepreneurial investment will be associated (cet. par.) with a high share of profits in the National Income, and a high rate of profit on capital. Thus high investment, through Keynes's 'widow's cruse', will produce the profits out of which further investment can be financed and, incidentally, the high rate of profit which will justify it and induce its continuation.

However, high investment would only lead to a high growth rate in the long run if it had a favourable effect on the rate of technical progress, for it was shown in Chapters 2 and 3 that the long-term growth rate of a developed economy will tend towards $(a+n)$. Because k tends towards g, it will tend towards $(a+n)$ as g tends towards $(a+n)$, so high investment will not even lead to a high k in the long run if it fails to produce a high a. Then, from (4.10), it is clear that in the very long run high investment will only lead to a high r if it manages to raise a. The influence of entrepreneurial investment on a is therefore a matter of great importance, and much of Part II will be devoted to this problem. At this stage, it will be right to outline two of the Keynesian theories on this subject.

Kaldor has suggested that a will partly depend upon the rate of capital accumulation, but this makes surprisingly little difference to the analysis. He suggests that there is a technical progress function of the following type[1]:

$$a = A + B.(k-n) \quad \text{(where A and B are constants).} \quad (4.12)$$

In long-term equilibrium where $g = k = (a+n)$, there will then be the following equation for the rate of growth of the economy (substituting for a from (4.12)):

$$g = k = \frac{A}{1-B} + n. \quad (4.13)$$

It will be seen from (4.13) that the economy's long-term rate of growth will still depend entirely upon the model's parameters, A, B and n, even with Kaldor's assumption that a depends partly on k. Thus entrepreneurial investment will still have no effect upon the economy's rate of growth in the long run.

The situation is more favourable to investment if it is assumed that technical progress depends upon the share of investment (S) rather than the rate of growth of capital. For instance, the

---

[1] Kaldor, 'A model of economic growth'.

following is a possible alternative technical progress function to Kaldor's[1]:

$$a = A + B.S \qquad (4.14)$$

where A and B are constants. Here, higher entrepreneurial investment must raise the rate of technical progress, but it will not do so sufficiently to overcome the diminishing returns forces in the economy. This technical progress function, and others, will be discussed in detail in Chapter 6.

It is, however, possible to attribute more technical progress to entrepreneurial investment than these technical progress functions allow for, and this is achieved by attributing much to the 'animal spirits' of entrepreneurs. Suppose that a country's entrepreneurs are plentifully endowed with 'animal spirits', to use Keynes's phrase:

Most, probably, of our decisions to do something positive, the full consequences of which will be drawn out over many days to come, can only be taken as a result of animal spirits – of a spontaneous urge to action rather than inaction, and not as the outcome of a weighted average of quantitative benefits multiplied by quantitative probabilities. Entreprise only pretends to itself to be mainly actuated by the statements in its own prospectus, however candid and sincere. Only a little more than an expedition to the South Pole, is it based on an exact calculation of benefits to come. Thus if the animal spirits are dimmed and the spontaneous optimism falters, leaving us to depend on nothing but a mathematical expectation, enterprise will fade and die; – though fears of loss may have a basis no more reasonable than hopes of profit had before.[2]

If entrepreneurs have ample 'animal spirits', they will undertake much investment. If the argument of Chapters 1, 2 and 3 is accepted, this investment will lead in time to a lower rate of return on capital, and a rate of return which falls in relation to the rate of interest (which is determined by monetary factors in Keynesian theory) with the result that the funds available for reinvestment (which are partly a function of the excess of profits over interest costs) and the financial inducement to invest must fall. This may well have been Keynes's own view of the matter at times, for there is his well-known phrase,

[1] W. A. Eltis, 'Investment, technical progress and economic growth', *Oxford Economic Papers*, vol. xv (Mar 1963) pp. 37-9.
[2] Keynes, *The General Theory of Employment, Interest and Money*, pp. 161-2.

'Two pyramids, two masses for the dead, are twice as good as one; but not so two railways from London to York',[1] which appears to point to the importance he attached to diminishing returns from a capital stock which was excessive to requirements. There are numerous further statements by him to this effect. An interpretation of his position might be that 'animal spirits' could lead short-sighted men to build a second railway line from London to York, but even 'animal spirits' could hardly be expected to produce the capital for a third. On this interpretation, 'animal spirits' will influence investment in the short term, but they will not disturb the long-term proposition that the capital an economy can absorb through time without diminishing returns is limited. This is not the only view of the matter which can be taken.[2]

Suppose the entrepreneurs who run industry wish to achieve rapid growth of their firms. In the first instance, they will undertake high rates of investment. Then will come setbacks, as universally high investment runs towards diminishing returns to capital. The rate of return on capital will fall, and the funds available for reinvestment will dwindle. At this point, faint-hearted men will revise their expectations downwards, but men with 'animal spirits' will seek to circumvent diminishing returns. They will look for improvements to their production methods which will raise their profits (by economising in labour, etc.) and so provide the funds for further expansion. They will seek ways of achieving the expansion they desire with lower capital inputs. If this is difficult, they will find out whether other firms, and the industry of other countries, manage to produce their products with less labour and less capital, and they will seek to imitate the techniques of others where these are superior to their own. Given sufficient pressure to achieve targets, they will, if necessary, invent superior methods, but successful copying of the methods of others will suffice for all but the most efficient firms in the world.

On this view, entrepreneurs with 'animal spirits' who set themselves high targets can be expected to fulfil them. Desired expansion rates will be translated into actual expansion rates, and thus, in the long run, g, the actual rate of growth, k, the rate of growth of capital, and $(a+n)$ will come to equal the rate of growth that entrepreneurs

[1] Keynes, *The General Theory of Employment, Interest and Money*, p. 131.
[2] A more optimistic view of what can be achieved through 'animal spirits' is suggested by Joan Robinson in her *Essays in the Theory of Economic Growth*, II, 'A model of accumulation'.

desire. Through the mechanism described above, a will adjust so that it becomes sufficient for the 'desired' growth rate. Through (4.10), r will become high if the desired growth rate, and therefore a and k, are high, and this will make the whole process viable.

Through similar reasoning, an economy with sluggish 'animal spirits' and a low desired growth rate will not need to improve its production methods to fulfil its narrow aspirations, so it will not improve them (and executives sufficiently unaware of their company's ethos to suggest improvements will be regarded as a nuisance and kept down or out). k, a and g will consequently be low, and r as well.

There are two lines of evidence in favour of this view. First, Leibenstein's celebrated article on X-efficiency, which suggests that there is generally a wide gap between the best production methods in industry and those in general use, even in the U.S.A., points to evidence which is generally helpful to this line of argument.[1] It suggests that firms can generally advance their efficiency very substantially by simply correcting faults in their current practices, which should be a reasonably straightforward task if the desire to do this is sufficiently strong.

Second, it is notable that technology advanced exceptionally rapidly in the two twentieth-century world wars, which suggests that what is discovered per annum in peacetime conditions may be rather slight in relation to what is discoverable. If the pressure of war can increase the ratio of what is discovered to what is discoverable, sufficiently strong 'animal spirits' might have the same effect, for these might place an economy's approach to the improvement of its technology on a 'wartime' basis. Generally, societies and economies will be run so that only a fraction of what is possible will be achieved.

The above theory has important implications if it is correct. In Part II there will be an analysis of the precise interrelationships between investment and technical progress which are needed to produce a situation where 'animal spirits' can overcome the diminishing returns factors.

Saving, Investment and Employment

Entrepreneurial investment also plays a crucial role in Keynesian analyses of the problem of whether growth will take place with continuous full employment.

[1] H. Leibenstein, 'Allocative efficiency versus X-efficiency', *American Economic Review*, vol. LVI (June 1966).

D

Harrod has argued that there are two growth rates on which attention should be focused.[1] One is the 'natural' rate of growth, g_n, which is the fastest rate of growth which can be maintained in the long run. This will be $(a+n)$. The other is the 'warranted' rate of growth, g_w, and this is the rate of growth which will maintain a capital–output ratio of V_r when full-employment saving is invested. V_r is the capital–output ratio which entrepreneurs wish to maintain, and they will only be content that growth is occurring at the right rate if a capital–output ratio of V_r is maintained. With a savings ratio of S, the only growth rate which will maintain a capital–output ratio of V_r is S/V_r, and this is g_w, the 'warranted' rate of growth.

Since a, n, S and V_r are all parameters, $(a+n)$, the 'natural' rate of growth, will only equal S/V_r by the fluke that $(a+n) = S/V_r$. This means that g_n will generally differ from g_w. If $(a+n)$ exceeds S/V_r, i.e. if g_n exceeds g_w, there will be insufficient saving to exploit the economy's opportunity for growth with consequent persistent tendencies towards excess demand and/or structural unemployment. If g_w exceeds g_n, there will be more saving at full employment than can be invested to the satisfaction of entrepreneurs, with the result that full-employment saving will tend not to be invested, with consequent persistent tendencies towards unemployment. Thus with Harrod's assumption of a given V_r, the likelihood is very strong that an economy will suffer from persistent unemployment or inflation.

In Chapter 2 this problem did not arise, for a production function was assumed where V could take any value. Then the problem of a possible discrepancy between the 'natural' and 'warranted' rates of growth could not appear, for a value could always be found for V which would equate $(a+n)$ to S/V, the 'warranted' rate of growth.

There is, however, a serious Keynesian objection to the suggestion that V can take any value. If the neoclassical theory of the production function is accepted (and it is this which leads to the suggestion that Harrod's problem does not arise, so it can be used to criticise this supposed refutation of Harrod), a higher V is associated with a lower marginal product of capital, and therefore a lower rate of profit. However, if the assumption that investment equals full-employment saving is to be plausible, the rate of profit must be sufficient to cover the rate of interest, and whatever risk premium entrepreneurs require. According to Keynesian theory, the liquidity trap will set an irreducible minimum to the rate of interest if the economy is to be viable. If

1 Harrod, 'An essay in dynamic theory', and *Towards a Dynamic Economics*.

there is an irreducible minimum to the rate of interest, there will be a minimum marginal product of capital which is acceptable, and therefore a maximum to V. If V exceeds this maximum, V_{max}, the marginal product of capital will be too low, and the consequent rate of profit unacceptable to entrepreneurs.

Given this, the lowest the 'warranted' rate of growth can fall to is S/V_{max}, and this may exceed $(a+n)$. In that event, g_w would inevitably

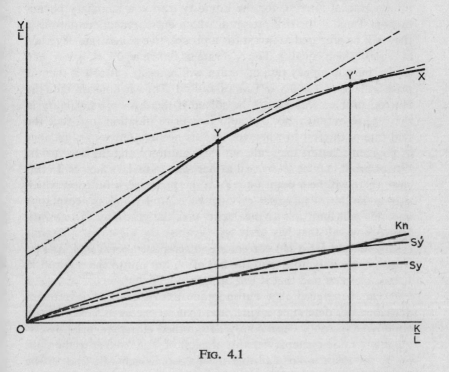

FIG. 4.1

exceed g_n, with consequent tendencies towards secular unemployment. The highest value S can take if this problem is to be avoided is $(a+n) \cdot V_{max}$.

In terms of the Solow–Johnson diagram which was used in Chapter 2, the slope of the tangent at Y shows the lowest rate of profit which is acceptable to entrepreneurs. If S'_y cuts K_n to the right of Y, as in Fig. 4.1, the supposed equilibrium at Y' is an impossible one, for the slope of the tangent at Y' is necessarily less steep than the tangent at Y, with the result that the rate of profit at Y' will be unacceptable to entrepreneurs. To make the economy viable, saving must fall to the schedule shown by the dotted line, S_y.

It is to be noted that if the lower limit to the rate of profit is set by the Keynesian liquidity trap, a sufficient rate of price inflation would apparently lead to a solution to the problem. Suppose the *real* marginal product of capital is r at Y, and r' at Y', and that i is the irreducible minimum to which the rate of interest can fall. i is a money rate of interest, for the liquidity trap is a monetary phenomenon. Then, if the risk premium which entrepreneurs require is q, they will be prepared to invest for a prospective *money* rate of return of $(i+q)$, which equals r. The *real* rate of return at Y', r', is less than $(i+q)$, but the money rate of return will reach $(i+q)$ or r if there is price inflation of $(i+q-r')$ or of $(r-r')$. Thus it appears that the Harrod problem can always be solved if there is both flexibility in the capital–output ratio, *and* sufficient price inflation to reduce the real rate of interest to whatever level is needed. Obviously, balance of payments factors may rule out this solution,[1] and the floor to the rate of profit may be set by real rather than monetary factors. In this case, there will be a point like Y on the production function which shows the lowest marginal product of capital which is acceptable, and this will limit the savings ratio that the economy can absorb. Up to now, all that has been said against the view that a flexible capital–output ratio can correct any discrepancy between g_n and g_w is that it *can* only do this to the left of Y, but not to the right of Y. It has not been said that it *will* do this.

It can be argued that autonomous entrepreneurial investment decisions will determine saving, and that an excess of saving at full employment over independently determined entrepreneurial investment will cause unemployment to the left of Y, as well as to the right of Y, for there is no plausible mechanism which will lead to the investment of this saving.

If there is to be an entrepreneurial investment function which is independent of saving, something must be said about this. In

[1] It might be thought that the adverse international effects of domestic price inflation at an annual rate of $(r-r')$ could be compensated by depreciation in the exchange rate of $(r-r')$ per annum. This would not, in fact, provide a solution to the problem, for depreciation in country H's exchange rate by $(r-r')$ relatively to the exchange rate of country X requires that H's interest rate be higher than X's by $(r-r')$ if there is to be equilibrium in its capital account. If X's interest rate is at the same liquidity-trap level, i, as H's, the interest rate in H will then have to exceed i by $(r-r')$, which means that H's *real* rate of interest will not be reduced.

economic theory, it is widely argued that entrepreneurial investment will vary with the rate of return on capital. Some entrepreneurs will relate the expected rate of return from investment to their cost of finance, possibly with the assistance of d.c.f. techniques, and they will invest more where r is higher in relation to their cost of finance. Other entrepreneurs may use payback criteria, and here more investment will generally fulfil any given payback criteria where the

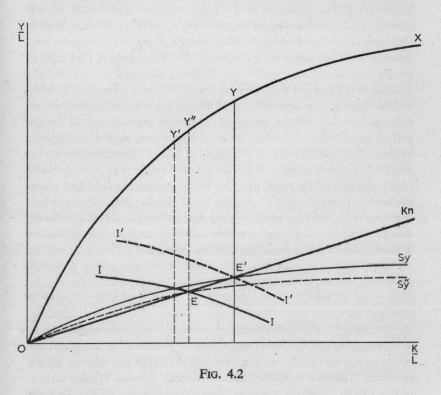

FIG. 4.2

achievable r is higher. Other entrepreneurs may invest a given proportion of their net or gross profits, and here, where r is higher, profits/capital will be higher, and if a given proportion of profits is invested, investment/capital will be higher. Many entrepreneurs are likely to be guided by more than one of these criteria, but they all have the effect that entrepreneurial investment will be higher where r is higher.

In Fig. 4.2, the rate of profit is the slope of the successive tangents to OX, and these slopes fall as capital per worker rises. If entrepreneurial investment varies with the rate of profit, it will be higher to the left of the diagram than it is to the right. II is an investment function which shows this, for II falls from left to right, and thus shows lower entrepreneurial investment where the rate of profit is lower.

In Fig. 4.2, II cuts S_y to the left of Y, so it cuts S_y to the left of the neoclassical equilibrium. The only apparent possibility of an equilibrium for the economy is at Y' where planned investment equals planned saving. However, investment per worker at Y' exceeds that shown by K_n, so capital per worker will be rising, which means that the economy will move to the right of Y'. The moment that capital per worker exceeds that at Y', the economy moves to the right of Y', and the rate of profit will then be lower (for a tangent to OX must be less steep to the right of Y'). With a lower rate of profit, investment per worker will be less, but saving per worker will be higher with a higher capital–labour ratio and therefore higher output per worker. Then, to the right of Y', planned saving must exceed planned investment at full employment (for it will be seen that S_y is above II at all points to the right of Y'). With planned saving exceeding planned investment at full employment, the National Income and employment must fall, which means that full employment cannot be maintained at Y', and the economy certainly cannot find its way to Y as it is supposed to do in neoclassical theory.

Full-employment equilibrium is, in fact, only possible at Y'' where II cuts K_n. For this equilibrium, the saving function must be the dotted line S_y'' which passes through E. At Y'', with S_y'', K_n and II passing through one point, E, capital per worker will be constant, and planned saving will continuously equal planned investment at full employment; but the economy will only find Y'' if S_y adjusts (or is adjusted) so that it passes through E. With the higher saving function, S_y there must be unemployment as was shown above. If the saving function is lower than S_y'' it will cut II to the right of E with the result that capital per worker falls; but this will raise the rate of profit, and make planned investment exceed planned saving at full employment with inflationary consequences. The only saving function which avoids both unemployment and excess demand is S_y''.

It will be seen that once an investment function is specified, with planned investment depending upon the rate of profit, the saving function must be accommodated to this, or it will cause trouble.

Hence, the investment function determines what will happen in equilibrium.

This is the Keynesian proposition that the entrepreneurial investment function (rather than the saving function) is the one that matters, and the one that determines capital per worker, the rate of profit, the capital–output ratio, the share of profits, etc. In the real world, it is scarcely plausible that K_n, S_y and II will pass through the same point without government intervention. Then the equilibrium position shown by the diagram must be an equilibrium that has been achieved with the help of government intervention. The government could either intervene to make the saving function pass through E, with suitable monetary and fiscal policies to influence saving in the direction desired. Alternatively, the government could leave the saving function alone at S_y, and seek to cause the investment function to shift to the dotted line $I'I'$, which would produce full equilibrium at the neoclassical Y. If the government can shift both the saving and investment functions at will, it can achieve either *full* equilibrium, and what happens will depend upon its decisions.

It is, however, possible, and some neoclassical economists would argue this, that governments have little power to influence an economy's saving function, since a community's saving habits are deep-rooted and only very slightly amenable to monetary and fiscal policies. Extra government saving might simply lead to less private saving, and so on. On the other hand, it might be argued, investment decisions can be influenced by government policy. With the world like this, the equilibrium at E' (where S_y cuts K_n) would be the one that mattered, and II would have to be made to pass through E'. The analysis of Chapter 2, where the economy's equilibrium capital per worker, etc., depended on S_y and K_n, would then be the right initial approach to the problem.

On the other hand, many Keynesians would argue that II depends upon deep-rooted psychological factors which are not easily amenable to government influence, while S_y can be shifted according to fairly clear consumption function formulae. With this view of the matter, E, the point where II cuts K_n, is the only possible equilibrium for the economy, and talk about the saving function is largely irrelevant to the problem of the economy's equilibrium, for S_y can be shifted in whatever way the community wishes, while II cannot.

No more need be said at this stage. Much more needs to be known before it can be said which view comes nearer to the truth.

Conclusion

It has been shown in this chapter that entrepreneurial investment decisions may play a much larger role than that allowed to them in Chapters 1, 2 and 3. They may play a major role in the determination of the share of profits and the rate of profit, and these may be determined with scant reference to marginal productivity. It may even be possible for entrepreneurs to obtain whatever growth rate they seek, free from the constraints of diminishing returns. Leaving aside these possibilities, the need for the expected rate of return on investment to cover interest rates and risk factors must surely set a lower limit to the marginal product of capital, which means that there will be situations where the maintenance of full employment requires that an economy's saving function be modified. In these situations, saving will need to be accommodated to investment. Indeed, if entrepreneurial investment decisions are sufficiently autonomous of saving and other influences, it may always be the case that saving has to be accommodated to investment, and it will then be the investment decisions that matter. A number of the unsettled questions in growth theory occur where there is a contradiction between Keynesian theory and neoclassical theory, and attempts will be made in Parts II and III of this book to resolve some of these contradictions. Before this is done, however, something must be said about a number of problems in capital theory which cast doubt on certain simple neoclassical propositions. Chapter 5 will be concerned with these problems.

5

Some Problems in Capital Theory

IN Chapters 1, 2 and 3 it was taken for granted that capital and what it produces can be measured in the same units. This is implicit in the Cobb–Douglas and CES production functions which suggest that there is a clear relationship between the quantity of *capital* and the quantity of *output*. It is implicit in the differentiation of such functions to obtain the marginal products of labour and capital. It is implicit in the type of argument where it is supposed that if a given fraction of the value of output is invested and added to the capital stock, this will increase by precisely the value of output times this fraction, with predictable effects on the following year's potential output.

However, a country's capital stock will consist of a collection of capital goods with clear physical specifications, which, together with quantities of other factors, produce given quantities of various goods. It is an improvement in this physical capital stock which permits increased real production. The capital stock can also be thought of as a sum of 'values' (measured in terms of some *numéraire*) of all items of equipment and working capital. An increase in the valuation of the capital stock will not necessarily permit increased real production, or even an increase in the value of production, for the value of the capital stock will depend (among other things) upon the rate of profit in the economy, and an economy's value of capital might rise relatively to the value of what is produced through a change in the rate of profit, while, at the same time, the physical effectiveness of capital fell. Some changes in economic variables will directly influence the value of capital, while others will influence its physical specification.[1]

[1] A distinction between capital as a collection of physical items of equipment, and capital as a sum of 'values', has been central to much of Joan Robinson's work in capital theory. See, for instance, 'The production function and the theory of capital', *Review of Economic Studies*, vol. XXI (1953-4); *The Accumulation of Capital*; and 'Solow on the rate of return', *Economic Journal*, vol. LXXIV (June 1964).

D*

A savings ratio or an investment ratio is essentially a value ratio, and an increase in the saving and investment ratios means that a higher proportion of the value of output is accumulated for future use, but if there is an equal rise in the cost of capital relatively to consumer goods, no extra physical equipment would be accumulated, and the economy's rate of growth could not be expected to rise. The relationship between investment and growth (i.e. the production function and what follows from it) must be a physical relationship and not a value relationship, for it is certain specific changes in technical capital which will produce changes in physical output. Technical progress and biases in this are physical changes in the conditions in which an economy operates. The capital–output ratio, however, is a value concept, and this could change (through a change in the relative prices of capital and consumer goods) without an equivalent change in the economy's physical capacity to produce.

An appreciation that the value of capital and physical capital may change in divergent ways enormously complicates economic theory, and greatly reduces what can be clearly said about the major economic relationships. For this reason, assumptions are generally made which eliminate these difficulties, or sweep them under the carpet. The propositions of Chapters 1, 2 and 3 hold if it is assumed that the economy produces only one good which can be used as a capital or consumer good. Then an increase in the investment ratio must mean that there is increased physical investment of this good, and an increase in the capital–output ratio must mean that more physical capital is used to produce a unit of output. At the same time, increased technical progress must increase the value of what can be produced (in terms of the single good). Indeed, as value can be measured in terms of this single good, value and physical quantity must come to the same thing. The same result is produced if it is assumed that all goods are manufactured by the same process, for if this is the case, the relative values of different goods cannot diverge, and value (with any good taken as *numéraire*) and physical quantity must always move proportionately. As soon as it is admitted that different goods are produced by different processes, the argument becomes more complicated, and the results of Chapters 1, 2 and 3 need to be modified. In Chapter 4, however, all the equations were in value terms, so the problems described above do not arise provided that no attempt is made to introduce a production function into a Keynesian model.

A recognition that there is a dichotomy between value and technical relationships will particularly complicate the set of problems associated with the production function. The precise way in which it complicates these problems will be best seen if a result which is common to all one-good-model production functions (including the Cobb–Douglas and CES production functions) is presented. With all these functions, an increase in the wage by ∂w in terms of the goods which capital produces will reduce profit per worker by ∂w with all techniques of production, and the rate of profit will then fall by $\partial w/(K/L)$ with all techniques. Hence, $\partial r = -\partial w/(K/L)$, and

$$\frac{\partial r}{\partial w} = -\frac{1}{K/L}. \tag{5.1}$$

Suppose that there are two alternative techniques of production, A and B, where output per worker is higher with A. Then, with one-good-model assumptions, A is bound to have a higher capital–labour ratio, so its capital–labour ratio can be written as $(K/L)+$ while B's is written as (K/L). Then with each small rise in the wage, the rate of profit will fall by $\partial w/(K/L)+$ with A, and by $\partial w/(K/L)$ with B, so the relative profitability of A will rise steadily as the wage rises. If it is less profitable than B at a low wage, its profitability will rise relatively to B's as the wage increases, and there will be one particular wage where its profitability 'catches up' with B's, and the two techniques will then be equally profitable. At a higher wage than this, A will be the more profitable technique, while B will be more profitable at a lower wage. There can then be only one 'switching wage' between A and B.

This result is illustrated in Fig. 5.1, where the factor-price curves of A and B which show the relationship between the rate of profit and the wage with each technique are shown. These have a constant slope of minus the capital–labour ratio (from (5.1)), so they will be drawn as downward-sloping straight lines with one-good-model assumptions where a particular technique will have the same capital–labour ratio at all rates of profit. A's slope will be $-(K/L)+$ and B's will be $-(K/L)$, and they can obviously intersect only once.

This appears to be an obvious general result, and it is not immediately clear that it depends on restrictive one-good-model assumptions, but this is in fact the case. Once one-good-model assumptions are dropped, there will frequently be cases where it cannot be said that A, the technique with higher output per worker, clearly has a higher capital–labour ratio than B. A's physical capital will differ from B's, and it may have a higher 'value', i.e. a higher K/L, at some rates of profit, while the 'value' of B's physical capital may be higher at other rates of profit. Then the above account of a single switching point between A and B at *one* particular wage will not hold. In terms of the factor-price frontier diagram, the factor-price curves of A and B will cease to be straight lines once one-good-model

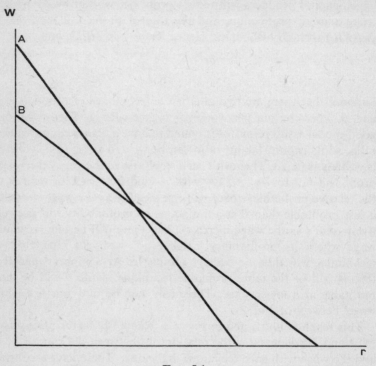

FIG. 5.1

assumptions are dropped, which means that they will be able to intersect more than once as in Fig. 5.2.

A number of authors have recently shown that there may be two or more switching points between techniques of production with different outputs per worker, i.e. there may be several wage rates and several rates of profit at which two techniques of production are equally profitable.[1] In the example illustrated in Fig. 5.1 where only

[1] See Robinson, *The Accumulation of Capital*, pp. 109-10; P. Sraffa, *Production of Commodities by Means of Commodities* (Cambridge U.P., 1960) pp. 34-40, 81-7; J. R. Hicks, *Capital and Growth* (Oxford U.P., 1965) pp. 148-69;

one switching point was possible, any increase in the wage above
the single 'switching wage' made the more labour-productive technique, *A*, the more profitable one. However, it has been widely
shown that where there is a departure from one-good-model assumptions so that the relative capital–labour ratios of *A* and *B* cannot be
clearly specified, an increase in the wage above a 'switching wage'
may make the more labour-productive technique, *A* or the less
labour-productive, *B*, the more profitable of the two. Joan Robinson
has called a switch to a technique with higher output per worker at
a higher wage (i.e. a switch in the orthodox direction) a *forward*

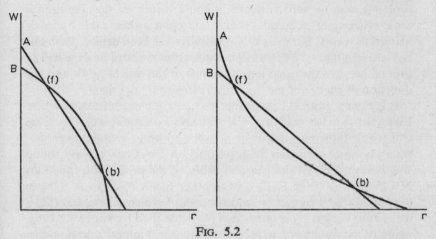

FIG. 5.2

switch, and a switch to a technique with lower output per worker at
a higher wage a *backward* switch.[1] In Fig. 5.2 the forward switching
points are marked (*f*) and the backward switching points (*b*). If all
switches were forward switches there would be little to worry about,
for any technique which was superseded by another with higher
output per worker as the wage rose could not 'come back' at a still

Luigi L. Pasinetti, 'Changes in the rate of profit and switches of technique',
David Levhari and Paul A. Samuelson, 'The nonswitching theorem is false', and
Michael Bruno, Edwin Burmeister, and Eytan Sheshinski, 'Nature and implications of the reswitching of techniques', all in *Quarterly Journal of Economics*,
vol. LXXX (Nov 1966); Joan Robinson and K. A. Naqvi, 'The badly behaved
production function', *Quarterly Journal of Economics*, vol. LXXXI (Nov 1967);
and Harcourt, *Some Cambridge Controversies in the Theory of Capital*, for a
general summary and survey of the debate.
[1] Backward switches can also be referred to as *capital-reversing*, see Harcourt,
p. 124.

higher wage. Techniques could then be ordered monotonically to show their order of adoption at successively higher wage rates, and something like the neoclassical production function could then be arrived at. The existence of backward switches prevents this. If a higher wage may be associated with the adoption of techniques with lower output per worker, a technique which was superseded by another with higher output per worker at one wage might come back as the most profitable one at a still higher wage. Then nothing resembling the neoclassical production function could exist. If it could be shown that backward switches are overwhelmingly less probable than forward switches, it could be argued that the monotonic ordering of techniques would represent a reasonable approximation to reality, but even this possibility has been denied. Pasinetti has asserted that '. . . there is no connection that can be expected in general between the direction of change of the rate of profit and the direction of change of the "quantity of capital" per man'.[1]

It is clearly of great importance to know the circumstances where backward switches may occur. If plausible assumptions can be made which rule these out, it will be possible to order techniques monotonically with the result that production functions can be found which have many of the characteristics of the production functions of Chapters 1, 2 and 3. If, on the other hand, Pasinetti is right in supposing that it cannot be said that backward switching and therefore capital-reversing is much less probable than forward switching, many of the results of Chapters 1, 2 and 3 will appear questionable.

The principal problems discussed above arise because different capital and consumer goods are produced by different processes, with the result that changes in the relative value of the various capital and consumer goods can occur without equivalent physical changes. The relationships between the technical conditions of production and their 'value' consequences must therefore be analysed. The reasons for divergences between technical and value relationships, once one-good-model assumptions are abandoned, will first be outlined with the help of a model where capital and consumer goods are produced by different techniques in different sectors of the economy. The model will then be used to analyse the circumstances where there will, and where there will not, be multiple switching between techniques. The exposition of the model is, perhaps necessarily, a little technical,

---

[1] Pasinetti, op. cit., p. 517.

and some readers may wish to go straight to the conclusions of the
chapter on p. 122.

*The Value of Capital and Physical Capital in a Two-Sector Model

The nature of the problem can be seen with the following very simple
two-sector model.[1] The version of the model which will be used in
this section will be simpler than the one in the next section where the
possibility of multiple switching will be analysed. The simpler version
of the model in this section will suffice to show the principal effects of
the assumption that capital and consumer goods are produced by
different processes, so that there is a departure from the one-good-
model assumptions of Chapters 1, 2 and 3.

It will be supposed that there are two kinds of capital good in an
economy. One of these produces the economy's single consumer
good, and this will be called a machine. The other produces machines,
and it can also reproduce itself, and this will be called a *basic*
machine tool. It is well known that machine tools are the only man-
made thing which reproduces. In the next section, *basic* machine
tools will be distinguished from *secondary* machine tools, but this
distinction will be avoided in this section to simplify the initial
argument, and it will therefore be assumed here that basic machine
tools produce machinery of all kinds in the investment sector, while
machines produce consumer goods in the consumption sector. The
main effects of the assumption that capital and consumer goods are
produced by different processes will be brought out most simply if
attention is focused on the relationships directly due to this. The
complicating effects of technical progress will therefore be avoided
at the start of the argument.

The costs of producing basic machine tools, machines and
consumer goods will be defined entirely in technical terms, and
the 'value' consequences of the technical assumptions will then be
derived.

Perhaps the simplest technical assumptions which bring out the
main features of the argument are the following. M men need to work
with basic machine tools for one period to produce the basic machine

---

[1] The model used is very similar to that devised by Sir John Hicks in *Capital
and Growth*, chap. 12 and 13. More basically, the method used to show the
connection between value relationships and physical relationships originated
with Ricardo's *Principles of Political Economy and Taxation*, chap. 1, 'On Value'.

tool which one worker can use. Basic machine tools can also be used to produce the machines which are used to produce the model's single consumer good by a number of alternative possible techniques, $1...n$. The number of workers who must work with basic machine tools for one period to produce a machine which can equip a worker with techniques $1...n$ is $m_1...m_n$, and output per worker with these machines will be $q_1...q_n$. Hence, m_b workers working with basic machine tools for one period will produce the machine which will equip one worker to produce consumer goods by technique b, and this worker's consumer-good output per period will be q_b. Capital letters, i.e. M, will always be used to refer to the various investment sector coefficients, and lower-case letters, i.e. m_b and q_b, will refer to consumption sector coefficients.

It will be assumed that there is a uniform wage of w per period which all workers are paid, and a rate of profit of r which is earned with all capital. Both new machines and new basic machine tools depreciate at a proportional rate of d per period. At the start of the argument, the complicating effect of gestation periods will be avoided with the assumption that production is completed in one period in each sector.

The price for which basic machine tools are sold, P, can be deduced very simply from the technical conditions of production. P will equal the wage costs of producing a machine tool, $M.w$, plus one period of profit on the M machine tools which are used to produce it, which comes to $r.M$ times the value of a new machine tool, or $r.M.P$, plus the depreciation of M machine tools over one period which is $d.M.P$. Hence, $P = M.w+(r+d).M.P$, i.e.

$$P = \frac{w.M}{1-(r+d).M}. \tag{5.2}$$

A basic machine tool worked by one worker produces $1/M$ machine tools per period, so its output per period, Q, will be sold for P times $1/M$. Then (from (5.2)):

$$Q = \frac{w}{1-(r+d).M}. \tag{5.3}$$

m_b men work with new machine tools for one period to produce the machine which a worker uses with technique b, so p_b, the price of a machine used to equip one worker with technique b, will be m_b times Q. Then (from (5.3)):

$$p_b = \frac{w.m_b}{1-(r+d).M}. \tag{5.4}$$

q_b, the output per period of a machine worked by one worker, using technique b, will be sold for the equivalent of the labour costs of operating the machine, w, plus the capital cost which is $(r+d).p_b$. Then (from (5.4)):

$$q_b = \frac{w(1+(r+d)(m_b-M)}{1-(r+d).M}. \tag{5.5}$$

The wage in terms of consumer goods can be derived from (5.5):

$$w = q_b\left(\frac{(1-(r+d).M)}{1+(r+d)(m_b-M)}\right). \tag{5.6}$$

For some purposes the wage will be the appropriate *numéraire* for the model, and for others the consumer good will be the appropriate *numéraire*. (5.6) permits all values to be expressed in terms of the consumer good, and this can be used to substitute for w in (5.2), (5.3) and (5.4).

$$P = q_b\left(\frac{M}{1+(r+d)(m_b-M)}\right) \tag{5.7}$$

$$Q = q_b\left(\frac{1}{1+(r+d)(m_b-M)}\right) \tag{5.8}$$

$$p_b = q_b\left(\frac{m_b}{1+(r+d)(m_b-M)}\right). \tag{5.9}$$

Technical progress could now be brought into the argument very simply with the help of equations (5.6) to (5.9). It could be supposed that $q_b = q_b.e^{a.t}$ (where q_b is output per worker at time 0), i.e. that output per worker with new machines rose through time at an exponential rate of a. Then, if this left M, m_b, r and d unaltered (i.e. if technical progress was something like Harrod-neutral except that here there are two sectors), the wage would rise at an exponential rate of a (in terms of consumer goods) (from (5.6)), and P, Q and p_b would rise at the same exponential rate of a (from (5.7), (5.8) and (5.9)). On the other hand, the formulae below for the capital–output ratios and shares of wages in the two sectors ((5.10) to (5.13)) would be independent of a if $q_b.e^{a\cdot t}$ were substituted for q_b, so the assumption of neutral technical progress would leave these unaltered. The analysis of the relationship between technical progress and growth is not a primary concern of this chapter, but it is useful to know that the argument could be extended very simply to allow for this. It is perfectly adequate for the purposes of this chapter to revert now to the assumption that q_b is a constant.

The capital–output ratios in the investment and consumption sectors, V and v, and the shares of wages in output, X_{wi} and X_{wc}, can be deduced very simply from the equations.

$$V = \frac{P}{Q} = M \qquad \text{(from (5.7) and (5.8))} \qquad (5.10)$$

$$v = \frac{p_b}{q_b} = \frac{m_b}{1+(r+d)(m_b-M)} \quad \text{(from (5.9))} \qquad (5.11)$$

$$X_{wi} = \frac{w}{Q} = 1-(r+d)M \qquad \text{(from (5.3))} \qquad (5.12)$$

$$X_{wc} = \frac{w}{q_b} = \frac{1-(r+d).M}{1+(r+d)(m_b-M)} \quad \text{(from (5.6))}. \qquad (5.13)$$

Thus V, the capital–output ratio in the investment sector, is simply the technical coefficient, M, and the wage, the rate of profit, etc., do not enter into its determination. This is because the assumptions of a one-good model hold in the sector of the economy where capital reproduces, and here any change in the rate of profit, etc., will affect capital and its products equally, so that the capital–output ratio is entirely a technical matter. This is not the case in the consumption sector, where (from (5.11)) it will be seen that the capital–output ratio equals the technical coefficient m_b where $M = m_b$, but not otherwise. In all other cases, a change in r will be associated with a change in the capital–output ratio, even though there is no change in the technical conditions of production. r and w can take a wide range of values depending upon the factors influencing the distribution of income. This will then influence the capital–output ratio in the consumption sector which will influence the growth consequent upon a particular savings ratio.

This means that the influence of the savings ratio upon the growth rate will not be simply a technical matter. The amount of machinery which savings (a 'value' concept) will be transformed into will depend

upon the distribution of income, and since growth will depend upon
the 'amount of machinery', the effect of saving on growth will be
even less straightforward than appeared to be the case in earlier
chapters.

The algebraic relationship between S, the share of saving and
investment in income, and μ, the proportion of basic machine tools
which is used to produce machinery for the investment rather than
the consumption sector – a technical relationship which determines
the economy's growth rate – can be derived from the assumptions
of the model. It will be simplest to work with the assumption of unlimited labour to bring out some of the fundamental characteristics
of two-sector models. The argument could easily be extended to deal
with the case of a limited labour force that must be fully employed.
With unlimited labour, it can be shown that the economy's growth
rate must be $((\mu/M)-d)$.[1]

If there are L_t basic machine tools worked by L_t workers at time t,
$\mu.L_t$ will be producing machine tools, and $(1-\mu).L_t$ will be producing machines for the consumption sector. These will provide equipment for $(\mu.L_t)/M$ workers in the investment sector per period, and
$((1-\mu).L_t)/m_b$ workers in the consumption sector, and these newly
equipped workers will produce $(Q.\mu.L_t)/M$ and $(q_b(1-\mu).L_t)/m_b$
per period. Then the ratio of investment to consumption output by
newly equipped workers will be $(Q/M).\mu:(q_b/m_b).(1-\mu)$. In long-
run steady growth, this will also be the ratio of gross investment to
consumption. The share of investment in output (which equals S,
the share of *gross* saving in income) can be deduced from this ratio,
i.e.

$$S = \frac{\frac{Q}{M}.\mu}{\frac{q_b}{m_b}(1-\mu)+\frac{Q}{M}.\mu}. \tag{5.14}$$

[1] If all basic machine tools are used to reproduce further machine tools, the
rate of growth of the stock of basic machine tools will be $(1/M-d)$. If a fraction,
μ, of machine tools is used to produce machine tools, the rate of growth of the
stock of basic machine tools will be $(\mu/M-d)$, and this will also be the rate of
growth of the stock of machines if μ is constant. With μ constant, the ratio of the
stock of machines to the stock of machine tools will be constant, and this means
that consumer-goods production will grow at the same rate as machinery
production. $(\mu/M-d)$ will then be the economy's steady growth rate. (Cf.
Hicks, *Capital and Growth*, pp. 143-5.)

Substitute for Q from (5.8), and note that

$$\frac{M}{m_b}(1+(r+d)(m_b-M)) = \frac{V}{v}$$

(from (5.10) and (5.11)). Then:

$$S = \frac{1}{1+\dfrac{V}{v}\left(\dfrac{1-\mu}{\mu}\right)} \tag{5.15}$$

$$\mu = \frac{1}{1+\dfrac{v}{V}\left(\dfrac{1-S}{S}\right)}. \tag{5.16}$$

(5.16) allows a value share of saving, and value capital–output ratios in the investment and consumption sectors, to be translated into a technical rate of growth. In a one-good model, v would equal V, so that $\mu = S$. Here v may be greater or less than V. If v is greater, i.e. if the consumption sector is more capital-intensive (in value terms) μ will be less than S, while μ will exceed S is the investment sector is more capital-intensive. Once the technical conditions of production are specified, there will always be an equation like (5.16) to show how a one-good model's value share of saving needs to be modified to take account of the assumption of production in two sectors, so that technically meaningful statements about the relationship between saving and growth can be derived.

The other type of problem which is due to the dichotomy between 'value' and technical relationships is the set of problems associated with the production function. These problems will be analysed in detail in the next sections where the circumstances where there may be multiple switching will be discussed, but before this, a very simple result will be arrived at which will show the principal effect on the production function of the assumption of production in two sectors. It was shown in (5.1) that $\partial r/\partial w$ will equal $-1/(K/L)$ with one-good-model assumptions. $\partial r/\partial w$ will now be found for the model based on two-sector assumptions which has been used in this section. Differentiate (5.6) with respect to r:

$$\frac{\partial r}{\partial w} = -\frac{(1+(r+d)(m_b-M))^2}{m_b \cdot q_b}. \tag{5.17}$$

Substituting from (5.9), (5.12) and (5.13):

$$\frac{\partial r}{\partial w} = - \frac{1}{p_b} (X_{wi}/X_{wc}). \tag{5.18}$$

As p_b is the value capital–labour ratio in the consumption sector, (5.18) shows that two-sector assumptions have a very simple effect on the basic neoclassical one-good-model result that

$$\frac{\partial r}{\partial w} = - \frac{1}{K/L} = - \frac{1}{p_b}$$

in this case. With the two-sector assumptions made here, $-1/p_b$ is multiplied by the ratio of the share of wages in the investment sector to the share of wages in the consumption sector, and these are of course the same in a one-good model. If X_{wi} exceeds X_{wc}, i.e. if capital intensity is higher in the consumption sector, a small increase in the wage will have a larger adverse effect on the rate of profit than it does where capital intensity is higher in the investment sector. (5.18) is a very simple equation, and it suggests that it may be possible to modify one-good-model production functions very simply to take account of two-sector assumptions.

Up to this point, the argument of this chapter suggests that traditional one-good-model theory needs to be modified in two respects to take account of two-sector assumptions. It needs to be modified to take account of the fact that a value share of saving will not necessarily correspond to the technical resources invested (and this can be done with the help of easily derivable equations such as (5.16)), and the fact that

$$\frac{\partial r}{\partial w} = - \frac{1}{p_b} (X_{wi}/X_{wc})$$

instead of $-1/(K/L)$. However, before it can be concluded that the problems raised by departures from one-good-model assumptions can be dealt with as easily as this, the possibility that there will be backward as well as forward switching between techniques must be examined. If the possibility of backward switching or capital-reversing is at all widely prevalent, there will be no clear production function for an equation like (5.18) to modify.

Backward switching becomes a possibility as soon as the factor-price curves of the various techniques cease to be straight lines. It is evident from (5.17) that they will only be straight lines where $m_b = M$, i.e. where capital intensity is the same in the investment and consumption sectors. Otherwise, where $M > m_b$, i.e. where capital intensity is higher in the investment sector, the factor-price frontier will slope downwards with an increasing slope (for $\partial^2 w / \partial r^2 < 0$), and it will slope downwards with a diminishing slope where $m_b > M$ (when $\partial^2 w / \partial r^2 > 0$). These possibilities are illustrated in Fig. 5.3. Backward

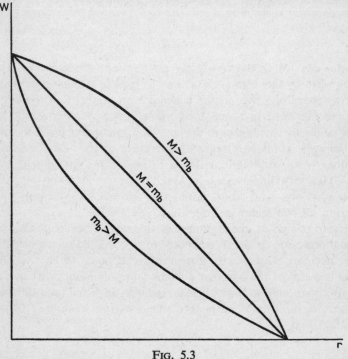

FIG. 5.3

switching is clearly a possibility where capital intensity differs in the two sectors, and the conditions where this will occur will now be analysed.

The Possibility of Multiple Switching – with Unit Gestation Periods

The analysis of this section will start with the problem of whether there can be more than one rate of profit at which two techniques of production are equally profitable with the assumptions that were made in the last section. The techniques which will be considered are any two techniques, 1 and 2, where output per worker is higher with 1 than with 2, i.e. q_1 exceeds q_2. Then 1 must be the more profitable technique at any wage exceeding q_2, for it can earn a profit at a wage exceeding q_2, while technique 2 must make a loss. If there is only one switching point between 1 and 2, the switch must be a forward switch, for 1, the more labour-productive technique, is the more profitable at a high wage. Hence there can only be backward switching between 1 and 2 if there is multiple switching, and the circumstances where there may be multiple switching will therefore also be those where there may be backward switching and capital-reversing.

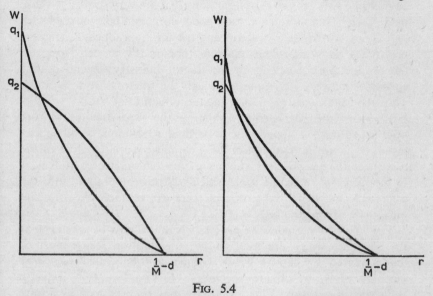

FIG. 5.4

With the assumptions of the last section, techniques 1 and 2 will earn the same rate of profit at the same wage where (from (5.6)):

$$w = q_1\left(\frac{1-(r+d).M}{1+(r+d)(m_1-M)}\right) = q_2\left(\frac{1-(r+d).M}{1+(r+d)(m_2-M)}\right).$$

Then:

$$r = \frac{q_1-q_2}{(q_1-q_2).M+q_2 m_1-q_1 m_2} - d. \qquad (5.19)$$

There can be only one solution to (5.19), so it is clear that techniques 1 and 2 will be equally profitable at only one rate of profit. Hence, there will be only one switching point between 1 and 2, and this will be a forward switch. Fig. 5.4, which shows the possible factor-price curves of the two techniques, shows why only one switching point is possible. The assumption that the same machine tools are used to produce the machines needed for techniques 1 and 2 means that the same rate of profit of $((1/M) - d)$ must be earned with all techniques on the horizontal axis where the wage is zero (from (5.6)). As the factor-price curves fall at either a continuously increasing or a continuously diminishing rate, they can only intersect once if they must both arrive at the same point on the horizontal axis, as in Fig. 5.4.

This is a surprising result, because Hicks has shown that there can be multiple switching with assumptions that are very similar to those made here.[1] Hicks's consumption good, corn, can be produced with two alternative kinds of tractor, and tractors reproduce, so tractors play much the same role as machine tools in this model. However, the production coefficients in his tractor industry depend on the consumer industry technique for which the tractors are to be used. Thus the coefficients regulating the reproduction of 'steam' tractors differ from the coefficients regulating the reproduction of 'oil' tractors, so tractors are specific to particular techniques, and he preferred to avoid the assumption of a capital-good equivalent to the *basic* machine tool. Hicks's tractors are much more nearly equivalent to the *secondary* machine tools which will now be brought into the argument, and it will be seen that there can be multiple switching once these are introduced.

The view of the productive process which will now be taken is that the machines which are used in the consumption sector must be manufactured by capital goods (which will be called *secondary* machine tools) which are specific to the consumption industry technique in question. Thus electricity may be produced by a dam or a conventional power station, and earth-moving equipment will be used to make a dam, while electrical machinery will be used to provide the equipment for a power station. In this case, earth-moving equipment and electrical machinery will be regarded as *secondary* machine tools.

It will be assumed that M workers work with *basic* machine tools for one period to produce the *basic* machine tool one worker uses, as before, and that the price of this machine tool is P. However, $M_1 \ldots M_n$ workers will need to work with *basic* machine tools for one period to produce the *secondary* machine tools, worked by one worker, which are needed for techniques $1 \ldots n$. The prices of these secondary

[1] Hicks, *Capital and Growth*, chaps. 12 and 13.

machine tools are $P_1...P_n$, and their output per period is $Q_1...Q_n$. With technique b, M_b workers will work with basic machine tools for one period to produce the secondary machine tool a worker can use, and m_b workers will then work with this secondary machine tool for one period to produce the b technique's machine, which will have a price of p_b, and produce q_b of the consumer good per period. The equations for the price and output per period of a basic machine tool are the same as in the last section, but new equations are needed for the price and output per period of secondary machine tools and machines. These are as follows:

$$P_b = \frac{w.M_b}{1-(r+d).M} \tag{5.20}$$

$$Q_b = \frac{w(1+(r+d)(M_b-M))}{1-(r+d).M} \tag{5.21}$$

$$p_b = \frac{w.m_b(1+(r+d)(M_b-M))}{1-(r+d).M} \tag{5.22}$$

$$q_b = \frac{w(1+(r+d)(m_b-M)+(r+d)^2.m_b(M_b-M))}{1-(r+d).M}. \tag{5.23}$$

The relative profitability of techniques 1 and 2 will now be compared, and it will be supposed as before that 1 is more labour-productive than 2 in the consumption sector, so that q_1 exceeds q_2. Where 1 and 2 are equally profitable at the same wage, (5.23) shows that:

$$w = \frac{q_1(1-(r+d).M)}{1+(r+d)(m_1-M)+(r+d)^2m_1(M_1-M)}$$

$$= \frac{q_2(1-(r+d).M)}{1+(r+d)(m_2-M)+(r+d)^2.m_2(M_2-M)}.$$

Then:

$$(r+d)^2(q_1m_2(M_2-M)-q_2m_1(M_1-M))$$
$$+(r+d)(q_1(m_2-M)-q_2(m_1-M))+(q_1-q_2) = 0. \tag{5.24}$$

(5.24) is a quadratic equation in $(r+d)$, so there may well be two positive roots, which means that there may well be two rates of profit at which techniques 1 and 2 are equally profitable. There is then a distinct possibility that there will be backward switching, for if there are two switching points, one must produce a backward switch. In terms of the factor-price frontier diagrams, the same rate of return $((1/M)-d)$, will again be earned with both techniques on the horizontal axis where $w = 0$, but $\partial^2 w/\partial r^2$ will not be persistently positive or negative with each technique, so the factor-price curves can intersect twice, even though they reach the horizontal axis at the same point as in Fig. 5.5.

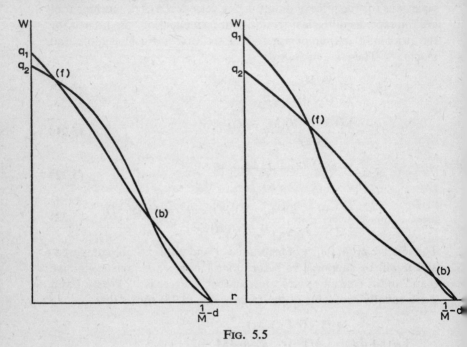

FIG. 5.5

The conditions where there will be two positive roots can be found with the help of the well-known proposition that the solutions to $a.x^2+b.x+c = 0$ are

$$x = \frac{-b \pm \sqrt{b^2 - 4ac}}{2a}.$$

From this it is evident that there will be two positive real roots where:

(i) a and c have the same sign.

(ii) b and c have opposite signs.

(iii) $b^2 > 4ac$.

With (5.24):

$a = q_1 m_2 (M_2 - M) - q_2 m_1 (M_1 - M)$.

$b = q_1 (m_2 - M) - q_2 (m_1 - M)$.

$c = q_1 - q_2$.

As c is defined positive, since it is given that q_1 exceeds q_2, conditions (i), (ii) and (iii) amount to:

(i) $q_1 m_2 (M_2 - M) - q_2 m_1 (M_1 - M) > 0$.

(ii) $q_2 (m_1 - M) - q_1 (m_2 - M) > 0$.

(iii) $(q_1 (m_2 - M) - q_2 (m_1 - M))^2$
$$- 4(q_1 - q_2)(q_1 m_2 (M_2 - M) - q_2 m_1 (M_1 - M)) > 0.$$

There is, however, a further condition which must be fulfilled if there is to be multiple switching in this case where there are at most two switching points. The rate of profit must always be such that the price of machine tools is positive, for otherwise a positive rate of return could be earned by making a loss with negatively priced machine tools. It is evident from (5.2) and (5.20) that machine tools will be positively priced provided that $1/M > (r+d)$. The higher rate of return which can be earned in (5.24) is

$$\frac{-b + \sqrt{b^2 - 4ac}}{2a},$$

and $1/M$ must exceed this, i.e.

$$\frac{1}{M} > \frac{-b + \sqrt{b^2 - 4ac}}{2a}$$

$$a \pm b.M + c.M^2 > 0.$$

The condition that $(a - b.M + c.M^2) > 0$ cannot possibly prevent reswitching, for a and c will be positive and b negative if (i) and (ii) hold with the result that $(a - b.M + c.M^2)$ must be positive. However, the condition that $(a + b.M + c.M^2) > 0$ may prevent reswitching, even if (i) and (ii) hold. $(a + b.M + c.M^2) > 0$ amounts to:

(iv) $M_2.m_2.q_1 > M_1.m_1.q_2$.

This is a condition additional to (i), (ii) and (iii) which must be met if there is to be reswitching. In consequence there will be only two positive real rates of profit at which techniques 1 and 2 are equally profitable if (i), (ii), (iii) and (iv) all hold, and these conditions will all hold if:

$$1 < \frac{m_1}{m_2} \cdot \frac{q_2}{q_1} < \frac{M_2}{M_1} < \frac{m_1}{m_2} \cdot \frac{q_2}{q_1} + \frac{(M(q_1 - q_2) - (q_2 m_1 - q_1 m_2))^2}{4(q_1 - q_2) \cdot q_1 m_2 \cdot M_1}.$$

$$(5.25)$$

It is immediately evident that there cannot be reswitching if $M_1 = M_2$. Thus there can only be reswitching if different secondary machine tools are needed for the two techniques. Moreover, M_2 will need to exceed M_1 if there is to be any possibility of reswitching. This means

Table 5.1

RANGE OF VALUES OF M_2/M_1 WHERE THERE WILL BE RESWITCHING

	$M = 2$ $M_1 = 4$	$M = 2$ $M_1 = 1$	$M = 4$ $M_1 = 2$	$M = 1$ $M_1 = 2$
$\frac{q_1}{q_2} = 1\cdot1$	–	–	1·10–1·12	1·10–1·11
$\frac{q_1}{q_2} = 1\cdot5$	1·50–1·51	1·50–1·54	1·50–1·52	1·50–1·58
$\frac{q_1}{q_2} = 2\cdot0$	2·00–2·06	2·00–2·25	–	2·00–2·28

that the capital equipment for the technique which is less labour-productive in the consumption sector will need to be manufactured in a more capital–intensive way than the equipment which is more labour–productive.[1] But this is not all. (5.25) shows that there will only be reswitching if the ratio of M_2 to M_1 lies in a particular range, and it may be a narrow range. Unfortunately the rather complicated term on the extreme right of (5.25) – which is due to condition (iii) – does not apparently simplify, so the range of values for M_2/M_1 where there will be reswitching will need to be shown in Table 5.1.

This is calculated for ratios of q_1 to q_2 of 2:1, 1·5:1 and 1·1:1, and for convenience $q_2 = 1$, so that the assumed values for q_1 are 2, 1·5 and 1·1. If there is to be any possibility of reswitching, the

---

[1] Cf. Bruno, Burmeister and Sheshinski, op. cit., p. 534; and W. A. Eltis, *Economic Growth: Analysis and Policy* (Hutchinson, 1966) p. 65.

consumer industry equipment for technique 1 will be manufactured less capital-intensively than the equipment for technique 2, and as 1 is more labour-productive in the consumption sector, its capital coefficient in the consumption sector will then need to be very much higher than 2's. It is conservatively assumed that m_1/m_2, the ratio of the consumption sector capital coefficients, will be $(q_1/q_2)^2$. This is equivalent to a capital elasticity of $\frac{1}{2}$ in the consumption sector (ignoring the handicap that the equipment for technique 1 is manufactured less capital-intensively). It will be appreciated that these assumptions give technique 2 rather greater advantages than it is actually likely to enjoy, so that the possibilities of reswitching will be over- rather than understated.

If $m_2 = 2$, the range of values for M_2/M_1 where there will be reswitching is as shown in Table 5.1.

It will be seen that the range of values for M_2/M_1 where there will be reswitching is generally quite narrow, but this is not always the case. There appears to be a distinct chance of reswitching where there is a considerable difference between q_1 and q_2, and also a considerable difference between M_1 and M_2. This suggests that the possibilities of reswitching may be greatest where techniques are fundamentally different. There will not be reswitching where the capital equipment for alternative techniques is produced by similar firms using similar combinations of labour and capital. Thus there is unlikely to be reswitching where the possible techniques require alternative electric generators or alternative automatic lathes. Where this type of choice is involved, M_1 will generally be much the same as M_2 with the result that there will not be reswitching. The possibility of reswitching will most often arise where there is a choice between very different technologies. The choice between a dam and a conventional power station where M_1 and M_2 are likely to differ markedly has already been mentioned. With nuclear power stations providing a further method of generating electricity, the possibility that there will be an 'unorthodox' production function for electricity is very clearly present. The same problem could arise with the various container industries, canning, bottling and packaging, where radically different techniques will be involved. On the other hand, there may be less risk of unorthodox effects with industries like the steel and motor-car industries, where the equipment for alternative techniques generally comes from similar firms which produce equipment in fairly similar ways. Here M_1 should not differ markedly from M_2.

The low range of values of the coefficients which produce reswitching in Table 5.1 is partly due to the role that *basic* machine tools play in the present model, for the factor-price curves of the two techniques must reach the horizontal axis at the same point where these are used to manufacture machinery at any stage of production. If the assumption of *basic* machine tools is dropped, and replaced by the assumption that the machinery used for technique 1 is entirely independent of the machinery for technique 2, as in Hicks's model, the factor-

Table 5.2

RANGE OF VALUES OF M_2/M_1 WHERE THERE WILL BE RESWITCHING

	$M_1 = 1$	$M_1 = 2$	$M_1 = 4$
$\dfrac{q_1}{q_2} = 1 \cdot 1$	1·01–1·05	1·01–1·03	1·01–1·02
$\dfrac{q_1}{q_2} = 1 \cdot 5$	1·01–1·30	1·01–1·15	1·01–1·07
$\dfrac{q_1}{q_2} = 2 \cdot 0$	1·01–1·68	1·01–1·34	1·01–1·17

price curves of the two techniques will reach the horizontal axis at different points, and there will then be reswitching over a rather wider range of the coefficients. With the same assumptions as for Table 5.1, reswitching will occur in the circumstances shown in Table 5.2 where the techniques are entirely independent.[1]

It is evident that reswitching is rather more of a possibility with these assumptions, and the serious possibilities of reswitching occur where q_1 and q_2 are rather far apart, so this is most likely to occur where techniques of production are fundamentally different.

[1] With the assumptions equivalent to those made by Hicks (*Capital and Growth*, p. 149), M_2 should be substituted for M with technique 2, and M_1 for M with technique 1. Then, using (5.23):

$$(r+d)^2[(q_1-q_2)M_2M_1+q_2M_2m_1-q_1M_1m_2]$$
$$+(r+d)[(q_2-q_1)(M_2+M_1)+q_1m_2-q_2m_1]+[q_1-q_2]=0.$$

This equation is used to calculate the critical values of the coefficients in Table 5.2, with the assumptions about the relationship between m_1, m_2, q_1 and q_2 that were made for Table 5.1.

It is arguable that the assumptions which produced the results illustrated in Table 5.2 have exaggerated the possibility of reswitching quite considerably, for the table is based on the assumption that the machinery needed for the two techniques is entirely distinct at every stage of production. In practice there will certainly be common items (or items produced with similar capital coefficients), and this will be particularly the case in the firms that produce equipment for the investment sector, but in addition there will be a number of common items in the firms which produce consumption sector equipment for the two techniques. Thus, rather similar buildings, vehicles and basic machinery are often likely to be used for very different kinds of machinery production at the level of both the basic and the secondary capital-goods industries. This means that a certain proportion of the equipment in all industries with all techniques will almost always be produced by what have been called 'basic machine tools' in the present model, and only a certain proportion by equipment specific to the technique in question. It was shown at an early stage of the argument that there cannot be reswitching where the machines for techniques 1 and 2 are entirely the product of the same machinery. It has been shown that there may be reswitching in circumstances where the machines needed for techniques 1 and 2 are the product of different secondary machine tools which were produced by the same basic machine tools at an earlier stage of production, and that reswitching will occur more frequently than this where all the equipment with the two techniques is distinct. Any real situation is likely to lie somewhere between these situations, with the result that Table 5.2 will somewhat overstate the possibilities of reswitching, and equation (5.25) and Table 5.1 may also overstate this.

But even (5.25) and the tables suggest that the likelihood of reswitching may be rather less great than some authors have supposed. The principal condition for not more than one switching point between two techniques which Bruno, Burmeister and Sheshinski have suggested, and they use the term 'nonswitching condition' to refer to a condition which ensures that there will be no more than one switching point, is based on Descartes's rule of signs which states that the number of real positive roots to a polynomial is equal to the number of variations in sign of the coefficients, or is less than this number by a positive integer.[1] All that this condition states for the quadratic case is that there cannot be reswitching if there is only

[1] Bruno, Burmeister and Sheshinski, op. cit., p. 544.

one change of sign, for there will then be at most one positive real root. This merely states that there cannot be reswitching if conditions (i) and (ii) (out of (i), (ii), (iii) and (iv) outlined earlier) fail to hold; and that there may be reswitching if (i) and (ii) hold. But this is only half the answer to the problem. Condition (iv), which is based on the need for all capital goods to be positively priced, must also hold if there is to be reswitching, and condition (iii), which ensures that real rates of return will be earned, must hold, but there is no derivation of equivalent conditions in the work of Bruno, Burmeister and Sheshinski. It is therefore hardly surprising that their sufficiency conditions for non-switching are 'highly restrictive'.

It would be a tiresome mathematical task to derive the conditions equivalent to (iii) and (iv) for a model with more stages in the productive process than has been assumed here. The equation for r would then be a cubic, or a polynomial of higher degree, and the reswitching (and corresponding non-switching) conditions would almost certainly be exceedingly complex. Given this, it is possible that complete reswitching and non-switching conditions for such cases will not be derived for some time. Until such cases are analysed completely – and the analysis will need to go further than Descartes's rule of signs – it will be impossible to refute or confirm assertions that reswitching is as probable as non-switching in such cases.

There is no need to be as agnostical as this about cases such as the quadratic case which can be analysed completely. Here, there may be reswitching where q_1 and q_2 are rather far apart, but otherwise the likelihood appears to be slight, especially where there are capital goods equivalent to the *basic* machine tools of the present model.

This is to summarise the situation where production with all techniques is completed within a unit gestation period. There are further possibilities of multiple switching when variability in the gestation period is allowed for, and these possibilities will be analysed in the next section.

The Possibility of Multiple Switching – with Prolonged Gestation Periods

Up to this point in the argument, it has been assumed that each process of production is completed within a unit gestation period. Traditional capital theory has been much concerned with the effect of time or the 'period of production' on the value of capital, the technique of production, etc. Some of the multiple switching effects which have been noted in recent literature have been associated with complexities due to long periods of production.[1] The assumption of a unit gestation period avoided the problems associated with the need for different time periods for different processes of production, and this assumption must now be dropped.

To bring out the effect of long gestation periods most simply and clearly (and particularly their effect on the possibility of multiple switching), a comparison will be made between the profitability of producing a quantity X of a particular good by two very simple techniques. One of these will be called the 'fixed capital technique', and here the good will be produced by labour and fixed capital in a unit period. The other will be called the 'gestation technique', and here the good will be produced by labour without supporting capital over several periods. To make the fixed capital technique as simple as possible, it will be assumed that the good which is produced by the process is itself used as the capital good with which labour is equipped. This is analogous to the technique for producing basic machine tools which was analysed in earlier sections.

The comparison between these two simple methods of producing X will bring out the main problems which follow from the assumption of prolonged gestation periods. Once this case is understood, the analysis of other and more complex cases will be quite straightforward.

With the fixed capital technique, suppose that X is produced by L workers working for one period with $M.X$ of the good, and that the good does not depreciate when it is used as capital. The capital–output ratio with the fixed capital technique will then always be M, for X is produced with one-good-model assumptions. X will be worth the wage bill, $w.L$, plus the capital cost of producing X which is r times the capital required, or $r.M.X$. Then $X = w.L + r.M.X$, i.e.:

$$X = \frac{w.L}{1 - r.M} \qquad (5.26)$$

[1] The original Ruth Cohen 'curiosum', and Sraffa's startling result that techniques cannot generally be ordered monotonically to show a series of techniques adopted as the rate of profit falls, which are fundamental to subsequent work on capital theory both depend upon gestation effects. See Robinson, *The Accumulation of Capital*, pp. 109-10, and Sraffa, *Production of Commodities by Means of Commodities*. The reswitching examples cited by Pasinetti, op. cit., also depend upon gestation effects.

E

$$\frac{w}{X} = \frac{1-r.M}{L}. \qquad (5.27)$$

With the gestation technique, X is produced through the continuous employment of h workers for j periods up to the unit gestation period of the fixed capital technique. X's value during the unit gestation period will then be the discounted cost of the wages of h workers for j periods, and since the 'present value' of a wage of w paid t periods previously is $w.e^{rt}$, X will be worth $h.\int_0^j w.e^{rt}dt$, i.e.:

$$X = h.w\left(\frac{e^{rj}-1}{r}\right). \qquad (5.28)$$

$$\frac{w}{X} = \frac{r}{h(e^{rj}-1)} \qquad (5.29)$$

and by Taylor expansion:

$$\frac{w}{X} = \frac{1}{h.j.(1+\frac{1}{2}r.j+\frac{1}{6}r^2.j^2+\frac{1}{24}r^3j^3...)}. \qquad (5.30)$$

The possible forms that (5.27) and (5.29) (the factor-price equations with the two techniques) can take are illustrated in Fig. 5.6. The factor-price equation of the fixed capital technique (5.27) will simply be drawn as a downward-sloping straight line, but the factor-price equation of the gestation technique (5.29) is more complex than this. It slopes downwards to the right (for $\partial(w/X)/\partial r<0$), and its gradient will diminish (for $\partial^2(w/X)/\partial r^2>0$), while r will become very large as w/X tends to zero, so it will asymptotically approach the horizontal axis. It will be noted that there may be no switching point between the two techniques (as in (a)), one switching point (as in (b)) or two switching points (as in (c)). There will only be two switching points, i.e. there will only be reswitching where the two following conditions are fulfilled, as in (c):

(i) The gestation technique must pay a higher wage than the fixed capital technique on the vertical axis where the rate of profit is zero.

(ii) The gestation technique must pay a lower wage than the fixed capital technique at some rate of profit, in which case, if its factor-price curve starts higher, it must intersect the fixed capital technique's factor-price curve twice.

Condition (i), a higher (w/X) where the rate of profit is zero, will be fulfilled if L is greater than $h.j$ (from (5.27) and (5.30)). Now $h.j$ is the number of workers who need to be employed for one period to produce X with the gestation technique, and this must be less than L, the number of workers who need to be employed for a period with

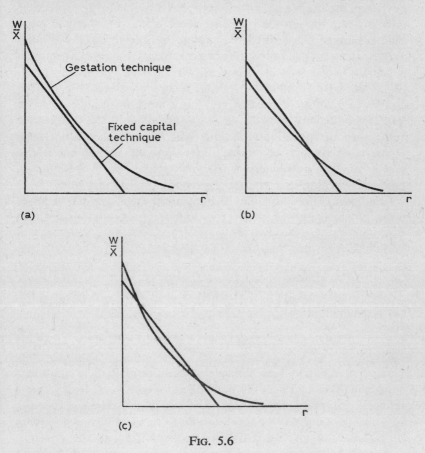

(a)   (b)

(c)

FIG. 5.6

the fixed capital technique. Thus the first condition that must be met if there is to be reswitching is that the gestation technique must use less labour than the fixed capital technique. It must thus require less labour to produce X with labour and the passage of time alone, than with labour and supporting fixed capital. It hardly needs to be said that this condition will very rarely be fulfilled, and this can be seen from the following proposition. Suppose there is a given amount of labour producing a particular output in one period without supporting fixed capital. There are two alternative ways of increasing output per worker. One is to equip the workers with supporting fixed capital. The other is to do the job more slowly, so that instead of employing L workers for one period, L/j workers are employed for j periods. It is only if doing the job more slowly raises labour productivity more than the use of supporting fixed capital that condition (i) will hold, and the chances of this are surely remote apart from cases where time is actually productive, as with trees, wine and oak chests, the traditional 'period of production' capital theory problems. If condition (i) fails to hold, i.e. if fixed capital has a more favourable effect on labour productivity than the mere passage of time, the factor-price curve with the gestation technique will start on the vertical axis below the fixed capital technique's factor-price curve as in Fig. 5.6(b), and it can then only intersect this once. However, if condition (i) holds, reswitching also requires that condition (ii) must hold.

Condition (ii) requires that the gestation technique pay a lower wage at some rate of profit to produce the position shown in Fig. 5.6(c) rather than that shown in Fig. 5.6(a). This condition will be fulfilled provided that (from (5.27) and (5.30)):

$$\frac{1-r.M}{L} > \frac{1}{h.j(1+\frac{1}{2}rj+\frac{1}{6}r^2j^2+\frac{1}{24}r^3j^3\ldots}$$

i.e. provided that:

$$1+r(\tfrac{1}{2}j-M)+\tfrac{1}{2}r^2j(\tfrac{1}{3}j-M)+\tfrac{1}{6}r^3j^2(\tfrac{1}{4}j-M) > \frac{L}{h.j}. \quad (5.31)$$

Now since $L/(h.j)>1$ as a result of condition (i), it is clear that condition (ii) cannot possibly be fulfilled unless $j>2M$, for a j of less than $2M$ will make the left-hand side less than 1. There is then the very strong non-switching condition that there will be non-switching if j is less than $2M$, i.e. if the gestation period with the gestation technique is less than twice the capital–output ratio with the fixed capital technique. Unfortunately there is not an equally clear reswitching condition. All that can be said is that there will be reswitching if j exceeds $2M$ by a sufficient margin.[1]

---

[1] In Sraffa's analysis, a rising rate of profit first raises and then lowers costs of production (expressed in terms of a 'standard commodity'), producing possible reswitching effects where j exceeds $1/R$, where R is the maximum rate of profit the

Where reswitching occurs because conditions (i) and (ii) are satisfied, the ratio of capital per worker with the gestation technique, $(K/L)g$, to capital per worker with the fixed capital technique, $(K/L)f$, changes very considerably, and this is the fundamental factor responsible for reswitching. The formula for $(K/L)g/(K/L)f$ is[1]:

$$\frac{\left(\dfrac{K}{L}\right)g}{\left(\dfrac{K}{L}\right)f} = \frac{j}{2M}.(1-rM).(1+\tfrac{1}{3}rj+\tfrac{1}{12}r^2j^2+\tfrac{1}{60}r^3j^3... \qquad (5.32)$$

and reswitching can be explained in the following way. j must exceed $2M$ to fulfil condition (ii), and this means that the gestation technique will be the more capital-intensive of the two at very low rates of profit. At high rates of profit, the gestation technique has very low relative capital intensity, and techniques with low capital intensity are normally preferred at high rates of profit. The gestation technique can then win through at two very different rates of profit because its relative capital intensity is so highly variable. However, it can only win through to produce reswitching if *neither* of two very stringent non-switching conditions is satisfied:

1. There will be, at most, one switching point where labour productivity is lower where labour works without supporting fixed capital with the gestation technique, than where labour works with capital equipment with the fixed capital technique.

2. There will be, at most, one switching point if the gestation period with the gestation technique is less than twice the capital–output ratio with the fixed capital technique.

At least one of these non-switching conditions will almost always be satisfied, but the generality of this result is clearly restricted by the

---

system can produce (*Production of Commodities by Means of Commodities*, pp. 34-40). In this case R is $1/M$ with the fixed capital technique, so the Sraffa criterion would appear to suggest possible reswitching if $j > M$. However, Sraffa's entire costs are incurred j periods in the past, while here costs are incurred continuously for $2j$ periods, so the two criteria are approximately equivalent.

[1] Capital per worker with the gestation technique is $1/r$ times profit per worker with this technique, or $w.\left(\dfrac{e^{rj}-rj-1}{j.r^2}\right)$ (from (5.28)), while capital per worker with the fixed capital technique is

$$\frac{M.X}{L} = \frac{w.M}{1-rM} \qquad \text{(from (5.26))}.$$

narrowness of the cases considered. Most actual techniques will contain elements of the gestation technique analysed here (since longer gestation periods will sometimes raise output per worker) and elements of rather more complicated fixed capital techniques than the one considered in this section. Where two techniques, A and B, each use gestation periods and fixed capital, the difference between them can be represented as so much extra gestation in technique A against so much extra fixed capital in technique B, with the result that any comparison of their relative profitability can be made along the lines of the analysis of this section. There will only be reswitching between such techniques if the extra gestation in A is equivalent to more than twice the extra incremental capital–output ratio in B, *and* if A also uses less labour to produce a particular output.

There will, of course, be further difficulties where the production of fixed capital is itself complex as in earlier sections of this chapter, for here the possibility of reswitching is rather generally present, though only the possibility, hardly the probability. If there is reswitching between complex techniques which include both gestation and fixed capital, this will be much more generally due to complexities in the manufacture of fixed capital, than to gestation effects. It must, of course, be remembered that the gestation period will be of significance in the range of activities where time is actually productive.

One final point about gestation should be noted. Even if it is accepted that gestation effects will rarely be strong enough to produce reswitching, there is an important aspect to gestation, and that is that where gestation is important, the concepts of capital intensity or capital per worker are particularly unclear. (5.32) showed the ratio of capital per worker with the gestation technique to capital per worker with the fixed capital technique, and both were clearly defined technical processes. The ratio varied from above unity to zero as the rate of profit rose from zero to $1/M$. A change in the rate of profit will therefore have a peculiarly great effect on value relationships like capital per worker (with unaltered technical relationships) where gestation plays an important role in production.

Conclusion

Recent developments in capital theory make it impossible to confine the analysis of growth to models with one-good assumptions. Joan

Robinson, Hicks, Sraffa, Pasinetti, Samuelson, Bruno, Burmeister and Sheshinski, and others, have shown that there is no presumption that the simple neoclassical results derived from such models will hold in a more complex world. An attempt therefore had to be made to analyse how far the simple propositions of one-good-model growth theory need to be modified to take account of complexities in the manufacture of capital equipment.

A possible conclusion of this chapter is that growth theory can be extended quite simply from one-good-model to two-sector assumptions, provided that all consumption and investment sector equipment is manufactured by the same basic equipment. Given this assumption, capital intensity can be allowed to differ in the two sectors, and the effects of differences can be analysed. Such differences will amend basic neoclassical equations in fairly simple and straightforward ways – as with (5.16) and (5.18) in this chapter. Moreover, there is no possibility of multiple switching where the capital equipment for alternative techniques is manufactured with the same basic equipment, so techniques can be ordered monotonically to show their order of adoption at successfully higher wage rates.

Once the assumption that all capital equipment is manufactured with the same basic equipment is dropped, the situation becomes much more complex, for capital per worker may not be clearly higher (in value terms) with one technique than another. It may be higher with a first technique at some wage rates, and with a second at other wage rates, with the result that the relative profitability of techniques may alternate with multiple switching points between them. Ambiguity in the relative value of the capital needed for alternative techniques will generally be the ultimate factor behind multiple switching, and this can be due to a variety of causes. Hicks has suggested that the basic cause of this ambiguity may be differences in the ratio of costs which must be incurred prior to final production to costs incurred in the process of final production.[1] Two narrower causes of ambiguity have been distinguished and analysed in this chapter, namely, a need for specific secondary capital equipment in the investment sector to manufacture particular consumption sector equipment, and different gestation periods with alternative techniques.

Where both *basic* and *secondary* investment sector equipment is used to manufacture consumption sector equipment, there is a

[1] J. R. Hicks, 'A Neo-Austrian growth theory', *Economic Journal*, vol. LXXX (June 1970).

possibility of multiple switching where the equipment which is more labour-productive in the consumption sector is manufactured with less capital-intensive *secondary* equipment. For there to be possible multiple switching or capital-reversing over a significant range of the coefficients, output per worker in the consumption sector must apparently be very different with the two techniques. This means that multiple switching will be much more of a possibility where techniques involve radically different economic processes than where they are alternative versions of the same basic process. The possibility of multiple switching does not appear to be very great, even where the above condition is fulfilled, provided that some common equipment is used to manufacture the equipment for the two techniques, but it cannot be ignored. This means that in practical cases, the choice of technique (in a planning process) must involve a very careful analysis of the various stages by which capital equipment is produced (and these may sometimes exceed the two stages suggested above with additional 'unorthodox' effects), for a change in factor prices may have unexpected effects on the relative profitability of alternative techniques if the technical processes by which capital is manufactured differ substantially.

The argument of the last section of the chapter suggests that the complexities due to gestation may not be as damaging to the conclusions of traditional capital theory as some have supposed, and they will certainly be less damaging than the assumption of different capital intensities in the manufacture of equipment. The practical possibilities of reswitching due primarily to gestation effects may be thought to be remote (except where time is particularly productive), given that this will only occur where taking time over production adds more to labour productivity than the use of fixed capital – and that the time taken must exceed twice the capital–output ratio of a fixed capital technique.

Even if it can be shown that extreme 'unorthodox' effects like reswitching will not generally occur (and there are cases where this cannot be shown), there is a thread in capital theory which is unfavourable to simple propositions which should not be lost sight of. There will scarcely ever be a clear and simple connection between the 'value' of capital and its technical specifications. Most published statistics on shares of investment, capital–output ratios and the like show *value* relationships, and account should also be taken, wherever this is possible, of known technical relationships. For instance, it

may sometimes be possible to take relative prices of capital and consumer goods into account (where the prices of particular capital
goods can be specified), and this may show that two countries with
very different shares of investment do much the same investment
(with one importing capital equipment from the other), while, on
the other hand, supposed similarities may hide very substantial
differences.

PART II

A Model of Equilibrium Growth

6

The Determination of the Rate of Technical Progress

Introduction

IT is clear from almost all approaches to what determines an economy's equilibrium rate of growth that the rate of technical progress will have a dominant influence upon it. The rate of technical progress will also be a major factor in the determination of an economy's capital–output ratio, its rate of profit and its distribution of incomes. How the rate of technical progress is determined will therefore be a matter of the utmost importance.

Something was said about the determinants of technical progress in earlier chapters, but this problem must now be analysed more fully. In the real world, an economy's rate of technical progress will clearly depend upon a large number of factors, many of which fall outside the usual boundaries of economics. A view which is widely taken is that the influence of these 'non-economic' factors is all important, and that the influence of factors normally analysed by economists in the context of growth models is relatively slight. With this view of the matter, it can be assumed that there is an exogenously given rate of technical progress of a or m – for this is given exogenously so far as an economic model which ignores scientific activity, educational structure, trades union activity, managerial skills, attitudes to change, the rapidity with which foreign technical advances are adopted, and so on, is concerned. This case has been fully dealt with in earlier chapters where exogenously given rates of Hicks- or Harrod-neutral technical progress were assumed at various stages.

This approach to the problem is the simplest, but it may ignore important aspects of the real world, for factors which are customarily included as variables in an economic model may influence the rate and bias of technical progress in important ways. In particular, it can be argued that the rate of technical progress will be influenced by some aspect of an economy's investment activity. It might be influenced by the rate of growth of the capital stock,[1] or the share of the National Product invested, or the accumulated sum of past investment,[2] or the period of time over which the capital stock is replaced.[3] Technical progress will be endogenous to the processes analysed by growth models rather than something which is exogenous to those processes in so far as the rate of technical progress depends upon investment.

In this chapter the reasons for expecting a positive relationship between the rate of investment and the rate of technical progress will be analysed. The central arguments will rest upon two propositions: that the incentive to develop superior capital goods will vary with the quantity of a new capital good that can be sold; and that weaknesses in the design of plant and machinery will be eradicated as more of a particular type of capital good is used or produced. These propositions will be analysed in turn. An object of the analysis will be to derive a plausible 'technical progress function', i.e. a plausible functional relationship between the rate of investment and the rate of technical progress, which is compatible with steady growth. It will be argued that there may well be a strong relationship between the rate of investment and the rate of technical progress, and that this will differ, with important consequences for growth theory, from the relationships suggested by Kaldor and Arrow.

Investment, Research and Development, and Technical Progress

The first reason for expecting an association between the rate of investment and the rate of technical progress is that it will be more profitable to invent and develop superior methods of production where the rate of investment is high. The reasoning behind this argument can be seen with the help of Figs. 6.1 and 6.2. Here, the schedule RR shows the amount that must be spent on research and development per annum in order to discover how to produce capital equipment which will permit reductions in unit costs of production with new equipment at various proportional annual rates. RR will cut the vertical axis because it is reasonable to suppose that some

---

[1] See Kaldor, 'A model of economic growth'.
[2] See Arrow, 'The economic implications of learning by doing'.
[3] See Eltis, 'Technical progress, profits, and growth'.

minimum sum must be spent on research and development before results begin to be achieved. Once results are achieved, it is reasonable to suppose that a high annual rate of cost reduction will be more expensive than a low rate, and that beyond a certain point it will become increasingly expensive to reduce costs at a higher proportional rate. With these assumptions, RR will slope upwards at an increasing rate, as in Fig. 6.1. More formally, if X is the annual cost

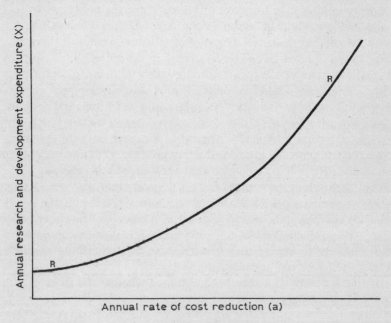

Annual rate of cost reduction (a)

FIG. 6.1

of research and development, and the annual rate of cost reduction is a, it is being assumed that $dX/da > 0$, and that dX/da varies with a so that $d^2 X/da^2 > 0$. A number of crucial assumptions are embodied in this RR function, and these must be discussed before the RR function can be used in the subsequent analysis.

The expression of the results of research and development expenditures as an annual rate of cost reduction is what is necessary if this is to influence an economy's equilibrium rate of growth, but it is not obvious that the results of research and development can be properly expressed in these terms. It could be argued that successful research will produce a given once-for-all reduction in costs, and that further reductions will be progressively more difficult to obtain, with the result that RR should be drawn as a *static* curve with cost of research and development instead of *annual* cost of research and development on the vertical axis, and reduction in cost instead of *annual* reduction in cost on the horizontal. Then the diagram would suggest that it is progressively more difficult and expensive to reduce costs of production, with the result that no *steady* rate of technical change could emerge from the analysis. There are objections to this view and arguments in favour of the view which is taken in Fig. 6.1 that RR can be drawn as a dynamic schedule. If there were diminishing returns to research and development in the sense that discoveries in one industry typically became progressively more expensive through time, companies would maintain research and development departments during the period when research could be fruitful, and contract them when the cost of further discoveries passed a certain point; but this is not what is typically observed. Research and development departments generally grow, and many produce a continuous stream of results. There is no evidence that their growth is generally associated with falling profitability. This suggests that discoveries may often be jumping-off points for further discoveries, with the result that the concept embodied in Fig. 6.1 of a research department of a given size producing results at a certain annual rate may approximate more closely to reality than the concept of diminishing research opportunities in any one direction.[1]

If this is accepted, it may be questioned whether the slope of RR should become steeper as the annual rate of cost reduction is increased. If discoveries are often starting-points for further discoveries, there is apparently no reason why doubling research expenditure should not double or treble the annual results achieved. The fundamental basis for an increasing upward slope to RR rests on an obvious principle which has been documented as a result of work done in the RAND Corporation.[2] The cost of a new development will increase if the time-span within which it must be completed is contracted beyond a certain point. Thus, writing in 1973, the aggregate cost of reaching

[1] Cf. J. Conlisk, 'A neoclassical growth model with endogenously positioned technical change frontier', *Economic Journal*, vol. LXXIX (June 1969), where it is argued that research and development expenditure in an economy's 'productivity sector' produces technical progress as an 'output'.

[2] See Edwin Mansfield, *The Economics of Technological Change* (Longmans, 1969) pp. 72-5.

Mars by 1978 must be greater than the cost of reaching Mars by 1983, which means that *annual* research and development expenditure would need to be more than doubled in the period 1973-8 to double the annual rate of technical progress, i.e. to achieve ten years' progress in five. That is the basis for the increasing upward slope of *RR*.

A further difficulty is associated with uncertainty. To draw *RR* is implicitly to assume that entrepreneurs expect particular rates of research and development expenditure to produce particular rates of cost reduction, but this ignores uncertainty, which is likely to be particularly great where research and development is concerned. A question which then arises is how far a function like *RR* can allow for uncertainty. The rates of cost reduction that entrepreneurs expect from particular rates of research and development expenditure can be represented by a single schedule in an uncertain world only if this shows something as simple as, for instance, the weighted average of the various possible rates of cost reduction multiplied by their (subjective) probabilities. Otherwise the results of research and development will need to be represented in more than one dimension, for instance by the expected yield and the degree of risk (or variance). If the initial argument is to be kept simple, it will be desirable to represent expected results by a single rate of cost reduction, and the argument could always be extended to deal with uncertainty in a more sophisticated way by making use of some of the results of portfolio theory – with firms undertaking a portfolio of risky research projects It will be assumed that the fundamental problems can be analysed without this.

A final problem is due to the fact that *RR* shows the expected rate of cost reduction of *existing products* when, in the real world, a very high proportion of research and development activity is associated with new products and improvements to products. The problems associated with this necessarily have to be tackled wherever the growth of a country's National Product is measured, for qualitative changes then have to be expressed as an increase in quantity. It can perhaps be assumed in the present argument that a quality change which raises the value of a product of unchanged real cost at a rate of *a* (in the estimation of the statisticians who compute the real National Product) can be represented as a rate of cost reduction (of an unchanging product) of *a*. Then cost reduction and product improvements will have the same analytical effect, and they can equally be regarded as technical progress. In both cases, firms will find that technical progress adds to their potential profits, and it will now turn out that this plays a significant part in the determination of the amounts they will find it profitable to spend on research and development.

In Fig. 6.2 a further curve, DD, has been added to RR, and this shows the amount that firms expect to earn from successful research and development activity. It can be supposed that the development of capital equipment which permits production with unit costs which are lower by a proportion of a (or the production of an equivalently

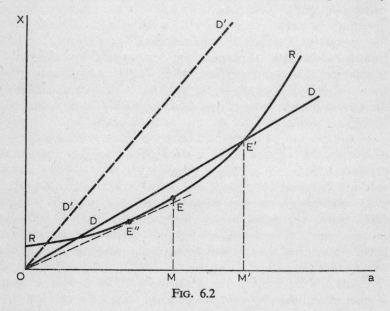

FIG. 6.2

superior product) will allow the firm responsible for these developments to charge a price for the equipment it markets (or to obtain a royalty from other firms licensed to market it) which is higher than it otherwise would be by a proportion of $u.a$ (where u is a constant). Thus it is assumed for simplicity that a firm can expect to earn twice as much extra profit from marketing equipment which permits the exploitation of 10 per cent technical progress as it can earn as a result of 5 per cent technical progress. If a firm expects to sell equipment which is worth I per annum, and it makes a discovery which cuts costs by a proportion of a, it can expect to obtain extra profits of I times $u.a$ per annum. This extra profit is shown as the schedule DD, and it will be a straight line, passing through the origin, with a slope of $u.I$. With these assumptions, the extra profits from successful research and development will be proportional to the percentage cost reductions which are made possible by the development, and proportional to total expected sales of equipment. Thus it is assumed that twice as much extra profit will be earned from a particular cost reduction in an economy where there is twice as much investment in equipment to which the cost reduction is relevant.

The costs of research and development and returns from this must clearly be measured in the same units. Initially, it will be assumed that the relative prices of capital goods (which influence I and therefore DD) and research and development activity (which influences RR) are given and constant. This assumption will be relaxed in a later stage of the argument, where it will be found that a continuous increase in the cost of research and development activity relatively to capital investment may play an important role in the growth process.

A profit-maximising firm will push research and development expenditure to the point where the extra profits obtained from the development of superior capital equipment exceed the cost of developing such equipment by the greatest possible amount, and this is found where the gap between DD and RR is maximum, i.e. at E where DD and RR are parallel.

There will naturally be cases where expected sales of equipment are so low that DD is entirely below RR, and then the point where DD and RR are parallel will show a loss, with the result that research and development will not be viable and the firm will not have a research department. However, where DD is above RR as in Fig. 6.2, the firm will earn maximum profits by pushing research and development to the point where DD and RR are parallel, and in Fig. 6.2 the firm will find it optimal to spend EM on research and development per annum, and reduce costs in consequence at a rate of OM per annum. A firm which expects to market capital goods worth $2I$ instead of I will have the DD curve $D'D'$ where each point on $D'D'$ has twice the height on the vertical axis of the corresponding point on DD, but it will have exactly the same RR curve as the other firm. $D'D'$ is parallel to RR at E', and this shows the annual amount that the firm with twice the original firm's market for capital goods will choose to spend on research and development, while OM' shows the annual rate of cost reduction that it will achieve. The second firm will spend more, and it will achieve more, for OM' is bound to exceed OM.

A question that immediately arises is whether a firm which expects to sell twice as much equipment as another will achieve twice, more than twice, or less than twice the annual rate of cost reduction of the other firm. It turns out that these are all possible. Doubling expected sales of equipment will double the slope of DD, and the new equilibrium will be where the slope of RR is also doubled, i.e. where its dX/da is doubled. This means that the critical point where the rate of technical progress is proportional to expected sales of equipment will occur where a is proportional to dX/da, i.e. where d^2X/da^2 is a constant. A functional relationship between X and a which will produce this result (and satisfy the assumptions on which RR is drawn that dX/da and $d^2X/da^2 > 0$) is $X = A + B \cdot a^2$ (where A and B are constants, A being the intercept of RR on the vertical axis in Figs. 6.1 and 6.2), so that

$$a = \sqrt{\frac{X-A}{B}}.$$

This allows fully for diminishing returns to research and development by making technical progress vary approximately with $\sqrt{X}$, and it also produces the result that doubling the expected sales of equipment will double the rate of technical progress. The relationship between a and X could clearly be stronger or weaker than this; for instance, $X = A + B \cdot a^{1 \cdot 5}$ where doubling investment would more than double technical progress, and $X = A + B \cdot a^{2 \cdot 5}$ where this would less than double technical progress.

A faster rate of technical progress must, of course, require a more than proportional increase in research and development expenditure – i.e. in annual investment in research and development as opposed to investment in new equipment. The average cost of technical progress in terms of expenditure on research and development will be X/a, or the slope of a line from the origin to RR in Fig. 6.2, and this will be minimum at E''. Any move up RR beyond E'' must raise the slope of a straight line from the origin, so it must raise the cost (in terms of research and development activity) of an extra 1 per cent per annum on the rate of technical progress. Hence, if doubling the expected demand for equipment doubles the rate of technical progress, it will more than double required research and development expenditure.

The results obtained so far have depended upon the assumptions that firms undertaking research and development seek to maximise their profits, and that there is no entry into research and development. However, the abnormal profits made by firms undertaking research and development, shown by a gap between DD and RR, might well attract other firms into this activity. Suppose initially that there is free entry. In this case firms will always enter where DD is above RR.

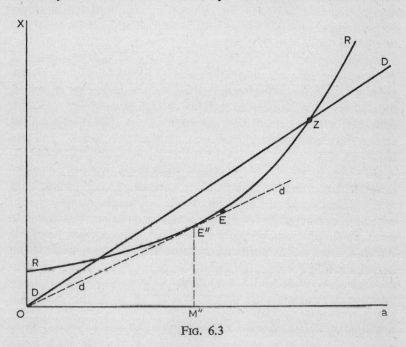

FIG. 6.3

With the entry of each extra firm seeking to develop better equipment, the expected sales of equipment per firm will fall with the result that the slope of DD will fall for each firm. So long as DD is above RR at any point, abnormal profits can be earned through research and development, so the limit set by free entry is that entry will continue until DD has fallen to dd which is tangential to RR at E'' in Fig. 6.3. The position of E'' is independent of an economy's rate of investment, etc., for it can be found by simply drawing a tangent from the origin to RR, so it will simply be a function of the schedule RR. This means that any connection between aggregate investment and the distance along RR which it pays firms to choose will completely disappear where free entry into research and development is assumed. Where expected sales of equipment are high, more firms will engage in research and development, but individual firms will not push expenditure further along their research and development functions. This would be beneficial to technical progress in that a larger number of research and development departments should increase the range of what is discovered, but this is not a benefit which will show in the analysis represented by Figs. 6.1, 6.2 and 6.3. Here, there will simply be more firms, each offering new equipment which permits an annual rate of cost reduction of OM''.

It then appears that where there is free entry into research and development, the rate of cost reduction achieved will vary with expected sales of equipment only in the rather imprecise sense that the number of firms engaged in research and development will vary with this, with the result that something extra should be achieved where more equipment is marketed, though how much extra can hardly be clear.

However, it will not be rational for the firms originally engaged in research and development to allow themselves to be pushed back to E''. If they could anticipate that this would be the consequence of earning abnormal profits at E, they would realise that they would do much better (in terms of market share, size and aggregate profits – though there would be no abnormal profits) by pushing research and development to Z where DD and RR intersect. This would represent the maximum research and development activity which was compatible with normal profits, and it would represent the maximum financially sound rate of technical advance that a firm could achieve. It would also preclude loss of markets through entry. Z is clearly a position of *long-run* profit maximisation in an industry where entry is thought to be the likely consequence of abnormal profits.[1]

The dominance of research and development in computers, chemicals, aircraft, and so on, by a few firms with giant research departments suggests that it may be more realistic to argue that firms carry out as much research and development as they can afford, than to assume that they limit it so as to maximise short-run profits and invite consequent entry. Naturally, it may be that Z is chosen because the motivation of managements in these cases is biased towards

[1] Cf. R. F. Harrod, 'Theory of imperfect competition revised', in *Economic Essays* (Macmillan, 1952).

technical progress and the achievement of technical excellence,[1] with the result that the principal objective of those responsible for the management of a firm is movement as far as possible along RR. Financial constraints will limit such movement to the point Z. Whether this is the reason why Z might be preferred to E, or whether it is long-run profit maximisation, it appears that the argument that the final equilibrium position will be at E'' is not a strong one. If there is profit maximisation and no fear of entry, equilibrium will be at E. With either the anticipation of entry, *or* a preference for sales, growth or technical progress maximisation over profit maximisation, the firm will choose Z. E'' will only be reached if the firm pursues profit maximisation in the short run, and completely fails to take the possibility of entry into account where this is indeed a possibility.

It has already been shown that where equilibrium is found at E, a higher expected rate of investment might increase the rate of technical progress in the same, a higher, or a lower proportion. Where firms reach equilibrium at Z, the same result will follow,[2] so the rate of technical progress may vary more or less than proportionately with the expected market for equipment. As with the equilibrium at E, there will be a need to increase investment in research and development more than proportionately with the rate of technical progress, but a doubled market for equipment is as likely to lead to a more than doubled rate of technical progress as to a less than doubled rate.

Figs. 6.1, 6.2 and 6.3 show the incentive to the individual firm to undertake research and development, but if there are barriers to entry into research and development, or if firms choose points such as Z (in Fig. 6.3) on their research and development functions which preclude entry, the number of firms undertaking research and development in each industry will not change significantly, and RR in Figs. 6.1, 6.2 and 6.3 will then represent the position of an industry. An increase in an industry's expected demand for capital equipment (and in equilibrium, this means an increase in actual investment as

---

[1] Cf. J. K. Galbraith, *The New Industrial State* (Hamish Hamilton, 1967).

[2] Doubling expected investment will double the slope of DD, so it will double X/a at Z. Technical progress will also double at Z provided that, on RR, a doubles where X/a doubles, i.e. provided that X varies with a^2 or that a varies with $\sqrt{X}$. It is clearly compatible with the general principle of diminishing returns to research and development (and the assumptions on which RR is drawn that both dX/da and $d^2X/da^2 > 0$) that a should vary more or less than proportionately with the square root of research and development expenditure, so a may vary more or less than proportionately with the expected market for equipment.

well) will then shift the point of equilibrium to the right, with the result that there will be a higher rate of technical progress, though whether this will be higher in a greater or a smaller proportion than the rate of investment is not clear. Similarly, the rate of technical progress in the whole economy will vary (less or more than proportionately) with the rate of investment.

The case for expecting an endogenous relationship between investment and the rate of technical progress is therefore strong, and this follows directly from the assumption that there is a schedule such as RR which allows an annual rate of expenditure on research and development to be transformed into an annual rate of cost reduction. The case for the existence of a schedule of this kind is therefore crucial to the argument, but once this is accepted, the rest follows fairly straightforwardly.

It is now necessary to see how the argument will work out in the very long run. This is necessary, because a technical progress function which can be of use in a growth model must show the long-term equilibrium relationship between investment and technical progress. No attempt will be made at this stage to prove that there will be steady growth with particular technical progress functions. Instead, the object will be to show the form that technical progress functions must take if steady growth is to be a possibility. The procedure will therefore be to assume some of the conditions necessary for steady growth (such as a constant share of saving and investment, a constant capital–output ratio, a constant share of wages), and to find forms for technical progress functions which will permit steady growth where these conditions hold. Whether there will, in fact, be steady growth where the technical progress function takes these forms is a problem which will be considered in later chapters, but there will be no possibility at all of steady growth if the technical progress function does not permit it in the conditions postulated.

Suppose an economy saves and invests a constant share of a growing National Product. Then investment will grow at the same rate as the National Product, and in Figs. 6.2 and 6.3 the slope of the DD curve will rise through time. If the RR curve does not also rise, i.e. if the 'real' expenditures needed to produce various rates of cost reduction do not grow with the National Product, E (where DD is parallel to RR) and Z (where DD and RR intersect) will move continuously to the right, with the result that there will be a continuous increase in the rate of technical progress until RR becomes vertical. There will then be no possibility of steady growth until *RR* becomes vertical. This is a perfectly plausible result, for there has arguably been a fairly continuous increase in the rate of technical progress in the past 150 years, especially in the U.S.A., and this has been accompanied by growth in research and development in relation to the National Product.[1] More attention will be devoted to the possibility that there may be an increasing rate of technical progress in a growing economy below; but this is not the only result that is possible. There is also the possibility of steady growth.

Suppose that a given rate of *employment* in research and development (with a given ratio of labour costs to total costs) will produce given annual rates of cost reduction. It may be more plausible to assume this than to assume that given resources in terms of final physical outputs will produce constant research and development results. With economic growth, a university department with given staffing will become steadily more expensive in terms of an economy's final physical outputs as the real wages and salaries of professors and their secretaries increase with other incomes. If the cost of a department had to be kept constant in terms of the economy's physical outputs, its staffing would steadily decline, and it could hardly be expected to achieve a constant stream of results. For this, constant employment would surely be necessary, and in so far as industrial research and development corresponds to university research, it will be right to assume that constant employment in research and development will be required if a constant rate of cost reduction is to be achieved. With this assumption, *RR* will be constant as a schedule on a diagram where the vertical axis is denominated in 'wage units'. If an economy with a constant labour force and a constant share of wages invests a constant fraction of its output, investment will also be constant in wage units. Investment will grow in physical units with the growth of final outputs, but any rise in output will be associated with an equal rise in output per worker (because of the assumption of a constant labour force) and in wages

[1] Statistics on technical progress in the nineteenth century are not generally thought to be very meaningful. For the twentieth century, it has been estimated that the growth in total factor productivity in the U.S.A. was 1·8 per cent per annum from 1900 to 1929, 2·3 per cent from 1929 to 1948, and 2·8 per cent from 1948 to 1966. The ratio of research expenditure to GNP approximately trebled from 1930 to 1944, and it doubled between 1953 and 1966. W. Fellner, 'Trends in the activities generating technical progress', *American Economic Review*, vol. LX (Mar 1970).

per worker (because the share of wages is constant), so any rise in physical investment will be associated with an equal rise in the wage. With investment constant in wage units, there will be no tendency for DD to alter if the vertical axes of Figs. 6.2 and 6.3 are denominated in wage units. With no tendency for DD to shift in relation to RR as economic growth takes place, steady growth will be a possibility, and there will be particular possible equilibrium points – where DD and RR are parallel, and where they intersect. The rate of technical progress will be constant at each of these points.

Suppose two economies with different shares of investment are compared, where both have *the same* constant labour force. Then both will have the same RR schedule (measured in wage units), but the one with a higher share of investment will have higher investment measured in wage units, and therefore a higher DD curve. This will be parallel to (or intersect) the RR curve further to the right, so the economy with a higher share of investment will have faster technical progress, and a faster equilibrium rate of growth. The rate of technical progress may vary more or less than proportionately with the share of investment, for reasons which were outlined earlier.

Suppose now that both economies have the same share of investment and that both have constant employment, but that one has a *larger* labour force than the other. Both will have the same RR line (measured in wage units), but the one with higher employment will have higher investment (measured in wage units) so it will have a higher DD curve, and therefore a faster (though constant) rate of technical progress. Hence, on this analysis, the rate of technical progress should vary with the size of the labour force, as well as the share of investment.

The evidence is perfectly compatible with this rather startling result. The argument points to a strong connection between the rate of technical progress and *aggregate* sales of capital goods, which will depend on factors such as the share of investment and the *level* of employment. This suggests that economies with large potential markets for capital equipment, the U.S.A. and the European Common Market economies for instance, should enjoy more technical progress than economies with smaller domestic markets which are precluded by tariffs from selling in large international markets. This may be one of the most fundamental if not the most fundamental argument in favour of large common markets for manufactured goods.

The argument suggests that a technical progress function which takes account of the effect of research and development expenditures on the rate of technical progress is likely to take the following form. The rate of technical progress will be proportional, less than proportional, or more than proportional to S, the share of investment in the National Product, and L, the level of employment, provided that this is constant. Where comparisons between economies with different levels of employment are avoided, the rate of technical progress will depend simply on S, and the following function will produce the desired result:

$$a_r = A_r + B_r . S \qquad (6.1)$$

where a_r is the rate of technical progress attributable to research and development, while A_r and B_r are constants, with A_r either positive or negative. If A_r is positive, a_r will vary less than proportionately with S, while it will vary more than proportionately if A_r is negative.

This technical progress function can be expected to apply to economies with a constant share of investment and constant employment. Suppose, however, that an economy has a constant share of investment and *growing* employment. Then, measuring in wage units, RR will not shift through time, but DD will rise continuously with the growth of the labour force. Then the points where DD and RR are parallel and where they intersect will shift continuously to the right, and this must mean a rising rate of technical progress through time. Hence, there is apparently no possibility of a steady rate of technical progress, and of steady growth, where the labour force is growing. The only possibility of steady technical progress with a growing labour force would arise if the research and development expenditure that was required to achieve a given annual rate of cost reduction was a constant fraction of the National Product. This would mean that if two economies were similar in every respect except that one had labour growth while the other did not, the one with labour growth would need to spend *increasingly* more than the other to achieve the same research and development results. There is no plausible reason why this should be, and it would indeed be peculiar if the cost of research and development needed to increase with the rate of growth of employment.

This means that in so far as the rate of technical progress depends upon research and development, there is likely to be an increasing rate of technical progress where the labour force is growing – and the labour force grows in most developed economies.[1] Steady growth will be possible only if it is assumed that the sectors of the economy where the rate of technical progress is influenced by research and development expenditure are so unimportant in relation to the economy as a whole that they can safely be neglected. This will be a justifiable assumption in some cases, especially if attention is focused on growth in the nineteenth and the earlier part of the twentieth century. In such cases the rate of technical progress will depend principally on other factors, and a steady rate of technical progress will be possible.

In the chapters that follow in Part II, the awkward analytical case of a rising rate of technical progress with growing employment will be ignored, for these chapters will be concerned with steady growth situations. Where the labour force grows in these chapters, it will have to be supposed that the technical progress resulting from research and development is negligible in relation to technical progress from other sources. However, the matter cannot be left like this. It is plausible that there will be a rising rate of technical progress where there is a growing labour force, and the labour force grows in most economies. It will turn out that accelerating technical progress will play an important role in the argument of Chapter 11 of this book, which is concerned with growth in conditions where disequilibrium growth is inevitable.

Before the argument of this chapter can be taken further, the second principal endogenous relationship between investment and technical progress, the relationship based on 'learning by doing' effects, must be analysed.

'Learning by Doing' Technical Progress Functions

The best-known form of the argument that a high rate of investment will be associated with rapid technical progress because weaknesses in the design and development of capital equipment will be eradicated more quickly is due to Arrow.[2] His model owes much to evidence

---

[1] Cf. William D. Nordhaus, *Invention, Growth and Welfare* (Cambridge, Mass.: MIT Press, 1969) p. 106: 'The assumption that technical change is a function of the relative amount (of either the labour force or production) devoted to research is not satisfactory. Empirical studies . . . indicate that the absolute amount of resources devoted to research should be the determining variable. The correct formulation does not allow a steady state equilibrium.'

[2] Arrow, 'The economic implications of learning by doing'.

obtained from the U.S. aircraft industry,[1] where it was found that if successively produced airframes were given serial numbers rising from 1 upwards, the cost of airframes varied with $N^{-\frac{1}{3}}$, where N was the serial number of an airframe. This is a plausible relationship, for it is fully to be expected that 'learning', an element in total technical progress, will depend upon cumulative output.

If proportionality between unit costs, and N^{-b}, where b is a constant, applies universally, the basic equation for unit costs H will be as follows:

$$H = J.N^{-b} \tag{6.2}$$

where J is a constant.

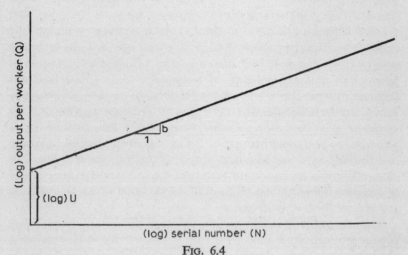

FIG. 6.4

If the share of wages is constant, labour costs will be a constant proportion of unit costs, so labour costs will be a constant proportion of H, and a constant proportion of $J.N^{-b}$. Labour productivity is the inverse of labour inputs per unit of output, so labour productivity (Q) will vary in inverse proportion with $J.N^{-b}$. Hence:

$$Q = U.N^b \tag{6.3}$$

where U is a constant. Taking the log of (6.3):

$$\log Q = \log U + b.\log N. \tag{6.4}$$

(6.4) is plotted in Fig. 6.4. This shows labour productivity rising

[1] T. P. Wright, 'Factors affecting the cost of airplanes', *Journal of the Aeronautical Sciences*, (1936); and H. Asher, *Cost–Quantity Relationships in the Airframe Industry*, R-291 (Santa Monica, Calif.: RAND Corporation, 1956).

along a straight log line on a double log scale, where the axes are independent of the passage of time. It is as if there is a succession of possible techniques of production, *1, 2, 3, 4, 5*, etc., with successive labour productivities which ascend along a straight log line on a double log scale. Investment in *1* will automatically make investment in *2* with a consequent rise in productivity a possibility, and this will make possible investment in *3* which will lead to a further increase in labour productivity, and so on. At the same time, an economy which stagnates for generations using *2*, cannot start to use *5* until it has first invested in *3* and learnt to use it, and then gone on to *4*. Whether *3* and *4* are used only briefly or for generations is immaterial. What matters is that an economy must be equipped with *3* and *4* before it can begin to use *5*. Thus investment automatically leads to technical progress, and it is a *sine qua non* for technical progress.[1] In Fig. 6.4 there is not a series of distinct techniques of production, but a succession of techniques with infinitesimal differences between them, and labour productivity rises as the economy moves up the schedule. The same general principle applies that the economy must pass along all the low points on the schedule if it is to reach any particular high point. This is a general principle involved in a learning-by-doing technical progress function, and it is plausible that it describes an important feature of the real world. It is now time to examine the particular features of the function which follow from the precise form of (6.2) and (6.3).

The effect of (6.3) is that each doubling of the serial number raises labour productivity 2^b times; and each increase in the serial number in the ratio $q:1$ raises labour productivity q^b times. This technical progress in the ratio $q^b:1$ will be achieved over any period, however short or long, in which the serial number is raised q times. Labour productivity will rise q^b times in ten years if it takes ten years to raise the serial number q times, and it will rise q^b times in a year if the serial number is raised q times in a year. Halving the period over which the serial number is raised q times would involve doing the same amount of investment in half the time, which would double the amount of investment which was done in a given period. Then technical progress in the ratio $q^b:1$ would be achieved in half the former time, which would mean that the annual rate of technical progress was doubled. Hence, doubling the rate of investment (in

[1] Cf. M. FG. Scott, 'Supply and demand refurbished', *Oxford Economic Papers*, vol. xix (July 1967) p. 163.

the sense that the same investment is done in half the former time) will double the rate of technical progress, and it follows from this that the annual rate of technical progress will be proportional to the rate of investment.

More simply, if something (investing; raising the serial number; anything) is done in half the former time, the rate at which it is done per unit of time will be doubled, and (as the technical progress which follows from a particular amount of investment is independent of the time taken to complete it) the consequences of this (whatever it is) will come through twice as fast per time unit. Then doubling investment, per time unit, must double technical progress, per time unit; so the annual rate of technical progress will be proportional to annual investment.

For growth equilibrium, a technical progress function must be capable of producing a steady rate of technical progress where a constant share of the National Product is saved and invested, and the circumstances where a learning-by-doing technical progress function is compatible with this will now be analysed. The eventual function must be one where doubling investment doubles the rate of technical progress, but it does not follow that a function will necessarily be found where doubling *any constant* share of investment will produce a constant doubled rate of technical progress. A constant share of investment may produce an increasing or a declining rate of technical progress, and in this case doubling this constant share would double the increasing or declining rate of technical progress.

Technical progress will occur at a constant rate through time if the serial number is raised at *any* constant proportional rate, for successive increases in the serial number in the ratio $q:1$ will advance labour productivity in constant successive steps of $q^b:1$. Then what is needed for a steady rate of technical progress is *any* steady proportional rate of increase in the serial number.

Up to now, exactly what the serial number is applied to has not been specified. It could apply to successively produced machines, each worked by one worker, or to successively produced machines where each produces the same quantity of output; or to cumulative gross investment, or to cumulative net investment, each measured in terms of consumer goods.

Arrow in fact applies the serial number to cumulative gross investment since the beginnings of industrialisation. In steady growth, with any particular depreciation assumption, net investment will be a constant fraction of gross investment, so it will be equivalent to Arrow's assumption to assume that the serial number is applied to c times cumulative net investment, i.e. to c times the net capital stock, where dc/dt is zero in steady growth. Then, substituting $c.K$ for N in (6.3):

$$Q = U.(c.K)^b. \tag{6.5}$$

Total output at time t, Y_t, will be output per worker (Q) times the total labour force, which will be $L_0.e^{nt}$, where L_0 is the labour force at time 0, and n is the rate of growth of the labour force, i.e.

$$Y_t = Q.L_0.e^{nt}. \tag{6.6}$$

Substituting for Q from (6.5):

$$Y_t = U.(c.K)^b.L_0.e^{nt}. \tag{6.7}$$

Differentiating (6.7) with respect to t:

$$\frac{1}{Y} \cdot \frac{dY}{dt} = n + b \cdot \frac{1}{K} \cdot \frac{dK}{dt} + b \cdot \frac{1}{c} \cdot \frac{dc}{dt}. \tag{6.8}$$

In steady growth, the rate of growth of output $((1/Y).(dY/dt))$ will equal the rate of growth of capital $((1/K).(dK/dt))$, and g and k can be written for these. Also, in steady growth, $dc/dt = 0$. Then, where $g = k$, and $dc/dt = 0$:

$$g = \frac{n}{1-b}. \tag{6.9}$$

This is Arrow's equation for the only possible rate of steady growth which can follow from his assumptions.[1] The rate of growth of productivity (p) will be $(g-n)$, so (from (6.9)):

$$p = n\left(\frac{b}{1-b}\right). \tag{6.10}$$

It is evident from (6.9) and (6.10) that, except where $b = 1$, the equilibrium rate of growth is very narrowly restricted. Even though doubling investment doubles technical progress, the only possible rate of *steady* growth will be solely a function of the rate of growth of the labour force, and the technical coefficient, b. Investment will not influence it at all. The reason for the independence of steady growth rates of investment, and their dependence on the rate of growth of the labour force, even though 'learning by doing' *should*

---

[1] Arrow, 'The economic implications of learning by doing', p. 165.

make investment the dominant influence, can be explained quite simply.

It was explained earlier that a q times increase in the serial number will raise output per worker q^b times. With proportionality between the serial number and the capital stock, this means that a q times increase in the capital stock will raise output per worker q^b times, and if b is less than *one*, this means that a q times increase in the capital stock will raise output per worker less than q times. With steady growth, output must increase at the same rate as capital. If labour productivity rises less than q times when the capital stock and output rise q times, labour requirements will increase, but if the labour force is constant, more labour cannot be made available. This means that a q times increase in output cannot be arranged. Then no growth at all is possible if the labour force is constant (and b is less than one), a result that is shown by (6.9) and (6.10). It will still be true that raising the capital stock twice as fast will raise labour productivity twice as fast – the propositions arrived at earlier – but in steady growth it will also raise labour requirements twice as fast, and this will vitiate the whole process for an economy with a constant labour force. Then the freedom to enjoy a wide range of growth rates which should result from freeing the rate of technical progress from any time constraint apparently fails to materialise. Instead, the steady growth rate is dominated by the discipline of the annual rate of labour growth, and there can be no technical progress if there is no quantitative or qualitative growth in the labour force.

It is, however, possible to define a learning-by-doing technical progress function which is very similar to Arrow's, but where any steady growth rate is possible, and where the rate of growth will depend substantially upon the share of investment.

With Arrow, a q times increase in the capital stock will increase labour productivity q^b times, and each successive increase in the capital stock by a fixed proportion will produce the same increase in labour productivity. Suppose that the unit for an increase in the capital stock is stated differently. Suppose the unit is the complete replacement of the capital stock by another with the same capital–output ratio, and that this always raises labour productivity in the ratio $e^G : 1$, where G is a constant. e^G can be 1·02 or 2·50: this will not affect the argument. With this assumption, the main essentials of a learning-by-doing technical progress function are retained. It is the act of investment that produces technical progress. An economy

F

moves up a straight log line as it replaces successive capital stocks, as with Arrow's function, and a succession of techniques, *1, 2, 3* and *4*, must be passed through before *5* can be used. Technical progress is defined independently of time, for given investment – replacing the capital stock with another with the same capital–output ratio – will produce the same e^G times advance in labour productivity, whether it takes one year or a hundred. The results are, however, very different from those arrived at with Arrow's technical progress function.

If it takes T years to replace the capital stock with another with the same capital–output ratio, labour productivity will rise e^G times in T years, which means that it will rise at an annual rate of $e^{(G/T)}$, or at an annual exponential rate of G/T. The period needed to replace the capital stock, T, will vary in inverse proportion with S, for if there is twice as much investment each year, the capital stock will be replaced in about half the time. If $T = D/S$, where D is a constant, the annual rate of technical progress due to learning-by-doing effects, a_z, will be $(G/D).S$ where G and D are constants. If the constant B_z is substituted for G/D, a learning-by-doing technical progress function which is very different from Arrow's is arrived at, i.e.

$$a_z = B_z.S. \tag{6.11}$$

The economy's rate of steady growth will be this plus n. With the slight modification to Arrow's formulation made here, *any* rate of technical progress will be compatible with steady growth, and any rate of steady growth will be possible. There will be an infinite range of possible rates of technical progress, and the rate an economy actually achieves from learning-by-doing effects will depend entirely on investment, and it will be proportional to the share of investment.[1]

There is no reason why bringing learning-by-doing effects into the argument should produce results which are more restrictive than those in a Cobb–Douglas world. Learning-by-doing assumptions should increase the influence an economy's saving and investment decisions can have upon its equilibrium growth rate. The formulation of learning-by-doing effects which is made here has that consequence, and as a result it is clear that the element of overall technical progress which is due to such effects will be proportional to the share of investment.

[1] This technical progress function, and the results which follow from it, were outlined in Eltis, 'Technical progress, profits, and growth'.

A Comprehensive Technical Progress Function

It can be argued that total technical progress will be due to a wide range of factors. There will be factors which are entirely exogenous to economic models as these are usually defined. These may be assumed to produce technical progress at an annual rate of A_e. Then there is the technical progress which is endogenous to the investment process, which can be divided into technical progress which is due to the investment process's stimulus to research and development activity, and to the learning effects which will go along with continuous investment. It has been argued that in steady growth with a constant labour force, these will produce annual technical progress of $A_r + B_r . S$ (where A_r can be positive or negative) and $B_z . S$ respectively. Adding these effects together, it is to be expected that total technical progress, a, will depend on the following equation:

$$a = (A_e + A_r) + (B_r + B_z) . S. \qquad (6.12)$$

The constants $(A_e + A_r)$ can be replaced by the constant A, which will be positive assuming that the technical progress which is due to factors which are exogenous to the investment process (A_e) amounts to more than the constant (and possibly) negative term (A_r) which is needed to allow for the possibility that higher investment may stimulate a more than proportionately higher rate of technical progress from research and development. The constants $(B_r + B_z)$ can be replaced by the constant B. Then:

$$a = A + B . S. \qquad (6.13)$$

(6.13) easily simplifies into the limiting cases where technical progress is entirely exogenous (and B is zero so that $a = A$), or entirely due to investment (where A is zero so that $a = B . S$). A technical progress function for the real world should lie in between the limits where $a = A$ and $a = B . S$, which points to the plausibility of the function shown by (6.13).[1]

The relationship between A and B will vary quite considerably between economies. The world's technical leaders will obtain much of their technical advance from their own research and development, which will give them a relatively high B_r, while backward economies which rely mainly on foreign technology will have negligible B_r's. There is no reason why B_z, the learning function, should be stronger

---

[1] This technical progress function was used in Eltis, 'Investment, technical progress, and economic growth', in 1963.

for the technical leaders, but their higher B_r's should ensure that they have relatively higher B's and therefore a higher proportion of endogenously determined technical progress.

Where the labour force grows, steady growth is only possible where research and development produces negligible technical progress in relation to other sources. This will not be the case with most advanced economies, and this means that research and development is likely to produce a growing rate of technical progress in such economies, with important implications for growth theory.[1] These will play their part in the argument of Chapter 11.

The technical progress function arrived at in this chapter is very different from Kaldor's pioneering technical progress function which is illustrated in Fig. 6.5.[2] There, the vertical axis shows the rate of growth of labour productivity, while the horizontal axis shows the rate of growth of capital per worker. The technical progress function, *PP*, cuts the vertical axis to show that there will be some growth in labour productivity, even where capital per worker is constant, because of factors contributing to technical progress which are independent of capital accumulation. After this, the rate of growth of labour productivity is assumed to vary with the rate of growth of capital per worker. The 45° line shows all points where capital per worker and output per worker grow at the same rate, and as capital and output will grow at the same rate in steady growth, an economy in steady growth must be somewhere on the 45° line. It must, at the same time, be somewhere on its technical progress function, and if it is to be on this as well as the 45° line, it must be at *X* where the two lines intersect. This will be the only point where equilibrium growth is possible. Then *OQ* and *OK* will be the only growth rates of output and capital per worker which are compatible with steady growth. Therefore, if two economies have the same technical progress function, *PP*, but different saving and investment propensities, both will

[1] There are also important implications for the future. If the growth rate doubles as a result of accelerating technical progress, the growth achieved over any given period will be *squared* – since an exponential is doubled – which means that science fiction results may be achieved with frightening rapidity. It must be remembered that in the real world technical progress usually takes the form of new products rather than a cheapening of existing products, and in the twentieth century these have created as many social problems as they have solved. In many cases legislation has had to be passed to control their unfavourable side-effects – or even new institutions set up; and this can hardly be done in time in every case, where new products arrive with increasing rapidity.

[2] Kaldor, 'A model of economic growth'.

have exactly the same growth rates of output and capital per worker. This means that there is no endogenous relationship at all between investment and the equilibrium rate of technical progress in Kaldor's model, for his technical progress function is so specified that only one point on it is compatible with equilibrium growth.

The same result follows mathematically. Kaldor's algebraic formulation of his technical progress function is:

$$(g-n) = A_1 + A_2(k-n) \qquad (6.14)$$

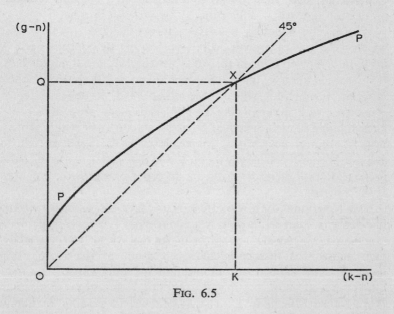

FIG. 6.5

where A_1 and A_2 are constants. This formulation makes PP a straight line, while he draws it as a concave curve, but this does not affect the result that there is only one possible rate of technical progress in equilibrium where $g = k$. If a is written for $(g-n)$ in (6.14), and $g = k$:

$$a = \frac{A_1}{1-A_2}. \qquad (6.15)$$

Hence a is a constant, and if the constant, A, is substituted for $A_1/(1-A_2)$, Kaldor's technical progress function becomes (6.13) with $B = 0$, i.e. he would have arrived at the same result if he had assumed that the rate of technical progress was exogenously given.

Indeed, with (6.14), he has assumed a function which implies a Cobb–Douglas relationship between output, capital and labour, for (6.14) can be rewritten as:

$$g = A_1 + A_2 . k + (1 - A_2) . n. \tag{6.16}$$

Integrate (6.16) with respect to time:

$$Y = D_1 . e^{A_1 . t} . K^{A_2} . L^{(1 - A_2)} \tag{6.17}$$

where D_1 is a constant.[1] It is naturally also the case that Kaldor's technical progress function will be arrived at if a Cobb–Douglas production function is differentiated with respect to time.

Superficially, Kaldor's (6.14) is almost identical to (6.13), but whether the rate of growth of productivity partly depends upon S (as in (6.13)) or on k (as in (6.14)) is a matter of crucial importance. If it depends upon k, this is simply another way of making Cobb–Douglas assumptions, If, on the other hand, it depends on S, economies with different saving and investment propensities will have different rates of technical progress, and different steady growth rates. If the argument of this chapter is accepted, it will be right to assume that a will depend partly on S, and that saving and investment propensities will therefore influence an economy's growth rate, even in the long run.

Both Kaldor and Arrow wrote long and forceful passages to argue that there is likely to be a strong endogenous relationship between investment and technical progress in the real world. Unfortunately, their subsequent mathematical specification of the relationship precluded any endogenous connection in equilibrium – in their growth models. With the specification of a technical progress function adopted here, that $a = A + B . S$, it will be possible to obtain results in the chapters that follow which are in line with the view of the technical process which Kaldor and Arrow initiated.

[1] See H. A. J. Green, 'Growth models, capital and stability', *Economic Journal*, vol. LXX (Mar 1960); and J. Black, 'The technical progress function and the production function', *Economica*, vol. XXIX (May 1962).

7

The Influence of Technical Progress Functions on Steady Growth Relationships

IN Chapter 6 it was argued that a plausible form for a technical progress function might be $a = A + B \cdot S$, where A and B are constants. A function of this kind will have a considerable influence on the steady growth relationships between the principal economic variables. This can be seen most simply if this technical progress function is substituted in the basic equations, $g = a + n$ and $V = S/(a+n)$, which were found in Chapter 2. Substituting $A + B \cdot S$ for a in these:

$$g = A + n + B \cdot S \qquad (7.1)$$

$$V = \frac{S}{A + n + B \cdot S}. \qquad (7.2)$$

Then, with this technical progress function, the equilibrium rate of growth will vary with the share of investment, and the capital–output ratio will vary less than proportionately with the share of investment. The results arrived at earlier will be modified to the greatest extent where the rate of technical progress is proportional to the share of investment, so that $a = B \cdot S$ (and $A = 0$). The effect of the technical progress function in this limiting situation is shown most clearly if it is assumed that growth is entirely due to technical progress. Then, with both A and n equal to zero:

$$g = B \cdot S \qquad (7.3)$$

$$V = \frac{1}{B}. \qquad (7.4)$$

Thus, if there is a constant labour force, and the rate of technical progress is proportional to the share of investment, the rate of growth will also be proportional to the share of investment, while the capital–output ratio will be a constant derived from the technical progress function itself. Then economies with different shares of investment will have different rates of steady growth, but they will all have the same capital–output ratio, $1/B$. This can be contrasted with the basic results arrived at in Chapter 2 which followed from the assumption that the rate of technical progress is an exogenously given constant. In that case, economies with different shares of investment all had the same rate of growth, but their capital–output ratios differed, and these were proportional to their shares of investment.

This extreme example brings out the crucial effect that technical progress functions can have upon steady growth relationships. The effect that the particular technical progress function considered here will have on the rate of profit, the share of profits, and the elasticities of the rate of profit and the rate of growth with respect to the share of investment, will be more complex than the effects shown in (7.1), (7.2), (7.3) and (7.4), but these will be equally important. What will matter particularly from the point of view of later chapters are the relationships between r, S and g, for the rate of profit will play an important role in the investment function which will be brought into the argument in the next chapter. In this chapter, the necessary steady growth relationships between r, S and g will be outlined. When the influence of r upon g and S through the investment decision is also brought into the analysis, there will be sufficient equations to simultaneously determine r, S and g, and this will provide the basis for the analysis of equilibrium growth relationships in a model where decisions to devote resources to capital investment and research and development are fully taken into account. It will be a major aim of this chapter to provide some of the basic relationships which are needed for this. The influence of the technical progress function upon the other variables will also be shown. This will be done for three types of model. First, the various relationships will be shown with Cobb–Douglas assumptions. Then they will be shown with CES assumptions, and finally they will be shown with vintage assumptions.

The Influence of the Technical Progress Function on a Cobb–Douglas Economy

Where $a = A + B \cdot S$ in a Cobb–Douglas economy, the rate of growth and the capital–output ratio must be those shown by (7.1) and (7.2).

The share of profits will be α, as it always must be with a Cobb–Douglas, and the rate of profit will be α/V, so this can be found from (7.2). Then the various steady growth relationships will be:

$$g = A + n + B.S$$

$$V = \frac{S}{A + n + B.S}$$

$$X_p = \alpha$$

$$r = \frac{\alpha(A + n + B.S)}{S} \qquad (7.5)$$

In the limiting situation where the rate of technical progress is proportional to the share of investment so that $A = 0$ and n is also zero, $V = 1/B$, $X_p = \alpha$ and $r = \alpha.B$, so the capital–output ratio, the rate of profit and the share of profits will each be the same with all values of S. Their values will simply depend upon the parameters, α and B. (7.5) shows that more generally, r will vary inversely with S, but not in inverse proportion as it does where the rate of technical progress is exogenously given. Then doubling S will less than halve r. The elasticity of r with respect to S is found by differentiating (7.5) with respect to S, i.e.

$$\text{Elasticity of } r \text{ with respect to } S = -\frac{A+n}{A+n+B.S}. \qquad (7.6)$$

Thus the elasticity of r with respect to S will be -1 where the rate of technical progress is exogenously given so that $B = 0$, and it will be zero (i.e. the rate of profit will be the same with all shares of investment) in the other limiting situation where the rate of technical progress is proportional to the share of investment, and there is no labour growth. Then the elasticity of r with respect to S must lie within the range, $-1 \ldots 0$, where technical progress depends partly on investment, and the production function is Cobb–Douglas.

The elasticity of the rate of profit with respect to the rate of growth can be derived quite simply from the elasticity of r with respect to S:[1]

$$\text{Elasticity of } r \text{ with respect to } g = -\frac{A+n}{B.S}. \qquad (7.7)$$

---

[1] Since $g = A+n+B.S$, the elasticity of g with respect to r is

$$(B.S)/(A+n+B.S) \qquad (7.8)$$

times the elasticity of S with respect to r.

F*

Then the elasticity of r with respect to g cannot be positive, and its negative value will vary inversely with the proportion of growth that is due to endogenously determined technical progress.

The position will be a little more complicated than this with CES assumptions.

The Influence of the Technical Progress Function on a CES Economy

Where $a = A + B.S$ in a CES economy, the rate of growth and the capital–output ratio must again be $A + n + B.S$ and $S/(A + n + B.S)$, while X_p and r can be found by substituting $A + B.S$ for a in (2.6) and (2.7). Then the various steady growth relationships will be:

$$g = A + n + B.S$$

$$V = \frac{S}{A + n + B.S}$$

$$X_p = J. \left(\frac{A + n + B.S}{S} \right)^{\left(\frac{1}{\sigma} - 1 \right)} \tag{7.9}$$

$$r = J. \left(\frac{A + n + B.S}{S} \right)^{\frac{1}{\sigma}}. \tag{7.10}$$

In the limiting situation where $a = B.S$ and n is zero, $V = 1/B$ as with Cobb–Douglas assumptions, while $X_p = J.B^{(1/\sigma - 1)}$ and $r = J.B^{(1/\sigma)}$, so as in the Cobb–Douglas case, V, X_p and r will each be the same with all values of S. Their values will simply depend on the parameters, J, σ and B.

The elasticity of the rate of profit with respect to the share of investment is found by differentiating (7.10) with respect to S:

$$\text{Elasticity of } r \text{ with respect to } S = -\frac{1}{\sigma} \left(\frac{A + n}{A + n + B.S} \right) \tag{7.11}$$

Thus the elasticity of the rate of profit with respect to the share of investment will be $-1/\sigma$ where the rate of technical progress is given exogenously (so that $B = 0$), and it will be zero where the rate of technical progress is proportional to the share of investment and there is no labour growth. Then the elasticity of the rate of profit with respect to the share of investment must lie within the limits $-1/\sigma \ldots 0$.

The elasticity of the rate of profit with respect to the rate of growth can again be derived from the elasticity of r with respect to S and (7.8):

$$\text{Elasticity of } r \text{ with respect to } g = -\frac{1}{\sigma}\left(\frac{A+n}{B.S}\right). \qquad (7.12)$$

Then the elasticity of the rate of profit with respect to the rate of growth cannot be positive, so with A, n and B given, a higher rate of growth will always be associated with the same or a lower rate of profit. The negative value of the elasticity of the rate of profit with respect to the rate of growth will vary inversely with σ and the proportion of growth that is due to endogenously determined technical progress.

The introduction of a technical progress function will cause more trouble with a vintage model; but it will nevertheless be desirable to work out its full effects with vintage assumptions. Without vintage assumptions, depreciation is either ignored, or allowed for in a rather arbitrary way. In the above equations, it must either be assumed that there is no depreciation, or that S is *net* investment so that depreciation is already allowed for. Then V is the *net* capital–output ratio, and so on. However, there is an important relationship between depreciation and other variables, and this will have a considerable effect upon the relationship between the rate of profit and the share of investment. Vintage theory is necessary to bring out this relationship. The mathematics of vintage growth with a technical progress function is a little complex, so the principal relationships will be arrived at and set out in the concluding section of this chapter, and this can be regarded as an appendix by those who are interested only in the general results arrived at. The very much simpler account of vintage growth with the technical progress function, $a = A+B.S$, which now follows will rely on some of the results arrived at in the concluding section of the chapter.

The Influence of the Technical Progress Function on a Vintage Economy

As vintage theory is a little more complex than the analysis of Cobb–Douglas and CES economies, it will be best to start by showing the effects of the very simple technical progress function where technical progress is proportional to the share of investment so that $a = B.S$. This will show the maximum extent to which a technical progress function can modify the earlier argument. The effects of the more comprehensive technical progress function, $a = A + B.S$, will lie between the results obtained where $a = B.S$, and the results obtained in the earlier analysis where a was constant, but it will be easier to understand this more realistic case if the effects of the simpler limiting technical progress function are first understood.

It has been shown that where $a = B.S$, and Cobb–Douglas or CES assumptions are made, the capital–output ratio, the share of profits and the rate of profit are independent of the share of investment. Indeed, it was possible to express each of these in terms of the model's parameters alone. The same basic result is arrived at with vintage assumptions, and here R, the *gross* rate of return with new plant, is invariant with respect to S, while C, the *gross* capital–output ratio with new plant, and X_p, the share of *gross* profits in gross output, will vary only slightly with respect to S.

R, the gross rate of return with new plant, must always equal the constant, B, which is the inverse of the ICOR when $n = 0$ (from (3.28)), i.e.

$$R = \frac{1}{\text{ICOR}} = B. \tag{7.13}$$

If the gross rate of return always equals the constant, B, there can be little variation in the capital–output ratio which profit-maximising entrepreneurs choose, for the profit-maximising capital–output ratio must lie within a narrow range if technical progress is Harrod-neutral, and the gross rate of return must always be B. It is shown in (7.19) that this is indeed the case, and C varies only something like $X_w/4$ times as much with respect to S where $a = B.S$ as it does where $a = A$. If the gross rate of return with new plant is invariant with respect to S, and the gross capital–output ratio varies only slightly, it must follow that the share of gross profits in gross output varies only slightly with respect to S. (7.20) shows that the elasticity of X_p with respect to S will be only slightly greater than the elasticity of C with respect to S where $a = B.S$. Hence, where $a = B.S$, R will not vary at all with respect to S, and C and X_p will vary so little that it will not be a gross oversimplification to see a vintage world where technical progress is entirely endogenous as one where R, C and X_p are independent of S. A vintage economy with twice the share of investment of an otherwise similar vintage economy will then have the same gross rate of return, and it would not be a great error to think of it as having about the same C and about the same X_p, for these will differ relatively slightly.

If higher investment has little effect on the capital–output ratio, its predominant effect must be on the life of plant, for a higher share of investment must either raise the capital–output ratio or reduce the life of plant. (7.18) shows that the elasticity of the life of plant with respect to the share of investment will not differ very markedly from $-\frac{3}{4}$ where $a = B.S$ and θ does not differ too much from θ^*. Thus, where technical progress is entirely endogenous, a higher share of investment must produce a much shorter life of plant. This can be contrasted with the situation where $a = A$ when higher investment raises or lowers the life of plant depending on whether θ is greater or less than θ^*.

If the effects of the technical progress function, $a = B.S$, with vintage and non-vintage assumptions are compared, the main point that emerges is that r, V and X_p are all independent of S with non-vintage assumptions, while with vintage assumptions only R, the gross rate of return, is independent of S. The capital–output ratio and the share of profits will both vary with S, but the differences in the capital–output ratio and the share of profits between economies that are due to different shares of investment should be slight. The same cannot be said of r, the *net* rate of return on capital.

An equation for r where $a = B.S$ shows that r will vary strongly with the life of plant[1]:

$$r = B - \frac{2}{T}\left(1 - \frac{T}{6}(r+B.S) + \frac{T^2}{36}(r^2 - r.B.S + B^2 S^2)...\right). \quad (7.14)$$

It is evident that r varies strongly with T, and as there is a strong inverse relationship between the life of plant and the share of investment (with an elasticity between these of the order of $-\frac{3}{4}$), there must also be a strong inverse relationship between the rate of profit and the share of investment. The reason for this is that a shorter life of plant substantially increases the rate of depreciation, and so a higher share of investment which must shorten the life of plant increases depreciation substantially at the same time. In terms of the formula shown in (7.14), B is the *gross* rate of return which is the same with all values of S, and

$$\frac{2}{T}\left(1 - \frac{2}{T}(r+B.S)...\right),$$

[1] Substitute $B.S$ for a and g (which are equal where $n = 0$) in (3.29).

which must be deducted from this to produce r, the net rate of return, is the rate of depreciation with new plant. A higher S must raise the rate of depreciation because it must reduce T substantially, so r, the net rate of return, which is $(R-\text{Depreciation}) = (B-\text{Depreciation})$ must be low where depreciation is high, and depreciation will necessarily be high where S is high.

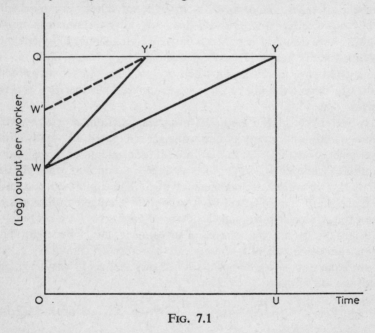

FIG. 7.1

The basic argument can be demonstrated with the diagram which was used in Chapter 3 to show that there must be an inverse relationship between r and S. Fig. 7.1 shows the gross quasi-rents earned with a machine which is worked by one worker during its whole working life. It produces an annual gross output of OQ throughout its life of T years, and this is shown by the horizontal line QY. The wage (in terms of its product) is OW when the machine is new, and it gradually rises to UY, so the wage through time is shown by WY. Then the total gross quasi-rents which are earned throughout the machine's lifetime are represented by the triangle QWY, and r is the rate of discount which equates QWY to the cost of the machine – C times annual gross output, or C times OQ.

Now suppose that S is doubled where the technical progress function is $a = B.S$ as is being assumed here. This will double the rate of technical progress, so it will double the annual rate of increase of the wage, i.e. the slope of WY will be doubled. Suppose, to simplify the diagrammatic representation of the argument, that a doubled S has its entire effect on T and none on C, which will be quite nearly the case.[1] With its entire effect on T and none on C, a doubled S will halve T,[2] so the line showing the wage during the machine's lifetime will reach QY in half the former time. As it rises twice as steeply, its starting-point on the vertical axis will be unchanged, for a line which starts at W and rises twice as steeply as WY will reach QY at Y', where Y' bisects QY. The total quasi-rents which must be discounted to equal C times OQ will then be shown by the triangle QWY' instead of QWY. The r which will discount QWY' so that it equals C times OQ will clearly be substantially lower than the r which equates QWY to the same capital cost. Hence a higher S would be very clearly associated with a lower r in a situation where doubling investment doubled technical progress, if it also halved the life of plant.

Of course, raising S to halve T would reduce r much more sharply than this if the rate of technical progress was given exogenously as in Chapter 3. With technical progress constant, the wage follows the dotted line $W'Y'$, and halving T then reduces the quasi-rents which must be discounted to equal C times OQ from QWY to $QW'Y'$ instead of just to QWY'. It is, however, a matter of some importance that doubling investment will reduce the rate of profit, even where this doubles the rate of technical progress. It will, of course, reduce the rate of profit much more sharply where the rate of technical progress is exogenously given.

The formula for the elasticity of r with respect to S is outlined in the final section of the chapter. Unfortunately it is rather complex, but Table 7.1 shows the elasticity of the rate of profit with respect to the share of investment where $a = B.S$ and higher investment has its entire effect on the life of plant, for various values of X_p and r/g. For purposes of comparison, Table 7.1 also shows (in parentheses) the elasticity of r with respect to S where $a = A$ and higher investment again has its entire effect on the life of plant. The results in the

---

[1] A higher S would have less than one-quarter of its effect on C and more than three-quarters on T where $\theta = \theta^*$, and its full effect would be on T and none on C where $\theta = 0$.

[2] This will be evident if $B.S$ is substituted for $(a+n)$ in (3.14).

table below can be contrasted with the non-vintage result that the elasticity of r with respect to S is 0 where $a = B.S$ (and $n = 0$) with all values of X_p and r/g.

It is evident that with vintage assumptions, the elasticity of r with respect to S is very clearly negative, but as the diagrammatic argument showed, completely endogenous technical progress will greatly lessen the reduction in the rate of profit that is associated with a higher share of investment. For instance, an economy with a rate of profit that is three times its rate of growth and a share of gross profits in gross output of one-third, will have an elasticity of r with respect to S of -0.84 where technical progress is wholly endogenous,

Table 7.1

VALUE OF ELASTICITY OF r WITH RESPECT TO S WHERE $a = B.S$

X_p	r/g			
	1·5	2·0	3·0	4·0
0·25	-3.03 (-8.34)	-2.20 (-6.26)	-1.32 (-4.17)	-0.90 (-3.13)
0·33	-2.05 (-6.36)	-1.44 (-4.77)	-0.84 (-3.18)	-0.56 (-2.39)
0·40	-1.53 (-5.34)	-1.06 (-4.00)	-0.61 (-2.67)	-0.39 (-2.00)
0·50	-1.04 (-4.35)	-0.70 (-3.26)	-0.38 (-2.17)	-0.23 (-1.63)

and -3.18 where it is exogenously given, and higher investment has its entire effect on the life of plant. Hence, a rise in the share of investment of one-third would be associated with a reduction in the rate of profit by almost one-quarter, even if the rate of growth of productivity increased by a third. The profitability of investment would be almost completely destroyed if the rate of growth of productivity was not raised at all. The implications of this are so important that the factors which influence the elasticity of r with respect to S in vintage and non-vintage models will be discussed further in a later section of this chapter.

The effect of the technical progress function, $a = B.S$, on the major economic variables in a vintage economy can now be summarised as follows. The gross rate of return on capital will equal B with all shares of investment, and the gross capital–output ratio with new plant and the share of gross profits in gross output will vary only slightly with S. However, because depreciation will vary with S, there will be a significant inverse relationship between the *net* rate of return on capital and the share of investment.

The effects of the more general technical progress function, $a = A + B.S$, will be more complex than this, but they will clearly lie somewhere between the results obtained where $a = A$ and $a = B.S$. For instance, R, the gross rate of return with new plant, must again be the inverse of the ICOR so that:

$$R = \frac{1}{\text{ICOR}} = \frac{A}{S} + B. \qquad (7.15)$$

Thus where $a = A$ so that $B = 0$ the gross rate of return varies in inverse proportion with S. Where $a = B.S$ so that $A = 0$, it equals the constant B with all values of S, and where $a = A + B.S$ it varies inversely with S, but not quite in inverse proportion. The equations in the final section of the chapter suggest that C will also vary more with respect to S where $a = A + B.S$ than it does where $a = B.S$. The crucial relationship between r, the *net* rate of return, and the share of investment is, however, again a little complex. Here:

$$r = \left(\frac{A}{S} + B\right) - \frac{2}{T}\left(1 - \frac{T}{6}(r + A + B.S)\right.$$

$$\left. + \frac{T^2}{36}(r^2 - r(A + B.S) + (A + B.S)^2)...\right). \qquad (7.16)$$

It is again evident that the influence of S upon r will depend partly on how it influences T. A higher S is bound to reduce $((A/S) + B)$, the term corresponding to R, the gross rate of return, but it may have any kind of effect on

$$-\frac{2}{T}\left(1 - \frac{T}{6}(r + A + B.S)...\right),$$

the term corresponding to the rate of depreciation. If a higher S reduces T (as it always does where $a = B.S$), it will raise the rate of depreciation and in this case r must be reduced, for the gross rate of return falls and the rate of depreciation rises at the same time, so that r, which is $(R - \text{depreciation})$, is doubly reduced. However, if a higher S raises T, it will reduce the rate of depreciation with the result that r may not be reduced. Thus a higher S is only *certain* to reduce r if it also reduces T, i.e. if the elasticity of T with respect to

S is negative. It turns out (from (7.22)) that the relationship between S and T is close to the following:

Elasticity of T with respect to $S \gtrless 0$ where

$$\theta \gtrless \theta^* \left[1 + \left(\frac{B.S}{A} \right)(X_w + \tfrac{1}{3}X_p) \right]. \qquad (7.17)$$

Thus a higher S is bound to reduce T, and therefore r, provided that θ does not exceed something like

$$\theta^* \left[1 + \left(\frac{B.S}{A} \right)(X_w + \tfrac{1}{3}X_p) \right].$$

Where technical progress was exogenously given in its entirety (so that $B = 0$), a higher S only reduced T where θ was less than θ^*, but the chances that a higher S will reduce T are somewhat increased where technical progress is part endogenous. Then θ may need to exceed θ^* quite substantially if a higher S is to raise T. Of course, even then, a higher S may not raise r, for a higher S will not raise r wherever it lengthens T. Depreciation will need to be cut quite substantially to counteract the adverse effect of a higher S upon $((A/S) + B)$, the gross rate of return, but nothing clear and simple can be said where a higher S lengthens the life of plant and so reduces the rate of depreciation.

The mathematical formula for the elasticity of r with respect to S is again highly complex (see (7.21)), though it is clear from this that a higher S will be associated with a lower r unless θ is well above 2.[1] There is a simple relationship between r and S with non-vintage assumptions (i.e. (7.11)), and it is clearly important to decide whether this will provide an adequate guide to the general relationship between r and S, or whether an attempt must be made to derive a simpler account of the vintage relationship between r and S. The very important relationships between r, S and g with vintage and non-vintage assumptions will therefore be discussed further in the next section.

The Relationship between r and S with Vintage and Non-Vintage Assumptions

A number of propositions about the relationships between r, S and g have been arrived at in this chapter, and they must now be brought

---

[1] The elasticity of r with respect to S must be negative unless the negative value of $(U.X_w)/(1 + U.X_w)$ substantially exceeds 1, and this will only happen if θ is well above 2 (from (3.45)).

together and if possible clarified. Something has already been said about the importance of these relationships. Clearly, if the rate of profit influences the rate at which entrepreneurs are prepared to accumulate capital (and it will be argued that it does), the influence of capital accumulation itself upon the rate of profit will be highly relevant to the simultaneous determination of the equilibrium values of the major economic variables.

The various accounts of the relationship between r and S which have been arrived at are, unfortunately, not at all simple. The situation is quite straightforward with non-vintage assumptions. Then, when $n = 0$, the elasticity of r with respect to S is

$$-\frac{1}{\sigma} \cdot \left(\frac{A}{A+B.S}\right) \text{ (from (7.11)),}$$

which provides a clear and simple account of the relationship between r and S. It suggests that the elasticity of r with respect to S cannot be positive: that it is zero where technical progress is entirely endogenous (so that $A = 0$), and that its negative value will vary with A, and inversely with σ. This is as simple a formula as is likely to be found, and it takes account of a technical progress function with both exogenous and endogenous technical progress, and an elasticity of substitution between labour and capital which can take any value. It will be desirable to accept this formula and abandon the far more complex vintage formula unless it misses something important. The case for abandoning the vintage formula in favour of the non-vintage formula will be overwhelming if it turns out that the vintage formula arrives at much the same answer in far more complex terms – but it does not arrive at the same answer.

Where $a = B.S$, the vintage elasticity of r with respect to S is negative, and quite strongly negative. The non-vintage elasticity of r with respect to S is zero. The elasticity of r with respect to S cannot be positive with the non-vintage formula, but with vintage assumptions it can be positive, though only if θ is rather high. Then the simple non-vintage formula cannot be used as an approximation for the much more complex vintage formula, for there are fundamental differences in kind between the results obtained. The question which then arises is which of these *fundamentally different* sets of results is to be preferred. The answer must be that the vintage formula allows for everything that the non-vintage formula allows for, and for something extra. The additional variable it allows for is the life of plant, and it is the influence of this upon r that produces the very different results that are arrived at in the two cases. The vintage approach must then be the preferred approach, for the something extra it allows for cannot safely be ignored.

A key relationship that is obscured in non-vintage theory is the interconnection between the life of plant and the rate of depreciation. This is an absolutely secure relationship and none could doubt that it is strong. Every airline is perfectly aware that if aircraft have a life of five years instead of ten, annual depreciation will be a higher ratio of the cost of a plane, and accountants' formulae for depreciation allow for this kind of effect. The Australian tax department actually allows twice straight-line depreciation, i.e. depreciation at a rate of $2/T$, which is curiously similar to the 'correct' rate of depreciation found in Chapter 3,

$$\frac{2}{T}\left(1 - \frac{T}{6}(r+a) + \frac{T^2}{36}(r^2 - ra + a^2)...\right). \qquad (3.27)$$

But the effect of T on the rate of depreciation can hardly be expected to come through clearly with non-vintage theory, and some have even contrived to miss it with vintage theory by assuming 'radiation depreciation' in a vintage model. It will turn out that it is this relationship that is largely responsible for the different results that are obtained with vintage and non-vintage models.

It might be thought that the relationship between depreciation and the life of plant can be implicitly allowed for in a non-vintage model. With vintage assumptions, S is the share of *gross* investment in the *Gross National Product*, while it is the share of *net* investment in the *Net National Product* with non-vintage assumptions. Then the relationship between depreciation and the life of plant could apparently be dealt with in a non-vintage world by estimating the net savings ratio 'correctly', so that the ratio of net to gross investment was always reduced or increased to the 'correct' extent where there was a change in the life of plant. Then the 'correct' relationship between depreciation and the life of plant would be implicit in S, and in capital stock statistics. This can be done in theory, but it will hardly occur in practice. Economic theorists frequently assume radiation depreciation in non-vintage models, and this will kill any connection between depreciation and the life of plant. Statisticians estimating the capital stock, or net investment, often estimate the ratio of net to gross investment rather arbitrarily, with the result that a higher share of gross investment is thought to mean that the share of net investment is higher in the same, or a greater, proportion. There is then considerable danger that the relationship between depreciation and the life of plant will be obscured unless it is brought out explicitly as it is with vintage theory.[1]

Then vintage and non-vintage theory will generally produce different results where the life of capital is significantly shortened or lengthened, for this will raise or lower depreciation sharply with consequences that are not reliably 'caught' with non-vintage assumptions. A significant shortening of the life of plant will occur, for instance, where S is increased with entirely endogenous technical progress. Since a higher S will only slightly raise the capital–output ratio where $a = B.S$, its predominant effect must be on the life of plant which will be sharply reduced. This must raise the rate of depreciation, and so work against r. But this is not noticed with non-vintage theory where the elasticity of r with respect to S is zero where $a = B.S$. It is unmistakably noticed as soon as a model is formulated where the life of capital is a variable, and the elasticity of r with respect to S then clearly comes out negative as in Table 7.1. This is an example of a situation where the implications of a shortening of the life of plant will be missed with non-vintage theory. The implications of a lengthening of the life of plant may also be missed. This will occur where S is increased in a world where labour and capital are highly substitutable, and technical progress is mainly exogenous. This cannot fail to reduce the rate of depreciation which will have a favourable effect on the rate of profit that may outweigh other unfavourable effects. This produces the result that the elasticity of r with respect to S can be positive, i.e. that a higher S can be associated with a higher r (with obvious reswitching implications) where labour and capital are highly substitutable. This effect is

[1] There is even difficulty with non-vintage theory where the capital stock is measured 'correctly', for this will produce a very odd technical progress function. If S is 'correct' net investment, and $a = A + B.S$, only higher *net* investment will produce more technical progress, but it is not at all clear why a given rate of gross investment should produce more technical progress where it lengthens the life of plant than where it shortens it – but it will certainly produce more *net* investment where it lengthens the life of plant and thus reduces depreciation. Thus the assumption that gets the rate of profit right, namely that depreciation varies inversely with T, gets the technical progress function wrong, and vice versa. Vintage theory avoids this difficulty by attributing technical progress to gross investment, and using the extra variable, T, to assist in the calculation of the true net rate of return on capital.

caught with vintage theory which shows that the elasticity of r with respect to S can be positive if θ is sufficiently high, and the proportion of endogenous technical progress is sufficiently low, but it is entirely missed with non-vintage theory.

If vintage theory is to be preferred to non-vintage theory because it catches additional important interrelationships of these kinds (which are otherwise sometimes certain to be missed), though at a considerable cost in terms of extra complexity, something must be said about the implications of this for the relationship between r and S. The full vintage formula for the elasticity of r with respect to S in

Table 7.2

THE ELASTICITY OF r WITH RESPECT TO S

$$\left(\text{where } \tfrac{2}{3} > \frac{B.S}{A+B.S} > \tfrac{1}{3}, \text{ and } 1 > \theta > \tfrac{1}{3} \right)$$

X_p	r/g			
	1·50	2	3	4
0·25	$-2\cdot25 - -4\cdot70$	$-1\cdot71 - -3\cdot58$	$-1\cdot17 - -2\cdot45$	$-0\cdot91 - -1\cdot87$
0·33	$-1\cdot61 - -3\cdot52$	$-1\cdot23 - -2\cdot67$	$-0\cdot86 - -1\cdot87$	$-0\cdot70 - -1\cdot48$
0·40	$-1\cdot27 - -2\cdot88$	$-0\cdot98 - -2\cdot22$	$-0\cdot71 - -1\cdot57$	$-0\cdot59 - -1\cdot28$
0·50	$-0\cdot95 - -2\cdot29$	$-0\cdot75 - -1\cdot77$	$-0\cdot57 - -1\cdot30$	$-0\cdot50 - -1\cdot09$

the final section of this chapter (7.21) is appallingly complex, and some values of this elasticity are therefore set out in Table 7.2. This gives the highest and lowest possible values of the elasticity of r with respect to S on the assumption that θ lies in the range $\tfrac{1}{3}$–1, and that at least one-third and not more than two-thirds of technical progress is endogenous to the investment process. A number of studies were referred to in Chapter 2 where values of σ in the range 0·5–0·7 were found, and the assumption that $\theta = \tfrac{1}{3}$–1 places only a little weight on these studies and makes considerable allowance for the distinction between θ and σ. If $1 > \theta > \tfrac{1}{3}$, and $\tfrac{2}{3} > (B.S)/(A+B.S) > \tfrac{1}{3}$, then the highest negative value of the elasticity of r with respect to S will occur where only one-third of technical progress is endogenous, and θ is as low as $\tfrac{1}{3}$, while the lowest negative value will be found where two-thirds of technical progress is endogenous, and $\theta = 1$. The elasticity of r with respect to S will approximate towards the upper rather than the lower end of the ranges given in Table 7.2 where θ is closer to $\frac{1}{3}$ than to 1, and where most technical progress is exogenous rather than endogenous.

With non-vintage assumptions, the elasticity of r with respect to S is $-0.33 - -2.00$ with all values of X_p and r/g where

$$\frac{2}{3} > \frac{B.S}{A+B.S} > \frac{1}{3},$$

and $1 > \sigma > \frac{1}{3}$ (and $n = 0$), so vintage assumptions pin this down into a rather narrower range. It is evident from Table 7.2 that with vintage assumptions the negative value of the elasticity of r with respect to S is highest where the share of profits is low, and the ratio of the rate of profit to the rate of growth is low. It varies inversely with both of these. The ratio of the rate of profit to the rate of growth has a considerable influence on the elasticity of r with respect to S, and this will be very strongly negative as the 'golden rule' where the rate of profit equals the rate of growth is approached. In a typical developed economy, the rate of profit might be about three times the rate of growth, and the share of gross profits might be about 0.33, and in this case the elasticity of r with respect to S would be $-0.86 - -1.87$, and near to the upper end of this range if most technical progress was exogenously given, and the elasticity of substitution between labour and capital was quite low.

The elasticity of r with respect to g is always $(A+B.S)/(B.S)$ times the elasticity of r with respect to S (from (7.8)), so this will be $1\frac{1}{2}$–3 times the figures shown in Table 7.2 if $\frac{2}{3} > (B.S)/(A+B.S) > \frac{1}{3}$. In each case, the first figure in Table 7.2 is raised $1\frac{1}{2}$ times to show the elasticity of the rate of profit with respect to the rate of growth, and the second figure 3 times. Thus the elasticity of r with respect to g will be $-1.29 - -5.61$ where $X_p = 0.33$ and $r/g = 3$. It will be evident that the elasticity of r with respect to g will be much more strongly negative than the elasticity of r with respect to S.

It appears that the elasticities of r with respect to S and g may be quite strongly negative with vintage assumptions, and these are the appropriate assumptions. A higher share of investment is likely to reduce the rate of profit near to proportionately at the very least, and it may reduce the rate of profit much more sharply than this. That is perhaps as much as can be said at this stage about the factors influencing the elasticity of the rate of profit with respect to the share of investment. It will play a considerable part in the analysis in Chapters 9 and 10.

The Principal Effects of the Technical Progress Function

It can be concluded that the assumption of a technical progress function of the form $a = A + B.S$ leads to considerable changes to the steady growth characteristics of advanced economies. In the limiting case where $a = B.S$, the rate of return on capital, the share of profits and the capital–output ratio will each be independent of S with both Cobb–Douglas and CES assumptions, and fairly similar results are obtained with vintage assumptions. With the more general technical progress function $a = A + B.S$, these ratios will all vary less with respect to S than they do where $a = A$, which means that a principal effect of the technical progress function is that the variability of these ratios is substantially reduced.

There is, however, one important relationship which does not clearly conform to this pattern, and that is the vintage relationship between the net rate of return on capital and the share of investment. Here two sets of forces are at work. On the one hand, higher investment will reduce R, the gross rate of return with new plant, to the extent that technical progress is exogenously given. On the other hand, the influence of higher investment upon depreciation can go either way. If these two sets of forces reinforce each other, then the elasticity of r with respect to S can be quite sharply negative, while it can even be positive if they work in opposite directions. The likelihood is that the two sets of forces will reinforce each other, for they will do this unless θ, the gross elasticity of substitution between labour and capital, exceeds something like

$$\theta^* \left[1 + \left(\frac{BS}{A} \right) (x_w + \tfrac{1}{3} x_p) \right],$$

and there is no empirical indication that it is plausibly as high as this. Then higher investment is likely both to reduce the gross rate of return with new capital and to increase the rate of depreciation, thus doubly reducing r. The elasticity of r with respect to S may then be rather sharply negative.

An interesting feature of the analysis is that there must undoubtedly be a negative relationship between r and S where technical progress is entirely endogenous. This is relevant to Joan Robinson's argument (which was referred to in Chapter 4) that entrepreneurs with animal spirits may achieve the growth rates they desire because they will simultaneously achieve rapid technical progress and a high rate of profit as a result of exceptional capital accumulation. If higher investment must be associated with a lower rate of profit in the long run where doubling investment doubles technical progress, once the influence of higher investment upon the life of plant (and therefore the rate of depreciation) is taken into account, it is difficult to see how entrepreneurs will be able to achieve their desired expansion rates. The entrepreneurs with animal spirits will certainly invest heavily, but they may run into serious financial troubles as growing interest and amortisation absorb an increasing proportion of their gross profits. It may be that businesses which exercise greater prudence will then come to dominate industry, so that the 'representative' entrepreneur will be less expansionist. However, it is too early to reject the animal spirits argument out of hand. This rested partly on the Keynesian theory of how the rate of profit is determined, while the argument of this chapter has been essentially neoclassical – although Joan Robinson and Kaldor have worked with very similar vintage assumptions.[1] The compatibility with vintage theory of the Keynesian theories of the determination of the rate of profit and the share of profits will be discussed in later chapters, and a final judgement on the animal spirits argument should be postponed until these are reached.

The main relationships from this chapter which will be used in later chapters are the various equations relating r to S and g. It will be argued in the next chapter that entrepreneurs will accumulate capital more rapidly where they expect to earn a higher rate of profit. If, in addition to a relationship between capital accumulation and the rate of profit of this kind, there is the strong negative relationship between the rate of profit and investment that has been discussed, then the rate of profit and the rate of accumulation will be simultaneously determined; and if both functions are sharp, quite small changes in the profit rate or in accumulation may suffice to restore equilibrium where there are departures from this. Before the argument can proceed to this point, it must be discovered whether there are indeed strong grounds for supposing that there is an investment function where entrepreneurs accumulate capital more rapidly where the rate of profit is high.

[1] See Robinson, 'A neo-classical theorem', and N. Kaldor and James A. Mirrlees, 'A new model of economic growth', *Review of Economic Studies*, vol. XXIX (June 1962).

*The Mathematics of Vintage Growth with the Technical Progress Function $a = A + B.S$

Where the technical progress function is $a = A + B.S$, the mathematical formulae for the elasticities of T, C, X_p and r with respect to S can be found by substituting for $(S/a).(\partial a/\partial S)$ in (3.44A), (3.46A), (3.47A) and (3.49A). Where

$$a = A + B.S, \qquad \frac{S}{a} \cdot \frac{\partial a}{\partial S} = \frac{B.S}{A + B.S},$$

and substituting this:

$$\frac{S}{T} \cdot \frac{\partial T}{\partial S} = \left(\frac{A}{A+B.S}\right) \cdot \left(-\frac{U}{1+U.X_w}\right)$$

$$+ \left(\frac{B.S}{A+B.S}\right) \cdot \left(-\frac{\frac{3}{4} - \frac{a.T}{32} + \frac{T^2}{240}(r^2 - ra - \frac{3}{16}a^2)\ldots + U.X_w}{1+U.X_w}\right).$$

$$(7.18)$$

$$\frac{S}{C} \cdot \frac{\partial C}{\partial S} = \left(\frac{A}{A+B.S}\right) \cdot \left(\frac{1}{1+U.X_w}\right)$$

$$+ \left(\frac{B.S}{A+B.S}\right) \cdot \left(\frac{X_w\left(\frac{1}{4} + \frac{a.T}{32} - \frac{T^2}{240}(r^2 - ra - \frac{3}{16}a^2)\ldots\right)}{1+U.X_w}\right). \quad (7.19)$$

$$\frac{S}{X_p} \cdot \frac{\partial X_p}{\partial S} = \left(\frac{A}{A+B.S}\right) \cdot \left(-\frac{U\left(1 - \frac{a.T}{6} - \frac{a^2T^2}{36} + \frac{a^3T^3}{270}\ldots\right)}{1+U.X_w}\right)$$

$$+ \left(\frac{B.S}{A+B.S}\right) \cdot \left(\frac{\frac{1}{4} - \frac{a.T}{96} - \frac{T^2}{240}(r^2 - ra + \frac{131}{48}a^2)\ldots}{1+U.X_w}\right). \quad (7.20)$$

$$\frac{S}{r} \cdot \frac{\partial r}{\partial S} \simeq \left(\frac{A}{A+B.S}\right)\left(-\frac{3}{r.T}\left[e^{\frac{T}{6}(r-\frac{1}{2}a)} + \left(\frac{U.X_w}{1+U.X_w}\right) \cdot e^{-\frac{T}{6}(r-3\frac{1}{4}a)}\right]\right)$$

$$+ \left(\frac{B.S}{A+B.S}\right) \cdot \left(-\frac{2\frac{1}{4}}{r.T}\left[e^{-\frac{T}{6}(r+\frac{13}{12}a)} + \frac{1}{3} \cdot \left(\frac{U.X_w}{1+U.X_w}\right) \cdot e^{-\frac{T}{6}(r-\frac{3}{4}a)}\right]\right).$$

$$(7.21)$$

The argument in earlier sections has been quite largely concerned with the relationships between T and S, X_p and S, and r and S, and these will now be analysed further.

The most useful equation to describe the relationship between T and S is the one for the value of θ where higher investment neither raises nor lowers the life of plant. This can be derived from (7.18), (3.21) and (3.42):

$$\frac{S}{T} \cdot \frac{\partial T}{\partial S} \gtreqless 0 \text{ where}$$

$$\theta \gtreqless \theta^* \cdot \left(\frac{1 + \left(\frac{B.S}{A}\right).X_w}{1 - \left(\frac{B.S}{A}\right).\left(\frac{1}{3}X_p - \frac{raT^2}{36} - \frac{a^2T^2}{360}\cdots\right)} \right). \quad (7.22)$$

It will only introduce slight inaccuracy (with reasonable values of $r.T$ and $a.T$) if this is approximated as:

$$\frac{S}{T} \cdot \frac{\partial T}{\partial S} \gtreqless 0 \text{ where } \theta \gtreqless \theta^* \left[1 + \left(\frac{B.S}{A}\right).(X_w + \tfrac{1}{3}X_p) \right].$$

The most useful equation to describe the relationship between X_p and S is the one for the value of θ which neither raises nor lowers the share of profits. This is derived from (7.20) and (3.42):

$$\frac{S}{X_p} \cdot \frac{\partial X_p}{\partial S} \gtreqless 0 \text{ where}$$

$$\theta \gtreqless \theta^* \left(\frac{1}{1 + \tfrac{1}{3}.\left(\frac{B.S}{A}\right).\left(1 - \frac{aT}{6} - \frac{T^2}{45}(r^2 + \tfrac{1}{4}ra - \tfrac{1}{2}a^2\cdots)\right)} \right). \quad (7.23)$$

The relationship between r and S is so complicated that two tables were used earlier in the chapter to show the values of the elasticity of r with respect to S on various assumptions. Table 7.1 was estimated on the assumption that technical progress was either wholly endogenous or wholly exogenous, and that higher investment had its entire effect on the life of plant (which will be the case where $\theta = 0$). Where $\theta = 0$,

$$\frac{U.X_w}{1 + U.X_w} = 1,$$

which makes the approximations for $(S/r).(\partial r/\partial S)$ (from (7.21))

$$-\frac{3}{r.T} \cdot e^{-\frac{1}{2}(rT + \frac{1}{3}aT)}$$

where technical progress is wholly endogenous, and $-(6/r.T)e^{\frac{1}{4}aT}$ where the rate of technical progress is exogenously given. These approximations are used to calculate the figures in Table 7.1, and their accuracy was discussed in Chapter 3 (pp. 67-8) and in the article referred to there. (3.20) can be used to show that $a.T = 0.55$ where $X_p = 0.25$, $a.T = 0.76$ where $X_p = 0.33$, $a.T = 0.95$ where $X_p = 0.40$, and $a.T = 1.26$ where $X_p = 0.50$. $r.T$ is r/g times $a.T$.

Table 7.2 is based on the assumption that $1 > \theta > \frac{1}{3}$, and $\frac{2}{3} > (B.S)/(A+B.S) > \frac{1}{3}$, and the table gives the upper and lower limits to $(S/r).(\partial r/\partial S)$ where θ and $(B.S)/(A+B.S)$ lie within these limits. The highest negative value of $(S/r).(\partial r/\partial S)$ will be found where $\theta = \frac{1}{3}$ and $(B.S)/(A+B.S) = \frac{1}{3}$, when (substituting in (3.45)):

$$\frac{U.X_w}{1+U.X_w} = \frac{1 - \dfrac{aT}{24} + \frac{1}{36}r^2T^2 + \frac{1}{36}raT^2 - \frac{1}{15}a^2T^2}{\frac{4}{3} + \left(1 - \dfrac{aT}{24} + \frac{1}{36}r^2T^2 + \frac{1}{36}raT^2 - \frac{1}{15}a^2T^2\right)} = U_1$$

in the formula below. Then, substituting for $(B.S)/(A+B.S)$ and $(U.X_w)/(1+U.X_w)$ in (7.21):

$$\frac{S}{r}.\frac{\partial r}{\partial S} \simeq -\frac{2}{r.T}(e^{\frac{1}{4}(rT-\frac{1}{4}aT)} + U_1.e^{-\frac{1}{4}(rT-3\frac{1}{4}aT)})$$

$$-\frac{0.75}{r.T}(e^{-\frac{1}{4}(rT+\frac{11}{12}aT)} + \frac{1}{3}U_1.e^{-\frac{1}{4}(rT-\frac{3}{4}aT)}). \quad (7.24)$$

Similarly, the lowest negative value of $(S/r).(\partial r/\partial S)$ will be found where $\theta = 1$ and $(B.S)/(A+B.S) = \frac{2}{3}$, when:

$$\frac{U.X_w}{1+U.X_w} = -\frac{1 - \frac{3}{8}aT - \dfrac{r^2T^2}{60} + \dfrac{raT^2}{60} + \dfrac{a^2T^2}{42}}{4 - (1 - \frac{3}{8}aT - \frac{1}{60}r^2T^2 + \frac{1}{60}raT^2 + \frac{1}{42}a^2T^2)} = U_2$$

below, and:

$$\frac{S}{r}.\frac{\partial r}{\partial S} \simeq -\frac{1}{r.T}(e^{\frac{1}{4}(rT-\frac{1}{4}aT)} + U_2.e^{-\frac{1}{4}(rT-3\frac{1}{4}aT)})$$

$$-\frac{1.5}{r.T}(e^{-\frac{1}{4}(rT+\frac{11}{12}aT)} + \frac{1}{3}.U_2.e^{-\frac{1}{4}(rT-\frac{3}{4}aT)}). \quad (7.25)$$

(7.24) and (7.25) are used to provide the figures in Table 7.2, with X_p and r/g substituted for $a.T$ and $r.T$ in the same way as in Table 7.1.

8

The Rate of Profit and Investment

THE equilibrium relationship between the rate of profit and aggregate saving and investment will be analysed in this chapter. It will be argued that both planned saving and planned entrepreneurial investment will vary strongly with the rate of profit, and the reasons for this will be outlined. The object of the analysis will be to obtain plausible saving and investment functions which can be used (together with the equations from Chapters 6 and 7) to determine the equilibrium values of the economy's major variables.

The derivation of a savings function with a strong relationship between saving and the rate of profit is quite straightforward, and this follows directly from the Keynesian theories of distribution which were outlined in Chapter 4. It was argued there that the proportion of profits saved can be expected to be much higher than the proportion of wages and salaries saved, with the result that an increase in profits/capital, i.e. in the rate of profit, will be associated with an increase in saving/capital. This means that a savings function can be expected to show a strong interconnection between the rate of profit and the ratio of saving to the capital stock.

There are also plausible reasons why there should be an equilibrium relationship between the rate of profit and planned entrepreneurial investment. In earlier chapters it was argued that there are three reasons for supposing that planned entrepreneurial investment will be high where the rate of profit is high and expected to remain high. First, entrepreneurs will have strong incentives to invest if they use discounted cash flow techniques for investment appraisal and the rate of profit is high relatively to the rate of interest. Second, they will have strong incentives to invest if they use given payback criteria to appraise prospective investment projects and the rate of profit is high, for more projects will then pass any specific payback test. Third, they will find it easier to finance investment where the rate of profit is high and they rely heavily on internal finance, for profits/capital will then be high with the result that investment/capital can be high in so far as profits are reinvested. But it could be argued that these are essentially short-term considerations.

In a short-run disequilibrium situation, it is possible to argue with Keynes that the rate of profit and the rate of interest will be determined by different sets of factors with the result that the rate of profit can be low while the rate of interest is high, and vice versa, and there will clearly be much more investment where the rate of profit is high and the interest rate low, than in the reverse situation. It is, however, more difficult to establish that there can be relative divergences between the rate of profit and the rate of interest in steady growth comparisons, for it is not obvious that two economies with different relationships between the rate of profit and the rate of interest can be in equilibrium; and if it were a condition of equilibrium growth that a high rate of profit must be associated with a high rate of interest, any favourable relationship between the rate of profit and planned entrepreneurial investment would disappear. Indeed, there might well be an unfavourable relationship, for the capital stock would be higher (*cet. par.*), the lower the rates of profit and interest, and this means that steady growth investment would also be higher at a low rate of interest (and profit) than at a high rate.

It is equally difficult to establish that arbitrary payback criteria will influence steady growth investment. Payback periods may be arbitrarily fixed in an actual economy over a particular period of time, and higher profit rates will then mean that more prospective projects can pass these tests; but constant payback periods can hardly form a basis for the analysis of equilibrium growth paths. Rational entrepreneurs will generally expect prospective investments to pass stiffer tests where there is much investment opportunity than where there is little, and if this is accepted, the payback period must be regarded as a variable and not a constant. Once it is recognised that a higher rate of profit may be associated with shorter payback requirements, any favourable relationship between the rate of profit and planned entrepreneurial investment will disappear.

A connection between the rate of profit and the funds available for reinvestment is perhaps a more promising basis for a steady growth relationship between the rate of profit and planned entrepreneurial investment, but there are difficulties even here, for it is to be expected that an economy with extensive investment opportunity and relatively little finance will evolve institutions which facilitate the use of external finance. Hence the degree to which firms must rely on internal finance can hardly be treated as a constant in steady growth comparisons. Moreover, profits can be consumed as well as invested, and retained earnings will not necessarily be used to increase a firm's fixed capital. It is therefore far from clear that there will necessarily be a close connection between profits and reinvestment in steady growth.

These considerations point to the possibility that any favourable relationship that there is between the rate of profit and planned entrepreneurial investment may be essentially short-term. If this is so, it will play a part, possibly an important part, in the theory of effective demand, employment and fluctuations, but it will have nothing whatsoever to do with equilibrium growth paths. There are, however, two lines of argument which can be used to establish a steady growth relationship between the rate of profit and planned entrepreneurial investment.

The first rests on deep-rooted psychological considerations based on the proposition that accumulation and consumption meet quite distinct desires. As Ricardo put it in a letter to Malthus in 1814: 'We all wish to add to our enjoyments or to our power. Consumption adds to our enjoyments, – accumulation to our power . . . .'[1] If accumulation and consumption satisfy distinct needs, entrepreneurs and wealth owners can be expected to have preferred combinations of consumable current income and growth, with the result that the effect of the rate of profit on their desired rates of accumulation can be plotted. Where the rate of profit is higher, they will be able to enjoy both a higher ratio of consumption to capital and a faster rate of growth of their capital, for consumption/capital and investment/capital can both be higher where profits/capital are higher. Moreover, wealth owners will expect a higher *permanent* income from given wealth at a higher rate of profit if they are on a steady growth path, and if equilibrium consumption depends upon 'permanent incomes', it is reasonable to suppose that they will take part of the benefit from a higher rate of profit in the form of a higher ratio of consumption to capital, and part in the form of a higher rate of growth of their capital, i.e. a higher *investment/capital*. If there are mechanisms to transpose these preferences into decisions to invest and consume, and

---

[1] Ricardo, *Works* (ed. Sraffa), vol. VI, pp. 134-5.

it will be argued in this chapter that there are, especially with steady-state assumptions, a higher rate of profit will be associated with both a faster rate of growth and a higher ratio of consumption to capital.

A second line of argument which reinforces this one is based on an extension of Kalecki's principle of increasing risk.[1] It can be argued that the risks which companies are prepared to incur will vary with the excess of the rate of profit over the rate of interest, and a greater willingness to take risks should produce more company borrowing and more company investment. This means that if the risks that companies take are regarded as variable and not something that is given, economies can be in equilibrium growth with very different relationships between the rate of interest and the rate of profit. Two economies might then have the same rate of profit, but one could have a much higher rate of interest than the other, for instance if a higher proportion of its investment was in the public sector with the result that its government had to offer higher interest rates to persuade wealth owners to hold more government stock in their portfolios. The entrepreneurs in this economy would then take fewer risks because the rate of interest was higher relatively to the rate of profit, and they would then invest less in the aggregate. The need for public sector finance will obviously not be the sole factor influencing the equilibrium relationship between the rate of interest and the rate of profit: international capital movements and monetary factors will also be highly relevant. However, it is clear that once risk is brought into the argument so that different equilibrium relationships between the rate of interest and the rate of profit are possible, a higher rate of profit may widen the gap between the rate of interest and the rate of profit, and so raise aggregate entrepreneurial investment along a steady growth path.

The reasons for expecting a favourable relationship between the rate of profit and planned saving and planned entrepreneurial investment will be analysed in the sections that follow. The economy's saving function will be derived first, and the investment function will be derived after this. In equilibrium growth, saving must equal investment, so the saving and investment functions that are arrived

---

[1] M. Kalecki, *Essays in the Theory of Economic Fluctuations* (Allen & Unwin, 1939) chap. 4. Modern portfolio theory has arrived at the same result. See, for instance, R. S. Hamada, 'Portfolio analysis, market equilibrium and corporation finance', *Journal of Finance*, vol. XXIV (Mar 1969).

at must be compatible. It will turn out that this basic condition for equilibrium growth can be satisfied.

The Rate of Profit and the Savings Function

There is no difficulty in establishing a basis for a long-term relationship between saving and the rate of profit, for this follows directly from the savings functions that were discussed in Chapter 4. Pasinetti's is the most useful of these, and he arrived at the proposition that in steady growth (from (4.11)):

$$k = S_c.r \qquad (8.1)$$

i.e. the relationship between the economy's rate of growth of capital and its rate of profit will simply depend on S_c, the savings propensity of 'pure capitalists' who have no earned income. If S_c is given, a doubled rate of profit will be associated with a doubled ratio of saving to capital, and a doubled rate of growth of capital.

(8.1) can be represented as the schedule, SS, in Fig. 8.1. This passes through the origin, and it slopes upwards to the right with a gradient of $1/S_c$. Clearly, doubling the rate of profit is here associated with a doubled rate of growth of capital. An alternative schedule, $S'S'$, is also illustrated in Fig. 8.1, and it can be argued that this is a more plausible form for the savings schedule of an individual country in a world economy. Some countries invest a high proportion of their saving overseas, while much of the growth of others is financed with foreign capital, and outflows and inflows of capital that persist for generations have played a most important role in the development of many economies. The schedule $S'S'$ represents the saving available to an individual country after such international capital movements have been allowed for. It is drawn on the assumption that the country will enjoy a net capital inflow if its rate of profit exceeds a particular rate, and in Fig. 8.1, $S'S'$ is drawn to the right of SS where the rate of profit exceeds r^*. Thus foreign investment will increase the rate of growth of capital the country can finance wherever its rate of profit exceeds r^*. Conversely, some proportion of the country's saving will be invested overseas rather than at home where the rate of profit is low, and in Fig. 8.1, $S'S'$ is drawn to the left of SS at rates of profit of less than r^* to show this. The fact that $S'S'$ is less steep than SS means that doubling the rate of profit will more than double the rate of growth of capital that can be financed. This is obviously important,

G

because it means that small differences in the rate of profit between economies may be associated with much larger differences in their rates of growth of capital, and this will matter in Chapters 9 and 10 where the various parts of the model are brought together to show how

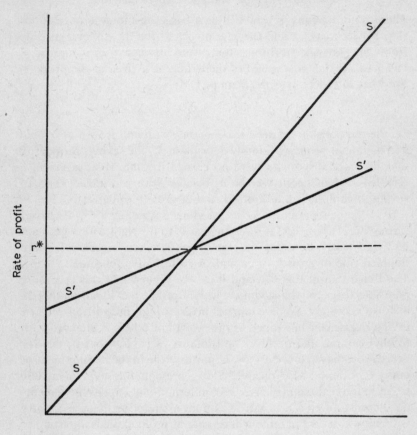

FIG. 8.1

the economy's equilibrium rate of profit and its equilibrium rate of growth are determined.

The schedule $S'S'$, the country's saving schedule with international capital movements allowed for, can be written as:

$$k = S_c . r + S_f . (\tilde{r} - r^*) \tag{8.2}$$

where S_f is a constant describing the relationship between net over-seas investment and $(r-r^*)$. From (8.2), it is clear that:

$$\text{Elasticity of } k \text{ with respect to } r = 1 + \frac{S_f \cdot r^*}{k} \qquad (8.3)$$

so the elasticity of the rate of capital accumulation with respect to the rate of profit will exceed 1 if there is any sensitivity of inter-national capital flows to the country's rate of profit.

Clearly, (8.2) is a saving function where the rate of capital accumu-lation a country can finance may be very sensitive to the rate of profit. With neoclassical theory, investment will correspond to full-employment saving, and if the rest of the argument was entirely neoclassical, (8.2) would provide a sufficient basis for the analysis of later chapters. (8.2) shows that, from the supply side, the rate of growth of capital will vary more than proportionately with the rate of profit. It was shown in Chapter 7 that higher investment and faster capital accumulation will always be associated with a lower rate of profit in given technical conditions. It will be shown in Chapters 9 and 10 that these two relationships permit the simultaneous deter-mination of an economy's equilibrium rate of profit and its equili-brium rate of growth.

However, a savings function alone will not suffice for a Keynesian analysis of the growth process, for in Keynesian theory investment decisions will be independent of saving decisions, and aggregate saving will then have to come into line with aggregate investment. The next sections will therefore be concerned with the derivation of an investment function. It will turn out that its mathematical form is similar to that of (8.2), and that there will be complete compatibility between the investment function and the saving function that has been arrived at.

Preferences between Income and Growth and the Investment Function

In this section of the chapter, it will be argued that planned entre-preneurial investment and the rate of growth of the capital stock will vary strongly with the rate of profit, because wealth owners will wish to make use of the opportunities for growth that are provided by a higher rate of profit to expand their wealth more rapidly. To establish this, it must be shown that entrepreneurial investment will be strongly influenced by private wealth owners' preferences between consu-mable current income and growth in equilibrium conditions. This is by no means obvious in view of the apparent divorce between management and ownership in much of modern industry.

There are, however, some companies that are managed by their owners, and here wealth owners will directly control all decisions and the relationship between income and growth will automatically be the one that they desire. There are other companies where directors have large shareholdings, or large shareholders such as insurance companies effectively appoint to directorships, and the preferences of wealth owners will then again have considerable influence. In other cases, the owners of a company's capital will not exercise immediate control, but it can be argued that the indirect influence they can exercise (through the share portfolios they decide to hold) will suffice to ensure that the equilibrium relationship between income and growth will be the one that wealth owners desire. If wealth owners exercise such indirect control, then the relationship between the rate of profit and planned entrepreneurial investment will depend on how their preferences between consumable current income and growth are affected by the opportunity to enjoy either a higher rate of growth of capital, or a higher ratio of consumption to capital which is provided by a higher rate of profit. It will be argued, as Malthus suggested, that they will make use of at least a part of the extra command over resources which a higher rate of profit provides to maintain a faster rate of accumulation of their capital.[1] If they do this, the capital stock will grow more rapidly where the rate of profit is higher, which means that there will be a favourable relationship between the rate of profit and planned entrepreneurial investment.

It must first be established that the relationship between consumable current income and growth will be the one that wealth owners desire where they do not directly manage the companies they own. This will first be established with highly restrictive assumptions, and it will then be shown that the argument can be very widely generalised.

It will be assumed at the start of the argument that profits are either retained or distributed as dividends, and that retained earnings which are always reinvested provide the entire finance for investment, while aggregate dividends are consumed. It will be assumed that all companies earn the same riskless rate of profit (on the depreciated replacement cost of their assets), and that there is no taxation of profits or dividends.

[1] Malthus, *Principles of Political Economy*, pp. 370-4. Cf. p. 8 above.

If the rate of profit is r so that net profits/capital is r, companies can maintain a ratio of dividends/capital of r, i.e. a dividend yield of r (where this is expressed as a ratio of dividends to capital measured at replacement cost), if their entire profits are distributed, or a ratio of net investment/capital of r, i.e. a rate of growth of capital of r, if their entire profits are reinvested, or they can maintain some combination of these. The various combinations of dividend yield and growth which are open to a company are shown by the straight line, DG, in Fig. 8.2, where the maximum dividend yield the company can maintain is OD, the maximum rate of growth of capital is OG, and $OD = OG = r$. There will be a series of lines parallel to DG which show the dividend yields and growth rates which companies can maintain at successively higher rates of profit.

Fig. 8.2 also shows a series of 'wealth owners' indifference curves' between the dividend yield and growth, $W''W''$, $W'W'$ and WW, and these are drawn concave to the origin because wealth owners can be expected to have a preferred combination of income and growth which means that they will only be prepared to sacrifice one of these at the margin for increasing amounts of the other.[1]

Wealth owners will wish to reach the highest possible indifference curve, and this will be WW which is tangential to DG at X, and if they reach this, they will enjoy a dividend yield of Od and a rate of growth of capital of Og. X will be chosen without difficulty where companies are managed by their owners, or where wealth owners have considerable influence over the decisions taken by directors, but it may be thought that there will be little pressure to choose X where managements hold few shares, and banks and insurance companies with large shareholdings do not fill directorships. Suppose some companies (called D companies below) choose X_d where dividend yields are higher and growth is less than at X, while others (called G companies) choose X_g where growth is higher and dividend yields are lower. Then shareholders can obtain the dividend yield and growth rate at X by holding the shares of D and G companies in a particular proportion in their portfolios. For instance, if the stock exchange values all companies at the replacement cost of their physical assets (i.e. if all valuation ratios are 1), then where $X_d X = X X_g$, wealth owners will achieve the combination of dividend yield and growth at X by holding half their wealth in D and half in

[1] Cf. J. Hirshleifer's use of shareholder indifference curves in *Investment, Interest and Capital* (Englewood Cliffs, N.J.: Prentice-Hall, 1970).

G company shares. If $X_dX > XX_g$, they will wish to hold more of their wealth in G shares, and vice versa. If the aggregate value of the D and G shares available corresponds exactly to the proportions of their portfolios that wealth owners wish to hold in these types of share, then the dividend yield and the growth rate of companies as a

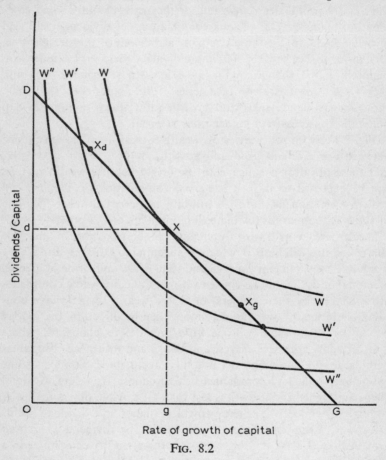

FIG. 8.2

whole will correspond exactly to wealth owners' preferences, i.e. the growth rate of companies as a whole will have a weighted average of Og, and the dividend yield a weighted average of Od, and X will show the combination of yield and growth of companies as a whole. Suppose, however, that most companies are G companies (because managements want more growth and lower dividends than wealth owners), while wealth owners need to hold half their wealth in G companies and half in D companies to achieve the optimum portfolio mix shown by X. Then if all valuation ratios were 1, there would be excess demand for D company shares and excess supply of G shares. In consequence, the prices of D shares would be bid up relatively to those of G shares, i.e. the valuation ratios of D companies would exceed 1 while the valuation ratios of G companies would become less than 1.[1] Conversely, with more D company shares than wealth owners wished to hold, the prices of G company shares would be bid up relatively to those of D company shares, so that G company shares had the higher valuation ratios. Thus, wherever the combination of current yield and growth that is offered by companies differs from the combination that wealth owners prefer, then the shares of companies that offer yield will be bid up relatively to those that offer growth if companies in the aggregate offer too little yield, and vice versa.[2]

The question that then arises is whether companies will be under any particular pressure to alter their dividend ratios as a result of shareholder pressures of these kinds. It can be shown that companies cannot afford to regard their share price as unimportant. Suppose that D and G companies have identical real capital assets at a particular point of time, and identical profits, and that wealth owners have excess demand for the shares of D companies and excess supply of G company shares where both have valuation ratios of 1. Then the prices of the shares of D companies (P_d) will be bid up relatively to the prices of the shares of G companies (P_g), so that $P_d > P_g$. G

---

[1] Some wealth owners may seek to obtain a high current income from their portfolios by holding a growth portfolio and selling off part of it each year. This w ill produce an excess supply of G company shares each year, and reduce their price relatively to the price of D shares in just the same way as attempts by wealth owners to hold a higher proportion of D shares in their portfolios than companies make available.

[2] Modigliani and Miller have shown that, in equilibrium, the value of a single company's shares will be independent of its rate of dividend. See Franco Modigliani and Merton H. Miller, 'The cost of capital, corporation finance, and the theory of investment', *American Economic Review*, vol. XLVIII (June 1958). However, there can only be *general* (as against partial) equilibrium if the overall relationship between income and growth is the one that wealth owners prefer. If this condition is not fulfilled, individual share prices will not be in equilibrium and wealth owners will bid up the prices of shares which offer favoured distribution ratios, and bid down shares with relatively unfavoured distribution ratios, until the overall balance of consumable current income and growth is compatible with equilibrium.

company shareholders will then be prepared to accept P_g D shares for every P_d G shares that they hold, so D company managements can make takeover bids for G companies on terms where a D company will acquire a G company for an increase in the number of its shares in the ratio $(1+(P_g/P_d)):1$. Then the D company will double its real capital assets (for both firms have the same real capital) at the cost of a less than doubling of the number of D shares outstanding. This move will be in the interests of the D company's shareholders (for aggregate profits and dividends can double while the number of shares is less than doubled), and it will leave the G company's shareholders indifferent, for the value of their shareholdings will not fall. However, it will deprive the management of the G company of a company to manage, which means that managements will be under exceedingly strong personal and financial pressures to choose payout ratios which maximise their share price if there is any possibility of takeover as a result of dividends which leave shareholders on a lower indifference curve than the best possible one. And there is a further argument which points in the same direction, which is that managements which seek expansion through takeover will need a high share price if they are to take over other companies on favourable terms. As a recent American textbook on mergers and acquisitions states:

> This compelling interest in a high stock price . . . is characteristic of those publicly held companies which seek to achieve growth through acquisitions. And there are sound reasons for this interest. Publicly held companies usually use their common stock, or securities convertible into their common stock, as the currency with which to buy other companies. The higher the price of their stock, the fewer shares they need to issue to pay for a given acquisition.[1]

Thus both managements which are motivated towards rapid expansion and managements which wish to preserve their position will have strong incentives to choose payout ratios which maximise the share price. It is to be noted that market pressures will not necessarily work to raise the payout ratio. Companies as a whole may invest and expand less than wealth owners wish, and in this case the companies which reinvest most will be preferred, with the result that they

---

[1] J. L. Harvey and A. Newgarden (eds.), *Management Guides to Mergers and Acquisitions* (New York: Wiley, 1969) p. 96.

will tend to take over companies which devote too small a proportion of their resources to expansion.

With transactions costs, and some imperfection in the market, takeovers will only be practicable where the relative share values of two companies differ more than nominally from the relative value of their real assets, and this means that managements will be able to depart from wealth owners' preferred payout ratios to a limited extent without incurring the risk of takeover,[1] but large departures will be unwise, and there is no doubt about what equilibrium payout ratios will need to be. Clearly, in equilibrium, the payout ratios of companies as a whole will average the payout ratio at X where DG is tangential to the highest possible wealth owners' indifference curve. At X, wealth owners as a whole will be in equilibrium, individual wealth owners will be in equilibrium, and company managements will not be able to raise their share price by altering their distribution ratios, so they will have the greatest possible chance of continuing to manage their companies.

Fig. 8.3 shows a series of such equilibrium points, and these can be used to produce a schedule which shows the equilibrium relationship between planned entrepreneurial investment and the rate of profit. DG, $D'G'$ and $D''G''$ show the opportunities open to wealth owners at successively higher rates of profit, while WW, $W'W'$ and $W''W''$ are wealth owners' indifference curves between consumable current income and growth. The tangency points between these curves are X, X' and X'', and these show the equilibrium relationship between planned entrepreneurial investment and the rate of profit. In Fig. 8.3 the equilibrium points fall on a straight line passing through the origin, and with such a line the ratio net investment/net profits will be the same at all rates of profit, and the ratio dividends/net profits will also be the same at all rates of profit. If the ratio net investment/ net profits is x, then net investment/capital $= x$(net profits/capital) so that:

$$k = x.r. \qquad (8.4)$$

This is the investment function which would follow from the assumption that wealth owners' preferred ratio of growth to currently consumable income is the same at all rates of profit, and that this ratio is $x : (1-x)$. This is not the only form the investment function

[1] There is considerable analysis of the constraints on managerial policy which are due to the possibility of takeover in Robin Marris, *The Economic Theory of 'Managerial' Capitalism* (Macmillan, 1964).

G*

can take, for the successive points of equilibrium need not fall on a straight line passing through the origin. Wealth owners' preferences might correspond to those shown in Figs. 8.4 or 8.5. In Fig. 8.4 the successive points of equilibrium fall on a straight line which intersects the vertical axis at D_0. Then there will be no accumulation at all

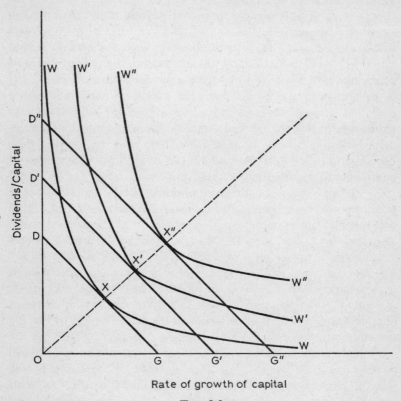

Rate of growth of capital

FIG. 8.3

where the rate of profit is less than OD_0, and a fixed proportion of the profits in excess of those needed to provide this minimum dividend yield will be reinvested. If x is the proportion of profits which is reinvested after the minimum dividend requirement has been met, net investment/capital will equal $x \cdot$ (net profits/capital$-d_0$) where d_0 (which equals OD_0) is the minimum dividend requirement, i.e.

$$k = x(r - d_0). \qquad (8.5)$$

This is the form the investment function will take if wealth owners have minimum income needs to which they give priority, and a preferred ratio of growth to further income once these minimum needs have been met.

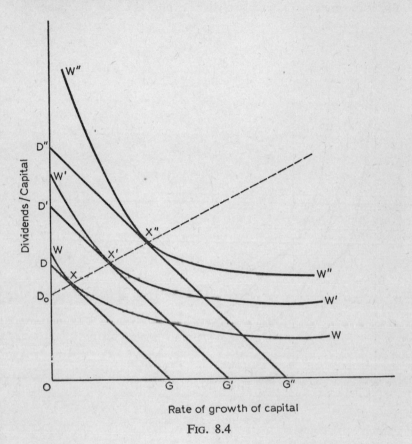

FIG. 8.4

With both (8.4) and (8.5), the rate of growth of capital will be higher at a higher rate of profit, but wealth owners' preferences between income and growth will not necessarily take the form that produces this result. In Fig. 8.5 the successive points of equilibrium fall on a vertical line which intersects the horizontal axis at G_0, so the rate of growth of capital will be OG_0 at all rates of profit in excess of OG_0. Here wealth owners are assumed to attach priority to the achievement of a particular rate of growth of capital, and then use any further resources at their disposal to produce consumable current income. The result of this is that planned entrepreneurial investment will be independent of the rate of profit (provided that this exceeds OG_0). Clearly, an indifference map could also be drawn where the preferred rate of growth of capital is lower, the higher the

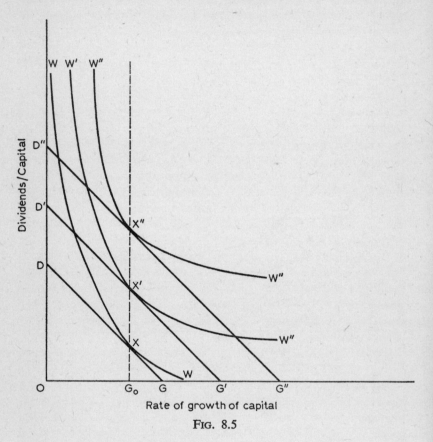

FIG. 8.5

rate of profit, i.e. where accumulation is an inferior good relatively to consumable current income. This means that there will only be a favourable relationship between the rate of profit and planned entrepreneurial investment if the indifference map which results from wealth owners' preferences between income and growth takes a particular form. Then nothing conclusive can be said about the relationship between the rate of profit and planned entrepreneurial investment until further considerations are brought into the argument. This can be done very simply.

A higher rate of profit will increase the incomes of wealth owners with particular wealth holdings, and if depreciation is correctly calculated, a higher rate of profit will provide such wealth owners with higher *permanent incomes*. The 'permanent income hypothesis' or 'normal income hypothesis' which relates personal saving to permanent incomes has produced excellent results, and it may point to the nature of the basic relationship between wealth owners' preferences for income and growth. Where the permanent income hypothesis has been tested, it has been widely found that personal saving is something like proportional to permanent incomes.[1] Thus a proportion, S, of permanent incomes is saved. Extending this to the analysis of wealth owners' preferred relationship between consumable current income and growth, it might be reasonable to suppose that they will wish to devote a proportion, S, of the resources at their disposal to accumulation, and the remaining $(1-S)$ to the provision of consumable current income. This is precisely the relationship illustrated in Fig. 8.3, which led to (8.4) – though there the proportion of net profits devoted to accumulation was x instead of S. (8.4) showed that where a constant proportion of net profits, x, is devoted to accumulation, while the remaining $(1-x)$ is distributed, k, the rate of growth of capital, will equal x times the rate of profit in steady growth. Thus the permanent income hypothesis points to an investment function where the rate of growth of capital is proportional to the rate of profit.

It may appear surprising that a relationship between planned entrepreneurial *investment* and the rate of profit can be derived from a hypothesis about the proportion of incomes which is *saved*. This has been possible because it has been assumed that planned entrepreneurial investment is identical to the retained earnings of companies. It might be thought that the results which have been arrived at will depend upon this and other arbitrary assumptions which have been made. The most crucial assumptions which have been made are

[1] See, for instance, Milton Friedman, *A Theory of the Consumption Function* (Princeton U.P., 1957) chaps. iv and v; F. Modigliani and A. Ando, 'The permanent income and the life cycle hypothesis of saving behaviour: comparisons and tests', in *Proceedings of the Conference on Consumption and Saving*, vol. II (Philadelphia, 1960); and A. Ando and F. Modigliani, 'The "life cycle" hypothesis of saving: aggregate implications and tests', *American Economic Review*, vol. LIII (Mar 1963).

that retained earnings provide the entire finance for investment, and that all companies earn the same riskless rate of return on capital. It will now be shown that the same results will follow without these assumptions.

It can be envisaged that wealth owners will hold real assets such as real estate, and a portfolio of shares of very different kinds, equity, fixed-interest, convertible stock, and so on, in a large number of different companies which have different earnings prospects involving differences in risk, etc. At the same time, companies will finance investment in a large number of different ways, including the reinvestment of profits, issues of equity and fixed-interest stock, borrowing from banks and other financial institutions, and so on. Wealth owners will hold portfolios with the combination of prospective income, capital appreciation and risk which they consider to be ideal, while companies will issue the various types of share in preferred proportions. They will use the finance they raise and the profits they earn to make contractual and discretionary payments to wealth owners, and to invest in real assets, with the result that they hold 'portfolios' of real assets.

In this more general model, equilibrium will take much the same form as in the earlier more restrictive analysis. If companies in the aggregate accumulate more capital and provide less consumable current income than wealth owners as a whole desire, the equity shares of companies which are expected to provide consumable current income rather than growth will be preferred relatively to those which provide growth rather than income, and this will put pressure on companies to provide the desired balance between consumable current income and growth. The same consideration will also now apply if companies as a whole take more or less risk of various kinds than wealth owners' preferences call for; so in equilibrium, both the distribution ratio and the degree of risk-taking will conform to wealth owners' preferences.

However, there are a number of difficulties with this line of argument which must be discussed before it can be concluded that, in equilibrium, the rate of growth of capital will depend solely on wealth owners' preferences between consumable current income and growth. In the earlier analysis, the rate of accumulation depended solely upon the preferences of existing wealth owners, because companies could not borrow so their sole source of finance was the reinvestment of profits, and this was directly or indirectly controlled by existing wealth owners. With the present more general analysis, it might be thought that companies will be less dependent on the preferences of existing wealth owners because of their ability to borrow in a wide variety of ways. However, it can be shown that these possibilities will not affect the conclusions which have been arrived at.

Companies may be able to borrow in a variety of ways, but they will borrow from wealth owners with particular preferences between consumable current income and growth. The wealth owners who lend to companies will receive equivalent claims on companies in the form of shares or acknowledgements of debt, and if these claims provide more growth and less current income or more income and less growth than wealth owners as a whole prefer, the relative prices of the various types of claim will alter so that companies are put under pressure to alter their investment plans and distribution ratios. The fact that some wealth owners will be *new* wealth owners who acquire wealth as a result of saving from current *earned* income (when formerly it was assumed that only the preferences of those who received *profit* incomes on existing wealth were relevant) will not affect the analysis, for the *new* wealth owners will have preferences between current income and growth in the same way as other wealth owners, and with a higher expected rate of profit they will place their wealth so that they can expect to obtain a particular relationship between consumable current income and growth. If wealth owners as a whole wish to receive a proportion, x, of the total returns from their wealth in the form of accumulation, the rate of growth of their capital will need to be $x.r$ in equilibrium, which means that (8.4) will hold with the more general assumptions which have now been made.

Then wealth owners' preferences between consumable current income and growth will determine the proportion of the nation's resources that is devoted to accumulation in equilibrium growth. It is to be noted that, once again, an *investment* function has been derived from premises which include the permanent income hypothesis about saving behaviour. Thus it appears that an investment function has been derived from a savings function, and in this case no assumption about the automatic reinvestment of company savings has been made. What has been assumed is that wealth owners *as a whole* have preferences between *the accumulation of their wealth* and consumable current income, and to satisfy their motives for accumulation they must collectively hold a certain proportion of their wealth in the form of equity shares in companies which are expected to achieve *real* growth of assets and earnings. The shares of companies which build up reserves, i.e. of companies which save without investing, may assist portfolio holders to hedge against certain kinds of risk, but they will in no way satisfy the motive for accumulation which will only be satisfied with the shares of companies which are expected to achieve rapid rates of real expansion. This means that an investment function genuinely results from the argument, given that in equilibrium the investment decisions taken by company managements must be in line with the rates of capital accumulation which wealth owners desire. There is, at the same time, an identical savings function. It will have been noted that (8.4) has precisely the same algebraic form as (8.1), the savings function based on Pasinetti's equation. This is not just a coincidence. The factors that determine x, wealth owners' preferences between accumulation and consumable current income, are precisely those that determine Pasinetti's S_c.

That there should be identity between a country's saving and investment functions along all equilibrium growth paths will appear surprising to Keynesians. Clearly, they can only be identical in equilibrium, for it is only then that the real assets of all companies will expand at precisely the rate that wealth owners desire, but even so it is clearly out of line with modern Keynesian theory to suggest that there will always be identity between an economy's saving and investment functions in equilibrium growth. What then is the point that has been missed?

The reason why Keynesian factors have played no part in the argument is that there has been no reference to monetary factors. There has also been no reference to the need for public sector finance and the effect of this on the rate of interest, and to the effect of international factors on this. It will be seen in the next section that there will no longer be identical saving and investment functions in equilibrium growth, once monetary factors and the rate of interest are brought into the argument.

The Rate of Interest and the Economy's Saving and Investment Functions

It must now be shown how monetary factors and wealth owners' preferences will both influence planned investment. Money is an asset (which is generally created without saving), but it provides neither currently consumable income nor growth. Instead, it provides liquidity. This means that the analysis of the last section will need to be modified.

With Keynesian monetary theory, companies and individuals will have a demand schedule for liquidity, and the quantity of money will provide a supply schedule (and the argument can obviously be extended to include schedules for near-money and near-liquidity), and in equilibrium money will be so priced, i.e. the rate of interest will be such, that the demand for liquidity equals the supply. Then the rate of interest will be determined independently of wealth owners' preferences between consumable current income and growth.

Whether the rate of interest will be high or low in relation to the rate of profit will depend on a number of factors. A most important one is public sector finance. If a high proportion of a nation's investment is in the public sector and this is financed by borrowing rather than taxation, governments will have to offer high interest rates to persuade wealth owners to hold a high proportion of government bonds in their portfolios, and this means that the interest rate that industry pays for fixed-interest finance will also be high. International capital movements will also influence the rate of interest. A high rate of capital inflow (because r exceeds r^*) will increase the aggregate saving available to a country in relation to its investment opportunity, and so reduce the interest rates governments must pay to finance any given proportion of public to private investment. In the long run, the interest rate will depend on broad considerations of these kinds, and in equilibrium growth, the money supply will need to be adjusted each year to produce the interest rate that just persuades wealth owners to hold the public debt that is issued annually, at constant interest rates.

It is now necessary to see how an interest rate, determined in this way, will affect the results which have been arrived at. Shares yielding fixed interest are always likely to form part of wealth owners' portfolios of assets and companies' portfolios of debt, and the question which must now be answered is how the yield of such shares will influence the various equilibrium relationships. The influence of a high rate of interest on companies will be considered first. Suppose that companies have substantial fixed-interest debt, and that the rate of interest is i. They will then be prepared to undertake projects with a secure prospective return which just exceeds i, but they will only be prepared to undertake risky projects if the prospective return exceeds i by a substantial margin. Then if r exceeds i by a small margin, only safe projects will be undertaken, while if r exceeds i by a substantial margin, many uncertain projects will be undertaken in addition. This means that a high rate of interest will reduce both the quantity of investment (at a particular rate of profit) and the degree of risk in the projects that are allowed to go ahead. The rate of interest will have a similar influence on portfolio holders. Where i is high, they can obtain a high and certain income and accumulate wealth in the form of government debt, provided that the government is prepared to make an increasing supply of this available (or provided that there is long-dated stock which gives secure capital growth). The proportion of their wealth which they will be prepared to make available to companies will then be lower, the higher the rate of interest; and they will be reluctant to encourage companies to invest for a risky prospective return of i where they can obtain a safe return of i from the government. Then the analysis of how high interest rates will affect both companies and portfolio holders points to the result that companies will invest less (and take fewer risks) where the rate of interest is high (in relation to the rate of profit) than where it is low.

Exactly how much the rate of interest will influence investment is far from clear. It might be thought, following Kalecki, that a function could be assumed where investment depends entirely upon the excess of the rate of profit over the rate of interest,[1] with the result that investment will be zero if the rate of profit equals the rate of interest. If uncertainty is attached to the yield and capital value of any one type of asset, wealth owners will be unwilling to hold their entire wealth in the form of any one asset, for they will obtain diminishing marginal satisfaction from each extra unit because of the risks involved in a large shareholding. In consequence, they will almost always wish to possess a number of different types of asset.[2] Then, if fixed-interest securities are available which offer 10 per cent, while company investment is expected to earn no more than 9 per cent, wealth owners might be theoretically expected to hold just fixed-interest securities in their portfolios, but if some of these were long-dated and there was slight doubt about the creditworthiness of the governments concerned (and there are few countries in the world which still

[1] Kalecki, *Essays in the Theory of Economic Fluctuations*, and *Studies in the Theory of Business Cycles 1933-9* (Blackwell, 1966) pp. 7-8.
[2] See, for instance, Sir John Hicks, *Critical Essays in Monetary Theory* (Oxford U.P., 1967) chap. 6, 'The pure theory of portfolio selection'.

pay interest on the long-dated bonds their governments issued in
1900), a part of portfolios would consist of assets of other types such
as land, property and industrial shares, even though these were all
expected to yield less than 10 per cent on a balance of probabilities.
It is by such caution that certain institutions and families manage to
retain their wealth through multifarious political upheavals. It is
thus to be expected that company investment, and investment of
other kinds, will continue, albeit at a diminished rate, even if the
rate of interest exceeds the rate of profit.

The principal effect of the rate of interest on investment is then
likely to be that there will be less investment and less risk-taking,
the higher the rate of interest in relation to the rate of profit, but
there is likely to be some investment, however high the rate of interest.

These effects of the rate of interest on investment will differentiate
a country's investment function from its saving function. Before
monetary factors and the need to finance the public sector were
brought into the argument, the equilibrium saving and investment
functions were both determined effectively by wealth owners' preferences between consumable current income and growth, and this
will still be largely true of the saving function, but investment will now
be able to come to less or more than the preferred rate of saving of
wealth owners. Where interest rates are high in relation to the rate
of return on capital, company investment will come to less than the
preferred accumulation of wealth owners, and the surplus will be
drawn into the public sector in conditions of equilibrium growth.
With very low interest rates, company investment will run ahead of
preferred accumulation, and public sector financing will make this
possible. Then steady growth assumptions entail that fiscal and
monetary policies balance out any differences between the private
sector's saving and investment functions.

An algebraic form for the private sector's investment function
which takes account of both wealth owners' preferences between
consumable current income and growth and the effect of the rate of
interest would be:

$$k = x_1.r + x_2.(r-i) \qquad (8.6)$$

where x_1 and x_2 are constants. It will be noted that this takes the
same general algebraic form as the saving function arrived at earlier
(8.2), where k equalled $S_c.r + S_f.(r-r^*)$. It is clear from the above
argument that for steady growth i will need to be adjusted so that
the two functions are brought into line with each other.

The investment and saving functions are so similar algebraically that it does not greatly matter from the point of view of the argument of later chapters which comes into line with which, but there is one important difference between them. There is no doubt with the saving function that capital accumulation will vary more than proportionately with the rate of profit, for the elasticity of k with respect to r equals $1 + (S_f . r^*)/k$ (from (8.3)), and r^* is a parameter that is exogenously given to any one economy. The equivalent equation from the investment function is:

Elasticity of k with respect to r

$$= 1 + \frac{x_2 . i}{k} (1 - \text{Elasticity of } i \text{ with respect to } r). \quad (8.7)$$

The difference between the two results is due to the fact that r^* is independent of r while i will very clearly vary with r.

It is clear from (8.7) that the rate of capital accumulation will vary at least proportionately with the rate of profit, and it will vary more than proportionately if a higher rate of profit is associated with a less than equivalently higher interest rate. A higher rate of profit will certainly be associated with a higher rate of interest because higher rates of return will need to be offered on public debt to compete with the higher yields obtainable from industrial shares, but this tendency should be partly offset by the stronger capital inflows from overseas that will be associated with a higher rate of profit. Moreover, international arbitrage is generally more sensitive to the rate of interest than to the rate of profit, and this is particularly true of short-term capital movements, and this should produce a situation where the rate of interest varies less between economies than the rate of profit. This suggests that the elasticity of i with respect to r will generally be less than 1, i.e. that differences in the rate of profit between economies will tend to be associated with smaller proportional differences in the rate of interest, and planned capital accumulation will then vary more than proportionately with the rate of profit (from (8.7)). Then doubling the rate of profit will more than double planned accumulation.

In earlier chapters, a number of functional relationships between investment and the rate of profit were arrived at which showed that a higher share of investment will generally be associated with a lower rate of profit. In this chapter, the factors influencing investment decisions have been analysed, and it has been argued that a higher

rate of profit will generally be associated with higher planned entrepreneurial investment. Clearly, if an economy is on a steady growth
path, entrepreneurs must be satisfied that they are investing at the
right rate, and the effects of their accumulation must be exactly
those shown in past chapters, so both sets of conditions will need to
be satisfied. In the next chapter various propositions from earlier
chapters will be brought together with the investment function
arrived at in this chapter to show how the equilibrium values of the
economy's rate of profit, its rate of growth and its share of investment will be simultaneously determined.

9

Profits and Growth

THE various threads of the argument can now be brought together
to show how the equilibrium values of the major economic variables
will be determined. In Chapter 2 it was pointed out that where an
economy is on a steady growth path, there must be microeconomic
equilibrium with producers and consumers satisfied that they are
investing, innovating and consuming at the right rates, as well as
macroeconomic equilibrium. The relevant microeconomic conditions
for equilibrium were analysed in Chapters 6 and 8 where it was argued
that these will be satisfied where the investment and technical progress
functions take particular forms. The macroeconomic conditions
were analysed in Chapters 2, 3, 4 and 7, which provide further
equations which must be satisfied if there is to be steady growth. The
equilibrium values of the major economic variables can be found if
these equations can be solved.

It will be found that there is a relatively simple approach to the
solution of the equations, for the rate of profit and the rate of growth
can be simultaneously determined by two schedules and these can
be derived from the results of past chapters. The essence of this
solution is contained in the passage of Malthus which was quoted in
Chapter 1, where he suggested that his theory of population will
apply equally to capital accumulation,[1] and the relevance of this to
the theory that has been developed in this book can be shown most
simply with the help of the following diagrammatic representation of
his argument.[2]

In Fig. 9.1, the horizontal axis shows the rate of population growth,
while the vertical axis shows the real wage. The schedule PP shows

[1] See p. 8 above.
[2] The diagrammatic representation of Malthus's theory of population which
follows is an extension of the diagram in T. Sowell, 'The general glut controversy
reconsidered', *Oxford Economic Papers*, vol. xv (Nov 1963). I am also indebted to
an unpublished paper on Malthus by Mr J. F. Wright.

the 'classical' relationship between the real wage and the rate of population growth. PP intersects the vertical axis (which shows zero population growth) at W_s, so the 'natural' or 'subsistence' wage is OW_s. PP slopes upwards to the right from W_s to show that there will be population growth at any wage exceeding OW_s, and that the rate of population growth will vary with the excess of the wage over the subsistence wage. PP thus shows the psychologically and sociologically determined supply curve of population. The other schedule, NN,

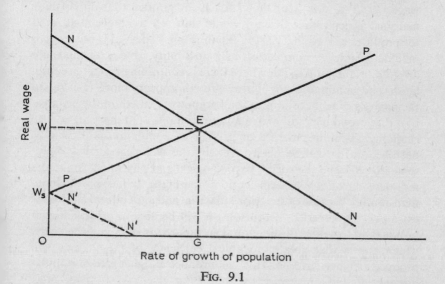

FIG. 9.1

which is implicit in the work of Malthus and Ricardo, shows the rate of growth of population that the economy can support. This depends on the rate of growth of circulating capital (i.e. the rate of growth of the 'wages fund'), and this will grow more rapidly in given technical conditions where wages are low so that profits (which are largely reinvested) are high, than where wages are high, leaving little surplus for accumulation. Then NN will slope downwards to the right to show that a country will only accumulate enough capital to support faster population growth at a lower wage. It will be shown that NN acts as a demand curve for population.

PP and NN intersect at E, and this shows the equilibrium wage, OW, where population and circulating capital (or the 'wages fund') grow at the same rate. If the wage is less than OW, circulating capital will grow more quickly than population and the available labour force, with the result that employers will bid up the wage towards OW, while capital will grow less quickly than population where the wage exceeds OW, thus reducing the wage. The equilibrium wage, OW, shows the only wage where the 'law of population' will produce a rate of population growth which will equal the rate of growth of the funds necessary for its maintenance.

Malthus and Ricardo took it for granted that this equilibrium wage would be OW_s, for they took it for granted that diminishing marginal agricultural efficiency would shift NN to an eventual $N'N'$ to produce a stationary-state equilibrium. They did not regard indefinite capital accumulation as a possibility,[1] but with hindsight an equilibrium point like E where there is continuing capital accumulation and continuing population growth appears more relevant to the analysis of real economies than arguments based on the proposition that economies will arrive at an inevitable stationary state. The economy's equilibrium rate of growth of population will then be positive, and it will be determined by the technical factors represented by NN and the social, psychological and physiological factors represented by PP. Where an economy has higher labour productivity than another because of superior industrial and agricultural efficiency, extra skills or superior institutions, it will be able to achieve higher profits (and therefore faster capital accumulation) at any given wage, which means that greater technical efficiency of these kinds will produce a higher NN line. This will produce a higher rate of population growth and a higher real wage if PP is given. At the same time, PP will be raised if a higher standard of living is, for any reason, a prerequisite for population growth, which means that Malthus's 'moral restraint' will produce a higher wage and a slower rate of population growth. Thus the technical factors produce what amounts to a demand curve for population, while the 'human' factors produce a supply curve, and these are sufficient to determine the economy's equilibrium rate of population growth and its equilibrium wage. It is

---

[1] How very long Malthus's long periods are is not always appreciated. Writing after Trafalgar in the third edition of his *Essay on Population* (1806), he considered the possibility that Britain might achieve continuous growth through a continuous increase in manufacturing output which could be traded for the extra food needed to feed a growing population. He thought that this could not provide a long-term solution to the problem of food supply, for (among other reasons) Britain could hardly be expected to have a 'commanding navy' for more than two or three hundred years (vol. II, pp. 273-6).

the use of two schedules of this kind to determine simultaneously the rate of population growth and the wage that is crucial, and two similar schedules can be used to analyse the determination of the equilibrium rate of capital accumulation and the equilibrium rate of profit.

This is illustrated in Fig. 9.2, which is Fig. 9.1 with only the lettering altered. Here the axes show the rate of profit and the rate of growth of capital in place of the wage and the rate of population growth. *KK*, which replaces the identically drawn *PP*, is the psychologically and sociologically determined supply curve of capital, and it

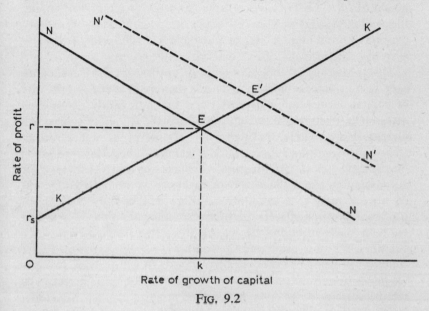

FIG. 9.2

illustrates the application of the 'law of population' to capital accumulation, for capital 'breeds' like population, a high rate of profit leading to high reinvestment and rapid accumulation. There is no capital accumulation where the rate of profit is as low as Or_s, the equivalent to the subsistence wage, and there is positive capital accumulation to the extent that the rate of profit exceeds Or_s. *NN* shows the effect of capital accumulation on the rate of profit, and it slopes downwards from left to right, for the rate of profit will be high where capital accumulates slowly relatively to population with the result that capital eventually becomes scarce, while it will be low where capital accumulates rapidly. The two schedules intersect at *E*, which shows the equilibrium rate of growth of capital, Ok, and the equilibrium rate of profit, Or. If the rate of profit is less than Or, capital will 'breed' less quickly than at E, so the rate of growth of capital will be less than Ok. This will eventually make capital scarcer relatively to labour than at E, with the result that the rate of profit will rise. If there is a loss of capital 'during a war which does not interrupt commerce', NN will rise temporarily to $N'N'$, i.e. capital will become scarcer relatively to population so it will earn a higher rate of profit at any given rate of accumulation, and if there is no shift in KK, i.e. 'if only the same habits of saving prevail among the capitalists as before', the new equilibrium will be at E' where both the rate of profit and the rate of accumulation will be higher than at E so that 'the recovery of the lost stock must be rapid'.[1]

That is Malthus's theory of population applied to capital accumulation. In long-run equilibrium, it makes the rate of profit and the rate of capital accumulation depend on a psychologically determined investment function, KK, which shows that the supply of capital will increase more rapidly, the higher the rate of profit, and a further technically determined function, NN, which can be referred to as the 'investment opportunity function'. This acts as a demand curve for accumulation, and it shows the long-run effects on the rate of profit of various rates of accumulation. There will be only one rate of profit and one rate of accumulation where the conditions represented by both these functions are satisfied, so they will determine the equilibrium rate of profit and the equilibrium rate of growth. Faster technical progress or faster population growth will provide stronger technical opportunities to absorb capital which will increase the relative scarcity of capital in the long run at any given rate of accumulation, so these will raise NN and (with KK given) produce a higher equilibrium rate of profit and a faster equilibrium rate of growth. A stronger psychologically or sociologically determined willingness to invest will shift KK to the right, which (with NN given) will produce a faster rate of capital accumulation and a lower rate of profit. Thus the technical and the 'human' factors will each play a part in the determination of the rate of profit and the rate of capital accumulation.

It is to be noted that it is the rate of growth of *capital* and not the rate of growth of *output* that is determined by these functions. It

[1] The quoted passages are from Malthus's *Principles of Political Economy* (1820) pp. 373-4.

would be anachronistic to interpose the modern steady growth result that $g = k$ into Malthus, but a modern version of the argument would certainly have $g = k$, so the economy's equilibrium rate of growth of *output* and its rate of profit would then be simultaneously determined by KK and NN.

It will turn out that the basic solution to the equations arrived at in earlier chapters of this book is precisely the same as that shown in Fig. 9.2, for KK and NN have their exact counterparts in Chapters 7 and 8. The investment and saving functions arrived at in Chapter 8 show that the rate of capital accumulation will be higher, the higher the rate of profit, so these are equivalent to KK. The functions corresponding to NN are to be found in Chapter 7, where the effects on the rate of profit of various rates of capital accumulation were analysed. It was shown there that faster capital accumulation (with given labour growth and a given technical progress function) always produces the same or a lower rate of profit with non-vintage assumptions, and with vintage assumptions faster capital accumulation must produce a lower rate of profit unless θ, the vintage elasticity of substitution between labour and capital, substantially exceeds 2. This means that there will almost always be a downward-sloping investment opportunity function like NN to show the adverse effects on the rate of profit of faster capital accumulation. Moreover, this downward-sloping function can only intersect the upward-sloping investment function at one point (as in Fig. 9.2), so there will almost always be a unique equilibrium rate of profit, and a unique rate of growth, and these will be determined in exactly the way that they are determined in Fig. 9.2.

The algebraic forms of the saving and investment functions that were found in Chapter 8 are $k = S_c.r + S_f.(r-r^*)$, and

$$k = x_1.r + x_2.(r-i)$$

((8.2) and (8.6)), and it was pointed out in Chapter 8 that the rate of interest will need to be such that these functions are compatible. In steady growth, g will equal k, so substituting g for k and rearranging:

$$r = \frac{S_f.r^*}{S_c+S_f} + g\left(\frac{1}{S_c+S_f}\right) \tag{9.1}$$

$$r = \frac{x_2.i}{x_1+x_2} + g\left(\frac{1}{x_1+x_2}\right). \tag{9.2}$$

(9.1) will be drawn exactly as KK in Fig. 9.2. It will intersect the vertical axis where $r = (S_f . r^*)/(S_c + S_f)$, and it will then slope upwards with a gradient of $1/(S_c + S_f)$. With (9.2), however, there is the problem that the rate of interest will not be independent of the rate of profit. Interconnections between r and i can be fully taken into account in the mathematical version of the argument that follows, but if (9.2) is to be drawn as a simple schedule like (9.1), intersecting the vertical axis where $r = (x_2 . i)/(x_1 + x_2)$, and then sloping upwards with a gradient of $1/(x_1 + x_2)$, it must be assumed that the rate of interest is independent of the rate of profit. There will still be a rising KK schedule where the rate of interest varies with the rate of profit, but it cannot be drawn straight from (9.2). It will, for instance, slope upwards to the right *from the origin* if the rate of interest varies proportionately with the rate of profit.

The functions equivalent to NN can be found with Cobb–Douglas, CES and vintage assumptions. In each case a production function and a technical progress function (and in the vintage case, a further function showing the necessary connection between C, r and T) are used to obtain an equation for r in terms of g.

Where the production function is Cobb–Douglas, there is an equation which shows the equilibrium relationship between r, S and g, i.e.

$$r = \frac{\alpha . g}{S}. \qquad (9.3)\,[1]$$

S can be eliminated from this equation by making use of the proposition, based on the technical progress function, that $g = A + n + B.S$ in steady growth, so that:

$$S = \frac{g - A - n}{B}. \qquad (9.4)$$

Then, from (9.3) and (9.4):

$$r = \frac{\alpha . B . g}{g - A - n}$$

and since $\dfrac{g}{g - A - n} = 1 + \left(\dfrac{A+n}{g}\right) + \left(\dfrac{A+n}{g}\right)^2 + \left(\dfrac{A+n}{g}\right)^3 \dots$

$$r = \alpha . B \left(1 + \left(\frac{A+n}{g}\right) + \left(\frac{A+n}{g}\right)^2 + \left(\frac{A+n}{g}\right)^3 \dots\right). \qquad (9.5)$$

---

[1] This is (2.4) with g substituted for $(a+n)$.

(9.5) is an exact counterpart to NN in Fig. 9.2. Like NN, it slopes downwards to the right, for where the parameters A, B, n and α are given and positive, a higher g must be associated with a lower r. Moreover, the height of this downward-sloping schedule will clearly vary with A, B, n and α. Then an economy with faster labour growth or a stronger technical progress function than another will have a higher rate of profit at all rates of growth.

There is a very similar equation for a CES economy:

$$r = J \cdot \left[B \left(1 + \left(\frac{A+n}{g} \right) + \left(\frac{A+n}{g} \right)^2 + \left(\frac{A+n}{g} \right)^3 \ldots \right) \right]^{\frac{1}{\sigma}} \quad (9.6)^1$$

where J is a constant. (9.6) must slope downwards to the right, like NN, and its height will depend upon A, B, n, J, and σ.

There is also a vintage equation for NN which is similar to (9.5) and (9.6):

$$r = B \left(1 + \left(\frac{A}{g} \right) + \left(\frac{A}{g} \right)^2 \ldots \right)$$

$$- \frac{2}{T} \left(1 - \frac{T}{6} (r+g) + \frac{T^2}{36} (r^2 - rg + g^2) \ldots \right). \quad (9.7)^2$$

Here r is a function of g and T. A higher g will be associated with a lower r so far as the first bracket,

$$B \left(1 + \left(\frac{A}{g} \right) + \left(\frac{A}{g} \right)^2 \ldots \right),$$

which corresponds to the *gross* rate of return, is concerned; but the second bracket,

$$\frac{2}{T} \left(1 - \frac{T}{6} (r+g) \ldots \right),$$

corresponding to depreciation, complicates the situation. It follows from the argument of Chapter 7 that this will rise with g (where A and B are given) provided that θ does not exceed something like

$$\theta^* \left[1 + \left(\frac{B \cdot S}{A} \right) (X_w + \tfrac{1}{3} X_p) \right],$$

and the view was taken in Chapter 7 that θ should not generally be as high as this.[3] Then a higher g can be expected to reduce the term

---

[1] Substitute g for $(a+n)$ in (2.7). Then use (9.4) to substitute for S.
[2] Use (9.4) with $n = 0$ to substitute for S in (3.29), and substitute g for a.
[3] See pp. 166-72 above.

corresponding to the gross rate of return, and raise depreciation at the same time, which will accentuate the extent to which a higher g is associated with a lower r. Then (9.7) will slope downwards, like NN, both because a higher g reduces

$$B\left(1+\left(\frac{A}{g}\right)+\left(\frac{A}{g}\right)^2 ...\right),$$

and because it raises

$$\frac{2}{T}\left(1-\frac{T}{6}(r+g)...\right).$$

Of course, this is conditional on the upper limit that has been placed on the value of θ, and (9.7) could even slope upwards if θ substantially exceeds 2, but it is most unlikely that it does.

Then there will generally be a downward-sloping function like NN with each of the models that has been considered. (9.5), (9.6) and (9.7) show the precise form of NN which follows from the specific assumptions of perfect competition, production functions with particular mathematical forms, and the technical progress function $a = A + B . S$. Without these assumptions there will still be a function corresponding to NN which slopes downwards to the right, for faster capital accumulation must reduce the scarcity of capital in relation to other factors of production in conditions of equilibrium growth, which must have an effect on what capital can earn. Imperfections in competition might allow entrepreneurs to resist the lower rate of return that should follow from a relative redundancy of capital, but with given market imperfections, i.e. with specified monopoly and trades union power, they will find it harder to earn a high rate of return where capital is redundant than where it is scarce. This means that there will still be a downward-sloping function, but its height will depend on competitive conditions as well as on the technical coefficients which influence the height of NN in (9.5), (9.6) and (9.7).

The recent work in capital theory which was discussed in Chapter 5 has shown that higher capital – labour ratios will not always be associated with a lower rate of profit, once the heterogeneity of capital goods is allowed for, but the argument of that chapter suggested that the orthodox relationship will hold in the great majority of cases.[1] It is only in very particular circumstances that

[1] Joan Robinson and K. A. Naqvi, in 'The badly behaved production function', explain why more restrictive conditions are needed for 'backward' than for 'forward' switches. (pp. 581-2).

higher capital per worker will be associated with a higher rate of return on capital, but the fact that this may sometimes happen means that NN will not slope downwards smoothly as in Fig. 9.2, but its broad sweep will be downwards, and this is all that is necessary for the main argument that follows.

The saving and investment functions, (9.1) and (9.2), will undoubtedly slope upwards, and any given saving or investment function must then intersect the relevant investment opportunity function, and it can be assumed that it will only intersect this once.[1] There will then be a unique equilibrium rate of profit and a unique rate of growth, and these will be determined in the manner that has been outlined.

In the remainder of this chapter, something will be said about the general implications of this solution, which are far-reaching. In the next chapter, the detailed mathematical results which follow from the solution will be discussed.

Before the general implications of the argument are discussed, it may be worth while to show that the same results can be arrived at more generally with both vintage and non-vintage assumptions.

With non-vintage assumptions, the equilibrium values of r, g, S and i need to be determined, and it can be shown that there will always be sufficient equations for this.

If the argument of Chapter 8 is accepted, an economy will always have an investment function where the rate of capital accumulation varies with the rate of profit, and inversely with the rate of interest. The investment function need not be of the linear form suggested in (8.6), but there will be a function of the general form $k = f(r, i)$, and since $g = k$ in equilibrium:

$$g = f(r, i). \qquad (9.8)$$

If the argument of Chapter 6 is accepted, the rate of technical progress will vary with the economy's share of investment. The relationship need not be linear, but there will still be a function of the general form $a = f(S)$, and since $g = (a+n)$:

$$g = f(S, n). \qquad (9.9)$$

[1] If the 'broad sweep' of NN is downwards to the right, but there are also aberrant upward movements (due to reswitching), NN may intersect KK more than once if its *upward slope* temporarily exceeds that of KK. This requires, not merely that the technical coefficients produce multiple rates of return, but also that the upward slope of NN (which normally slopes downwards) be rather steep where KK intersects it, so it should be safe to disregard this possibility.

Provided that it is accepted that there will always be some kind of relationship between the technical conditions of production, the relative scarcity of factors of production, and factor returns, then there will be an equation of the general form $r = f(V)$, and since $V = S/g$ in steady growth:

$$r = f(S/g). \tag{9.10}$$

Finally, if the argument of Chapter 8 is accepted, then the interest rate will be a function of monetary factors (M); fiscal factors, and in particular the proportion of private saving used in the public sector which will depend on (I_g/S_g); the rate of profit which will influence the interest rate which must be paid to draw private sector saving into the public sector; and the relationship between the rate of profit and the particular profit rate where there are no net international capital movements into or out of the country $(r-r^*)$. Thus:

$$i = f(M, I_g/S_g, r, (r-r^*)). \tag{9.11}$$

(9.8), (9.9), (9.10) and (9.11) provide sufficient equations to determine the equilibrium values of the model's four variables, r, g, S and i, if it is assumed that n, M, I_g/S_g and r^* are given. The solution to the equations can be illustrated diagrammatically by dividing them into pairs, which then become the schedules of Fig. 9.2. NN is obtained from (9.9) and (9.10), and where S is eliminated from these, $r = f(g, n)$. KK is obtained from (9.8) and (9.11), and (9.11) can be used to substitute for i in (9.8) to produce an equation of the form $g = f(r, M, I_g/S_g, (r-r^*))$. KK and NN can then be used to determine simultaneously the equilibrium values of r and g, as in the diagrammatic solution.

With vintage assumptions there are two further variables, T, the life of plant, and C, the gross capital–output ratio with new plant, which need to be determined, and the equation which makes the rate of profit a function of V or (S/g) (9.10) will not be available. There is therefore a need for three further equations, and these are provided by the specific vintage equations, (3.8), (3.9) and (3.10), which were outlined in Chapter 3.

There will then be sufficient equations to determine the equilibrium values of the variables with both vintage and non-vintage assumptions, and the simplest approach to a solution to these equations is through the two schedules, KK and NN, of Fig. 9.2. Precise form can be given to the equations as a result of the analysis of earlier chapters, and the detailed results which follow from these will be analysed in

Chapter 10. Before this, it will be useful to say something about the general implications of the argument. What follows will not depend on the detailed form of the equations. It will simply depend on the broad propositions that *KK* slopes upwards to the right, and *NN* slopes downwards. These propositions are sufficient to establish results which were understood by Malthus and, in addition, by Schumpeter, but which have since been lost sight of.

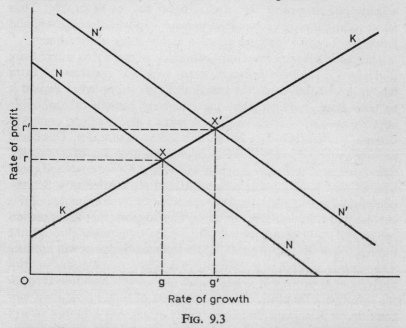

FIG. 9.3

The basic diagram will be used to compare economies with different opportunities for investment, and different preferences for accumulation. A comparison between economies with different opportunities for investment will be made first.[1]

Suppose there are two economies with the same investment function, where one has faster labour growth or faster labour-augmenting technical progress than the other. Then both economies will have the same *KK* line, but the economy with faster labour growth or faster technical progress will be able to earn a higher rate of profit at any given rate of accumulation, so its *NN* line will be above the

[1] There is a similar diagram, and an account of the results which follow in Eltis, 'Technical progress, profits, and growth'.

H

other economy's NN line. The long-term situation is illustrated in Fig. 9.3, where there is one investment function, KK, that is common to both economies, and two investment opportunity lines, NN and $N'N'$, where $N'N'$ is the opportunity line of the economy with faster labour growth, or faster technical progress. It intersects KK at X' which is above and to the right of X, and this means that the economy with faster labour growth or faster technical progress will enjoy both a faster rate of growth Og', and a higher rate of profit, Or'. Thus faster technical progress will lead to faster capital accumulation, and (which is not quite the same thing) a higher share of investment.[1]

This result has important implications. It suggests that where there is a given investment function, extra technical progress or extra labour growth will cause the investment that is needed to exploit it to take place, provided that the long-term growth of economies approximates to equilibrium growth paths – and it will be argued in Chapter 12 that there may be mechanisms to ensure this. This could provide a solution to one of the more puzzling problems of economics, namely whether technical progress will simply reduce costs and cause unemployment, or whether it can actually induce expansion. Schumpeter found a clear answer to this question,[2] and the argument of this chapter points in the same direction. This suggests that faster technical progress will be associated with higher investment through the mechanism of the rate of profit. Extra technical progress will produce a higher rate of profit at the old rate of capital accumulation, and this higher rate of profit will induce faster capital accumulation through the investment function, until the two sets of forces produce a new equilibrium at a higher rate of accumulation, and a higher rate of profit. That is how Malthus and Schumpeter saw the economic process, but their insights have been largely lost sight of, with the result that economic theory has produced no clear interconnecting force between technical progress and investment. Most economic theorists have been content to assume that an economy's share of investment is independent of technical progress and population

[1] The rate of capital accumulation is I/K, and S, the share of investment, is I/Y, so $S = (I/K).(K/Y)$. Then the relationship between the share of investment and the rate of capital accumulation will depend upon K/Y. A higher rate of capital accumulation will be associated with a higher share of investment unless there is at least an equal proportional fall in K/Y. It will be shown in Chapter 10 that this is not to be expected, with the result that faster capital accumulation can be expected to produce a higher share of investment. Much rests on this point.

[2] J. Schumpeter, *The Theory of Economic Development* (Cambridge, Mass.: Harvard U.P., 1934).

growth, with the result that these can only influence its capital–output ratio. Then any relationship between the share of investment in the National Income and the rate of growth should be entirely accidental, for it is just as likely that a high share of investment (i.e. a high savings ratio) will be associated with a low growth rate as it is that investment and the rate of growth will be positively correlated. It is well known that this is not borne out statistically, and Table 9.1 illustrates the well-known relationship that fast-growing economies invest more than those with slow growth rates.

Table 9.1

INVESTMENT, GROWTH AND INCOME DISTRIBUTION, 1955-69

	g	S (gross)	S (gross)/g	W/Y
U.K.	2·7%	16·0%	5·9	0·73
U.S.A.	3·8%	16·5%	4·3	0·70
France	5·4%	20·5%	3·8	0·62
Italy	5·6%	21·0%	3·75	0·57
West Germany	5·7%	23·5%	4·1	0·63
Japan	10·6%	30·5%	2·9	0·53

W/Y is the share of 'Compensation of Employees' in the National Income, and the figures for 1958, 1961, 1964 and 1967 from *National Accounts of OECD Countries 1958-67* are averaged. The figures for g and S (gross) are derived from the UN *Monthly Bulletin of Statistics*. Unfortunately, the *net* savings ratios of these countries, with depreciation measured on a comparable basis, are unavailable.

The connection between S and g that is illustrated in this table can hardly be compatible with the view that there is a random relationship between them, but that is the view of the matter that is generally taken by neoclassical growth theorists. The theory that has just been outlined provides one of several possible explanations of the very strong relationship between S and g,[1] namely that rapid technical

[1] Among the other possible explanations of the close connection between g and S that is illustrated in Table 9.1 are the following. (i) The connection may be entirely short-term, when all would agree that higher investment will produce faster growth. However, with this argument, higher investment should increase the growth rate, at most, proportionately (see pp. 42-4 above), while Table 9.1 shows that higher investment is associated with a more than proportionally

progress and labour growth produce a high rate of profit which induces rapid capital accumulation, while, at the same time, high investment produces rapid technical progress which contributes to rapid growth.

It is a characteristic of the theory that is being outlined that the share of investment is not something that is exogenously given to an economy. Instead, it is one of the 'outputs' of the model, where the 'inputs' or parameters include, not the share of investment, but 'wealth owners' preferences between income and growth', and the coefficients of the technical progress function. These parameters determine the slope and height of KK and NN which 'produce' the model's outputs, the rate of growth and the rate of profit – and, derivable from these, the share of investment. The actual mathematical relationships between investment on the one hand, and the technical opportunity for growth on the other, with Cobb–Douglas, CES and vintage assumptions, will be analysed in Chapter 10. However, the main outlines of the solution, namely that stronger opportunities for growth will produce faster growth, a higher rate of profit and more investment, can be stated very simply with the help of the diagrammatic representation of the argument that is provided by Fig. 9.3.

A situation where one economy has stronger preferences for growth than another is illustrated in Fig. 9.4, where two economies have the same investment opportunity function, NN, and different investment functions, KK and $K'K'$. The economy with stronger preferences for growth has the investment function $K'K'$, and its equilibrium rate of growth, Og', will be higher than the other economy's, while its equilibrium rate of profit, Or', will be lower. Thus stronger preferences for accumulation produce more accumulation, but at the cost of a lower rate of profit. This line of argument is well known, and it dates from Adam Smith's account of the rate of profit in the capital-saturated Dutch economy, but it is not a view of the matter that is universally accepted, for Joan Robinson has argued that a higher

---

higher growth rate. (ii) The evidence is compatible with the life-cycle hypothesis of savings behaviour, where faster growth produces a higher share of saving. Modigliani suggests that this may provide a good explanation of inter-country savings data in 'The life cycle hypothesis of saving and inter-country differences in the saving ratio', published in *Induction, Growth and Trade: Essays in Honour of Sir Roy Harrod*, ed. W. A. Eltis, M. FG. Scott and J. N. Wolfe (Oxford U.P., 1970).

desired rate of growth, due in her argument to stronger 'animal spirits', may increase the rate of profit instead of reducing it. She suggests that a higher desired rate of growth may sometimes call forth the innovations it needs so that it can be realised,[1] and if it is, the higher g that results will be associated with a higher r if S_p is given (from $g = S_p.r$). There are a number of points to note here. The equation $g = S_p.r$ is algebraically identical to one of the investment functions arrived at in Chapter 8, $g = x.r$. However, in her

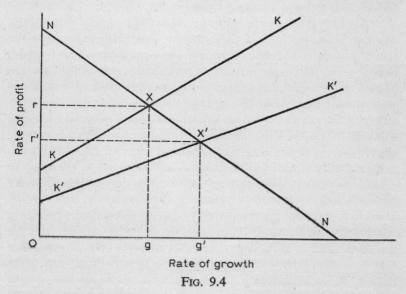

FIG. 9.4

argument, 'animal spirits' raise g, so they will raise r if S_p is given. With the present argument, the equivalent to stronger 'animal spirits' is 'stronger wealth owners' preferences for growth', and this raises x which acts against an increase in r. One question at issue between these two approaches is whether entrepreneurs can plausibly choose a rate of growth, or whether they are forced to choose between current income and growth. Joan Robinson's entrepreneurs who simply choose a higher g and consume a fixed proportion of the higher profits which are then earned are in an especially privileged position. They can choose growth without having to forgo income; in other words, they can expand their cake and eat it at the same time. The

[1] Robinson, *Essays in the Theory of Economic Growth*, II, 'A model of accumulation'.

alternative view suggests that entrepreneurs must choose between expansion and consumable current income. Then, if they choose faster expansion in given technical conditions, they are *ipso facto* choosing a lower ratio of consumption to capital. Thus a major question at issue is whether wealth owners merely have the power to choose between various permutations of current income and growth, or whether they have the power to impose a higher growth rate which will provide the resources for extra capital accumulation and higher dividends at one and the same time.

If they have the power to impose a rate of growth, can they impose any rate of expansion that they please? Clearly, they cannot if the rate of growth of the labour force and the technical progress function impose constraints in the form of an investment opportunity function like NN. If the argument of Chapter 7 is accepted, there will be a downward-sloping investment opportunity function unless θ is very high, and even then there will be an investment opportunity function that will limit the rate at which the economy can grow. If this is accepted, entrepreneurs will not be able to expand at whatever rate they please.

Entrepreneurs and wealth owners may still escape the need to choose between income and growth if they can exploit Keynes's 'widow's cruse', which may return to them whatever they spend.[1] Then they may still be able to enjoy higher investment and higher consumption at the same time. It would be widely agreed that this will be possible in an underemployed economy where anything that wealth owners spend will be returned to them without any other section of the community being one whit worse off, but is this abrogation of normal economics (where everything has a cost and nothing is obtained without the sacrifice of something else) equally possible in a fully employed economy? At full employment, wealth owners can only obtain extra resources by raising the rate of growth (and it has been argued that they cannot impose any growth rate they please if a technical progress function is specified), or by obtaining a higher share of profits in the National Income. If they can obtain whatever share of profits they wish (and that is what is believed by those who maintain that stronger preferences for growth are associated with a higher rate of profit), then they can accumulate more without consuming less, and vice versa, while workers will bear the cost. They cannot do this in a competitive economy for the rate and share of profits will then be otherwise determined, but what if

[1] See pp. 72-5 above.

there are innumerable imperfections in competition, and increasing returns to scale which have the effect of creating pockets of excess capacity?[1] A world of this kind will be a more complex one to analyse than a fully competitive world, but it does not follow because it is complicated that wealth owners can take what they wish with scant regard to other pressures. The effects of imperfect competition and increasing returns to scale on income distribution and the rate of profit will be analysed in Chapters 11 and 13, and it will turn out that no fully employed economy can be coherently imagined where wealth owners can obtain the total command over resources that they wish for. This is not unexpected, and it means that it is the *preferences* of wealth owners and entrepreneurs and not their *commands* that will influence what happens. Their preferences will certainly influence the rate of profit and the rate of growth, and it would be wrong to ignore the effect of their preferences as many do, but this does not mean that theirs will be the sole influence.

The argument of this chapter suggests that the rate of profit and the rate of growth will be determined by two sets of forces. There are the psychological and sociological forces represented by the investment function, KK, and the technical forces represented by the investment opportunity function, NN. Both sets of forces must play a part. It will be wrong to believe that the technical factors are all-important so that no part is played by the psychological factors represented by KK, and it will be equally wrong to attribute everything to entrepreneurial psychology, and use the general difficulties associated with capital measurement, imperfect competition and increasing returns to scale to suggest that technical factors play *no analysable part* in the growth process. Psychology has a part to play in economic phenomena, but its role must generally be circumscribed by technical factors. Entrepreneurs with 'animal spirits' will go bankrupt if net profits become less than interest payments on massive investment with a necessarily short life. Psychology plays its part in the investment function which represents one of the sets of forces which determine the rate of profit and the rate of growth of a developed economy, but this set of forces will interact with the technical forces represented by the investment opportunity function and this too must play a part, though not a part which excludes all else. Both are important, and their interaction will determine what will happen.

[1] See Kaldor, 'Marginal productivity and the macro-economic theories of distribution'.

10

The Determination of the Share of Investment, the Rate of Profit and the Rate of Growth

IT was shown in Chapter 9 that sufficient equations have now been arrived at to determine the equilibrium values of the share of investment, the rate of profit and the rate of growth. This means that it is now possible to analyse the full influence of opportunities for growth, and preferences between consumption and growth on the equilibrium values of these variables. Different economies will have different opportunities for growth, for the rate of growth of the labour force and the coefficients of the technical progress function will vary between economies. The extent to which opportunities for growth are exploited will also vary between economies, for the wealth owners of each country will have different preferences between consumption and growth. The opportunities for growth and the preferences between consumption and growth will determine the equilibrium values of S, r and g of each economy. It will be interesting to know how strong the various influences are, and there are questions of particular importance which it may be possible to answer.

It will be important to know something about the sensitivity of the share of investment and the rate of growth to the parameters of the investment function. It may be that stronger preferences for growth will produce much faster growth and much higher shares of investment, or it may be that the investment function will have relatively little influence so that economies with equal technical opportunities for growth and very different preferences between consumption and growth have much the same share of investment, and much the same rate of growth. It will be interesting to see how closely the results of the analysis approximate to either of these possibilities.

It will also be interesting to know whether greater opportunities for growth, i.e. a stronger technical progress function or faster labour growth, have a considerable effect on the share of investment, or only a slight effect. Greater opportunities for growth must obviously have a near to proportional effect on the *equilibrium* rate of growth, and it does not require technical analysis to demonstrate this, but it is much less clear how sensitive investment will be to stronger opportunities for growth. It is not even obvious that stronger opportunities for growth will necessarily influence investment in the expected direction.

A further point of interest will be the sensitivity of the capital–output ratio, the rate of profit and the share of profits to differences in the parameters. There have been suggestions by various authors at various times that some or all of these have been historically constant and/or similar between economies.[1] It would be a contribution towards the explanation of such phenomena if it turned out that the capital–output ratio, the rate of profit or the share of profits were much the same with very different investment and technical progress functions. It is, of course, inherently unlikely that clear-cut results about their plausible degree of variation will be found from *a priori* reasoning alone.

Attempts will be made to answer these questions in this chapter. They would ideally be answered with the help of expressions which stated the value of each of the variables in terms of parameters alone, but unfortunately this is impossible with CES and vintage assumptions. This is evident from (10.1) in the final mathematical section of the chapter, which is the simplest equation for g that can be found with CES assumptions. A glance at this equation will show that a convenient formula for g in terms of parameters alone cannot be found. The position will be no more manageable than this with vintage assumptions, for vintage equations have proved to be more complicated than the equivalent non-vintage ones at every stage of the argument. This means that convenient statements of the equilibrium values of S, r and g in terms of the model's parameters alone cannot be obtained.

[1] See, for instance, Kaldor, 'A model of economic growth'; M. Kalecki, 'The determinants of distribution of the National Income', *Econometrica*, vol. VI (Apr 1938); E. H. Phelps Brown and P. E. Hart, 'The share of wages in National Income', *Economic Journal*, vol. LXII (June 1952); and E. H. Phelps Brown and Margaret H. Browne, *A Century of Pay* (Macmillan, 1968) pp. 333-43.

There is, however, a relatively simple method of obtaining the results which are actually of most interest. These are the effects on the variables of differences in particular parameters between two economies. Thus it will be interesting to know how faster labour growth and a stronger technical progress function will influence the share of investment, the rate of profit and the rate of growth of non-vintage and vintage economies. The effect of a stronger investment function must also be found. It will turn out that the *elasticities* of S, r and g with respect to the parameters of the investment function and the investment opportunity function can be obtained quite simply, and this is the information about the solutions to the model which is actually of most interest.

The effects on S, r and g of stronger preferences for growth, i.e. the effects of a KK line that is further to the right, will be analysed first. After this, the effects of greater opportunities for growth, i.e. of a higher NN line, will be shown. The actual calculation of the elasticities is worked through in the final section of the chapter, 'The Solution of the Equations', and the results of this final section will be presented and discussed below. The effects on S, r and g of stronger preferences for growth, i.e. the effects of a KK line that is further to the right, will be analysed first. After this, the effects of stronger opportunities for growth, i.e. of a higher NN line, will be shown. The implications of the results will then be discussed.

The Effect of the Investment Function on S, r and g

In this section, the effect of the economy's saving and investment functions on the equilibrium values of S, r and g will be outlined. The investment and saving functions are mathematically very similar, and the effect of the investment function, $k = x_1.r + x_2.(r-i)$, will be outlined below, with i regarded as a variable that is solely a function of r and various parameters (from (9.11)). The effect of the savings function, $k = S_c.r + S_f(r-r^*)$, can easily be inferred from the results arrived at.

The investment function, $k = x_1.r + x_2(r-i)$, has two parameters, x_1 and x_2, and the effects of proportional changes in each of these could be obtained and compared. However, this would double the results to be presented, and much less than double the useful information obtained. The interesting questions can all be answered from the results that follow from the assumption that x_1 and x_2

always differ between economies in the same proportion. It will therefore be assumed throughout the chapter that $\partial x_1/x_1 = \partial x_2/x_2$. The effects of investment functions that differ between economies in this way will be outlined with, in succession, Cobb–Douglas, CES and vintage assumptions.

The effects of different investment functions in a Cobb–Douglas world are outlined in Table 10.1. E, which equals $(B.S)/(A+n)$,

Table 10.1

THE INFLUENCE OF THE INVESTMENT FUNCTION
IN A COBB–DOUGLAS WORLD

Elasticity of	With respect to	
g	x_1 and x_2	$\dfrac{E}{E+F}$
r	x_1 and x_2	$-\dfrac{1}{E+F}$
S	x_1 and x_2	$\dfrac{E+1}{E+F}$
V	x_1 and x_2	$\dfrac{1}{E+F}$
X_p	x_1 and x_2	nil

where $E = \dfrac{B.S}{A+n}$, and

$$F = 1 + \frac{x_2 . i}{g} . [1 - \text{Elasticity of } i \text{ with respect to } r]$$

describes a relationship that is familiar from past chapters, and E will be $\frac{2}{3}$ if four-tenths of growth is due to endogenously determined technical progress, and $\frac{1}{2}$ if one-third of growth is due to this. As F is

$$1 + \frac{x_2 . i}{g} [1 - \text{Elasticity of } i \text{ with respect to } r],$$

this must equal at least 1, and it will exceed 1 if interest rates differ proportionately less than profit rates between economies, and the greater sensitivity of interest rates to international capital movements suggests that interest rates may normally differ less. F will be $1\frac{1}{6}$ if $x_1 = x_2$, $r = 2i$, and the elasticity of i with respect to r is $+\frac{1}{2}$. Perhaps about the highest value of F might occur where $x_2 = 1\frac{1}{2}x_1$, $r = 1\frac{1}{2}i$, and the elasticity of i with respect to r is as little as $+\frac{1}{4}$ when F would be $1\frac{1}{2}$. F should then lie in the range 1–$1\frac{1}{2}$, but it is unlikely that it would often exceed $1\frac{1}{3}$, and about $1\frac{1}{6}$ is the kind of value that might most plausibly be expected.

The results in Table 10.1 can be contrasted with the elementary neoclassical results of Chapter 2. There higher investment was simply a higher S, not higher parameters of an investment function, and this had no effect on g, i.e. the elasticity of g with respect to S was nil. However, a higher S reduced r and raised V proportionately, i.e. these had elasticities with respect to S of -1 and $+1$. With the present model the various elasticities are influenced by both E and F. The rate of growth has an elasticity of $E/(E+F)$ with respect to the parameters of the investment function, i.e. of $+0.36$ if $E = \frac{2}{3}$ (so that four-tenths of growth is due to endogenously determined technical progress) and $F = 1\frac{1}{6}$. The rate of profit has an elasticity of $-1/(E+F)$ with respect to the parameters of the investment function, and the capital–output ratio of $+1/(E+F)$, which must be less than 1. It is 0.55 if $E = \frac{2}{3}$ and $F = 1\frac{1}{6}$. Thus the investment and technical progress functions of the present model damp the elasticities of r and V with respect to investment, possibly quite severely. The share of profits, which is always α with Cobb–Douglas assumptions, is of course insensitive to both the S of Chapter 2 and the investment function of the present model.

There is one final effect that is interesting, and this will become much more significant with CES and vintage assumptions. The elasticity of the share of investment with respect to the parameters of the investment function is $(E+1)/(E+F)$, which is less than 1. Thus a 50 per cent increase in investment at each rate of profit and interest will produce an *ex-post* increase in investment of less than 50 per cent. It is not much less with Cobb–Douglas assumptions: $(E+1)/(E+F)$ comes to $+0.91$ where $E = \frac{2}{3}$ and $F = 1\frac{1}{6}$, and in this case an increase in the coefficients of the investment function of 50 per cent will raise S about 45 per cent, but this effect will be accentuated with CES assumptions. There, higher investment will reduce the equilibrium share of profits (if $\sigma < 1$), which means that entrepreneurs will not be able to afford to raise *the share of investment* as much as they raise x_1 and x_2. But there is even an adverse effect on the share of investment with the present Cobb–Douglas assumptions where the share of profits does not fall, and this is due to an interesting feature of the investment function. With this, investment depends partly on the excess of the rate of profit over the rate of interest, and a given reduction in r will reduce $(r-i)$ by a greater proportion if F exceeds 1, with the result that aggregate investment which depends on both r and $(r-i)$ will be adversely affected. Now a higher x_1 and x_2 will always reduce r, and so 'squeeze' $(r-i)$, and this means that the share of investment will always rise less than x_1 and x_2 – even where these have no adverse effect on the share of profits.

It will be evident that the present model's investment and technical progress functions considerably damp the effect of higher preferences for growth on aggregate investment, the capital–output ratio and the rate of profit. It will be clear from Table 10.2 that some of these effects will be accentuated with CES assumptions if σ is less than 1.

Table 10.2 shows that the capital–output ratio and the share of profits could easily vary rather little with respect to the coefficients of the investment function. The elasticity of the capital–output ratio with respect to x_1 and x_2 will be reduced below 1 by a σ of less than 1, by the presence of endogenously determined technical progress, and by any sensitivity of investment to $(r-i)$. If $\sigma = 0.60$, which would be in line with the econometric studies referred to in Chapter 2, and if $E = \frac{2}{3}$ and $F = 1\frac{1}{6}$, then the elasticity of V with respect to x_1 and x_2 will be $+0.38$, while the elasticity of X_p with respect to the coefficients of the investment function will be only -0.26. In other words, if one economy invests 50 per cent more than another wherever both have the same rate of profit and the same rate of interest, the economy which invests more will have a capital–output ratio which is only about 19 per cent higher than the other's, and a share of profits which is something like one-eighth lower, which means that its share of wages will be much less than one-eighth higher since X_w normally exceeds X_p. Incidentally, its share of investment in the National Income will only be about 32 per cent higher, and its rate of profit a little less than one-third lower. Thus, with CES assumptions and a σ of less than 1, a stronger investment function has a much smaller proportional effect on the equilibrium share of investment, and the above example illustrates how strong these effects can be.

These are some of the implications of the model for a CES world. Differences in the investment function produce smaller differences in the equilibrium share of investment, and much smaller differences in the capital–output ratio and the share of profits, because endogenous technical progress, a σ of less than 1, and sensitivity of investment to $(r-i)$ combine to damp the effect of the investment function. It appears from Table 10.2 that the share of profits must vary even less than the capital–output ratio with respect to the investment function

Table 10.2

THE INFLUENCE OF THE INVESTMENT FUNCTION IN A CES WORLD

Elasticity of	With respect to	
g	x_1 and x_2	$\dfrac{\sigma.E}{F+\sigma.E}$
r	x_1 and x_2	$-\dfrac{1}{F+\sigma.E}$
S	x_1 and x_2	$\dfrac{\sigma+\sigma.E}{F+\sigma.E}$
V	x_1 and x_2	$\dfrac{\sigma}{F+\sigma.E}$
X_p	x_1 and x_2	$-\dfrac{1-\sigma}{F+\sigma.E}$

where $1>\sigma>0\cdot5$, which is interesting as the historical case for stability in income distribution is much stronger than the evidence in favour of a constant capital–output ratio.

Perhaps the main point of importance in this analysis of a CES economy is the presence of *three* possible damping effects which reduce the degree of variation of V, X_p and r. The stabilising effect of endogenous technical progress was given much emphasis in Chapter 7, but it is now joined by the possible stabilising effects of a σ of less than 1, and sensitivity of investment to the excess of the rate of profit over a rate of interest that varies less than the rate of profit.

It is now time to turn to vintage assumptions. Here it will be best to present the values of the various elasticities in a series of tables. These are presented as in Chapter 7 on the assumption that the value

Table 10.3

THE VINTAGE ELASTICITY OF g WITH RESPECT TO x_1 AND x_2

$$\left(\text{where } \tfrac{2}{3} > \frac{B.S}{A+B.S} > \tfrac{1}{3}; \ 1 > \theta > \tfrac{1}{3}; \ \text{and } F = 1\tfrac{1}{3} \ (\text{or } 1)\right)$$

| X_p | r/g | | | |
	1·5	2	3	4
0·25	0·052–0·18	0·065–0·23	0·093–0·30	0·12–0·35
	(0·066–0·23)	(0·085–0·28)	(0·12 – 0·36)	(0·15–0·42)
0·33	0·066–0·24	0·086–0·29	0·12 – 0·37	0·14–0·42
	(0·087–0·29)	(0·11 – 0·35)	(0·15 – 0·44)	(0·18–0·49)
0·40	0·080–0·28	0·10 – 0·34	0·14 – 0·41	0·16–0·46
	(0·10 – 0·34)	(0·13 – 0·40)	(0·18 – 0·48)	(0·21–0·54)
0·50	0·098–0·34	0·12 – 0·40	0·16 – 0·47	0·19–0·50
	(0·13 – 0·41)	(0·16 – 0·47)	(0·20 – 0·54)	(0·23–0·57)

of θ lies in the range $\tfrac{1}{3}$–1, and that at least one-third and not more than two-thirds of technical progress is endogenously determined. The values of the elasticities of the rate of growth with respect to the coefficients of the investment function are outlined in Table 10.3, which shows various possible values of this elasticity on the assumption that F is either $1\tfrac{1}{3}$, a rather high value, or (in brackets) 1. Most actual situations will lie between these. The low end of the ranges given below will be where $\theta = \tfrac{1}{3}$ and $(B.S)/(A+B.S) = \tfrac{1}{3}$, while the higher limit to the elasticities will occur where $\theta = 1$ and $(B.S)/(A+B.S) = \tfrac{2}{3}$.

With non-vintage assumptions, the equivalent value of this elasticity is 0·11–0·60 where $F = 1\tfrac{1}{3}$, and 0·14–0·67 where $F = 1$, so vintage assumptions pin this down within a narrower range of values. This is also true of the elasticity of the share of investment with respect to the coefficients of the investment function, where particularly interesting results are arrived at. The possible values of this elasticity are outlined in Table 10.4.

Table 10.4

THE VINTAGE ELASTICITY OF S WITH RESPECT TO x_1 AND x_2

$$\left(\text{where } \tfrac{2}{3} > \frac{B.S}{A+B.S} > \tfrac{1}{3}; \ 1 > \theta > \tfrac{1}{3}; \text{ and } F = 1\tfrac{1}{3} \text{ (or 1)} \right)$$

		r/g		
X_p	1·5	2	3	4
0·25	0·15–0·27	0·20–0·34	0·28–0·45	0·35–0·53
	(0·20–0·34)	(0·26–0·42)	(0·36–0·54)	(0·45–0·63)
0·33	0·20–0·35	0·26–0·43	0·35–0·55	0·43–0·63
	(0·26–0·44)	(0·33–0·53)	(0·45–0·65)	(0·55–0·73)
0·40	0·24–0·42	0·30–0·50	0·41–0·62	0·49–0·69
	(0·31–0·52)	(0·39–0·61)	(0·53–0·73)	(0·61–0·80)
0·50	0·30–0·52	0·37–0·60	0·48–0·70	0·56–0·75
	(0·38–0·61)	(0·47–0·71)	(0·61–0·81)	(0·70–0·86)

With non-vintage assumptions, the equivalent value of this elasticity is 0·33–0·90 where $F = 1\tfrac{1}{3}$, and 0·43–1·00 where $F = 1$, so vintage assumptions again produce results in a narrower range. Table 10.4 shows very clearly that the general result that the share of investment is rather insensitive to the coefficients of the investment function will hold over a very wide range of values of θ, $(B.S)/(A+B.S)$, X_p and r/g. There are apparently no plausible values of these where this elasticity exceeds 1, and it may be very small indeed. This reinforces the results obtained with CES assumptions, but there is now a further effect that weakens the impact of a stronger investment function on the share of investment. This is the connection between investment, the life of plant and the rate of depreciation which was of such importance in Chapter 7. If θ is less than about

$$\theta^* \left(1 + \left[\frac{B.S}{A} \right] . [X_w + \tfrac{1}{3} X_p] \right),$$

a higher share of investment will reduce the life of plant which will raise the rate of depreciation and sharply reduce the rate of profit. This will then have adverse effects on investment through the investment function. Table 10.4 shows the total effect of these complex influences, and it shows how easily a stronger investment function may increase the share of investment much less strongly because of its adverse effects on the rate of profit. A typical developed economy might have a share of profits of 0·33, an r/g of 3 and an F of $1\frac{1}{6}$, and in this case

Table 10.5

THE VINTAGE ELASTICITY OF THE ICOR WITH RESPECT TO x_1 AND x_2

$$\left(\text{where } \tfrac{2}{3} > \frac{B.S}{A+B.S} > \tfrac{1}{3}; \ 1 > \theta > \tfrac{1}{3}; \text{ and } F = 1\tfrac{1}{3} \text{ (or 1)}\right)$$

X_p	r/g			
	1·5	2	3	4
0·25	0·09–0·10	0·11–0·14	0·15–0·19	0·18–0·23
	(0·11–0·13)	(0·14–0·18)	(0·18–0·24)	(0·21–0·30)
0·33	0·11–0·13	0·14–0·17	0·18–0·23	0·21–0·29
	(0·15–0·17)	(0·18–0·22)	(0·21–0·30)	(0·24–0·37)
0·40	0·14–0·16	0·16–0·20	0·21–0·27	0·23–0·33
	(0·18–0·21)	(0·21–0·26)	(0·23–0·35)	(0·25–0·41)
0·50	0·18–0·20	0·20–0·25	0·23–0·32	0·25–0·37
	(0·20–0·25)	(0·24–0·31)	(0·27–0·41)	(0·29–0·47)

the elasticity of its share of investment with respect to the coefficients of its investment function would be 0·40–0·60, which means that if its entrepreneurs chose to invest 50 per cent more at each rate of profit and interest, they would eventually succeed in raising the share of investment only 20–30 per cent. This will obviously severely damp the sensitivity of the economy's major variables to the coefficients of the investment function. The sensitivity of the ICOR to x_1 and x_2 is outlined in Table 10.5.

Here the equivalent non-vintage formula for V provides an equally narrow range of values. Where $F = 1\frac{1}{3}$, the elasticity of V with respect to x_1 and x_2 is 0·22–0·30 where $1 > \sigma > \frac{1}{3}$ and $\frac{2}{3} > (B.S)/(A+B.S) > \frac{1}{3}$, and where $F = 1$ this elasticity will lie within the range 0·29–0·33.

Thus the vintage and non-vintage approaches to the problem agree on the astonishing result that the ICOR and the capital–output ratio are both highly insensitive to the coefficients of the investment function. These results can be contrasted with the basic neoclassical result that doubling the share of investment doubles both the capital–output ratio and the ICOR. With the present model, these will rise one-third or less with almost all values of the elasticity of substitution, etc.

Table 10.6

THE VINTAGE ELASTICITY OF X_p WITH RESPECT TO x_1 AND x_2

$$\left(\text{where } \tfrac{2}{3} > \frac{B.S}{A+B.S} > \tfrac{1}{3}; \ 1 > \theta > \tfrac{1}{3}; \ \text{and } F = 1\tfrac{1}{3} \ (\text{or } 1)\right)$$

		r/g		
X_p	1·5	2	3	4
0·25	−0·04−+0·08	−0·06−+0·10	−0·09−+0·13	−0·11−+0·15
	(−0·06−+0·10)	(−0·08−+0·12)	(−0·11−+0·16)	(−0·14−+0·17)
0·33	−0·06−+0·10	−0·09−+0·12	−0·12−+0·15	−0·16−+0·15
	(−0·09−+0·13)	(−0·11−+0·15)	(−0·16−+0·17)	(−0·21−+0·17)
0·40	−0·08−+0·11	−0·11−+0·13	−0·16−+0·15	−0·19−+0·14
	(−0·11−+0·14)	(−0·14−+0·16)	(−0·20−+0·17)	(−0·26−+0·16)
0·50	−0·12−+0·13	−0·15−+0·14	−0·22−+0·13	−0·30−+0·09
	(−0·15−+0·15)	(−0·19−+0·17)	(−0·28−+0·16)	(−0·37−+0·11)

Table 10.6 shows that the share of profits is almost wholly insensitive to the coefficients of the investment function. The insensitivity of the share of profits to x_1 and x_2 is even greater than that of the ICOR, and this time the non-vintage result is not similar to the vintage one. With equivalent non-vintage assumptions, the elasticity of the share of profits with respect to x_1 and x_2 is −0·44−0 where $F = 1\tfrac{1}{3}$, and −0·37−0 where $F = 1$. Thus vintage assumptions show that the share of profits will be particularly insensitive to the parameters of the investment function. The rate of profit is more sensitive to the parameters of the investment function than the share of profits and the ICOR, but Table 10.7 shows that the negative elasticity of r with respect to x_1 and x_2 will be less than 1.

With non-vintage assumptions, the equivalent values of the elasticity of r with respect to the coefficients of the investment function are $-0.30--0.67$ where $F = 1\frac{1}{2}$, and $-0.33--0.86$ where $F = 1$, so vintage assumptions also pin this elasticity into a narrower range of values. If X_p is 0.33, $r/g = 3$, and $F = 1\frac{1}{6}$ in a typical developed economy, then the elasticity of r with respect to the coefficients of the investment function will be $-0.50--0.75$, and an increase in investment of 50 per cent at each rate of interest and profit will

Table 10.7

THE VINTAGE ELASTICITY OF r WITH RESPECT TO x_1 AND x_2

$$\left(\text{where } \tfrac{2}{3} > \frac{B.S}{A+B.S} > \tfrac{1}{3}; \ 1 > \theta > \tfrac{1}{3}; \text{ and } F = 1\tfrac{1}{3} \text{ (or 1)} \right)$$

X_p	\multicolumn{4}{c}{r/g}			
	1·5	2	3	4
0·25	$-0.61--0.71$	$-0.58--0.70$	$-0.53--0.68$	$-0.48--0.66$
	$(-0.77--0.94)$	$(-0.72--0.90)$	$(-0.64--0.88)$	$(-0.58--0.85)$
0·33	$-0.57--0.70$	$-0.53--0.69$	$-0.47--0.66$	$-0.44--0.64$
	$(-0.71--0.91)$	$(-0.65--0.89)$	$(-0.56--0.85)$	$(-0.51--0.82)$
0·40	$-0.54--0.69$	$-0.50--0.68$	$-0.44--0.65$	$-0.41--0.63$
	$(-0.66--0.90)$	$(-0.60--0.87)$	$(-0.52--0.83)$	$(-0.47--0.80)$
0·50	$-0.49--0.68$	$-0.45--0.66$	$-0.40--0.63$	$-0.37--0.61$
	$(-0.59--0.87)$	$(-0.53--0.84)$	$(-0.46--0.80)$	$(-0.43--0.77)$

reduce the rate of profit by between one-sixth and one-quarter. This still shows rather less sensitivity than elementary neoclassical analysis, where an increase in S of one-half would reduce r by more than one-third if σ was less than 1.

It appears from the various tables that vintage economies with very different investment functions are likely to have very similar ICORs and very similar shares of profit. In addition, their shares of investment and rates of profit will differ much less than x_1 and x_2. Similar results were arrived at with CES assumptions with σ less than 1, though here there was rather greater variation in some of the major variables. What has emerged in this part of the argument is that the economy's major variables are rather insensitive to the parameters of the investment function. Whether they will be equally insensitive to the coefficients of the economy's investment opportunity function, i.e. to n and the coefficients of the technical progress function, remains to be seen. This question will be answered in the next section where the effects of a higher NN line will be analysed.

The Effect of the Investment Opportunity Function on S, r and g

An economy's opportunity for growth is governed by n, the rate of growth of its labour force, and A and B, the coefficients of its technical progress function, and it is the influence of these upon the equilibrium values of S, r and g that must be analysed. It will reduce the number of relationships that need to be analysed (without again significantly

Table 10.8

THE INFLUENCE OF THE INVESTMENT OPPORTUNITY FUNCTION
IN A COBB–DOUGLAS WORLD

Elasticity of	With respect to	
g	A, B and n	$\dfrac{F+E.F}{F+E}$
r	A, B and n	$\dfrac{1+E}{F+E}$
S	A, B and n	$\dfrac{(F-1)(1+E)}{F+E}$
V	A, B and n	$-\dfrac{1+E}{F+E}$
X_p	A, B and n	nil

reducing the information obtained) if it is assumed that A, B and n always vary between economies in the same proportion, so that $\partial A/A = \partial B/B = \partial n/n$.

The effects of different investment opportunity functions in a Cobb–Douglas world are outlined in Table 10.8. The first point to note here is that greater opportunities for growth will lead to a higher share of investment and a *more than proportional* increase in the equilibrium rate of growth, provided that F exceeds 1, i.e. provided that there is some sensitivity of investment to $(r-i)$. It is to be noted that the rate of growth must increase more than proportionately if S increases. This is because g (which equals $A+n+B.S$) will increase in proportion with A, n and B if S is constant, so if S increases, then g must increase more than proportionately. The reason why S must increase if investment is at all sensitive to $(r-i)$ is straightforward. The share of profits is always α with a Cobb–Douglas production function, and if the investment function was simply $k = x_1.r$, a fraction x_1 of net profits would always be invested so that S was always $\alpha.x_1$, and the elasticity of S with respect to A, B and n would then necessarily be zero. However, a higher A, B and n must raise r, and this is likely to raise $(r-i)$ more than proportionately, so it will raise investment if this depends on both r and $(r-i)$. There is thus a favourable counterpart to the 'squeeze' of $(r-i)$ that had an adverse effect on investment in the last section. Here, more favourable investment opportunities should raise $(r-i)$ more than proportionately, which will then raise the share of investment, and raise the growth rate by a greater proportion than the increase in A, B and n.

With Cobb–Douglas assumptions, stronger opportunities for growth will not raise the share of profits, but they will raise this with CES assumptions (and $\sigma<1$), and this will accentuate the extent to which more favourable investment opportunities raise the share of investment and the rate of growth. The influence of the investment opportunity function in a CES world is outlined in Table 10.9. It is evident from this table that greater investment opportunities will increase the share of investment (which will more than proportionately raise the rate of growth), provided that F exceeds σ, which means that the share of investment will increase unless σ is somewhat higher than has so far been supposed. If σ is 0.6, and four-tenths of growth is due to endogenously determined technical progress, and F is $1\frac{1}{6}$, then the elasticity of S with respect to the coefficients of the investment opportunity function will be $+0.60$, and the elasticity of the rate of growth with respect to these coefficients will be $+1.25$.

A very interesting result in Table 10.9 will be seen if this is compared with Table 10.2, which showed the influence of the investment function with CES assumptions. If these tables are compared, it will be seen that r, V and X_p each vary exactly $(1+E)$ times as much with respect to the coefficients of the investment opportunity function as they vary with respect to the coefficients of the investment function,

234 A MODEL OF EQUILIBRIUM GROWTH

The interesting point this brings out is that endogenous technical progress, which reduces the degree of variation in V, r and X_p that is due to differences in investment between economies, apparently increases the degree of variation that is due to differences in the technical opportunity for growth. The rather considerable potential for variation in A, B and n between economies, together with the greater sensitivity of r, V and X_p to these than to the coefficients of the investment function, suggest that the international variation of the

Table 10.9

THE INFLUENCE OF THE INVESTMENT OPPORTUNITY FUNCTION
IN A CES WORLD

Elasticity of	With respect to	
g	A, B and n	$\dfrac{F + E.F}{F + E.\sigma}$
r	A, B and n	$\dfrac{1 + E}{F + \sigma.E}$
S	A, B and n	$\dfrac{(F - \sigma).(1 + E)}{F + \sigma.E}$
V	A, B and n	$-\dfrac{\sigma + \sigma.E}{F + \sigma.E}$
X_p	A, B and n	$\dfrac{(1 - \sigma).(1 + E)}{F + \sigma.E}$

rate of profit, the capital–output ratio and the share of profits may be quite largely due to differences in the technical opportunity for growth. Then fast-growing economies can be expected to have higher rates of profit, higher shares of profit (provided that $\sigma < 1$) and rather lower capital–output ratios than slow-growing economies.

The variation in r, V and X_p that is to be expected as a result of different technical opportunities for growth is hardly likely to be negligible. Fast-growing economies appear to have potential growth rates which are rather more than twice those of slow-growing economies, so it is not unreasonable to suppose that some economies will have A's, B's and n's which are twice those of others. These will produce very different values of V, r and X_p unless their elasticities with respect to the coefficients of the investment opportunity function are very low, and they do not appear to be particularly low. If σ is 0·60, if four-tenths of growth is due to endogenously determined technical progress, and if F is $1\frac{1}{6}$, the elasticity of r with respect to A, B and n will be $+1·06$, while the elasticities of V and X_p with respect to these parameters will be $-0·64$ and $+0·43$ respectively. Then an economy with twice the technical opportunity coefficients of another would have (*cet. par.*) a share of profits which was about two-fifths higher, a rate of profit which was about *double* the other economy's, and a capital–output ratio which was about one-third lower. Incidentally, its rate of growth would be about two and a half times as high, for a discrepancy of $2:1$ in the values of A, B and n produces a discrepancy of about $2·5:1$ in the growth rate, so the two economies might have growth rates of 5 per cent and 2 per cent per annum. Most developed economies can be expected to come within this range, but there are exceptional economies which appear to have growth rates of the order of 8 to 10 per cent per annum. Such economies can be expected to have capital–output ratios which are very much lower than those of 'orthodox' economies, and shares of profit which are rather higher than the 25 to 40 per cent that otherwise appears to be normal. The post-Second World War Japanese share of profits of nearly 50 per cent which is indicated in Table 9.1 (p. 215 above) is particularly interesting in this context. Indeed, the general results of the model that the share of profits will vary with the rate of growth, and that the capital–output ratio will vary inversely with this, are very much in line with the evidence of Table 9.1.

It is very much a prediction of the model that the rate of profit will also vary strongly with A, B and n. The suggested elasticity of the rate of profit with respect to A, B and n, $+1·06$, is very high indeed, and the result that fast-growing economies can be expected (*cet. par.*) to have much higher rates of profit than slow-growing economies is an inevitable consequence of the investment function that has been assumed. If it was assumed that investment decisions were entirely independent of $(r-i)$, i.e. if it was assumed that $k = x_1 . r$ alone, then r could be expected to vary in proportion with g. With the assumption that investment depends partly on $(r-i)$, the elasticity of r with respect to g becomes $+1/F$ (from (10.21)), which is $+\frac{6}{7}$ if F is $1\frac{1}{6}$, and it will be $+\frac{2}{3}$ even if F is $1\frac{1}{2}$, which is the top of the range of possible values for F that has been suggested. Then doubling the rate of growth must apparently raise the rate of profit by a factor of at least two-thirds. This means that a strong positive association between the rate of profit and the rate of growth is an inescapable prediction of the model. The net rate of return on capital is exceedingly hard to measure, but it would certainly contradict one of the fundamental features of the model if it turned out that fast-growing economies like West Germany, Italy and Japan earned net rates of return on capital which were not significantly higher than those earned in the U.K. and the U.S.A. Table 9.1 suggests that since 1955 fast-growing economies have had higher shares of profit, i.e. higher P/Y's, and lower capital–output ratios, i.e. lower K/Y's than the U.K. and the U.S.A., so it is to be expected that statistical studies on the net rate of return (P/K) will show that they earn higher net rates of return on capital as the model predicts, for $P/K \equiv (P/Y).(Y/K)$.

Clearly, the model could make no attempt to explain a constant and internationally uniform capital–output ratio, a constant rate of profit, or a constant share of profits. On the contrary, the prediction that the rate of profit will vary with the opportunity for growth is a strong one. The predictions that the capital–output ratio will vary inversely with the opportunity for growth, and that the share of profits will vary positively with this, are nearly as strong. Then none of the 'great historical constancies' can be rescued, but the model is well in line with the stylised facts of Table 9.1.

This is perhaps all that can be said about the effects of the investment opportunity function with non-vintage CES assumptions. It is now time to turn to vintage assumptions. The effect of a stronger investment opportunity function with vintage assumptions is worked out in the concluding section of the chapter, and the elasticities of S, g and r with respect to A and B are outlined there in (10.24), (10.25) and (10.26). These produce results which are very similar to those produced by the CES equations. It was shown in Table 10.9 that with CES assumptions stronger investment opportunity will increase the share of investment where F exceeds σ, and this can be written as, $1+(F-1)>\sigma$. With vintage assumptions, the equivalent proposition (from (10.24)) is that stronger investment opportunity will increase the share of investment where

$$1+\left(\frac{F-1}{F}\right).H>\theta.$$

The similarity of the two propositions is obvious, and in both cases the elasticity of substitution can exceed 1 to the extent that F exceeds 1, if stronger investment opportunity is to be associated with a higher share of investment. The two propositions will be identical if $H = 1/F$. In fact H can be greater or less than $1/F$, it takes the form,

$$\frac{r.T}{3}\left[e^{\frac{T}{6}(r-3\frac{1}{2}g)} + \tfrac{1}{2}\theta\left(1 + \frac{T}{6}(r+g)...\right)\right]$$

so there is no presumption that greater investment opportunity will raise investment less or more with vintage than with non-vintage assumptions. Whether a higher A and B increase the rate of growth less or more than proportionately will depend on whether they increase the share of investment, so this too will depend on whether

$$1 + \left(\frac{F-1}{F}\right).H > \theta \text{ (from (10.25).)}$$

Then provided that θ does not exceed 1 quite markedly, stronger investment opportunity can be expected to increase the share of investment, and raise the rate of growth more than proportionately.

It appears that the vintage effects of the investment opportunity function may be rather similar to the non-vintage ones, but the vintage expressions in the concluding section are very much more mathematically complex than the equivalent non-vintage CES expressions in Table 10.9. It may be questioned whether much will be gained by obtaining usable approximations for them. The investment function produced very different results with vintage and non-vintage assumptions, and it was evident in Chapter 7 that the equations for the elasticity of r with respect to S were very different for the two cases. It was therefore essential to obtain *usable* vintage expressions for the various elasticities. With the investment opportunity function, vintage assumptions do not obviously produce results which are radically different from those produced by non-vintage ones. This was suggested as early as Chapter 3, where it turned out that the critical elasticity of substitution where faster technical progress raised the share of profits was 1 with both vintage and non-vintage assumptions. It has now been seen that whether greater investment opportunity increases the share of investment and raises the rate of growth more than proportionately will depend on the same basic factors with vintage and non-vintage assumptions. Then, in this analysis of the investment opportunity function, it may be possible to regard the much simpler non-vintage equations as surrogates for the vintage equations. This may not make very much difference.

The conclusion of this section is, then, that the effects of greater investment opportunity on the share of investment and the rate of growth will depend very much on the value of σ (or θ). Unless these exceed 1 quite significantly, greater investment opportunity will increase the share of investment, and raise the rate of growth more than proportionately. One of the great questions of economics that this result bears on is the effect of faster population growth on the rate of growth of the standard of living. Unless σ exceeds F, faster population growth will increase the equilibrium rate of growth more than proportionately, with the result that it will be associated with a faster rate of increase of output per worker.[1] Whether the 'standard of living' will then increase more rapidly will also depend on the effect of faster population growth on various amenities which have not been taken into account in the analysis of this book, but material production per head should certainly increase more rapidly, which will influence the rate of growth of the standard of living. This result may have some bearing on the relative growth rates of the U.K. and the U.S.A. in the past century, particularly when the further effect of growth in the labour force on research and development activity is taken into account.[2]

It appears that stronger opportunities for growth will also be associated with a markedly higher rate of profit, a higher share of profits, and a lower capital–output ratio. Observed international variation in r, V and X_p may well be associated with differences in the opportunity for growth, for it is to be expected that this will vary greatly between economies, and the capital–output ratio, the rate of profit and the share of profits will each be more sensitive to differences in the investment opportunity function than to differences in the investment function.[3] The likelihood of international uniformity in V, r or X_p is remote in view of the very different investment opportunities of different economies.

The Implications of the Results

The effects of the investment function and the investment opportunity function on the equilibrium values of S, r and g have now been

[1] Cf. Eltis, 'Investment, technical progress, and economic growth', p. 39, n. 2.
[2] See pp. 142-4 above.
[3] This is especially the case with the share of profits, which is almost wholly insensitive to the coefficients of the investment function in Table 10.6, one of the vintage tables.

analysed, so an attempt can be made to answer the questions that were raised at the start of the chapter.

The first question related to the sensitivity of the share of investment and the rate of growth to the parameters of the investment function. The rather surprising answer to this question appears to be that the elasticity of S with respect to x_1 and x_2 may well be rather less than unity. This is particularly likely to be the case with vintage assumptions, where attempts to invest more may well have a drastic adverse effect on the net rate of return on capital because the rate of depreciation may vary strongly with investment, and the aggregate increase in investment will not then be great. This means that attempts to invest more may reduce the rate of profit much more than they increase investment and the rate of growth. With non-vintage assumptions, the elasticity of S with respect to x_1 and x_2 will be reduced below 1 by both a σ of less than 1, and by any sensitivity of investment to the excess of the rate of profit over the rate of interest. Then the answer to the first question is that an increase in the amount that entrepreneurs are prepared to invest at each rate of profit and interest is likely to result in a rather smaller, perhaps a much smaller, eventual proportional increase in the economy's share of investment.

The second question related to the effect of an economy's investment opportunity function on its equilibrium share of investment. In other words, are greater opportunities for growth, i.e. higher values of A, B and n, likely to lead to a higher share of investment and a more than proportionately higher rate of growth? It appears that with non-vintage assumptions greater opportunities for growth will increase the share of investment where σ is less than F, and with vintage assumptions the share of investment will be raised, provided that θ is less than

$$1 + \left(\frac{F-1}{F}\right).H.$$

Thus, in each case, the expected result that greater investment opportunity will increase the share of investment is arrived at unless the relevant elasticity of substitution between labour and capital is rather high. The value of the elasticity of substitution between labour and capital will then have considerable bearing on whether greater opportunities for growth will increase or reduce the share of investment.

The third question that was raised at the start of the chapter related to the possible stability of the equilibrium values of the capital–output ratio, the share of profits and the rate of profit. The argument of this chapter suggests that these will be more sensitive to the coefficients of the investment opportunity function than to the coefficients of the investment function. The investment opportunity function will vary greatly between economies, and this means that it is to be expected that the rate of profit, the capital–output ratio and the share of profits will show quite considerable variation.

A major weakness in the argument has been that the results have rested on the assumptions of perfect competition in factor and product markets, and constant returns to scale. These weaknesses must be removed, and some of the effects on the argument of imperfect competition and increasing returns will be brought out in Chapters 11 and 13.

Much econometric work on national statistics rests on theoretical foundations which include the assumption of perfect competition and constant returns to scale. The weaknesses due to this may not much influence the quality of the results. This surprises many, but one of Milton Friedman's less controversial examples is very much to the point. He reminds us that the well-known proposition that a body which falls through the earth's atmosphere will accelerate at 32 ft per second[2] is based on the assumption that it falls through a vacuum. The proposition nevertheless predicts the acceleration of a hard ball (but not a feather) accurately.[1] All *testable* economic propositions necessarily rest on unreal assumptions, for, as Lewis Carroll's Sylvie and Bruno discovered, a map with a scale of a mile to a mile is no help at all. The quality of a theory depends on how well it can pass the tests of explanation and prediction.

There is much in the theory that has been outlined in this chapter that is testable. Clearly, the basic predictions like the one that fast-growing economies will have higher rates of profit, higher shares of profit, and lower capital–output ratios than slow-growing economies are likely to test well, for they are in line with what Kaldor has called 'the stylised facts'. It would be interesting to see whether the predictions can pass the test of more rigorous scrutiny than this.

The results of Part II of this book have, of course, rested on the assumption of steady growth. This is virtually inevitable in analysis

---

[1] Milton Friedman, *Essays in Positive Economics* (Chicago U.P., 1953) p. 16.

which makes use of simultaneous equations to determine the values of the economy's major variables, but more is clearly necessary before the results of a model can be confidently set against the growth of actual economies. The steady growth analysis of Part II of this book may be regarded as a starting-point for further analysis. Part III will be concerned with problems in disequilibrium growth, and it will turn out that the steady growth analysis of Part II will play an important role in this more general analysis of the growth process.

*The Solution of the Equations

The results of this chapter have depended on the solution of a system of equations that were arrived at in earlier chapters. These equations need to be analysed with Cobb–Douglas, CES and vintage assumptions. As the results of Cobb–Douglas assumptions are always the same as CES results with $\sigma = 1$, it will suffice if the equations are solved with CES and vintage assumptions, and the CES solutions will be found first.

An attempt will be made first to find straightforward expressions for the variables in terms of parameters alone. The investment and the investment opportunity functions of Chapter 9 provide two equations in terms of r and g alone, so it should be possible to use (9.1),

$$r = \frac{S_f . r^*}{S_c + S_f} + g\left(\frac{1}{S_c + S_f}\right),$$

and (9.6),

$$r = J\left[B\left(1 + \left(\frac{A+n}{g}\right) + \left(\frac{A+n}{g}\right)^2 ...\right)\right]^{\frac{1}{\sigma}}$$

to obtain an expression for g in terms of parameters alone. The following equation is obtained when r is eliminated from these two equations:

$$g + S_f . r^* = (S_f + S_c) . J . \left[B\left(1 + \left(\frac{A+n}{g}\right) + \left(\frac{A+n}{g}\right)^2 ...\right)\right]^{\frac{1}{\sigma}}. \quad (10.1)$$

This is an equation for g which is solely in terms of g and the various parameters, but it does not provide the possibility of obtaining a simple proposition for g. There is clearly only one solution for g, since a higher g raises the left-hand side and reduces the right-hand side, but it cannot be conveniently expressed. There will equally be no convenient expression for r and S. This means that the desired information must be obtained in the form of elasticities of the variables with respect to various parameters. The model is one where, with non-vintage assumptions, four general equations, (9.8), (9.9), (9.10) and (9.11), are used to determine the equilibrium values of the four variables, g, r, S and i. If these are differentiated with respect to any one parameter, for instance x_1, then four equations which are linear in terms of the elasticities of g, r, S and i will be obtained, and these can be solved straightforwardly. The argument of the book has provided precise non-vintage equations for (9.8), (9.9) and (9.10) from (9.2), (7.1) and (2.7), namely:

$$g = x_1 . r + x_2 . (r - i) \qquad (10.2)$$

$$g = A + n + B . S \qquad (10.3)$$

$$r = J . \left(\frac{S}{g}\right)^{-\frac{1}{\sigma}}. \qquad (10.4)$$

However, a precise form for the rate of interest equation, (9.11), has not been suggested. Rather than to select one arbitrarily, it will be best to write the elasticity of the rate of interest with respect to a parameter, for instance x_1, not as $(x_1/i) . (\partial i / \partial x_1)$, but as $(x_1/r) . (\partial r / \partial x_1)$ times $(r/i) . (di/dr)$, and to include $(r/i) . (di/dr)$, the elasticity of the rate of interest with respect to the rate of profit, in the solutions.[1] The differentiation of the three equations, (10.2), (10.3) and (10.4), with respect to, for instance, x_1 will then produce three equations which are linear in terms of *four* elasticities, those of g, r and S with respect to x_1, and the elasticity of i with respect to r. These can be solved to find the equilibrium values of the elasticities of g, r and S with respect to x_1, and the solutions will include the fourth elasticity, $(r/i) . (di/dr)$. An algebraic form for this could be found if precise form were given to (9.11), but the view is being taken that it will be more useful to allow for a general relationship between r and i in the solutions.

The elasticities of g, r and S with respect to x_1 and x_2, the parameters of the investment function, will be found first. The elasticities of the variables with respect to x_1 and x_2 could be found separately, but this would unnecessarily double the number of elasticities that need to be found. To avoid this, it will be assumed that x_1 and x_2

---

[1] $(r/i) . (di/dr)$ is a complete differential and not a partial differential because i is solely a function of r and parameters which otherwise play no part in the model (from (9.11)).

differ between the two economies in the same proportion so that $\partial x_1/x_1 = \partial x_2/x_2$, and the elasticity of g with respect to x_1 will then always equal the elasticity of g with respect to x_2, etc.

Differentiate (10.2), (10.3) and (10.4) with respect to x_1, substituting x_2/x_1 for $\partial x_2/\partial x_1$, and differentiating A, B, n, σ and J as constants:

$$\frac{x_1}{g}\cdot\frac{\partial g}{\partial x_1} = 1 + \left[1 + \frac{i\cdot x_2}{g}\cdot\left(1 - \frac{r}{i}\cdot\frac{di}{dr}\right)\right]\cdot\frac{x_1}{r}\cdot\frac{\partial r}{\partial x_1} \qquad (10.5)$$

$$\frac{x_1}{g}\cdot\frac{\partial g}{\partial x_1} = \left(\frac{B.S}{A+n+B.S}\right)\cdot\frac{x_1}{S}\cdot\frac{\partial S}{\partial x_1} \qquad (10.6)$$

$$\sigma\cdot\left(\frac{x_1}{r}\cdot\frac{\partial r}{\partial x_1}\right) = \frac{x_1}{g}\cdot\frac{\partial g}{\partial x_1} - \frac{x_1}{S}\cdot\frac{\partial S}{\partial x_1}. \qquad (10.7)$$

(10.5), (10.6) and (10.7) provide three linear equations to determine $(x_1/g).(\partial g/\partial x_1)$, $(x_1/r).(\partial r/\partial x_1)$ and $(x_1/S).(\partial S/\partial x_1)$, the elasticities of g, r and S with respect to x_1. The solutions are given in Table 10.2 with E substituted for $(B.S)/(A+n)$ and F substituted for

$$\left[1 + \frac{i\cdot x_2}{g}\left(1 - \frac{r}{i}\cdot\frac{di}{dr}\right)\right].$$

Since $V = S/g$, the elasticity of V with respect to x_1 will always be the elasticity of S with respect to x_1 *minus* the elasticity of g with respect to x_1. Similarly, since $X_p \equiv r.V = (r.S)/g$, the elasticity of X_p with respect to x_1 will be the elasticity of r with respect to x_1 *plus* the elasticity of S with respect to x_1, *minus* the elasticity of g with respect to x_1. This means that the elasticities of V and X_p with respect to x_1 can be derived from the solutions to (10.5), (10.6) and (10.7), and these are given in Table 10.2.

To obtain the elasticities of g, r and S with respect to the parameters of the investment opportunity function, it is assumed that A, B and n differ between economies in the same proportion. (10.2), (10.3) and (10.4) are then differentiated with respect to A, B/A being substituted for $\partial B/\partial A$, and n/A for $\partial n/\partial A$, while x_1, x_2, σ and J are differentiated as constants:

$$\frac{A}{g}\cdot\frac{\partial g}{\partial A} = \left[1 + \frac{i\cdot x_2}{g}\left(1 - \frac{r}{i}\cdot\frac{di}{dr}\right)\right]\cdot\frac{A}{r}\cdot\frac{\partial r}{\partial A} \qquad (10.8)$$

$$\frac{A}{g}\cdot\frac{\partial g}{\partial A} = 1 + \left(\frac{B.S}{A+n+B.S}\right)\cdot\frac{A}{S}\cdot\frac{\partial S}{\partial A} \qquad (10.9)$$

$$\sigma \cdot \left(\frac{A}{r} \cdot \frac{\partial r}{\partial A} \right) = \frac{A}{g} \cdot \frac{\partial g}{\partial A} - \frac{A}{S} \cdot \frac{\partial S}{\partial A}. \tag{10.10}$$

(10.8), (10.9) and (10.10) are solved to give the elasticities of g, r and S with respect to A. The elasticities of V and X_p with respect to A can be derived from these and the solutions are outlined in Table 10.9.

The elasticities of r, g and S with respect to the parameters must now be found with vintage assumptions. These add two further variables, C and T, to the model, so six variables, r, g, S, i, C and T, need to be determined, and six equations are needed for this. (10.2) and (10.3) hold with both non-vintage and vintage assumptions, and (9.11) can be used to deal with the relationship between r and i in the same way as with non-vintage assumptions, and this means that three further specifically vintage equations are needed. These are provided by the general vintage equations, (3.8), (3.9) and (3.10), and the precise form of these that was found in Chapter 3 is as follows (from (3.14), (3.23) and (3.35), with g substituted for a since $n = 0$):

$$S = \frac{g \cdot C}{1 - e^{-gT}} \tag{10.11}$$

$$C = \tfrac{1}{2} \cdot g \cdot T^2 \left(1 - \frac{T}{3}(r+g) + \frac{T^2}{12}(r^2 + rg + g^2) \right.$$

$$\left. - \frac{T^3}{60}(r^3 + r^2 g + rg^2 + g^3) + \frac{T^4}{360}(r^4 + r^3 g + r^2 g^2 + rg^3 + g^4) \ldots \right) \tag{10.12}$$

$$\left(\frac{1}{h \cdot \lambda} \right) \cdot C^{\frac{1}{\theta}} = T \left(1 - \frac{rT}{2} + \frac{r^2 T^2}{6} - \frac{r^3 T^3}{24} + \frac{r^4 T^4}{120} - \frac{r^5 T^5}{720} \ldots \right). \tag{10.13}$$

(10.2), (10.3), (10.11), (10.12) and (10.13) provide sufficient equations to determine the elasticities of r, g, S, C and T with respect to the parameters, the solutions containing terms in the elasticity of i with respect to r. The elasticities of g, r and S with respect to the parameters of the investment function will be found first, and it will be assumed that $\partial x_1/x_1 = \partial x_2/x_2$. The simplest approach to the solution of the vintage equations is to make use of the results of Chapter 7 which were based on four of the five equations, i.e. (10.3), (10.11), (10.12) and (10.13). The fact that (10.11) and (10.12) contain terms in g instead of a does not affect the usefulness of the results of Chapter 7, as a was differentiated as a variable throughout the chapter, and $a = g$ where $n = 0$.

The equation that was not taken into account in Chapter 7 is (10.2), and this provides the link between the elasticities of the variables with respect to S arrived at in Chapter 7, and the elasticities with respect to x_1 and x_2 that are now needed. Thus, differentiate (10.2) with respect to S, differentiating x_1 and x_2 as variables:

$$\frac{x_1}{S} \cdot \frac{\partial S}{\partial x_1} = \frac{1}{\dfrac{S}{g} \cdot \dfrac{\partial g}{\partial S} - \left[1 + \dfrac{i \cdot x_2}{g} \cdot \left(1 - \dfrac{r}{i} \cdot \dfrac{di}{dr}\right)\right] \cdot \dfrac{S}{r} \cdot \dfrac{\partial r}{\partial S}}. \tag{10.14}$$

Now

$$\frac{S}{g} \cdot \frac{\partial g}{\partial S} = \frac{B \cdot S}{A + B \cdot S}$$

where $n = 0$ (from (10.3)), and

$$\left[1 + \frac{i \cdot x_2}{g}\left(1 - \frac{r}{i} \cdot \frac{di}{dr}\right)\right] = F,$$

so that (10.14) can be written as:

$$\frac{x_1}{S} \cdot \frac{\partial S}{\partial x_1} = \frac{1}{\left(\dfrac{B \cdot S}{A + B \cdot S}\right) - F \cdot \left(\dfrac{S}{r} \cdot \dfrac{\partial r}{\partial S}\right)}. \tag{10.15}$$

Now various values of $(S/r) \cdot (\partial r/\partial S)$ with the present vintage assumptions were outlined in Table 7.2, and a similar table outlining various values of $(x_1/S) \cdot (\partial S/\partial x_1)$ can be derived very simply from this with the help of (10.15). This is done in Table 10.4. Moreover, all but one of the other important elasticities can be derived from (10.15). Thus, from (10.15) and (10.6), which holds with vintage assumptions:

$$\frac{x_1}{g} \cdot \frac{\partial g}{\partial x_1} = \frac{1}{1 - F \cdot \left(\dfrac{A + B \cdot S}{B \cdot S}\right) \cdot \left(\dfrac{S}{r} \cdot \dfrac{\partial r}{\partial S}\right)}. \tag{10.16}$$

And from (10.16) and (10.5):

$$\frac{x_1}{r} \cdot \frac{\partial r}{\partial x_1} = -\frac{1}{F - \left(\dfrac{B \cdot S}{A + B \cdot S}\right) \cdot \left(\dfrac{r}{S} \cdot \dfrac{\partial S}{\partial r}\right)}. \tag{10.17}$$

I

And since the ICOR equals S/g, then from (10.15) and (10.16):

$$\frac{x_1}{\text{ICOR}} \cdot \frac{\partial(\text{ICOR})}{\partial x_1} = \frac{1}{\left(\dfrac{B.S}{A}\right) - F \cdot \left(\dfrac{A+B.S}{A}\right) \cdot \left(\dfrac{S}{r} \cdot \dfrac{\partial r}{\partial S}\right)}. \quad (10.18)$$

Tables 10.3, 10.5 and 10.7 are derived quite straightforwardly from Table 7.2 and these equations.

The derivation of the elasticity of X_p with respect to x_1 and x_2 presents slightly more difficult problems, but this can be found with the help of the following equation (from (3.20) with g substituted for a):

$$\frac{x_1}{X_p} \cdot \frac{\partial X_p}{\partial x_1} = \left(\frac{x_1}{T} \cdot \frac{\partial T}{\partial x_1} + \frac{x_1}{g} \cdot \frac{\partial g}{\partial x_1}\right) \cdot \left(1 - \frac{g.T}{6} - \frac{g^2 T^2}{36} + \frac{g^3 T^3}{270} \ldots\right). \quad (10.19)$$

$(x_1/g).(\partial g/\partial x_1)$ has been found above, but $(x_1/T).(\partial T/\partial x_1)$ has not yet been found. This can be derived from the differentials of (10.11), (10.12) and (10.13) with respect to x_1, (10.15) and (10.16) being used to substitute for $(x_1/S).(\partial S/\partial x_1)$ and $(x_1/g).(\partial g/\partial x_1)$. Then:

$$\frac{x_1}{T} \cdot \frac{\partial T}{\partial x_1} =$$

$$-\frac{\left(\dfrac{A}{A+B.S}\right).U + \left(\dfrac{B.S}{A+B.S}\right)\left(\frac{3}{4} - \dfrac{gT}{32} + \dfrac{T^2}{240}(r^2 - rg - \frac{3}{16}g^2)\ldots + UX_w\right)}{(1 + U.X_w) \cdot \left(\left(\dfrac{B.S}{A+B.S}\right) - F \cdot \left(\dfrac{S}{r} \cdot \dfrac{\partial r}{\partial S}\right)\right)}. \quad (10.20)$$

Then, from (10.19), (10.20) and (10.16):

$$\frac{x_1}{X_p} \cdot \frac{\partial X_p}{\partial x_1} =$$

$$-\frac{\left(\dfrac{A}{A+B.S}\right).U - \left(\dfrac{B.S}{A+B.S}\right)\left(\frac{1}{4} + \dfrac{gT}{32} - \dfrac{T^2}{240}(r^2 - rg - \frac{3}{16}g^2)\ldots\right)}{\left(\dfrac{1 + U.X_w}{1 - \dfrac{gT}{6} - \dfrac{g^2 T^2}{36} + \dfrac{g^3 T^3}{270} \ldots}\right) \cdot \left(\left(\dfrac{B.S}{A+B.S}\right) - F \cdot \left(\dfrac{S}{r} \cdot \dfrac{\partial r}{\partial S}\right)\right)}. \quad (10.21)$$

Then, using (3.45), the elasticity of X_p with respect to x_1 will be:

$$-\frac{\frac{5}{21}+\dfrac{g.T}{11}+\dfrac{r^2T^2}{170}+\dfrac{rgT^2}{232}+\dfrac{g^2T^2}{310}\ldots}{\frac{1}{3}-F.\left(\dfrac{S}{r}.\dfrac{\partial r}{\partial S}\right)}$$

where $\theta=\frac{1}{3}$ and $(B.S)/(A+B.S)=\frac{1}{3}$, and it will be

$$+\frac{\frac{1}{3}-\dfrac{gT}{18}-\dfrac{r^2T^2}{135}+\dfrac{rgT^2}{135}-\dfrac{g^2T^2}{180}\ldots}{\frac{2}{3}-F.\left(\dfrac{S}{r}.\dfrac{\partial r}{\partial S}\right)}$$

where $\theta=1$ and $(B.S)/(A+B.S)=\frac{2}{3}$. Table 10·6 is calculated from Table 7.2 and these formulae.

The starting-point for the derivation of the elasticities of g, r and S with respect to A and B (where these vary between economies in the same proportion) is (3·53A) with g substituted for a. This is again based on four of the five equations that now need to be solved, and when the fifth, (10.2), is differentiated with respect to g (x_1 and x_2 now being differentiated as constants)

$$\frac{g}{r}.\frac{\partial r}{\partial g}=\frac{a}{r}.\frac{\partial r}{\partial a}=\frac{1}{1+\dfrac{x_2.i}{g}\left(1-\dfrac{r}{i}.\dfrac{di}{dr}\right)}=\frac{1}{F}. \qquad (10.22)$$

Where (10.3) is differentiated with respect to S (with $n=0$, and $(B/A).(dA/dS)$ substituted for dB/dS):

$$\frac{g}{S}.\frac{dS}{dg}=\frac{a}{S}.\frac{dS}{da}=\frac{1}{\left(\dfrac{B.S}{A+B.S}\right)+\dfrac{S}{A}.\dfrac{dA}{dS}}. \qquad (10.23)$$

(10.22) and (10.23) can be used to substitute for $(a/r).(\partial r/\partial a)$ and $(a/S).(\partial S/\partial a)$ in (3.53A) to produce the following equation for $(A/S).(\partial S/\partial A)$:

$$\frac{A}{S}.\frac{\partial S}{\partial A}=\frac{1-\theta+\left(\dfrac{F-1}{F}\right).H}{H_1-\left(\dfrac{B.S}{A+B.S}\right).\left[1-\theta+\left(\dfrac{F-1}{F}\right).H\right]} \qquad (10.24)$$

where

$$H = \frac{r.T}{3}\left[1 + \frac{T}{6}(r-3\tfrac{1}{2}g) + \frac{T^2}{90}(r^2 - 8\tfrac{1}{2}rg + 14\tfrac{1}{2}g^2)\ldots\right.$$
$$\left. + \theta\left(\tfrac{1}{2} + \frac{T}{12}(r+g) - \frac{T^2}{90}(r^2 + 2\tfrac{3}{4}rg + 3\tfrac{1}{4}g^2)\ldots\right)\right]$$
$$\simeq \frac{r.T}{3}\left(e^{\frac{T}{6}(r-3\frac{1}{2}g)} + \tfrac{1}{2}\theta\left[1 + \frac{T}{6}(r+g)\ldots\right]\right]$$

$$H_1 = 2 + \frac{T}{3}(r-2g) + \frac{T^2}{18}(r^2 - 4rg + 4g^2)\ldots$$
$$- \theta\left(1 - \frac{T}{6}(r+g) - \frac{T^2}{36}(r^2 - rg - 2g^2)\ldots\right)$$

It will be noted that the denominator of (10.24),

$$H_1 - \left(\frac{B.S}{A+B.S}\right)\left[1 - \theta + \left(\frac{F-1}{F}\right).H\right],$$

must be positive even if $(B.S)/(A+B.S) = 1$ and $F = 1\tfrac{1}{2}$, for this can then be written as:

$$1 + \tfrac{2}{9}T(r-3g) + \frac{T^2}{27}(r^2 - 4\tfrac{1}{4}rg + 6g^2)\ldots$$
$$+ \frac{\theta}{9}\left(T(r+\tfrac{3}{2}g) + \frac{T^2}{6}(r^2 - 2rg - 3g^2)\ldots\right.$$

and this means that the sign of (10.24) will simply depend on the sign of its numerator. Then, from (10.24) and (10.9) (which also holds with vintage assumptions)

$$\frac{A}{g}\cdot\frac{\partial g}{\partial A} = 1 + \frac{1 - \theta + \left(\dfrac{F-1}{F}\right).H}{\left(\dfrac{A+B.S}{B.S}\right).H_1 - 1 + \theta - \left(\dfrac{F-1}{F}\right).H}. \quad (10.25)$$

And from (10.25) and (10.8):

$$\frac{A}{r}\cdot\frac{\partial r}{\partial A} = \frac{1}{F} + \frac{1 - \theta + \left(\dfrac{F-1}{F}\right).H}{F\left(\dfrac{A+B.S}{B.S}\right).H_1 - F(1-\theta) - (F-1).H}. \quad (10.26)$$

A number of results can be derived from (10.24), (10.25) and (10.26), and the most important of these depend on the sign of (10.24).

PART III

Disequilibrium Growth

Part II

11

Economies of Scale and Growth

THE analysis of Part II of this book was largely confined to steady growth comparisons, and economies with different investment functions and different investment opportunity functions were compared to see how these would influence the equilibrium values of the major economic variables. However, because growth had to be 'steady', certain factors which play an important role in the growth and development of economies were neglected.

It is likely that increasing returns to scale play a considerable part in the growth process. Adam Smith and Allyn Young,[1] and more recently Hicks[2] and Kaldor,[3] have argued that this is so. There is much empirical evidence for increasing returns to scale in industry,[4] and there is moreover much macro- and microeconomic evidence in favour of Verdoorn's law which states that there is a strong interconnection between the rate of growth of productivity and the rate of growth of output, and this *may* be explained by increasing returns to scale.[5] However, as will be shown below, increasing returns are only compatible with steady growth where highly restrictive assumptions are made, and this is perhaps the main reason why growth models which allow for increasing returns to scale have not yet been fully worked out.

---

[1] Allyn Young, 'Increasing returns and economic progress', *Economic Journal*, vol. XXXVIII (Dec 1928).

[2] Hicks, 'Thoughts on the theory of capital – the Corfu Conference'.

[3] N. Kaldor, *Causes of the Slow Rate of Growth of the United Kingdom*, Inaugural Lecture (Cambridge U.P., 1966).

[4] See, for instance, Wiles, *Price, Cost and Output*, 2nd ed. appendix to chap. 12, and Walters, 'Production and cost functions', for a summary of the evidence.

[5] See, for instance, P. J. Verdoorn, 'Fattori che regolano lo svillupo della produttività del lavoro', *L'Industria* (1947); Kaldor, *Causes of the Slow Rate of Growth of the U.K.*; W. Beckerman and Associates, *The British Economy in 1975* (Cambridge U.P., 1965) chap. vii; and Kieran A. Kennedy, *Productivity and Industrial Growth: The Irish Experience* (Oxford U.P., 1971) chaps. 4, 6 and 7.

Another problem which was neglected in the 'steady growth' argument of Part II was the determination of the level of output in the short period and the relationship of this to steady growth paths. The relationship between Keynesian macroeconomic theory and the theory of equilibrium growth outlined in Part II clearly needs to be shown.

Once economies of scale (and, in consequence, imperfect competition also) have been brought into the argument, and Keynesian macroeconomic theory as well, it will be possible to discuss the theory of income distribution much more realistically than in Part II. There perfect competition, constant returns to scale, and equilibrium in factor and product markets were assumed throughout, with the result that marginal products were the sole determinant of factor returns. In the real world, income distribution will also depend on the market power of labour and capital and, as was shown in Chapter 4, the various Keynesian income flows, and the theory of income distribution must take these into account as well as the marginal products of the various factors.

In the next three chapters, an attempt will be made to deal with these problems. This chapter is concerned with the influence of increasing returns to scale on growth; Chapter 12 is concerned with the relationship between actual income levels and steady growth paths; and Chapter 13 is concerned with the problem of income distribution. A final chapter is concerned with some of the policy implications of the argument.

One major problem must be discussed before the effects of increasing returns to scale can be analysed. It is shown by Euler's theorem that the payment of its marginal product to each factor of production just exhausts total output where returns to scale are constant. With an increasing returns factor of z (so that a Q times increase in the quantity of each factor of production increases total output $Q.z$ times), it would require z times total output to pay each factor its marginal product, so all factors cannot receive their marginal products.[1] There must be imperfect competition causing at least one factor to receive less. If no factor can receive more than its marginal product, but factors can receive less, there will be a range of possible income distributions. If z is 1·25, and in order to receive its marginal product labour must receive 0·75 times total output, while capital must receive 0·50 times total output, the share of wages could be as

[1] See pp. 5-6 above.

high as 0·75 or as low as 0·50. The share of profits could be as high as 0·50 or as low as 0·25. Whether labour receives three-quarters of the National Product and capital one-quarter, or labour one-half and capital one-half, will depend on the relative bargaining power of labour and capital, the exact nature of various market imperfections, and Keynesian income flows.

This raises serious problems for growth theory, for the rate of profit and the share of profits can only be known when it is known how the 25 per cent of the National Income which might go to labour or capital (50 per cent if z is 1·50) will be allocated between them, and this will depend on a number of considerations some of which fall outside the usual boundaries of growth theory. The difficulties raised by this are among those that have prevented the evolution of fully developed growth models which allow for increasing returns to scale.

The problems raised by increasing returns can be divided into two parts. First there is the problem of what fraction of its marginal product each factor will receive, and second there is the problem of how increasing returns will then influence the growth rate, and the values of other major variables. In this book, the problem of income distribution will be analysed in Chapter 13, and the analysis of this chapter will be confined to the second of the two problems, namely how increasing returns to scale will influence the values of the major variables if the proportion of its marginal product that each factor receives is known.

It will then be assumed that the wage is p_1 times the marginal product of labour, and the rate of profit p_2 times the marginal product of capital. The factors influencing p_1 and p_2 will be discussed in Chapter 13. So far as the results arrived at in this chapter are concerned, p_1 and p_2 may depend on the relative bargaining power of factors, imperfections in competition, or Keynesian income flows, and what is necessary for the results that follow is merely that there should be some stability in p_1 and p_2. Clearly, there are some necessary restrictions on the values of p_1 and p_2. Since aggregate marginal products must amount to z times the income available for distribution, each factor could receive $1/z$ times its marginal product, i.e. p_1 and p_2 could both equal $1/z$, or if p_1 exceeds $1/z$, p_2 will be less than this, and vice versa.

The effects of increasing returns to scale on the rate of economic growth and the other major variables will now be analysed. The

I*

effects of economies of scale will first be analysed for the simple case of a Cobb–Douglas economy where, it will turn out, steady growth is a possibility, so the analysis of Part II can be modified to show the effects of increasing returns to scale on the equilibrium values of g, r, S, V and X_p. After this, the effect of increasing returns to scale will be shown with CES and then with vintage assumptions. It will be shown that these involve a necessary departure from steady growth, but it will nevertheless be possible to say something about how increasing returns will influence the development of economies.

Increasing Returns to Scale with Cobb–Douglas Assumptions

A Cobb–Douglas production function which allows for a returns to scale factor of z can be written as follows:

$$Y = (\beta . K^\alpha . L^{1-\alpha})^z. \tag{11.1}$$

L represents efficiency units of labour, and it grows at a rate of $(a+n)$ as in earlier chapters. The relationship between g, the rate of growth of output, k, the rate of growth of capital, and $(a+n)$ is found by differentiating this equation with respect to time, i.e.

$$g = z.\alpha.k + z.(1-\alpha).(a+n). \tag{11.2}$$

It can be shown that the rate of growth will be constant if output and capital grow at the same rate and $(a+n)$ is constant when:

$$g = (a+n).z.\left(\frac{1-\alpha}{1-\alpha.z}\right). \tag{11.3}$$

Thus increasing returns multiply the equilibrium growth rate (which is otherwise $(a+n)$) by an 'economies of scale multiplier' of

$$z.\left(\frac{1-\alpha}{1-\alpha.z}\right),$$

i.e. by a multiplier which exceeds z.[1]

Where output and capital grow at the same rate, V, the capital–output ratio, is S/g, so (from (11.3)):

$$V = \left(\frac{S}{a+n}\right).\left(\frac{1-\alpha.z}{z-\alpha.z}\right). \tag{11.4}$$

[1] Cf. F. H. Hahn and R. C. O. Matthews, 'The theory of economic growth: a survey', *Economic Journal*, vol. LXXIV (Dec 1964) p. 833.

Thus, if they leave S unaltered, increasing returns to scale reduce the equilibrium capital–output ratio, which is otherwise $S/(a+n)$, by a factor which exceeds z.

The equilibrium rate of profit is found by differentiating (11.1) with respect to K, noting that $r = p_2 . (\partial Y / \partial K)$.

$$r = \frac{\alpha . (a+n)}{S} . \left(p_2 . z^2 . \left[\frac{1-z}{1-\alpha . z} \right] \right). \qquad (11.5)$$

With constant returns to scale and perfect competition, the equilibrium rate of profit is $(\alpha . (a+n))/S$, so increasing returns alter the rate of profit by a factor of

$$p_2 . z^2 \left(\frac{1-\alpha}{1-\alpha . z} \right)$$

if S is unaltered. This could be less than 1 if p_2 is much less than p_1, but unless capital receives a much lower fraction of its marginal product than labour,

$$p_2 . z^2 \left(\frac{1-\alpha}{1-\alpha . z} \right)$$

will exceed 1, and increasing returns to scale will then raise the rate of profit if they leave S unaltered.

X_p, the share of profits, is $r . V$, so from (11.4) and (11.5):

$$X_p = p_2 . z . \alpha. \qquad (11.6)$$

With constant returns to scale and perfect competition, the share of profits is simply α with Cobb–Douglas assumptions, so this is altered by a factor of $p_2 . z$ which will exceed unity if capital loses a lower proportion of its marginal product than labour as a result of imperfect competition and increasing returns to scale, and it will be less than 1 if capital loses a higher proportion of its marginal product than labour.

(11.3), (11.4), (11.5) and (11.6) show that increasing returns to scale are perfectly compatible with steady growth in a Cobb–Douglas world, for g, V, r and X_p can all be constant if S and p_1 and p_2 are constant.

It was pointed out at the start of the chapter that a correlation between the rate of growth of labour productivity and the rate of growth of output has been very widely found. In equilibrium growth, the rate of growth of labour productivity is $(g-n)$, and if ψ is the increase in the rate of growth of labour productivity that is associated with a unit increase in the rate of growth of output, i.e. if ψ is the 'Verdoorn coefficient', then from (11.3):

$$\psi = \frac{1 - \dfrac{1}{z}}{1 - \alpha}. \tag{11.7}^1$$

Thus, if there are increasing returns to scale so that z exceeds 1, there will be a positive Verdoorn coefficient which will simply depend on the values of z and α. It can be shown that the 'economies of scale multiplier' is $1/(1 - \psi)$, so this is derived most simply from the Verdoorn coefficient.[2]

Up to this point of the argument of this chapter, it has been assumed that S and $(a + n)$ are given and constant. However, it was argued in Part II of this book that S and a are variables depending on the economy's fundamental parameters – the coefficients of the investment function and the investment opportunity function. Here, as in Part II, there are three equations to determine the equilibrium values of g, r and S.

The investment function is unaltered by increasing returns to scale, so this can be written as in Chapter 9:

$$r = \frac{x_2 . i}{x_1 + x_2} + g \left(\frac{1}{x_1 + x_2} \right). \tag{11.8}$$

The two other basic equations are modified by increasing returns to scale, and they are obtained by substituting $(A + B . S)$ for a in (11.3) and (11.5). Thus:

$$g = (A + n + B . S) . z . \left(\frac{1 - \alpha}{1 - \alpha . z} \right) \tag{11.9}$$

$$r = \frac{\alpha (A + n + B . S)}{S} . p_2 . z^2 . \left(\frac{1 - \alpha}{1 - \alpha . z} \right). \tag{11.10}$$

(11.8), (11.9) and (11.10) provide sufficient equations to determine the equilibrium values of g, r and S. The elasticities of g, r, S, V

---

[1] A higher rate of growth must be associated with a higher n (provided that the Verdoorn coefficient is less than 1), and this means that ψ can be written as $\dfrac{\partial(g - n)}{\partial n} \bigg/ \dfrac{\partial g}{\partial n}$ which can be found from (11.3).

[2] ψ, which is $\dfrac{\partial(g - n)}{\partial n} \bigg/ \dfrac{\partial g}{\partial n}$, can be written as $\left(\dfrac{\partial g}{\partial n} - 1 \right) \bigg/ \dfrac{\partial g}{\partial n}$. Then the 'economies of scale multiplier', which cannot differ from $\partial g / \partial n$, is $1/(1 - \psi)$. Cf. (11.3) and (11.7).

and X_p with respect to the model's various parameters (which now include z) can be found from these equations as in Chapter 10. The various elasticities are outlined in Table 11.1.

Table 11.1

Elasticity of	With respect to x_1 and x_2	With respect to A, B and n	With respect to z
g	$\dfrac{E}{E+F}$	$\dfrac{F+E.F}{F+E}$	$\left(\dfrac{1}{1-\alpha.z}\right) \cdot \left(\dfrac{F+E.F}{F+E}\right)$
r	$-\dfrac{1}{E+F}$	$\dfrac{1+E}{F+E}$	$\left(\dfrac{1}{1-\alpha.z}\right) \cdot \left(\dfrac{1+E}{F+E}\right)$
S	$\dfrac{E+1}{E+F}$	$\dfrac{(F-1)(1+E)}{F+E}$	$\left(\dfrac{1}{1-\alpha.z}\right) \cdot \left(\dfrac{(F-1)(1+E)}{F+E}\right)$
V	$\dfrac{1}{E+F}$	$-\dfrac{1+E}{F+E}$	$-\left(\dfrac{1}{1-\alpha.z}\right) \cdot \left(\dfrac{1+E}{F+E}\right)$
X_p	nil	nil	nil

Where $E = \dfrac{B.S}{A+n}$ and

$$F = 1 + \frac{x_2.l}{g}\,[1 - \text{Elasticity of } l \text{ with respect to } r].$$

The third column is derived on the assumption that $p_1 = p_2 = 1/z$, but this assumption is not needed for the derivation of the first two columns.

It will be seen that the results in the first two columns are independent of z. This means that these elasticities are exactly the same as those arrived at with constant returns to scale assumptions in Chapter 10 (see Tables 10.1 and 10.8). This is a remarkable result, and it suggests that increasing returns will not affect a number of the basic results arrived at in Chapter 10. The third column, which shows the elasticities of the major variables with respect to z, shows that an economy with a higher z than another will have (*cet. par.*) a higher g, a higher r, a higher S and a lower V than the other economy. These are the same results as those arrived at above, and they suggest that the most fundamental effects of increasing returns to scale on growth can be shown without the added complication of an argument that takes the investment function and the investment opportunity function into account.

The main effects of increasing returns to scale that have emerged from the argument are that they produce both an economies of scale multiplier and a Verdoorn coefficient, where these are alternative ways of looking at the same phenomenon. It is well known that these multiply the growth that is due to any other source, such as growth in the industrial labour force or more rapid technical advance, so economies of scale will magnify the advantages countries obtain from other sources of growth.[1] They will not, however, produce growth by themselves, i.e. if $(a+n)$ is zero in (11.3), g will be zero, however high z is. Economies of scale then have the effect of giving countries with faster industrial labour growth a faster rate of growth of productivity, and Kaldor has attributed the U.K.'s comparatively slow rate of growth of productivity since the Second World War to the comparatively slow rate of growth of the industrial labour force. This result follows directly from the economies of scale multiplier of (11.3) if differences in n between economies predominate over differences in a as Kaldor assumes.

Some readers may have noted that there is an interesting correspondence between the results arrived at above and the effects of 'learning by doing' in Arrow's model which was discussed in Chapter 6. The steady growth rate in Arrow's model is $n/(1-b)$ where b is a constant (from (6.9)), so the effect of 'learning by doing' with Arrow's assumptions is that a multiplier of $1/(1-b)$ is applied to the rate of growth of the labour force (in efficiency units) to produce the economy's steady growth rate. With increasing returns (and Cobb–Douglas assumptions), a multiplier of

$$z\left(\frac{1-\alpha}{1-\alpha.z}\right)$$

is applied to the rate of growth of the labour force (in efficiency units) to produce the economy's steady growth rate. This means that the effects of increasing returns and Arrow-type 'learning by doing'

[1] Cf. Denison, *Why Growth Rates Differ: Postwar Experience in Nine Western Countries*, chap. 17.

will be almost indistinguishable in conditions of steady growth, and if both are present, the total 'z effect' can be thought of as the sum of Arrow-type 'learning by doing' and increasing returns effects.

The analysis of this section has been confined to Cobb–Douglas assumptions, and these have prevented the share of profits from varying except as a result of a change in p_1/p_2. It will obviously be desirable to go on to CES assumptions, but it will turn out that these will prove to be incompatible with steady growth, so the present section will be the last in this book where the technique of steady growth comparisons can be used. From this point onwards, the argument will have to take secular and short-term changes in the values of the major variables into account.

It will be shown, however, that most of the effects of economies of scale on growth that have been arrived at here with Cobb–Douglas assumptions will still stand with CES assumptions and 'unsteady' growth. Some further important results will be arrived at in the next section, but an increasing returns CES production function produces a few mathematically technical interrelationships, and some readers may find the remainder of this chapter difficult, and therefore prefer to go straight to the conclusion of the chapter on p. 271.

*Economies of Scale and Growth with CES Assumptions

A CES production function which allows for a returns to scale factor of z can be written as follows:

$$Y = (\lambda(h \cdot K^{-u} + (1-h) \cdot L^{-u}))^{-\frac{z}{u}}. \tag{11.11}$$

L, which is labour in efficiency units, grows at a rate of $(a+n)$, and $u = (1/\sigma) - 1$. X_p and X_w can be found from the marginal products of labour and capital, which are obtained by partially differentiating (11.11) with respect to L and K. Thus:

$$X_w = \frac{p_1 \cdot z}{1 + \left(\dfrac{h}{1-h}\right) \cdot \left(\dfrac{K}{L}\right)^{(1-1/\sigma)}} \tag{11.12}$$

$$X_p = \frac{p_2 \cdot z}{1 + \left(\dfrac{1-h}{h}\right) \cdot \left(\dfrac{K}{L}\right)^{(1/\sigma-1)}}. \tag{11.13}$$

(11.12) and (11.13) show that distributive shares can only be constant through time if the economy's capital–labour ratio is constant. Thus, for steady growth, capital and labour must grow at the same rate (in efficiency units). The full implications of this will be seen once the equation showing the relationship between the rates of growth of capital, labour and output is arrived at, and this is obtained by differentiating (11.11) with respect to time:

$$g = k.z \left(\frac{1}{1 + \left(\dfrac{1-h}{h}\right) . \left(\dfrac{K}{L}\right)^{(1/\sigma - 1)}} \right)$$

$$+ (a+n).z. \left(\frac{1}{1 + \left(\dfrac{h}{1-h}\right) . \left(\dfrac{K}{L}\right)^{(1 - 1/\sigma)}} \right). \quad (11.14)$$

(11.14) is a most important equation. Since:

$$\frac{1}{1 + \left(\dfrac{1-h}{h}\right) . \left(\dfrac{K}{L}\right)^{(1/\sigma - 1)}} + \frac{1}{1 + \left(\dfrac{h}{1-h}\right) . \left(\dfrac{K}{L}\right)^{(1 - 1/\sigma)}} = 1 \quad (11.15)$$

certain problems occur wherever z exceeds 1. Clearly, where z exceeds 1, either g must exceed k, or both g and k must exceed $(a+n)$. Distributive shares will only be constant if $k = (a+n)$ to keep K/L constant, and in this case g must exceed k, so constancy of distributive shares entails a falling capital–output ratio. If, however, $g = k$ to keep the capital–output ratio constant, then (11.14) shows that both g and k will necessarily exceed $(a+n)$. There will then be a rising K/L, and (11.12) and (11.13) show that this will produce a continuous change in income distribution. If σ is less than 1 as is generally supposed, a rising capital–labour ratio will produce a continuous fall in the share of profits and a corresponding continuously rising share of wages in the National Income. Thus, with CES assumptions, increasing returns must apparently produce either a falling capital–output ratio, or a falling share of profits, or some combination of these, and these results do not rest on the assumption that $(a+n)$ is constant.

The difficulties produced by CES assumptions can be looked at in the following way. It was shown in Chapter 2 that labour-augmenting Harrod-neutral technical progress is compatible with steady growth where the production function is CES, while Hicks-neutral technical progress which augments both labour and capital is not. Now, in (11.14), z in effect augments the rates of growth of labour and capital z times, so its effect is analogous to that of Hicks-neutral technical progress. In an economy where capital and labour grow at the same rate, increasing returns provide a bonus the effect of which is identical to that of further Hicks-neutral technical progress of $(a+n)(z-1)$, i.e. it is as if the rate of growth of the *effective* labour force is $(a+n).z$ instead of $(a+n)$, and the rate of growth of the *effective* capital stock is also $(a+n).z$ instead of $(a+n)$. Thus Harrod-neutral technical progress and labour growth at rate $(a+n)$, together with increasing returns to scale, produce results that are theoretically analogous to those produced by Harrod-neutral technical progress and labour growth at rate $(a+n)$, and Hicks-neutral technical progress at rate $(a+n)(z-1)$. As only Harrod-neutral technical progress is compatible with steady growth if the production function is CES, what prevents steady growth is the Hicks 'capital augmentation' at rate $(a+n)(z-1)$ that follows from increasing returns. It is this 'capital augmentation' which reduces the share of profits (if $\sigma < 1$), or the physical capital–output ratio – for less physical capital is needed to produce given real effects.

There are two possible ways round this difficulty. First, a Kennedy technical possibilities function could be invoked to restore *ex-post* Harrod neutrality.[1] With this, the falling share of profits that results from 'capital augmentation' (where $\sigma < 1$) could be expected to bias technical advances in a labour-saving and capital-using direction, with the result that it would appear *ex post* that there had simply been Harrod-neutral technical progress. However, the adoption of a technical possibilities function has a number of consequential effects, including the one that the equilibrium distribution of incomes is determined by this function alone. A second way of avoiding the inconvenient 'capital augmentation' that is part of the Hicks-neutral effect of increasing returns to scale would be to attribute increasing returns solely to the effect of more labour. There is, however, no justification for this, particularly as one of the most fundamental effects of increasing returns to scale is that capital is used more effectively, the larger the size of plant. This would not be shown if economies of scale were solely derivable from a larger L. To attribute increasing returns to both extra labour and extra capital is more natural than to attribute these to extra labour alone, and this is exactly what is done in (11.11). It is unfortunate that steady growth

[1] See C. M. Kennedy, 'Induced bias in innovation and the theory of distribution', *Economic Journal*, vol. LXXIV (Sep 1964).

is then no longer a possibility, but this may well be a plausible result. There is, moreover, much that can still be said about the way economies will develop through time.

It is clear from (11.14) that increasing returns must produce a falling capital–output ratio, or a falling share of profits, or some combination of these, and it is in fact possible to say a great deal about the direction and the rate of change of these crucial variables. The first step is to consider the plausibility of the possibilities that have emerged, namely that the capital–output ratio will be constant while the share of profits falls continuously, or that the share of profits will be constant while the capital–output ratio falls. Consider the first of these possibilities. If capital increases at the same rate as output so that K/Y is constant, while P/Y falls continuously, then $(P/K).(K/Y)$ (which equals P/Y) must fall equivalently, and with K/Y constant, P/K, the rate of profit, must then fall at the same rate as P/Y. Thus equal growth rates of capital and output must produce a falling rate of profit, and the rate of profit will fall at exactly the rate at which the share of profits falls. If the argument of Chapter 8 is accepted, a falling rate of profit must produce a falling rate of capital accumulation, maybe not at once, but certainly the trend rate of capital accumulation should be downwards. If the rate of accumulation responds to the falling rate of profit, however slightly, capital will not continue to grow as fast as output. This means that capital must grow less quickly than output, with the result that a falling trend in the capital–output ratio is one expected result of increasing returns in a CES world.

Thus capital will not increase as rapidly as output. The alternative possibility that was considered above was that capital might increase so slowly in relation to output that the capital–labour ratio would not rise, with the result that distributive shares could then remain constant. Now $P/Y \equiv (P/K).(K/Y)$, and if P/Y is constant while K/Y falls, P/K must rise at exactly the rate at which K/Y falls. Thus the rate of profit must rise if capital grows so slowly that the share of profits is constant. A rising rate of profit could be expected to produce a rising rate of growth of capital, with the result that it is not to be expected that the rate of growth of capital will be held back sufficiently to prevent the share of profits from falling. It then appears that the rate of capital accumulation must be sufficient to produce a falling share of profits, but it will not be fast enough to increase capital at the same rate as output.

Hence it is to be expected that the trend in both the capital–output ratio and the share of profits will be downwards in a CES economy with increasing returns to scale. It can be shown that the rate of profit can also be expected to fall. An equation for the rate of profit (which equals $p_2 . (\partial Y / \partial K)$) is obtained by differentiating (11.11) with respect to K:

$$r = p_2 . \lambda . h . z . Y^{\left(\frac{u}{z} + 1\right)} . K^{-(u+1)}. \tag{11.16}$$

Differentiating (11.16) with respect to time:

$$\frac{1}{r} . \frac{dr}{dt} = \left(\frac{u}{z} + 1\right) . g - (u+1) . k. \tag{11.17}$$

It follows from (11.14) and (11.17) that the following equations will hold where the rate of profit is constant:

$$\frac{g}{a+n} = \frac{z}{1 - \sigma . (z-1) . \left(\dfrac{h}{1-h}\right) . \left(\dfrac{K}{L}\right)^{(1 - 1/\sigma)}} \tag{11.18}$$

$$\frac{k}{a+n} = \frac{1 + \sigma . (z-1)}{1 - \sigma . (z-1) . \left(\dfrac{h}{1-h}\right) . \left(\dfrac{K}{L}\right)^{(1 - 1/\sigma)}} \tag{11.19}$$

Since K/L must be rising, it follows that both $g/(a+n)$ and $k/(a+n)$ must fall where the rate of capital accumulation is just sufficient to keep r constant (provided that $\sigma < 1$).

If $(a+n)$ is assumed constant, then both g and k must be falling where the rate of profit is constant. However, if the investment function is taken into account, it is clear that a constant rate of profit will not induce a falling rate of capital accumulation, for this can be expected to produce a constant rate of accumulation. Then a constant rate of profit will induce more capital accumulation than is needed to sustain it, so the investment and production functions will only produce compatible results if the rate of profit falls very slightly through time thus producing a falling rate of capital accumulation through the investment function, and a falling rate of growth. Then, if $(a+n)$ is constant, the development of economies will be such that the capital–output ratio, the share of profits and the rate of profit can all be expected to fall, though, as will be shown below, their rates of fall will be quite slow.

However, before the rates of fall of V, X_p and r that are to be expected where $(a+n)$ is constant are analysed, it will be appropriate to refer back to a line of argument that emerged in Chapter 6. It was argued there that economies with a growing labour force can be expected to achieve results from research and development which produce a rate of technical progress that accelerates through time. This would produce a rising $(a+n)$, and inspection of (11.19) shows that k can be constant if $(a+n)$ rises at the same rate as

$$\left(1-\sigma.(z-1).\left(\frac{h}{1-h}\right)\left(\frac{K}{L}\right)^{\left(1-\frac{1}{\sigma}\right)}\right),$$

and k can increase through time if $(a+n)$ rises at a faster rate than this expression. This means that the rate of profit can rise and (through the investment function) induce a growing rate of capital accumulation if the rate of increase of $(a+n)$ (as a result of accelerating technical progress) exceeds the rate of increase of

$$\left(1-\sigma.(z-1).\left(\frac{h}{1-h}\right).\left(\frac{K}{L}\right)^{\left(1-\frac{1}{\sigma}\right)}\right).$$

This is not a simple condition (and a simple condition cannot apparently be derived from it), but it is evident that if the argument in Chapter 6 in favour of accelerating technical progress is accepted, then increasing returns may produce either a rising or a falling rate of profit, depending on the rate at which technical progress accelerates. This will not affect the propositions that increasing returns will produce a falling share of profits and a falling capital–output ratio, for these did not depend on the assumption that $(a+n)$ is constant. All that is affected is the proposition about the rate of profit, which will fall if $(a+n)$ is constant, and rise if $(a+n)$ accelerates at a sufficient rate.

The simplest assumption to work with is the one that $(a+n)$ is constant, and something will be said about the rates at which the share of profits, the capital–output ratio and the rate of profit can then be expected to fall. It is clear that the rate of growth of capital will be more than that needed to keep r constant, i.e. the rate of growth of capital will exceed

$$g.\left(\frac{1}{z}+\sigma.\left(\frac{z-1}{z}\right)\right) \quad \text{(from (11.17)),}$$

but it will be less than g, the rate of growth of output. If k must lie within these limits, then the rate of change of the capital–output ratio (which is $(k-g)$) must lie within the limits:

$$\frac{1}{V}\cdot\frac{dV}{dt} = 0...g\left(1-\frac{1}{z}\right).(\sigma-1).\qquad(11.20)$$

The rate of fall of the rate of profit will be nil if capital increases fast enough to keep this constant, and

$$\left(1-\frac{1}{z}\right)\left(\frac{1}{\sigma}-1\right).g$$

where capital increases at the same rate as output (from (11.17)), so if the rate of growth of capital lies within these limits:

$$\frac{1}{r}\cdot\frac{dr}{dt} = 0...g\left(1-\frac{1}{z}\right).\left(1-\frac{1}{\sigma}\right).\qquad(11.21)$$

Since $X_p \equiv r.V$, it follows that

$$\frac{1}{X_p}\cdot\frac{dX_p}{dt} = \frac{1}{r}\cdot\frac{dr}{dt}+\frac{1}{V}\cdot\frac{dV}{dt},$$

with the result that:

$$\frac{1}{X_p}\cdot\frac{dX_p}{dt} = g\left(1-\frac{1}{z}\right)(\sigma-1)...g\left(1-\frac{1}{z}\right)\left(1-\frac{1}{\sigma}\right).\quad(11.22)$$

It will be evident from (11.20), (11.21) and (11.22) that the rates of fall of the share of profits, the rate of profit and the capital–output ratio may be very slight. If $z = 1\frac{1}{2}$, which makes a generous allowance for increasing returns, and $\sigma = \frac{2}{3}$, the share of profits will fall at a rate of $g.(\frac{1}{5}...\frac{1}{6})$, so an economy with a growth rate of 3 per cent per annum, approximately the U.S. growth rate from 1900 to 1960, would experience a fall of $\frac{1}{300}$ to $\frac{1}{200}$ in its share of profits per annum, or a fall from, say, 30 per cent to 22–25 per cent in sixty years. The sum of the rates of fall of r and V will be no more than this, since $V.r \equiv X_p$, so these will fall at more modest rates. These suggested results of increasing returns are quite in line with such empirical evidence as is available, for it appears that both the share of profits and the capital–output ratio are now markedly lower in the U.S.A. than they were at the start of the twentieth century, and they have fallen fairly continuously.[1] As for the rate of profit, this may rise or fall depending on whether technical progress accelerates, and it certainly seems to have accelerated in the U.S.A., so there is no reason to expect a falling U.S. rate of profit.[2]

As with Cobb–Douglas assumptions, increasing returns to scale produce a Verdoorn coefficient, but this will not be constant with CES assumptions. ψ, the Verdoorn coefficient, is given below on the assumption that the rate of growth of capital is less than that needed to increase capital as fast as output, but more than that needed to maintain a constant rate of profit. Then, from (11.14) and (11.18), with $(p_1 . X_p)/(p_2 . X_w)$ substituted for $(h/(1-h)) . (K/L)^{(1-1/\sigma)}$:

$$\psi = \left(1 - \frac{1}{z}\right) . \left(1 + \sigma\left(\frac{p_1 . X_p}{p_2 . X_w}\right)\right) \cdots \left(1 - \frac{1}{z}\right)\left(1 + \frac{p_1 X_p}{p_2 X_w}\right). \quad (11.23)$$

Thus there is bound to be a positive Verdoorn coefficient, and its value will depend upon z, σ and income distribution. If σ is less than 1, ψ will fall slowly.

The 'economies of scale multiplier' for the same limiting rates of capital accumulation is $1/(1-\psi)$. Thus:

$$\frac{g}{a+n} = \frac{1}{1-\psi} = \frac{z}{1 - \sigma . (z-1) . \left(\dfrac{p_1 . X_p}{p_2 . X_w}\right)} \cdots \frac{z}{1 - (z-1) . \left(\dfrac{p_1 . X_p}{p_2 . X_w}\right)}.$$
$$(11.24)$$

[1] One estimate suggests that the 'property share' in the U.S. National Income fell fairly steadily from 30·6 per cent in 1900-9 to 22·4 per cent in 1954-63. (Bernard F. Haley, 'Distribution in the United States', in the Proceedings of the International Economic Association Conference on *The Distribution of National Income*, ed. Jean Marchal and Bernard Ducros, Macmillan, 1968.) John W. Kendrick and Ryuzo Sato have estimated that the property share fell from 28·0 per cent in 1919 to 22·2 per cent in 1960, and that the capital–output ratio fell very drastically from 4·58 to 2·62 in the same period ('Factor prices, productivity and economic growth', *American Economic Review*, vol. LIII, Dec. 1963). More conservatively, L. R. Klein and R. F. Kosobud have estimated that the ratio capital stock/Net National Product fell from 3·987 in 1900 to 2·55 in 1953 ('Some econometrics of growth: great ratios of economics', *Quarterly Journal of Economics*, vol. LXXV, May 1961). These estimates suggest that the rate of fall of the capital–output ratio may have been rather faster than that suggested by (11.20). This could be the result of a rising r, or technical progress nearer to Hicks than to Harrod neutrality, so that there was some capital augmentation from technical progress in addition to that produced by increasing returns to scale.

[2] See p. 141, n. 1 above.

This must exceed z. It is to be noted that the Verdoorn coefficient and the 'economies of scale multiplier' are not very sensitive to the rate of growth of capital within the limits assumed.

Kaldor has suggested that the Verdoorn coefficient may have been as high as 0·5 (with a consequent 'economies of scale multiplier' of 2) in developed economies in the period 1954-64.[1] If $(p_1 . X_p)/(p_2 . X_w)$ is one-third, and σ is two-thirds, Kaldor's estimate of a Verdoorn coefficient of 0·5 would imply a z of 1·60–1·69, which brings out the point that a z of rather less than 2 will produce an 'economies of scale multiplier' of 2. (11.24) makes it clear that the 'economies of scale multiplier' will always exceed z.

It is obviously impossible to show the precise effects of economies of scale on the investment opportunity function in a CES world, with the result that the long-run effects of increasing returns to scale on the equilibrium values of g, r and S cannot be shown. This is impossible because, in the absence of steady growth, no *equilibrium* values of any kind can be found. It is, however, possible to say something in general terms about the effects produced by the interaction of the investment function and the investment opportunity function.

It is immediately evident from (11.24) that g cannot become less than $(a+n).z$, however far X_p falls, so an economy with increasing returns must always have a potential growth rate that is at least z times as fast as that of an economy with constant returns and the same $(a+n)$.[2] Thus, while the growth rate of an economy with increasing returns will decline continuously as its share of profits falls, it will decline asymptotically towards $(a+n).z$.

An economy with increasing returns and another economy with constant returns and the same $(a+n)$ at each rate of profit are compared in Fig. 11.1, and both economies have the same investment function, KK. In the absence of accelerating technical progress, the economy with increasing returns will have a falling investment opportunity function because it will have a falling rate of profit at any constant rate of accumulation, so its investment opportunity function might fall from $N'N'$ to $N''N''$, $N'''N'''$, etc., but it cannot fall below the dotted line, $N*N*$, where accumulation at each rate of profit is about z times that of the economy with constant returns

[1] Kaldor, *Causes of the Slow Rate of Growth of the U.K.*
[2] The same result follows from (11.14) and (11.15), where k must always exceed $(a+n)$ (since a rising K/L is an inevitable consequence of increasing returns), with the result that g must always exceed $z(a+n)$ in (11.14).

and the investment opportunity function *NN*. The investment opportunity function of the economy with increasing returns will asymptotically approach $N*N*$ as its rate of profit falls, so its rate of growth will fall successively from Og' to Og'', Og''' and so on towards $Og*$, while its rate of profit will fall from Or' to Or'', Or''', etc., until it asymptotically approaches $Or*$, a much higher rate of

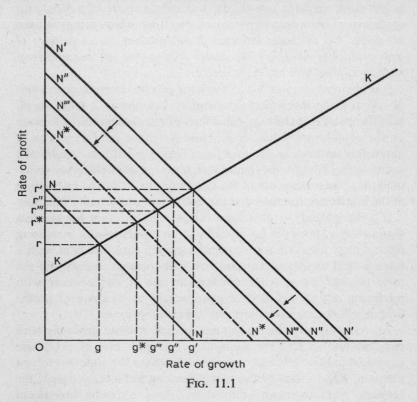

Fig. 11.1

profit than *Or*, the rate of profit of the economy with constant returns.

Thus the very interesting result can be arrived at that, in the absence of accelerating technical progress, increasing returns will be associated with a declining g, r, V and X_p in a CES world, but g cannot decline to less than z times the growth rate of a similar constant returns economy, and r must remain about this much higher than the rate of profit in a constant returns economy. V and X_p can apparently continue to decline indefinitely. With accelerating technical progress, there may of course be no decline at all in g and r, for these may both rise through time, but V and X_p will both fall continuously.

It will be seen that increasing returns to scale may have far-reaching effects on the development of economies. In this section the argument has been extended from Cobb–Douglas to CES assumptions. The effect of proceeding to vintage assumptions will be outlined in the next section.

Increasing Returns to Scale with Vintage Assumptions

Increasing returns may lead to greater efficiency, both because economies of scale increase the efficiency of new plant, and because the efficiency of all plant may vary with the aggregate output of an industry or an economy. Without vintage assumptions, the entire benefits from increasing returns must depend on an economy's aggregates, as in the last two sections where increases in K and L produced more than proportionate increases in Y. With vintage assumptions, the equivalent to this would be to assume that productivity with all plant of all vintages advanced at a rate depending on the rate of growth of aggregate output. But this will not be the sole effect of increasing returns, for plant of all vintages will not benefit equally. New plant can be expected to benefit particularly from a larger scale of production, so increasing returns will raise productivity with new plant to an extent depending on an increasing returns production function with new plant, and in addition they will raise productivity with all plant as aggregate output rises. These effects of increasing returns, first on new plant, and second on all plant, will be considered in turn.

It was pointed out in Chapter 3 that with vintage assumptions entrepreneurs will choose the technique of production with new plant by equating the capital cost of saving a worker to the discounted cost of a worker throughout the lifetime of plant, and with the constant returns production function used in Chapter 3,

$$Y^{-u} = \lambda(h.K^{-u}+(1-h).L^{-u}),$$

the capital cost of saving a worker can be written as

$$\left(\frac{1-h}{h}\right) \cdot \left(\frac{K}{L}\right)^{u+1},$$

while the cost of a worker throughout the lifetime of plant can be written as

$$\left(\frac{e^{-aT}-e^{-rT}}{r-a}\right) \cdot \frac{Y}{L}$$

at time 0.[1] With the equivalent increasing returns to scale production function with new plant which will take the same algebraic form as (11.11), the capital cost of saving a worker will still be

$$\left(\frac{1-h}{h}\right) \cdot \left(\frac{K}{L}\right)^{u+1},$$

but the discounted cost of a worker throughout the lifetime of plant will fall from

$$\left(\frac{e^{-aT}-e^{-rT}}{r-a}\right) \cdot \frac{Y}{L} \text{ to } p_3 \cdot \left(\frac{e^{-aT}-e^{-rT}}{r-a}\right) \cdot \frac{Y}{L},$$

where p_3 is the ratio of the wage to output per worker with the least productive plant in use. In consequence, it will be less worth while to use capital to save labour, so the capital–output ratio with new plant will be lower. Moreover, the rising capital–labour ratio with new plant that is to be expected for the same reasons as in the last section (for Y, K and L cannot grow at the same rate in (11.11)) will prevent the achievement of steady growth, and continuously increase the capital cost of saving a worker relative to the discounted cost of a worker, thus producing a falling capital–output ratio with new plant. Hence an increasing returns production function with new plant should produce both a lower capital–output ratio and a falling capital–output ratio – results similar to those arrived at for all plant in a non-vintage world.

The effect of increasing returns on r, the net rate of return, is obviously more difficult to analyse because this will depend partly on p_2, and partly on how increasing returns affect T, the life of plant – and this can hardly be elucidated without the technique of equilibrium comparisons which is ruled out by the impossibility of achieving steady growth.

It is clear, however, that there will be an 'economies of scale multiplier' as in the last section, though not a constant one, for the growth of labour productivity with new plant will be raised in the same way as productivity with all plant was raised in the last section,

[1] See pp. 61-2 above.

and the rate of growth of average labour productivity equals the rate of growth of productivity with new plant where T and the productivity gap between plant of various vintages is constant. While some change in T is to be expected through time, this will no more than modify the tendency for average productivity to move with the productivity of the newest plant, and this means that the 'economies of scale multiplier' and the Verdoorn coefficient will have much the same effect as in the last section.

Increasing returns which raise labour productivity with all plant will have very similar effects to those arrived at in the last section, for there productivity with all plant was raised equally. Thus there will be a Verdoorn coefficient and an 'economies of scale multiplier', and these will produce an NN line that is further to the right, thus raising both the rate of profit and the rate of growth.

The total effect of increasing returns in a vintage world will be an amalgam of their effect on productivity with all plant, and their rather more complex impact on new plant. When these effects are combined, it does not appear that vintage assumptions lead to any obvious modification of the results arrived at in the last section, and it may well be that the principal effects produced by increasing returns can be shown with the non-vintage CES model that was outlined there.

Conclusion

It will be seen that increasing returns may have far-reaching effects on the development of economies. The argument of this chapter suggests that economies of scale will lead to a falling capital–output ratio and a falling share of profits – trends which are fully in line with evidence from the U.S.A. in the twentieth century. Increasing returns may also produce a falling rate of profit, but it is possible that this may be counteracted by accelerating technical progress. Even so, the result arrived at is that either technical progress will accelerate, or alternatively that the rate of profit will fall (albeit to a rate that must be higher than the rate of profit in a similar economy with constant returns to scale), which has strong implications for the development of modern economies. These are the likely long-term effects of increasing returns to scale. The other effects of increasing returns are highly favourable to growth, for these apply a multiplier to the growth available from any other source. Where the Verdoorn coefficient is ψ, the 'economies of scale multiplier' will be

$1/(1-\psi)$, which means that material living standards will rise an extra $\psi/(1-\psi)$ per cent for each extra per cent the labour force grows – that is, living standards which ignore the costs of congestion which follow from faster population growth will rise at this rate. Whatever their long-term impact on the share of profits, there can be no doubt that increasing returns must have highly favourable effects on the growth and development of economies, and particularly those with rapid industrial labour growth.

12

The Relationship between Actual Growth and Equilibrium Growth

NOTHING was said in Part II of this book about the determination of the economy's level of output in the short period, for it was taken for granted that full employment and normal-capacity working would be maintained at all times. With continuous normal-capacity working, it could be assumed that entrepreneurs had a clear expected rate of profit to base their decisions on, and that this corresponded to the actual achieved rate of return on capital. Their investment depended solely on this (and its relationship to the equilibrium rate of interest), and it was assumed that full-employment saving automatically corresponded to investment, thus determined.

Where there are departures from normal-capacity working as there are in all economies at most times, investment will not be solely influenced by the equilibrium rate of return on capital. The actual degree of capacity working will have an important influence on investment, and entrepreneurs will also be influenced by the expected rate of growth. The degree of capacity working which has a significant influence on profits in the short run will also influence the share of saving in the National Income.

In this chapter the factors influencing planned investment and planned saving in the short period will be analysed, and the conditions which must be fulfilled if planned investment is continuously to equal planned saving at full employment and normal-capacity working will be discussed. The first part of the chapter will be concerned with this, and the conditions where continuous equilibrium growth will be achieved will be set out. After this, the effect of departures from equilibrium will be analysed; the stability of equilibrium will be discussed; and something will be said about the fluctuations of the National Income that are to be expected.

It will be seen that the analysis owes much to Harrod's growth model which has evolved continuously since 1939.[1] The model differs from the Harrod model in a number of respects, and there is a considerable debt to Kaldor's trade-cycle model of 1940.[2] There are particular departures from the Harrod model in the assumptions made about investment decisions, and the determination of g, the actual rate of growth.

The Conditions Necessary for Stable Equilibrium Growth

Equilibrium growth will be achieved if planned and actual investment are always exactly the amounts needed for this, and planned investment continuously equals planned saving at full employment and normal-capacity working. The factors which influence investment and saving decisions will therefore need to be analysed before the conditions necessary for continuous equilibrium growth can be outlined. The factors which influence investment decisions will be outlined first.

It will be assumed that planned entrepreneurial investment depends on the rate of profit for the reasons outlined in Chapter 8, but it will depend on other factors in addition. Suppose two economies earn the same rate of profit at normal-capacity working, and that they have entrepreneurs with identical investment functions. They may still have different rates of investment for two reasons: they may have different rates of capacity working, or different growth expectations. If one economy has a shortage of plant while the other has excess capacity, the one which is short of plant will invest more. If both economies enjoy the same degree of capacity working, but the entrepreneurs of one economy expect the rate of growth to be faster, then that economy will have higher investment. It then appears that the degree of capacity working, growth expectations and the rate of return on capital will each have some influence on planned entrepreneurial investment, and a theory must be outlined which allows each of these to have some effect. Fortunately there is a simple diagrammatic method of showing how these will each influence the investment function.

In Fig. 12.1 the horizontal axis shows the degree of capacity

[1] See in particular Harrod, 'An essay in dynamic theory' (1939), *Towards a Dynamic Economics* (1948), and 'Are monetary and fiscal policies enough?', *Economic Journal*, vol. LXXIV (Dec 1964).

[2] See N. Kaldor, 'A model of the trade cycle', *Economic Journal*, vol. L (Mar 1940).

working of the 'representative' firm. At 100, it has what it judges to be the ideal capacity to produce current output, and this corresponds (but not exactly) to the situation in Harrod's model where C, the actual capital coefficient, equals C_r, the desired capital coefficient. If the representative firm is producing at 99, it has 1 per cent excess capacity, and if it produces at 101, it is 1 per cent short of capital. The vertical axis shows investment by the representative firm expressed as a share of value-added.

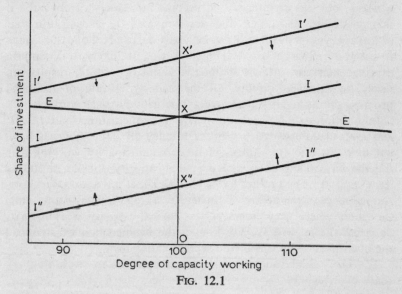

FIG. 12.1

EE shows the equilibrium share of investment by the representative firm that follows from the economy's fundamental equations of Part II. It is assumed that the economy's share of investment will be the same as the representative firm's share of investment in value-added, so the economy will achieve equilibrium investment where the representative firm invests the equilibrium share shown by EE. If the share of investment is on EE, the representative firm's rate of growth, and its rate of profit (at normal-capacity working), will be those that follow from the intersection of the investment function and the investment opportunity function of Part II.[1] It follows from

[1] EE slopes downwards slightly because a given *amount* of investment is needed each year to raise the capital stock at the equilibrium rate, so equilibrium investment will be a higher *share* of value-added where capacity working and value-added are low, than where these are both high.

this that on EE the economy's capital stock grows at just the rate necessary to provide full employment for the labour force, whatever its rate of growth (in natural or efficiency units). This equilibrium rate of growth will be referred to as g^*, and it corresponds to Harrod's 'natural' rate of growth. g^* will equal $(a+n)$ in the absence of increasing returns, and it will be assumed for simplicity that this condition holds at all degrees of capacity working. It is arguable that an economy's a may fluctuate to some extent with its degree of capacity working, but this chapter would become immensely complicated if this possibility was taken into account, and the assumption that $(a+n)$ always equals g^* may not be a particularly bad one. Decisions to spend on research and development, etc., are likely to depend on expected markets in the very long run, since profitable results can rarely be achieved rapidly, so the underlying rate of technical progress should fluctuate relatively little with capacity working.

In addition to EE, three alternative investment functions, II, $I'I'$ and $I''I''$, are illustrated in Fig. 12.1. They all slope upwards from left to right, and they intersect the normal-capacity working axis (i.e. the vertical axis showing a degree of capacity working of 100) at X, X' and X''. The upward slope of these functions shows the short-run influence of the degree of capacity working on investment, while the point where they intersect the normal-capacity working axis describes the growth expectations of the businessmen who control the investment decisions of the representative firm.

The investment functions are drawn upwards to show that the share of investment is always higher where the degree of capacity working is higher. With a rigid acceleration principle, the sensitivity of investment to the degree of capacity working is implausibly great, for this leads to much sharper fluctuations of investment than those experienced in developed economies since 1945, but there must be some kind of relationship between the degree of capacity working and planned entrepreneurial investment. The upward slope of II, $I'I'$ and $I''I''$ merely shows that planned investment is higher where the degree of capacity working is higher. It will turn out that this allows the effect of the acceleration principle to be shown as a special case, but less extreme sensitivity of investment to the degree of capacity working can also be shown.

The intersection of the investment function and EE describes the growth expectations of the representative entrepreneur. If he expects the equilibrium rate of growth, g^*, to be achieved, then at normal-capacity working his firm will invest exactly the amount needed to raise the capital stock at the equilibrium rate. The investment needed for this is shown by EE, and at normal-capacity working OX must be invested to raise the capital stock at the equilibrium rate, so the investment function of a firm that expects growth at the equilibrium rate will pass through X. Then II is an example of an investment function where growth at the equilibrium rate is expected. If the representative entrepreneur expects a faster growth rate than g^* at normal-capacity working, his firm will invest more than OX where the degree of capacity working is 100, with the result that the investment function will lie above X. In Fig. 12.1, $I'I'$ passes through X' which is above X, and this is the investment function for a representative entrepreneur who expects a faster rate of growth than g^*. Similarly, $I''I''$ which passes through X'' is the investment function where the representative entrepreneur expects a rate of growth of less than g^*. It will be seen that the expected rate of growth will have a considerable influence on the short-run investment function. It will be assumed that the expected rate of growth will tend towards any actual rate of growth which is steadily maintained, so the expected rate of growth will equal the actual rate of growth in equilibrium. Where the rate of growth fluctuates, however, there may be considerable differences between the expected rate of growth and the actual rate, and the expected rate will then independently influence investment decisions.

Before the argument proceeds further, a fundamental relationship between the investment function and EE will be outlined. Where investment is at the rate shown by EE, the capital stock is increased at the equilibrium rate, and this is just sufficient to keep the rate of profit constant (at normal-capacity working). If investment is less than that shown by EE, the capital stock is increased at less than the equilibrium rate with the result that capital will become scarcer in relation to other factors of production than in equilibrium conditions. This will raise the rate of profit at normal-capacity working, so the rate of profit will rise wherever investment is less than that shown by EE. Similarly, the rate of profit (at normal-capacity working) will fall wherever investment exceeds that shown by EE. The rate of profit will also vary with the degree of capacity working because higher utilisation ratios will produce a higher rate of profit, but if the advantages from overcapacity working and the adverse effects of excess capacity on the rate of profit are given, then the rate of profit

K

at *any* given degree of capacity working will move up and down with the rate of profit at normal-capacity working. Thus an economy working continuously at 105 will always have a higher rate of profit than a similar economy working at 100, and whether its rate of profit rises or falls will depend on whether its investment is less or more than that shown by *EE*. In consequence, the rate of profit will fall at *all* degrees of capacity working where the share of investment exceeds that shown by *EE*, so in Fig. 12.1 where *I'I'* is above *EE* throughout its length, the rate of profit must fall through time at all degrees of capacity working, with the result that *I'I'* will fall through time towards *EE*. Similarly, where the short-run investment function is *I"I"*, investment will be less than that needed to increase the capital stock at the equilibrium rate, so the rate of profit will rise through time and cause *I"I"* to rise towards *EE*. Thus the investment function will fall towards *EE* if it is above it, and rise towards *EE* if it is below it, and this will obviously prove to be a powerful equilibrating force. Its strength will depend on the elasticity of *r* with respect to *S* which played so large a part in earlier chapters.

This section of the present chapter is concerned with the conditions necessary for equilibrium growth, so there is no need to pay attention to the factors which may cause the investment function to shift upwards and downwards (which will only occur in disequilibrium situations). It is worth while, however, to have a complete grasp of the factors which determine the position, the slope and the rate of shift of the investment function. This will be above *X* if a faster rate of growth than the equilibrium rate is expected (and below it with a slower expected growth rate): it will slope upwards more steeply, the greater the sensitivity of investment to the degree of capacity working, and it will move down towards *EE* if it is above it, and rise towards *EE* from below.

The next step in the argument is to show how the degree of capacity working is determined at any time, and this will be done with the help of Fig. 12.2. Here, *II* shows planned investment as a share of the National Income in relation to the degree of capacity working in the economy as a whole. *SS* shows planned saving (as a share of the National Income) at different degrees of capacity working, and it slopes upwards from left to right for two main reasons. First, the share of profits is normally higher, the higher the degree of capacity working, and a higher proportion of profits is saved than of wages and salaries. Second, the high levels of income associated with high degrees of capacity working are likely to be regarded as temporary by some, and similarly the low income levels associated with low degrees of capacity working will also be widely regarded as transitory. This means that 'permanent incomes' will fluctuate less than actual incomes where factor returns fluctuate because of changes in the degree of capacity working. Actual incomes will exceed 'permanent incomes' at high-capacity working, and vice versa at low-capacity

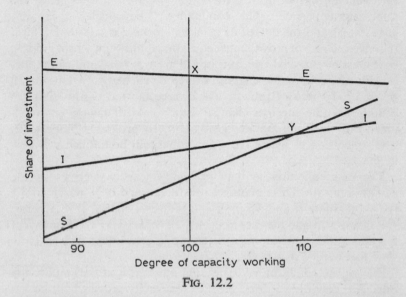

FIG. 12.2

working, and if saving is partly a function of the gap between actual and 'permanent incomes' as is widely supposed, then the share of saving will vary strongly with the degree of capacity working. For simplicity, it will be assumed that SS, the schedule showing the relationship between the share of saving and the degree of capacity working, does not shift through time. Thus planned saving will be a constant fraction of income at each degree of capacity working, and it will be a higher fraction of income, the higher the degree of capacity working.

II and SS cut at Y, which shows the degree of capacity working where planned saving equals planned investment. Y will show the equilibrium degree of capacity working at any time. The equilibrium at Y is stable if SS is steeper than II, and it is unstable if II is steeper than SS.[1]

The conditions where growth will be steady and stable at the equilibrium rate, g^*, where capital will increase at just the rate necessary to provide full employment for the labour force, whatever its rate of growth, can now be set out and outlined. For g, the actual rate of growth, continuously to equal g^*, four conditions must be satisfied. First, productive capacity must grow at the equilibrium rate. Second, output must grow at the equilibrium rate, i.e. at the same rate as capacity. This condition will be satisfied if capacity grows at g^* and the degree of capacity working is constant. Third, the expected rate of growth must equal the equilibrium rate of growth, so it must be expected that output will grow at the equilibrium rate. Fourth, there must be a stable degree of capacity working at all times, or the rate of growth will diverge far too easily from the equilibrium rate through chance disturbances to saving or investment, with the result that any kind of orderly progress is impossible. The circumstances where these conditions will be fulfilled will now be outlined.

The first condition is that productive capacity grows at the equilibrium rate. This condition will be satisfied if Y, which shows the point where II and SS intersect, is always on EE. If Y is below EE, investment and the rate of growth of capacity will be insufficient for the equilibrium rate of growth, while investment will be more than that needed if Y is above EE.

The second condition is that output must grow at the equilibrium rate. This condition will be satisfied if capacity grows at the equilibrium rate, and the degree of capacity working is constant, which will be achieved if the investment and saving functions intersect at a given point on EE. For this, II and SS must intersect on EE, and there must be no tendency for II and SS to shift.

The third condition is that the expected rate of growth must equal the actual and equilibrium rates. This condition will only be satisfied if II passes through X in Fig. 12.1, i.e. if investment is just sufficient for the equilibrium rate of growth at a degree of capacity working of

---

[1] If SS is steeper than II, planned saving will exceed planned investment to the right of Y, causing the degree of capacity working to fall towards that at Y, and planned investment will exceed planned saving to the left of Y, causing the degree of capacity working to rise. Hence, the equilibrium at Y is stable. It is unstable if II is steeper than SS because the degree of capacity working would always move further away from Y if it was at all away from that at Y. (See Kaldor, op. cit.)

100. Where the investment function intersects the normal-capacity working axis below X, the expected rate of growth is less than the equilibrium rate, while it exceeds the equilibrium rate where II is above X.

The fourth condition for steady and stable growth at the equilibrium rate is that the equilibrium at Y must be stable. This condition will be satisfied if SS is steeper than II. If II is steeper than SS, any chance disturbance will lead to very strong expansion or contraction.

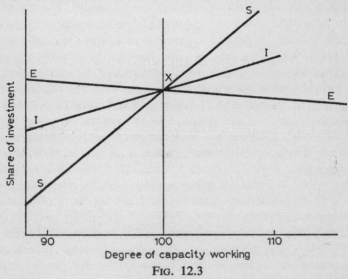

Fig. 12.3

The effect of these conditions is illustrated in Fig. 12.3. SS and II both pass through X where investment is just sufficient for the equilibrium rate of growth, the degree of capacity working is 100, and SS is steeper than II. At X, growth will continue at the equilibrium rate. Capacity will grow at the equilibrium rate. There will be no tendency for the degree of capacity working to alter, for SS will continue to pass through X, and with a constant rate of profit and exactly the rate of growth that entrepreneurs expect, and exactly the degree of capacity working they desire, II will not alter through time, so it will continue to pass through X. Moreover, the equilibrium at X is stable.

Some of these conditions are equivalent to the conditions for growth at the 'natural' rate in Harrod's argument. In the argument of this book, there are a number of possible equilibrium rates of growth, for the rate of technical progress is a variable and not a constant, but the particular equilibrium rate of growth that follows from the intersection of the investment function and the investment opportunity functions of Part II can be regarded as analogous to Harrod's 'natural' rate of growth. The condition arrived at here that SS must pass through X, i.e. that planned saving at normal-capacity working must just equal the investment needed for equilibrium growth, is equivalent to Harrod's condition that the 'natural' rate of growth must equal the 'warranted' rate of growth. The condition that II should pass through X, i.e. that planned investment at normal-capacity working must just equal the investment needed for the equilibrium rate of growth, is equivalent to the condition he was concerned with in 1964, that investment should be just sufficient for the 'natural' rate of growth where C equals C_r.[1] The condition that SS should be steeper than II is one which Kaldor has considered important,[2] but it is the opposite of the normal situation in the Harrod model. In the latter, a departure from equilibrium, i.e. a departure of the actual rate of growth from the 'warranted' rate, leads to a greater rise (or fall) in planned investment than in planned saving, which will produce unlimited expansion or contraction.

It is to be noted that much more is needed for growth at the equilibrium rate than equality between planned investment and planned saving at full employment. These will only be equal by chance, but even if they are equal, II must pass through X, i.e. growth expectations, etc., must be appropriate to the equilibrium rate of growth, and SS must be steeper than II if any kind of comfortable progress is to be possible. It is almost inconceivable that any actual economy could be continuously in this fortunate situation. The various factors which may produce departures from equilibrium growth will be considered in the next section.

Departures from Equilibrium Growth

There will be departures from equilibrium growth if any of the conditions outlined in the last section are not fulfilled. In this section, something will be said about the factors which may produce departures from equilibrium growth, and the effects of each of these will be analysed.

[1] Harrod, 'Are monetary and fiscal policies enough?'
[2] See Kaldor, op. cit., and 'A model of economic growth'.

There will be departures from equilibrium growth if saving or investment is inappropriate for this at normal-capacity working. The extent of any departures will clearly be much less severe where *SS* is steeper than *II* than in the reverse situation where *II* is steeper. In this section, the effect of inappropriate saving and investment schedules will be analysed first with the assumption that the savings schedule is steeper than the investment schedule. This will greatly reduce the extent of any departures from equilibrium, and it will be

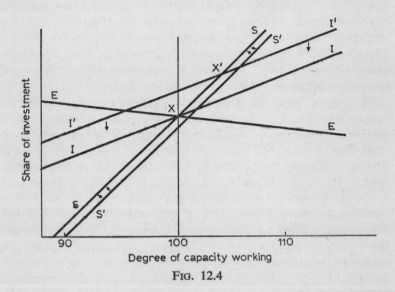

FIG. 12.4

useful to examine the nature and extent of the economy's equilibrating forces in the first place in the relatively simple conditions where *SS* is steeper than *II*. The effect of the more difficult situation where *II* is steeper (over at least part of the possible range of capacity working) will be analysed after this.

The first and simplest departure from equilibrium which will be examined is the effect of a small random movement of the savings schedule from *SS* to *S'S'* for one period (in Fig. 12.4), after which it returns to *SS*. The reduction in planned saving which temporarily shifts the savings schedule to *S'S'* raises the degree of capacity working from 100 to 101, and this means that actual output will rise 1 per cent faster than capacity while the degree of capacity working is rising, so that *g*, the actual rate of growth, will exceed *g**

by 1 per cent over the period of transition. This temporary increase in g may influence g_e, the expected rate of growth. If it does not, equilibrium will be rapidly restored. The investment function will not shift, and the return of the savings schedule to SS will reduce the degree of capacity working from 101 to the original 100, producing an actual rate of growth of 1 per cent less than g^* averaged over the period in which capacity working falls from 101 to 100. Growth can continue at rate g^* after this, provided that the temporary rise in g to a growth rate in excess of g^*, and its consequent temporary fall, have a negligible influence on the expected rate of growth. Thus the savings schedule can fluctuate about X without wider repercussions, provided that temporary fluctuations in g of the kind described have a negligible effect on g_e. The effect of short-term fluctuations in the investment schedule will be equally innocuous.

More complicated developments will follow a temporary fluctuation of saving (or investment) if this affects the expected rate of growth, but it appears that fluctuations in this will necessarily be limited. A *rising* g_e will be needed to produce a continuously rising degree of capacity working, so it is the rate of change of g_e (rather than g_e itself) that produces fluctuations in the degree of capacity working. As soon as g_e reaches a peak and ceases to rise further (following the shock producing a temporary fall in saving), the investment function will reach a peak (at, say, $I'I'$ in Fig. 12.4) and the degree of capacity working will then cease to rise further. The actual rate of growth will then become the same as the rate of growth of capacity, and in time the expected rate of growth will come down towards this. The investment function will fall back towards X for two reasons: first, because of the fall in the expected rate of growth which will follow the reduction in the actual rate of growth to equality with the rate of growth of capacity; and second, because at X' investment exceeds that needed for equilibrium growth which will produce a falling profit rate and so a falling investment function. The fall in the expected rate of growth and the rate of profit will bring the investment function down, and reduce the degree of capacity working towards 100. The falling investment function is likely to overshoot equilibrium, for the actual rate of growth will be less than the rate of growth of capacity while the degree of capacity working is falling, which may well cause g_e to fall below g^*, so small random movements of the saving and investment schedules, when these are otherwise compatible with equilibrium growth, will produce fluctuations in the degree of capacity working around 100 if g_e is sensitive to g over short periods.

It is to be noted that fluctuations due to a fluctuating expected rate of growth will be slight unless expectations are highly elastic. If the increase in g to a growth rate of g^* plus 1 per cent averaged over the period of transition produces only a slight once-for-all upward revision of g_e, the investment function will rise briefly and then fall back as soon as it is appreciated that output is merely rising at approximately g^*. A rise in g must produce immediate expectations of further increases in this if fluctuations in the expected rate of growth are to produce results that are at all significant. The assumption that a change in g will always produce a smaller change in g_e will be quite sufficient to contain such fluctuations within narrow bounds.

Thus the economy will remain close to its equilibrium growth path provided that temporary fluctuations in the savings and investment schedules are the sole source of disturbance, and provided that g_e is not particularly sensitive to short-term fluctuations in g. The effect of a long-term failure of the investment or saving function to pass through X must now be analysed, for this may produce more troublesome effects.

The effect of an inappropriate investment function follows quite straightforwardly from the above analysis, for $I'I'$ in Fig. 12.4 can be regarded as the investment function of an economy with an expected rate of growth that is substantially above g^* over more than a transitory period, while the savings function, SS, is the one appropriate for equilibrium growth. Here, with the degree of capacity working constant at 103 (where $I'I'$ intersects SS in Fig. 12.4), g will not exceed the rate of growth of capacity, so expectations of a rate of growth substantially faster than g^* can hardly be fulfilled, with the result that g_e should come down in time, however strongly expectations of a faster rate of growth are held; and the rate of profit will fall with investment above EE which will produce additional reductions in investment. The falling expected rate of growth and the falling rate of profit will gradually lower the investment function towards X. There is obvious risk of overshooting, but the tendency for an investment function that is above or below X because of an inappropriate expected rate of growth to produce correcting effects is clear and obvious.

The situation where the savings function is inappropriate for equilibrium growth is a more difficult one to analyse, and the effects

K*

of this on the growth process are more serious. This is the situation that corresponds to discrepancies between the 'natural' and 'warranted' rates of growth in Harrod's model, and these produce persistent unemployment or inflation. In the model outlined in this book, a savings function inappropriate for equilibrium growth may be due to a rate of interest that is above or below the one that produces identical savings and investment functions. It was argued in Chapter 8 that the private sector's planned investment will exceed the savings available to the private sector at full employment if the rate of interest is lower than the particular i that is compatible with long-term equilibrium and vice versa. As the relationship between private sector saving and investment depends on both the rate of interest and taxation and debt policies, low interest rates will not produce an excess of planned investment over planned saving if governments ensure that sufficient saving is made available to the private sector from public sources. Similarly, high rates of interest can be compensated through the use of potential private sector finance in the public sector. Then excessive saving can be due to too high an interest rate, or taxation that is excessive in relation to public expenditure. Similarly, insufficient saving can be due to a low interest rate, or insufficient taxation in relation to public expenditure. Whatever the ultimate cause of such discrepancies, there is no doubt that the savings schedule may be inappropriate for equilibrium over long periods, and the effects of this will now be analysed.

The situation where saving is insufficient for equilibrium is illustrated in Fig. 12.5. SS is below X, and it intersects II, the investment function appropriate for equilibrium growth, at X' where the degree of capacity working exceeds 100. Now X' must lie above EE, and this means that the rate of profit must be falling, which will produce a falling investment function. The degree of capacity working will fall as the investment function falls, and this means that g will be less than the rate of growth of capacity which should produce a fall in g_e, and this will also contribute to the fall of the investment function. Once the investment function is as low as Y' (where SS and EE intersect), investment will cease to exceed that needed for equilibrium growth, and the rate of profit will then cease to fall, and below Y' investment will actually be insufficient for equilibrium growth and the rate of profit will start to rise. The fall in the investment function is unlikely to stop at Y' because of the effect of the expected rate of growth, but the rising rate of profit as the investment function falls below Y' will arrest its fall in time, and once it ceases to fall (when it reaches, say, $I''I''$) it will start to rise because of the rising rate of profit. As the investment function rises above $I''I''$, the degree of capacity working will be rising which will have a favourable effect on both g and the expected rate of growth, and this will give the investment function further upward stimulus until Y' is reached, when the rate of profit will again start to fall. Capacity working will

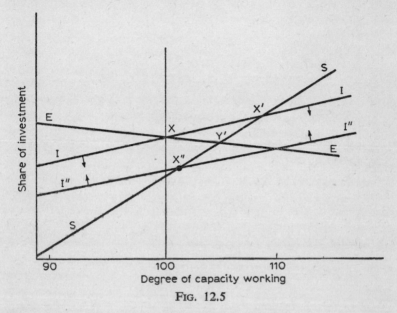

FIG. 12.5

then fluctuate around Y' (where the savings function and EE intersect), and the degree of fluctuation will depend on the sensitivity of g_e to g. At Y' there is excess demand for labour and abnormal-capacity working, and this will be the point around which fluctuations will occur where saving is persistently less than that needed for equilibrium growth.

It is to be noted that in this situation, where, in Harrod's terms, the 'natural' rate of growth exceeds the 'warranted' rate, capital increases at approximately the equilibrium rate and the Harrod problem is solved through the variability in the degree of capacity working that is allowed for in this model. The share of investment in the National Product that is needed for equilibrium growth is lower, the higher the degree of capacity working (i.e. EE slopes downwards), while the share of saving is higher, the higher the degree of capacity working. There must then always be a degree of capacity working where planned saving will equal the investment necessary for equilibrium growth, i.e. any *SS* line must intersect *EE* somewhere. The degree of capacity working where *SS* and *EE* intersect will exceed 100 where the savings schedule passes below *X*, and it will be less than 100 where saving is excessive at normal-capacity working,

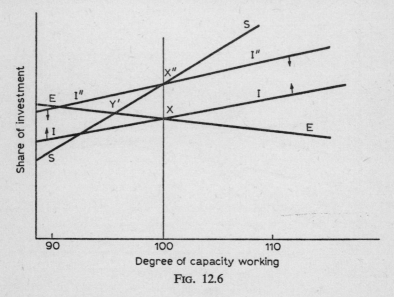

Fig. 12.6

as in Fig. 12.6 where the economy will fluctuate around *Y'*. Then where, in Harrod's terms, the 'natural' rate of growth differs from the 'warranted' rate, income will fluctuate around a degree of capacity working that differs from 100.

It then appears that capital will grow at approximately the equilibrium rate, even where the savings ratio is inappropriate for equilibrium growth. This will simply produce a persistent tendency towards over- or undercapacity working with consequent repercussions on the rate of inflation and the balance of payments, but there should be no long-run tendency for capital to grow at rates other than the equilibrium rate. These results have, however, been arrived at with the relatively simple assumption that the short-run savings function is always steeper than the short-run investment function. There will certainly be situations where the reverse is true, and this will produce the effect of Harrod's 'knife-edge', and much wider fluctuations.

Where the investment function is steeper than the savings function, expansion or contraction will be unlimited unless, following Kaldor, at least one of the functions is non-linear, as in Fig. 12.7 where the investment function is non-linear. Here, there are possible equilibrium degrees of capacity working at X, Y' and Y'', but the intersection point between II and SS at X is unstable, so the economy will always

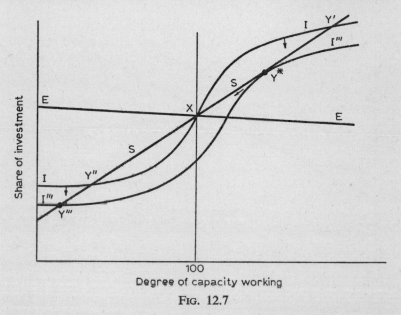

Fig. 12.7

tend to either Y' or Y''. As Kaldor pointed out in 1940, there are several reasons why the investment function may be non-linear. The sensitivity of investment to the degree of capacity working will be unusually low at high levels of economic activity because 'rising costs of construction, increasing costs and increasing difficulty of borrowing will dissuade entrepreneurs from expanding still faster – at a time when they already have large commitments'. Thus, ceilings will limit the physical output of the capital-goods industries, and financial ceilings will reduce the sensitivity of investment to the degree of capacity working where there is considerable overcapacity working. A further point, not mentioned by Kaldor, is that entrepreneurs may well expect that high levels of capacity working will

not be maintained for long, which means that they will not respond
to increases in capacity working with higher investment, once a
certain point is reached. At the lower end, the investment function
will be non-linear because only part of entrepreneurial investment
is sensitive to the degree of capacity working, the remainder being a
response to technical developments and autonomous factors.

In Fig. 12.7, the economy will tend to either Y' or Y'', because
the equilibrium at X is unstable. At Y', the degree of capacity

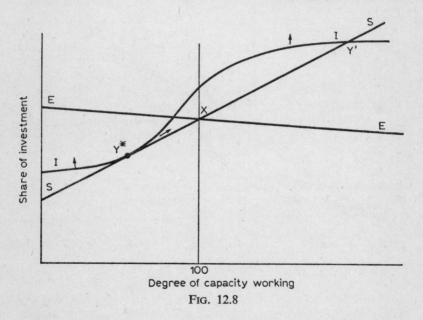

FIG. 12.8

working exceeds 100 and investment exceeds that needed for equilibrium growth, so the rate of profit must be falling. This must produce
a falling investment function, and output will grow less quickly than
capacity as this falls which will have adverse effects on the expected
rate of growth, and this will accentuate the rate of fall of the investment function. If SS passes through X as in Fig. 12.7, the falling
investment function must become tangential to SS above EE, so
there will be excessive capital accumulation until the investment
function falls to tangency with SS (at Y^*). The investment function
will then have fallen to $I'''I'''$. Once it falls below this, output will
fall to Y''', the lower equilibrium point. At the lower equilibrium
point, investment must be insufficient for equilibrium growth, and

the rising rate of profit that follows from this (at a given degree of capacity working) will gradually raise *II*, and rising growth expectations will then contribute to its rise until it is again tangential to *SS* as in Fig. 12.8. This mechanism, which is almost exactly as Kaldor described it in 1940 (the differences are the use made of the expected rate of growth, and the *EE* line), will produce fluctuations between the upper and lower equilibrium points. Equilibrium investment will be achieved in the long run, for the rate of profit will always be

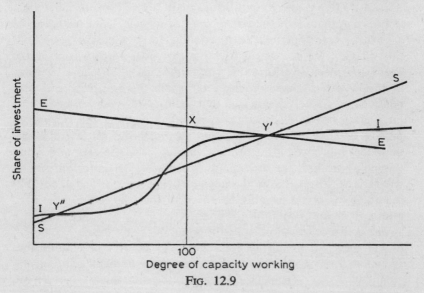

FIG. 12.9

rising (at a given degree of capacity working) where less than this is invested, and falling in the converse situation. If *SS* passes through *X* as in the above diagrams, the average degree of capacity working over the cycle will be 100, but it will be more than 100 if *SS* passes below *X*, and less than 100 if it is above *X*.

The case where *SS* is below *X* so that saving is insufficient for equilibrium growth at a degree of capacity working of 100 is an interesting one (and it is not implicit in Kaldor's account), for this raises the possibility of continuous stable growth without strong cyclical tendencies. In Fig. 12.9, *Y′*, the upper stable point, is on *EE* (which is possible because *SS* is below *X*) and in consequence the rate of profit will be constant at *Y′*. Random disturbances will shift the investment and saving functions, and cause slight fluctuations of the kind considered earlier, but a shift to the lower equilibrium point will be avoided provided that investment does not fall (or savings rise) to a position where there is tangency between the investment and savings functions. It might then appear that stable growth is possible at a position like Y' where saving is insufficient for equilibrium growth at normal-capacity working. There is unfortunately one difficulty.

In Fig. 12.9, II intersects the normal-capacity working axis below X (and it must do so if equilibrium is to be achieved on EE). This implies a g_e that is less than g^* at normal-capacity working. Clearly, growth for several periods at the equilibrium rate must raise g_e, and this will shift the investment function upwards, which will raise the degree of capacity working and g and thus raise g_e further. However, as the investment function rises, the share of investment will rise relatively to EE and this means that the rate of profit will be falling (at a given degree of capacity working) throughout the expansion process described above. The falling rate of profit will exercise the dominant influence on investment, once g_e ceases to rise, and from this point onwards the investment function will start to fall. There will then be fluctuations in the degree of capacity working about Y', but these might conceivably be so small that the economy avoids falling to its lower equilibrium point.

The converse situation is also a possibility, and this is illustrated in Fig. 12.10. If saving is more than that needed for equilibrium growth at normal-capacity working, there may be stable equilibrium at a low degree of capacity working, and this might even be an equilibrium point where there is no long-run tendency for the rate of profit to rise. The economy would then fluctuate in conditions where excess capacity and unemployment were the norm, and where booms were never quite strong enough to take the economy to its upper equilibrium point.

A situation where the investment function is steeper than the savings function over a certain range can then produce three basic types of cyclical process. If saving is just sufficient for equilibrium growth at normal-capacity working, i.e. if the 'natural' rate of growth equals the 'warranted' rate, then the economy will fluctuate between a high equilibrium point where there are shortages of capacity, and the investment-goods industries are producing to capacity, and a low equilibrium point where there is excess capacity, and negligible 'induced' investment. Where savings are insufficient for equilibrium growth at normal-capacity working, i.e. where the 'natural' rate of growth exceeds the 'warranted' rate, the economy may fluctuate about a rather higher capacity working rate, but alternatively, stable equilibrium could conceivably be maintained throughout, with relatively small fluctuations which never take the economy away from overcapacity working. If saving is more than that needed for equilibrium growth, there is a possible prospect of fluctuations about a low equilibrium point with continuous excess capacity.

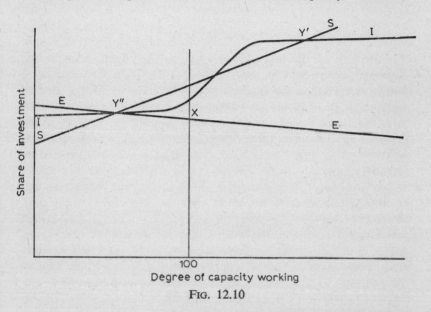

FIG. 12.10

It will be noted that there need only be serious disturbances to equilibrium growth where the investment function is steeper than the savings function over part of its range, and even then capital will grow at approximately the equilibrium rate in the long run apart from the situation where saving is excessive at normal-capacity working, where there may be persistent underemployment of labour and capital.

A very large number of possible types of fluctuation have been outlined in this section, and some of these have serious implications while others are relatively innocuous. Two points stand out. The first is that the position of the savings function in relation to X is of great importance. Where SS passes above X, excess capacity will be the norm, while overcapacity working will be the norm where SS is below X. However, the growth process is only likely to be particularly disturbed where the investment function is steeper than the savings function over part of its range, for fluctuations may then be quite extensive. The factors which influence the slope of the saving and investment functions are therefore of great importance, and this must now be discussed. The next section will be concerned with this problem.

The Stability of Equilibrium and the Extent of Fluctuations

The analysis of the last section suggests that fluctuations in the National Income will be relatively slight if the savings function is always steeper than the investment function (and g_e is not unduly sensitive to g). Fluctuations will be quite extensive where the investment function is steeper. The factors which influence the slope of the savings and investment functions are therefore of great importance, and they must now be analysed. The investment function will be considered first.

The investment function slopes upwards because businesses can be expected to invest more where they are short of capacity than where they have excess capacity, and the slope of the investment function will depend on the sensitivity of business investment to the degree of capacity working. If the capital–output ratio that business seeks to maintain is V_r, then approximately an extra V_r per cent of the National Product will need to be invested to make good each per cent by which businesses judge that the capital stock is deficient. If they plan to make good the shortage over j years, they will need to invest an extra V_r/j per cent of the National Product per annum for each per cent by which they judge the capital stock to be deficient. If they judge that overcapacity working of 1 per cent indicates a shortage of capital of 1 per cent, then the share of business investment will be V_r/j per cent higher where the degree of capacity working is 101 than it will be where this is 100 – and V_r/j per cent lower where it is 99. The slope of the investment function will then be V_r/j.

If j is one year, so that businessmen plan to make good a shortage of capacity in full in one year, investment will be higher by V_r per cent of the National Product for each per cent of overcapacity working, and lower by V_r per cent for each per cent of excess capacity – a situation similar to that produced by a crude acceleration principle. The slope of the investment function would then be V_r, which would exceed 1 quite substantially if V_r corresponds to the capital–output ratio (measured in years) with new plant. The slope of the savings function will correspond to the marginal propensity to save out of the increased incomes that are due to higher-capacity working, and this must be less than 1, and few would argue that it can be more than $\frac{1}{3}$–$\frac{1}{2}$. Then, where the slope of the investment function is V_r, i.e. where entrepreneurs seek to invest enough to correct for shortages or surpluses of productive capacity in one period, this must be steeper than the savings function, and these assumptions must produce instability. In the traditional multiplier–accelerator theory of the trade cycle, periods of very rapid expansion and contraction generally alternate, and this is the result of extreme sensitivity of investment to the degree of capacity working. Harrod's 'knife-edge' is due to the fact that any departure of the actual rate of growth from the 'warranted' rate will produce a larger increase (or fall) in planned investment than in planned saving leading to further expansion (or contraction), and this is again due to the sensitivity of investment to the degree of capacity working that is assumed. The assumption that entrepreneurs seek to make good shortages (or surpluses) of plant in one period must inevitably produce a similar result.

It can be argued, however, that the investment function need not be as steep as V_r. Its slope is V_r/j, and this will be less than V_r if entrepreneurs aim to adjust their plant to normal-capacity working over several periods. j will exceed 1 in so far as investment takes time (and expansion in some industries takes four years or more), and in so far as entrepreneurs regard periods of excess demand or supply as temporary. It will be evident that the slope of the investment function will be much less than V_r if j substantially exceeds 1, and it could perfectly plausibly be less than the slope of the savings function.

j, the period of time over which entrepreneurs correct for shortages or surpluses of plant, will depend on two sets of factors. It will depend partly on physical gestation periods, and it will also depend on the pace at which entrepreneurs *seek* to correct for apparent shortages or surpluses of plant. Physical gestation periods, which amount to four or more years in some sectors of the economy, will hardly come to more than two or three years, averaged over the economy as a whole, and they could well be less than this. V_r/j would then be $\frac{1}{3}V_r - \frac{1}{2}V_r$, which would exceed any plausible marginal propensity to save. Then the investment function would almost certainly be steeper than the savings function if physical gestation periods were the sole factor that influenced j. It is, however, also possible that entrepreneurs will not seek to correct sensitively for over- and undercapacity working because investment plans may be more dependent on long-term considerations than on short-term fluctuations. This requires that long-term expectations are firmly held and not easily changed. II may well be less steep than SS if j exceeds physical gestation periods for this reason, so the sensitivity of entrepreneurial plans to current conditions may be of decisive importance.

Joan Robinson pointed out how important it was that investment plans should depend predominantly on long-term considerations rather than current conditions in 1952, when she wrote:

... when the capitalists know that unpredictable disturbances are liable to occur, the inertia of the economy is destroyed. When the present state of affairs alone is certain, it has an undue influence upon behaviour. Thus, when output expands, for any reason, relatively to capacity, capitalists have a tendency to behave as though they expected the consequent high level of profit to be maintained in the future, and to plan investment accordingly. While investment is going on, profits rule all the higher; but the increase in capacity which is being created is doomed to bring the rate of profit below the level which caused it to be planned. Thus accumulation can take place only in a series of booms interrupted by slumps.[1]

Here, Joan Robinson's investment function differs slightly from the one assumed in this chapter, but the importance of the entrepreneurial time horizon is the same. Where 'the present state of affairs alone is certain', entrepreneurs will overcorrect for excess capacity and over-capacity working, with the result that there is upward and downward instability. Where an economy has settled down to fairly continuous growth, investment will not rise massively where there is 2 or 3 per cent overcapacity working, or fall where there is a little excess capacity. Investment plans are more likely to be based on expected

---

[1] Joan Robinson, 'The model of an expanding economy', *Economic Journal*, vol. LXII (Mar 1952) pp. 52-3.

long-term trends, and these may be adjusted rather slowly and slightly in response to short-term changes in the level of economic activity. j will then much exceed 1, with the result that the economy's savings function may well be steeper than its investment function, so that growth will indeed be stable and fluctuations slight.

The possibility that SS may be steeper than II does not rest solely on the above argument. Monetary factors have been ignored up to this point in the argument of this chapter, and these may produce a stable equilibrium where the 'real' factors would, by themselves, produce instability. If the money supply grows at the same rate as the money value of normal-capacity output, any increase in the degree of capacity working will be associated with tightening money markets and a rise in the rate of interest, while conversely a fall in the degree of capacity working will be associated with a fall in liquidity preference relatively to the money supply and a fall in the rate of interest. The rise in the rate of interest and the monetary tightening that is associated with a rise in the degree of capacity working will reduce planned investment relatively to planned saving at each degree of capacity working, which means that the slope of the investment function will be reduced relatively to that of the savings function. Similarly, the lower rate of interest associated with excess capacity will raise planned investment relatively to planned saving, and once again reduce the slope of the investment function relatively to that of the savings function. This will clearly increase the possibility that the savings function will be the steeper of the two. There is then a considerable possibility that the basic equilibrium position where the investment and savings functions intersect may be stable. If monetary factors are ignored, j may be large enough to make SS steeper than II. Even if II is still steeper than SS where only 'real' factors are considered, the additional influence of monetary factors may produce conditions of stable equilibrium.

The conclusion of the argument of this chapter must then be that an approximation to steady growth, and very wide fluctuations, are both possible. Some economies will enjoy stable growth with only slight fluctuations. These will be economies where entrepreneurial investment plans are based on realistic expected growth rates, and where these are only slightly adjusted when the rate of growth changes. Such economies will take short-run shocks in their stride, and their rates of growth, their rates of profit and their shares of investment should correspond quite closely to those arrived at in the equilibrium analysis of Part II. In other economies, the expected rate of growth will have less influence on investment decisions, and current capacity working and current profitability will matter more. Such economies will have steeper investment functions than savings functions, and if monetary factors are insufficient to produce stability, output may oscillate between high and low degrees of capacity working, or it may settle at a high or low point with the prospect that there might always be substantial fluctuations if a shock affected saving or investment sufficiently sharply. In such economies, the equilibrium results of Part II should give the values of the major variables averaged over long periods, but considerable short-run vicissitudes would be a possibility.

The one case which works out particularly badly for equilibrium growth theory is the one where the investment function is steeper than the savings function, and saving is more than that needed for equilibrium growth at normal-capacity working. In this case the economy may reach a low equilibrium point with continuous over-capacity working, and no long-run tendency for the degree of capacity working to reach a high equilibrium point. There will then be no tendency for the capital stock to grow at the equilibrium rate in the long run, and factory space may well grow less quickly than the labour force to produce structural unemployment. In other cases, the worst that can happen is fluctuation around the equilibrium rate of capital accumulation with the result that the equilibrium equations indicate what happens in the long run; and they will give quite good results for the short run as well if the relationship between II and SS is stable and the savings ratio is not too much out of line with the saving necessary for equilibrium growth.

It has, of course, been assumed throughout this chapter that there is an equilibrium growth path producing an equilibrium share of investment that is represented by EE in the diagrams. It emerged in Chapter 11 that where there are increasing returns to scale, equilibrium growth will only be possible in very special circumstances. The long-term investment function and the investment opportunity function will, however, intersect at all times, and this will produce a precise growth rate, profit rate and required investment share, though these may well shift through time. The effect of a changing EE line will be no more serious than the effects from a series of small consecutive shocks to the savings and investment functions. Investment will accommodate to a changing EE line if it can accommodate to changes in *II* and *SS* without serious fluctuations, and this means that the argument of this chapter can follow on quite naturally from the results of Chapter 11.

The conclusion of this chapter is, then, that economic growth will often correspond quite closely to equilibrium growth. In other cases, particularly where current economic conditions have a considerable influence on investment decisions, output will fluctuate quite considerably, but long-term trends in the major variables should still correspond quite closely to equilibrium trends apart from the case where an economy has both instability and excessive saving. However, where an economy is subject to strong fluctuations, the fluctuations themselves may exercise some influence on the technical progress and production functions, with the result that cyclical movements and entrepreneurs' response to these may play a role in the development of economies that is additional to the influence of the equilibrium relationships. This may obviously happen, but it is to be noted that it will only happen in particular circumstances.

13

The Problem of Distribution

MUCH has been said about income distribution in previous chapters. Two basic approaches to this have been outlined: the theories of Kalecki, Kaldor and Pasinetti which use Keynesian income flows to determine distribution, and the various theories which rely on the equation of the wage to the marginal product of labour – or, with vintage assumptions, to output per worker with the least productive plant in use. These approaches have produced results which are in many cases diametrically opposed to each other. As the theory of income distribution is, in Ricardo's words, 'the principal problem in Political Economy',[1] matters cannot be left in this unsatisfactory state. An attempt will therefore be made in this chapter to resolve some of the difficulties which are due to the opposed results of the two principal theories of distribution, and the theoretical chapters of this book will conclude with an account of the theory of income distribution which then emerges.

The Keynesian theories have produced a number of very useful results, and three particularly vital equations are the following. First, from Kalecki, and based simply on National Income accounting identities:

$$P \equiv I + C_p - W_s \tag{4.1}$$

where P is aggregate profits, I aggregate investment, C_p consumption from profits and W_s saving from wages. It is clear from this National Income accounting identity that aggregate profits must be higher where investment is higher, or where consumption out of unearned incomes is higher. Kaldor has produced a very similar equation (from (4.8)):

$$X_p \equiv \frac{I}{Y} \cdot \frac{1}{S_p - S_w} - \frac{S_w}{S_p - S_w} \tag{13.1}$$

---

[1] Ricardo, *Principles of Political Economy and Taxation*, in *Works* (ed. Sraffa) vol. I, p. 5.

where S_p is the proportion of *aggregate* profits saved, and S_w the proportion of wages and salaries saved. This equation can be derived from Kalecki's,[1] and like (4.1) it is derived directly from accounting identities (though I, S_p and S_w could refer to planned investment and savings propensities instead of actual *ex-post* saving and investment), and it shows that profits must vary directly with investment (though here it is the *share* of profits that varies with the *share* of investment) and inversely with the proportion of profits saved. For the customary interpretation of this equation, it must be assumed that in any economy at any one time, a higher I will always raise I/Y, so that where entrepreneurs raise planned investment, they also raise the share of investment in the National Income, and vice versa.

Pasinetti has shown that (13.1) can be much simplified in steady growth, for the proportion of the capital stock that workers and salary earners own will then be the same as their proportion of aggregate saving. Workers' saving will then have an entirely neutral effect on income distribution with the result that:

$$X_p = \frac{I}{Y} \cdot \frac{1}{S_c} \tag{13.2}$$

where S_c is the proportion of profits saved by 'pure capitalists' who have no earned income. (13.2) is not the mere result of accounting identities, so it is both more useful and less useful than (13.1). It is more useful because it makes the prediction that, in steady growth, X_p will be determined by I/Y and S_c alone, and it is less useful because there is no reason to expect it to be valid in the short period, while the more complex (13.1) must hold over all periods, however short.

At first sight, these Keynesian equations appear to provide the basis for a theory of distribution, for the first two, at any rate, must hold in all circumstances, and they present plausible propositions about distribution that are by no means obvious. There are, however, two weaknesses in these equations. Profits and the share of profits are determined by investment and the share of investment, but I and I/Y are themselves variables, and not parameters that are given to an economy. The variables I and I/Y will themselves be influenced by the distribution of incomes if investment is financed substantially from profits as it often is, so it is not clear whether profits determine investment or whether it is generally the other way round. Keynesians

[1] See p. 78 above.

maintain the latter, but this is not the only direction of causation that is possible. With the direction of causation unclear (or indeed whether there is causation), all that can be said is that (4.1) and (13.1) describe the relationship between actual profits and actual investment at all times, and this relationship must play a part in an overall system of equations that determine all the variables of an economy. It cannot be said from this relationship alone that the share of profits is determined by the share of investment.

The second limitation to the conclusions that can be directly derived from the Keynesian equations is more serious and fundamental. (4.1), (13.1) and (13.2) are derived from the condition that saving and investment are equal where product markets are cleared. There is no reference to factor markets in the derivation of these equations, so saving may be identical to investment with half the labour force unemployed, or with more vacancies than jobs. This would not invalidate (4.1) and (13.1), for these are valid wherever $I = S$. However, the lack of reference to the labour market means that further conditions will need to be met if labour market equilibrium at full employment is to be achieved as well as product market equilibrium. It follows from this that the Keynesian equations can produce no more than part of a theory of distribution.

The alternative theory, the marginal productivity theory and its vintage equivalent, has also produced some simple and useful results, but there are again serious weaknesses. The simplest marginal productivity proposition is, of course, the result that with Cobb–Douglas assumptions, full employment, and perfect competition in all markets, the share of profits equals the capital exponential, α. The formula for the share of profits is only slightly more complicated than this with CES assumptions, i.e. (from (2.6)):

$$X_p = J.V^{(1-1/\sigma)} \tag{13.3}$$

where J is a constant. In steady growth, V, the capital–output ratio, equals S/g which equals $S/(A+n+B.S)$, so that:

$$X_p = J.\left(\frac{S}{A+n+B.S}\right)^{(1-1/\sigma)}. \tag{13.4}$$

(13.4) brings out the familiar result that with marginal productivity assumptions, a higher share of investment will be associated with a lower share of profits when the elasticity of substitution between labour and capital is less than unity – the usual assumption. This is the opposite of the apparent results produced by the Keynesian models.

With vintage assumptions, the position is basically the same. Here, with a constant labour force (from (3.20)):

$$X_p = \frac{e^{aT} - aT - 1}{e^{aT} - 1} = \tfrac{1}{2}aT(1 - \tfrac{1}{6}aT + \tfrac{1}{360}a^3T^3...) \qquad (13.5)$$

where a is the rate of technical progress and T is the life of plant. It is clear that the share of profits will vary strongly with the product of a and T. A higher share of investment will raise a in so far as technical progress is endogenous to the investment process, but it will reduce T provided that the elasticity of substitution between labour and capital with new plant is less than about

$$\theta^* \left[1 + \left(\frac{B.S}{A} \right) (X_w + \tfrac{1}{3}X_p) \right] \quad \text{(from (7.17)).}$$

The effect of a higher S upon the product of a and T will then depend both on the elasticity of substitution between labour and capital, and the proportion of technical progress that is endogenous, and it can be shown that the critical value of the elasticity of substitution between labour and capital with new plant which determines whether higher investment will raise or lower the share of profits is of the order of

$$\theta^* \left(\frac{1}{1 + \tfrac{1}{3} \left(\dfrac{B.S}{A} \right)} \right) \quad \text{(from (7.23)).}$$

Higher investment will reduce the share of profits where the elasticity of substitution is less than this, and increase it where it exceeds this critical value.

Then, with both vintage and non-vintage assumptions, whether a higher share of investment raises or lowers the share of profits will depend on the elasticity of substitution between labour and capital, but the critical value of the elasticity of substitution differs in the two cases. The critical value of σ, the elasticity of substitution with non-vintage assumptions, is unity, and it is only where σ exceeds this that higher investment raises the share of profits. With vintage assumptions, the critical value of θ, the equivalent parameter, is rather lower than 1, less than 0·70–0·83 where technical progress is part endogenous, and higher investment will raise the share of profits where θ exceeds this.

Thus marginal productivity and the equivalent vintage theory produce results that are quite distinct from those produced by the Keynesian equations. With the Keynesian equations, a higher share of investment always raises the share of profits, while with vintage assumptions it will only do so if the elasticity of substitution between labour and capital is higher than some critical value. However, the marginal productivity results depend on a number of assumptions which much weaken their acceptability. In the first place, (13.3) (13.4) and (13.5) will only hold where there is perfect competition in all markets, constant returns to scale and full employment. Imperfect competition and increasing returns can to some extent be allowed for by assuming that factors receive given proportions of their marginal products, as in Chapter 11 where increasing returns were assumed, and with CES assumptions:

$$X_p = \frac{p_2 \cdot z}{1 + \left(\frac{1-h}{h}\right) \cdot \left(\frac{K}{L}\right)^{(1/\sigma - 1)}} \qquad (11.13)$$

where z is the returns to scale factor and p_2 the proportion of its marginal product that capital receives. A higher share of investment will raise the capital–labour ratio, and this will reduce the share of profits if σ is less than 1, as with perfect competition. Then, if there is some stability in p_2, imperfect competition will not change the fundamental nature of the marginal productivity results, for provided that a change in K/L is not accompanied by a continuous change in p_2 in a particular direction, higher investment will change income distribution in the same direction as it does in conditions of perfect competition. However, the influence of marginal products and the technical conditions of production that determine them will be weakened, for income distribution will also be influenced by p_1 and p_2, the proportions of their marginal products that labour and capital receive, and these will have an influence on distribution that may be as great as or greater than the influence of marginal products. Both sets of factors are taken into account in (11.13), and this equation shows that the share of profits will fall if K/L rises with σ less than 1, and that it will also fall if p_2 falls.

This qualification to the results of *simpliste* marginal productivity theory does not remove the contradictions between the results of the marginal productivity and the Keynesian theories of distribution. A higher share of investment at full employment will still raise the share of profits according to Keynesian theory, and reduce it according to marginal productivity theory (with $\sigma < 1$). There are, however, further weaknesses in marginal productivity theory.

The principal weakness that has not yet been considered is the one that was considered at length in Chapter 5. It was shown there that *simpliste* marginal productivity results depend crucially on the assumption that all the various goods that are produced in an economy are manufactured with the same technique of production so that their relative prices are constant, with the result that one-good-model assumptions are valid. Variability in the relative prices of capital and consumer goods will produce discrepancies between technical relationships like marginal products, and *value* relationships such as income shares. Moreover, *simpliste* marginal productivity results depend on the assumption that production functions are smooth and twice differentiable. The possibility that particular techniques may be the most profitable ones at more than one set of factor prices will prevent this, to put it mildly.

Wherever income distribution is derived from the partial differentiation of production functions with respect to capital and labour, it must be implicitly assumed that these difficulties are not fundamental. It may be supposed, for instance, that production functions are reasonably smooth within the plausible range of marginal products, and that differences in the rate of profit have only moderate effects on the relative prices of capital and consumer goods. The neoclassical results may provide an approximation to the true relationships and they may stand up to empirical testing if these assumptions are justified. It is obvious that the heterogeneity of capital and consumer goods will often matter, but it does not follow from the consequent failure of *simpliste* marginal productivity theory that income distribution can then be independent of the technical conditions of production, for a fundamental relationship resembling the marginal productivity one will still hold. This can be shown with the help of the vintage theory distribution diagram of Chapter 3.

Suppose that there is an economy with a heterogeneous collection of capital goods producing a variety of capital and consumer goods with a variety of techniques, and suppose that labour requirements with all capital equipment are fixed once this is installed, as with putty-clay vintage theory. This meets the conditions of those who are sceptical about the relevance of marginal products to income distribution.

The capital equipment capable of manufacturing *each* of the many products produced by the economy can be represented by a schedule such as the line *AB* in Fig. 13.1. This diagram resembles the vintage distribution diagram in Fig. 3.2, but Fig. 13.1 represents a single industry producing a single product, and not the whole economy. The capital equipment capable of manufacturing this product is listed along the horizontal axis in ascending order of labour productivity, and the distance along the horizontal axis shows the number

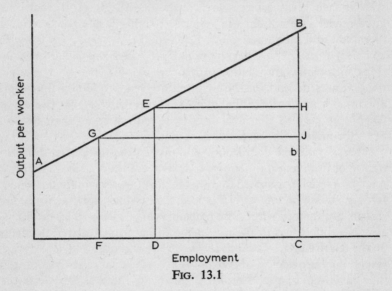

Fig. 13.1

of workers required to work each item of equipment, so that a capital good worked by 10 workers is represented by 10 units along the horizontal axis. The item of equipment with the highest labour productivity is *b*, and labour productivity with *b* is *BC*. If *CD* workers are employed in this industry, it will be most efficient to work the equipment between *C* and *D*, and total output of the good in question will then be *BCDE*. Suppose, to simplify the initial argument, that there is perfect competition in both the labour and the product market. Then with *CD* workers employed, the wage *in terms of this industry's product* will be *ED* for the reasons explained in Chapter 3,[1] and the industry's total wage bill will then be *EHCD*, and its aggregate profits *EBH*.

[1] See pp. 45-6 above.

There will be a similar diagram for each of the products that is manufactured in the economy. If the aggregate employment provided by all the industries (i.e. the sum of the *CD*'s of all the various diagrams) is less than the economy's available labour force, employment in some industries will need to be increased if full employment is to be achieved. If the industry represented in Fig. 13.1 is one of these, and its employment is increased from *CD* to *CF*, the wage bill, *measured in terms of the product of the industry in question*, will change from *EHCD* to *GJCF*, aggregate profits will rise from *EBH* to *GBJ*, and the share of profits will rise from *EBH/BCDE* to *GBJ/BCFG*. Thus any rise in employment in this industry must be associated with a rise in its share of profits, and a rise in aggregate profits measured in its product. A rise in employment in the economy as a whole will produce a net rise in employment but not necessarily an increase in employment in each industry, for employment might fall in industries producing 'inferior' goods where an increase in aggregate demand might reduce sales. These are hardly likely to amount to a significant proportion of industry, and the share of aggregate profits in the National Income will rise with an increase in employment provided that the higher profit shares in industries where employment rises have a greater effect on aggregate profits than the lower profit shares where employment falls, and they certainly should since it does not appear in practice that employment falls in a significant range of industries when general employment rises. There is, moreover, a further point in favour of the supposition that the aggregate share of profits will rise with aggregate employment, for as this rises, the relative prices of goods produced in industries with growing employment should rise relatively to those in any industries with declining employment as a result of normal supply and demand analysis, and as a result of this the 'weight' of industries with a rising profits share should be raised relatively to that of any industries with declining employment and a declining profits share. This suggests that the share of aggregate profits in the National Income will certainly vary with employment in the short run.

It can be concluded from this that the economy will have a particular share of profits at full employment. Where the share of profits is lower than this, some industries will be employing fewer workers so there will be less than full employment, while where the share of aggregate profits in the National Income is higher, wages in some industries will be below the equilibrium wages that produce just full employment, with the result that there will be excess demand for labour in some industries.

Thus where there is perfect competition in all markets, the hetero-geneity of capital and consumer goods will not disturb the basic marginal productivity proposition that there is a unique share of profits at full employment, which is *partly* determined by the technical conditions of production. With heterogeneous products, the full-employment share of profits will depend on the relative demand for different products at full employment (which will influence the relative prices of the different goods produced by industries with different shares of profit) as well as on the technical conditions of production, but there will be a determinate share of profits in the National Income which is quite independent of the Keynesian equations. It will clearly be impossible to arrive at this share of profits by partially differentiating any simple function, and the influence of the various factors that determine it will not be easy to disentangle, though it certainly appears that a higher share of investment may reduce it, for this will raise the share of investment in some industries, which will shorten the life of plant in these industries (unless the capital–output ratio with new plant is raised considerably) with adverse effects on their shares of profit, and very possibly in the aggregate share of profits also.

These results have depended on the assumption of general perfect competition which ensures that output per worker with the least productive plant in use equals the wage in each industry. If imperfect competition merely makes the equilibrium wage a fixed proportion of output per worker with the least productive plant as has so far been supposed, the general conclusions will be unaffected. In Fig. 13.2, where imperfect competition makes the wage. $E'D/ED$ times out-put per worker with the least productive plant in use, the share of profits is $E'EBH'/BCDE$ where CD workers are employed, and $G'GBJ'/BCFG$ where CF workers are employed, and this leaves the general results arrived at above unaltered.

It is obviously inconvenient to have to work with a large number of industries using a heterogeneous collection of capital goods and producing a variety of products with variable relative prices. The argument outlined above has been necessary because it was essential to show that the theory does not break down where there are hetero-geneous capital goods producing a variety of products, but now that

this has been shown, it will obviously be convenient to revert to the
expositional device of a vintage model producing a single product.
It will therefore be taken for granted from this point onwards that
an economy's entire capital stock can be represented on a single
diagram like Figs. 13.1 or 13.2. Then *CF* will represent the economy's
full labour force, and the economy's equilibrium share of profits at
full employment will be *GBJ/BCFG* where there is perfect competition, and *G'GBJ'/BCFG* where there is imperfect competition. This
equilibrium share of profits at full employment will be referred to

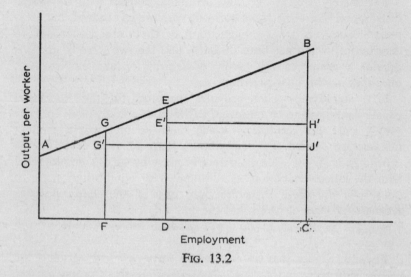

Fig. 13.2

as the 'equilibrium share of quasi-rent'. There must be unemployment
where the share of profits is less than this, and excess demand for
labour where the share of profits exceeds the 'equilibrium share of
quasi-rent'.

Then, to sum up, marginal productivity theory in this modified
vintage form stands out as something that is quite distinct from
Keynesian distribution theory. In this modified form, distribution
at full employment depends on the various factors which determine
the 'equilibrium share of quasi-rent'. These will include all the
technical factors which influence the life of plant and the productivity
gap between the plant of different vintages, such as the share of
investment, the rate of embodied technical progress, the rate of
growth of the labour force, and the rate of deterioration of plant as

L

it ages, so these will all influence distribution at full employment. This will also be influenced by all the factors that affect the relationship between average earnings and output per worker with the least productive plant in use, and the various imperfections in competition in factor and product markets, and the aims and achievements of trades unions, will all be relevant here. With all this said, something very like the basic marginal productivity result still holds, for there is a particular share of profits at full-employment equilibrium which is quite independent of Keynesian income flows.

Fortunately it turns out that there is no conflict with Keynesian distribution theory if this is correctly interpreted. Indeed, the Keynesian equations are complementary to the vintage approach to distribution which has been outlined, and the two lines of analysis provide a comprehensive theory of distribution and employment, once they are brought together.

It is employment that provides the clue, for the Keynesian equations describe distribution at any level of employment, for they simply state the conditions which must be met where product markets are cleared. The 'equilibrium share of quasi-rent', on the other hand, shows what distribution must be at full employment with the labour market in equilibrium. The 'equilibrium share of quasi-rent' therefore describes only one of the many possible Keynesian shares of profit, but the one it describes is the particular Keynesian profits share that will produce full-employment equilibrium.

It can be argued that the core of the theory of distribution is the relationship between these two shares of profit, the Keynesian share of profits of equation (13.1) and the 'equilibrium share of quasi-rent' of Figs. 13.1 and 13.2. Equation (13.1), which simply depends on an accounting identity, must always hold, so the actual share of profits must always be the one shown by this equation, but this will only equal the 'equilibrium share of quasi-rent' by a fluke. If the Keynesian share of profits is greater than the 'equilibrium share of quasi-rent', it follows that the wage must be less than the particular wage which produces labour market equilibrium at full employment. In consequence there will be excess demand for labour wherever the Keynesian share of profits exceeds the 'equilibrium share of quasi-rent'. This situation is illustrated in Fig. 13.3, where the 'equilibrium share of quasi-rent' is $G'GBJ'/BCFG$, and the Keynesian share of profits, $KGBM/BCFG$, exceeds this. Alternatively, it could be said that the aggregate profits that follow from Kalecki's equation (4.1) come to *KGBM* instead of *G'GBJ'*. In consequence, the wage is only *KF* instead of the equilibrium wage at full employment, *G'F*. With the wage as low as *KF*, it is profitable to work the equipment between *G* and *N* with the result that there are insufficient workers fully to utilise the more productive equipment between *G* and *B*, and this will give the employers owning equipment to the right of *G*

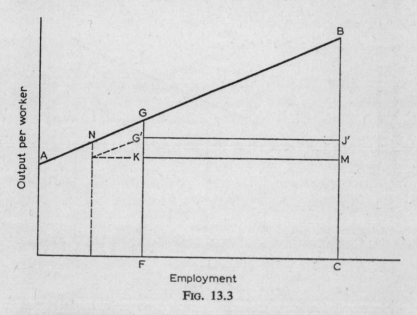

Fig. 13.3

incentives to offer higher wages to attract labour, with the result that there will be 'wage drift' at any wage less than *G'F*. However, so long as the Keynesian share of profits exceeds the 'equilibrium share of quasi-rent', the wage must remain less than the equilibrium one with the result that disequilibrium in the labour market will persist.

The opposite situation where the 'Keynesian share of profits' is less than the 'equilibrium share of quasi-rent' is illustrated in Fig. 13.4. Here, the Keynesian share of profits is only *E'EBH'/BCDE* while the 'equilibrium share of quasi-rent' is *G'GBJ'/BCFG*, with the result that the wage is *E'D* which is higher than *G'F*, the equilibrium wage at full employment. With the wage as high as *E'D*, employers will only find it worth while to employ *CD* workers, with the result that *DF* workers will be unemployed. This unemployment will persist so long as the Keynesian share of profits remains less than the 'equilibrium share of quasi-rent'.

In Fig. 13.3 the inflationary pressure in the labour market would be removed if the Keynesian share of profits was reduced, i.e. if there was less investment, or higher propensities to save out of wages and profits. This is a perfectly orthodox Keynesian result, for in the most elementary Keynesian theory lower planned investment or

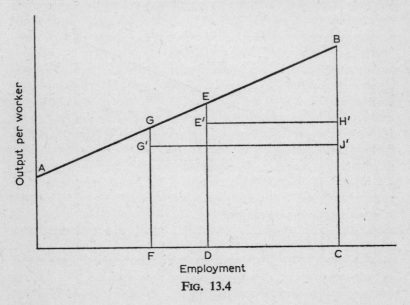

FIG. 13.4

higher planned saving reduces inflationary pressure. Similarly, the unemployment in Fig. 13.4, which is due to a Keynesian share of profits less than the 'equilibrium share of quasi-rent', can be removed if the Keynesian share of profits is raised sufficiently, i.e. if planned investment is raised or the savings propensities are reduced. This is again a Keynesian result of the utmost orthodoxy and simplicity.

What has emerged is an extension of the Keynesian theory of employment. This disregards distribution as it is usually stated, but it must obviously have implications for distribution as well as for output and employment. The usual Keynesian statement of the effect of an increase in investment is to say that this will raise effective demand through the multiplier, which will increase the demand for final products and labour in certain predicted proportions. In fact, an increase in investment will also raise aggregate profits (through

Kalecki's (4.1)), and with imperfections in competition given, the economy will only generate higher profits at a higher level of output and employment. Hence an increase in investment will raise output, employment *and profits*. Similarly, the reduction in effective demand that follows a fall in investment will be associated with a fall in aggregate profits, as well as with lower employment and output. Thus distributional effects run alongside the normal Keynesian mechanisms, and the elementary Keynesian propositions can easily be extended to bring in distribution. For instance, it is generally accepted in elementary Keynesian theory that an increase in a budget deficit raises aggregate demand, output and employment – and it can now be added (from (4.7)) that it raises profits as well, and higher aggregate profits will only be generated at a higher National Income.

Much of this emerged in Kaldor's celebrated 'Alternative theories of distribution', where important interconnections between Keynesian theory and the theory of distribution were set out. However, something was lost. Kaldor's equations show that higher investment (or a reduction in the propensity to save from wages or profits) has a corresponding effect on aggregate profits, but there is no connection between profits and employment. In Kaldor's argument, almost any share of profits is said to be compatible with full employment, with the result that an important element in Keynesian theory is missing. However, once the 'equilibrium share of quasi-rent' is brought into the argument, a complete Keynesian theory emerges, for then, in conditions of unemployment, higher investment raises employment as well as profits until the share of profits rises to equality with the 'equilibrium share of quasi-rent', after which higher investment will continue to raise profits, and at the same time produce excess demand for labour.

This missing element in Kaldor's theory of distribution comes out very clearly if the implications for income distribution of the short-run analysis of Chapter 12 are examined. There, it is very clear that a shift in the short-run saving or investment schedule will produce a shift in the degree of capacity working – an upward shift in *II* or a downward shift in *SS* causing an increase in the degree of capacity working and therefore an increase in employment. This increase in capacity working is also associated with an increase in the share of profits in the short run, for it is clear that the degree of capacity working and the share of profits must be closely associated in the short run. Now the *II* and *SS* schedules of Chapter 12 were specifically derived from Kaldor's trade-cycle model of 1940, where the degree of capacity working was determined in this way, but his more recent income distribution model has no interconnection between the saving and investment schedules and the degree of capacity working. Instead these simply determine distribution. It is agreed in the present argument that they determine distribution, and in the short run they influence this in the direction Kaldor's equations suggest, but they influence the degree of capacity working in addition, and this has important implications. Once the influence of *II* and *SS* on the degree of capacity working is recognised, it becomes clear that only one share of profits is compatible with normal-capacity working (i.e. working at *X* where the degree of capacity working is 100), and any deviation of the share of profits from this equilibrium share will be associated with a departure of the degree of capacity working from 100 in the same direction. The economy's actual share of profits is then determined by two sets of factors. First, there are the factors which determine what the share of profits is at normal-capacity working, or in terms of the argument of this chapter, the factors that determine the 'equilibrium share of quasi-rent'. These will include the long-term growth factors, and the various imperfections of competition which influence income distribution. The second set of factors which determine an economy's share of profits are the factors which determine the relationship between actual capacity working and normal-capacity working, i.e. the economy's saving and invest-ment schedules. These determine the Keynesian share of profits in terms of the argument of this chapter, and in terms of the argument of Chapter 12 they determine whether the degree of capacity working exceeds 100 with the result that the actual share of profits exceeds the equilibrium share, or vice versa.[1]

Thus investment, technical progress, labour growth, monopoly power, trades union power, etc., will influence distribution both through their effect on the equilibrium distribution of incomes at full employment, and through their short-run influence on the economy's actual degree of capacity working which will determine whether the actual share of profits is higher or lower than the equilibrium share. The theory that has been outlined allows the long- and short-run influence of each of these factors to be shown.

[1] D. W. Soskice outlined a similar approach to distribution in a paper he read in Oxford in 1969.

To illustrate this, something will be said below about the long-run and short-run effects on income distribution of higher investment, faster growth of the labour force, an increase in monopoly power by business, and an increase in trades union power.

Higher investment will reduce the life of plant (unless the capital–output ratio rises considerably) which will reduce the 'equilibrium share of quasi-rent'. Then, in the long run, a higher share of investment may tend to reduce the share of profits at full employment and normal-capacity working. However, in the short run a higher share of investment will raise the Keynesian share of profits which will raise the actual degree of capacity working with favourable effects on short-run profits. Then higher investment is likely to be immediately favourable to the share of profits, but it may be unfavourable in the longer term as the effects of a shorter life of plant on the 'equilibrium share of quasi-rent' work their way through.

Faster growth of the labour force should lengthen the life of plant with favourable effects on the 'equilibrium share of quasi-rent' and therefore the share of profits at full employment and normal-capacity working, and in the short run faster labour growth might well raise planned investment relatively to planned saving which would raise the share of profits in the short run. Then faster labour growth might well be favourable to the share of profits in both the long and the short run, and the effects of faster technical progress should be equally favourable. The favourable long-run effects of faster labour growth and faster technical progress were brought out in the equilibrium equations of Part II, and the same conclusions follow from the present more general analysis.

Stronger monopoly power should raise the proportion of its marginal product that capital receives relatively to the proportion that labour receives, with favourable effects on the 'equilibrium share of quasi-rent'. More precisely, greater monopoly power should reduce the marginal revenue product of labour relatively to its marginal physical product because individual firms will generally face less elastic demand curves, and this will reduce the wage relatively to output per worker with the least productive plant in use which will raise the 'equilibrium share of quasi-rent' and therefore the share of profits at full employment. If greater monopoly power succeeds in raising the share of profits in the short run, it may well raise planned saving (which will depend partly on current profits) relatively to planned investment with the result that short-run profits fall. If monopoly power raises the *share* of profits in the short run, and reduces *aggregate* profits, it must reduce employment. Then greater monopoly power, which will obviously be favourable to profits in the long run, might well have unfavourable effects on profits and employment in the short run.[1]

A factor that weakens the ability of modern industry to use monopoly power to achieve a higher share of profits is the increase in the ratio of salaried staff to the total labour force that is often associated with an increase in the size of firms. In the model so far, only wages and profits have been distinguished, but in a more general model the salaries of staff employed independently of current production lines would need to be paid from the 'equilibrium share of quasi-rent', so an increase in monopoly power which raised both the 'equilibrium share of quasi-rent' and the salary bill might leave the share of profits (at full-employment equilibrium) unchanged. The increase in the ratio of 'white-collared' to 'blue-collared' workers has been a persistent trend in the twentieth century, and the cost of white-collared workers can often be met only from increased profit margins in the activities concerned directly with current production, which requires an increase in the 'degree of monopoly'. The fall in the share of profits in the U.K. and the U.S.A. in the twentieth century has already been remarked on, and it may be that this has been partly due to an insufficient increase in the degree of monopoly to compensate for the increase in the proportion of salaried staff. It is as if Marx's prediction of a declining rate of profit because the capital–output ratio must rise faster than the degree of exploitation is coming true, only it is the ratio of 'indirect' workers to production workers that is rising and not the ratio of fixed capital to working capital. Obviously, it would be desirable to go on to a more general model where production workers and 'indirect' workers were distinguished to analyse this kind of effect. Clearly, monopoly power can only be translated into a higher share of profits if the salaries which must be met from the 'equilibrium share of quasi-rent' can be kept down.

Stronger trades union power which merely raises money wages faster will have no discernible effects on the aggregate share of wages. Faster wage increases have no clear effect on the 'equilibrium share of quasi-rent' (for faster increases in money wages do not obviously

[1] Cf. J. Steindl, *Maturity and Stagnation in American Capitalism* (Blackwell, 1952), and Kalecki, *Theory of Economic Dynamics*.

influence the relationship between the wage and output per worker with the least productive plant in use), so they do not patently influence the share of wages in the long run. It is not even clear that faster increases in money wages will reduce the share of profits in the short run, for to do so they must raise planned saving relative to planned investment, and they will only clearly do this if the money supply is not increased with inflation. It then appears at first sight that a scramble to raise money wages will have the sole effect of raising the wages of those whose product prices are pushed up relatively faster (since the equilibrium wage levels in different industries are determined in terms of the products of those industries) at the expense of those whose product prices rise relatively slowly, while the overall share of wages is unaltered.

This is not, however, all that union power can achieve if this is used in more subtle ways. A crucial relationship in the present theory is the one between the wage and output per worker with the least productive plant in use. This ratio will be depressed if the supply of labour to the individual firm is inelastic, for the marginal cost of labour (which is what entrepreneurs equate to the marginal revenue product of labour with the least productive plant) will then be much higher than the wage. It is in the interests of workers that the supply of labour to the individual firm should be as elastic as possible at the best wage that can be negotiated. Trades union activity can certainly produce a situation where employers must take on extra labour at an agreed rate of pay, and this will make the supply curve of labour to the individual firm elastic, and therefore bring the wage nearer to output per worker with the least productive plant. Trades unions can have an equally important effect on the wages paid to workers who produce with intra-marginal plant which earns high quasi-rents. Here businesses can afford to pay much higher wages than those paid with marginal plant, but with a perfectly competitive labour market all workers will receive the same wage. Unions can often negotiate higher wages for those working with more efficient plant so that part of the quasi-rent which would accrue to capital in perfect competition goes to labour instead. Subtlety is obviously needed if employers are to be faced with a horizontal supply curve of labour where they hire extra men, and with productivity-related wages for those at work, but policies to achieve both of these, through compulsory union membership on the one hand, and productivity bargaining on the shop floor to extract exceptional wages for those

L*

working with modern plant, are not uncommon. Employers will obviously wish to be free to hire non-union labour, and they will wish to obtain for profits the extra quasi-rents that follow from superior efficiency, by paying the same wages whatever the efficiency of plant. Their power to do this, and the power that workers have to prevent them, will have a considerable influence on the aggregate distribution of incomes in the long run.

It is to be noted that where unions manage to raise the wages paid to those who work with modern plant relatively to those who work with marginal plant, then the net rate of return on capital (which is the discount rate which equates the quasi-rents received throughout the lifetime of plant to its cost) will be adversely affected, perhaps very adversely affected, and investment and growth will then be lower than they would have been if wages were the same with all vintages.

These few brief remarks about how monopoly and trades union power may affect the analysis are designed to show how this will fit into the argument, rather than to pretend to say anything of particular importance. What is important is the basic division of the factors that influence distribution into the set of factors that influence the full-employment distribution of incomes through the 'equilibrium share of quasi-rent', and the short-run Keynesian income flows that determine the degree of capacity working, the level of employment, and the actual share of profits at all times.

The influence of the long-term growth factors on the 'equilibrium share of quasi-rent' was worked out most fully in Part II of this book, but the analysis there necessarily relied on perfect competition, constant returns to scale, and one-good-model assumptions. Once these assumptions are dropped, precise mathematical results can no longer be arrived at, and the argument must rely on much more general statements of the kind made in this chapter. However, the analysis in this chapter points in much the same direction as the mathematical analysis of Part II.

However, the equations of Part II only described the influence of one of the three sets of factors that determine income distribution, for this is also influenced by the market power of capital and labour, and Keynesian income flows. Hence the detailed studies that have been made of trades union power and industrial pricing policies are highly relevant to income distribution in the real world, for this will differ from the results of perfect competition analysis to a marked extent. Only the salient points about the influence of monopoly and trades union power can be outlined in a book that is basically about growth theory, but what can be said is exactly how the market power of capital and labour is relevant to income distribution. It is relevant because it influences the 'equilibrium share of quasi-rent', i.e. the distribution of income at full employment and normal-capacity working.

The Keynesian income flows are also relevant to the problem of distribution, and Kaldor and Kalecki were clearly right to see that in addition to the normal Keynesian equations which determine output and employment, there are further equations which relate to the distribution of incomes, but not surprisingly it turns out that these equations describe the distribution of incomes in the short period, and not the distribution of incomes at full employment. The conclusion of the analysis of this chapter is, then, that the Keynesian share of profits is always the economy's actual share of profits. However, the economy's share of profits at full employment, the 'equilibrium share of quasi-rent', depends on long-term growth forces and class power, and the relationship between this and the Keynesian profits share determines whether there will be unemployment or excess demand for labour. Thus it turns out that Keynesian income flows, market power, and the economy's capital structure, are all relevant to the problem of distribution.

14

Implications for Policy

IT is always dangerous to jump too rapidly from theory to policy. In a memorable passage which many economists must have taken to heart in recent years, Keynes wrote in 1930, six years before the *General Theory*:

> . . . it is characteristic of economics that valuable and interesting work may be performed and steady progress made for many years, and yet that the results will be almost useless for practical purposes until a certain degree of exactness and perfection has been reached. Half-baked theory is not of much value in practice, though it may be half-way towards final perfection.[1]

In many ways, the present state of growth theory resembles that of the theory of money and employment in the early inter-war years. A great deal of work is being done, but much of it has been destructive of results that were once believed, while a testable analysis of the growth process that meets the requirements of the critics of the old orthodoxy has been slow to evolve. Much modern analysis, and particularly the work on capital theory that was discussed in Chapter 5 of the present book, makes otherwise straightforward problems appear intractable. Other contributions rest to such an extent on the unrealistic assumptions of a single good, perfect competition and constant returns to scale that it is, in the words of the author of a recent account of neoclassical theory, 'a matter of faith' to believe that the results arrived at bear some relation to conditions in the known world.

The question that arises is whether it is safe to derive any policy conclusions from the analysis of the present book. Much of this has rested on highly abstract assumptions, and the precise mathematical results have almost without exception been based on the assumption

---

[1] Keynes, *A Treatise on Money*, vol. II, p. 406.

of steady growth. However, this can contribute to the analysis of policy problems, for the assumption of steady growth allows these to be tackled in two stages. The first stage which is safe is to proceed by comparing economies in steady growth to determine the policies with regard to research and development, capital investment, profits taxation, and so on, which are associated with faster steady growth rates. Whether it is possible to apply the answers derived from steady growth analysis to the problems of actual economies is another matter, and this is the second and more difficult stage of the analysis.

In this concluding chapter, these problems will be considered in turn. The first two sections of the chapter will be concerned with the policies that will contribute to faster growth on the assumption that steady growth is in some way achieved, and these sections will be concerned with policies to influence the investment opportunity function and the investment function, which determine the economy's equilibrium growth rate. After this, the applicability of these results to the growth of actual economies will be considered, and the chapter will conclude with some comments on the relevance of the argument of this book to the problems involved in the redistribution of incomes and wealth.

However, one fundamental problem must be discussed before the argument can proceed. A more favourable investment opportunity function or a stronger investment function will raise the economy's equilibrium rate of growth, but these will almost certainly also reduce the share of consumption in the National Product, so criteria are needed to decide whether prospective changes are, on balance, desirable. This raises very large problems about which much has been written.[1] It may be considered that the 'golden rule' (that consumption will be maximised eventually where the rate of profit equals the rate of growth[2]) provides a possible basis for policy, for this suggests that anything that increases investment will also raise eventual consumption provided that the rate of profit equals or exceeds the rate of growth after the change. However, the 'golden

[1] See, for instance, Hicks, *Capital and Growth*, part III; R. M. Solow, *Growth Theory: An Exposition* (Oxford U.P., 1970) chap. 5; E. Burmeister and A. R. Dobell, *Mathematical Theories of Economic Growth* (New York: Macmillan, 1970) chaps. 10-11; and the articles by Joan Robinson, J. E. Meade, D. G. Champernowne and J. Black in the 'Symposium on Production Functions and Economic Growth' published in the *Review of Economic Studies*, vol. XXIX (June 1962).

[2] See p. 31 above, where the 'golden rule' is explained.

rule' is only valid if there is no endogenous connection between the share of investment and the rate of technical progress. With the model outlined in the present book, any increase in the share of investment will raise the rate of technical progress and therefore the rate of growth of consumption, so a higher S must always produce higher ultimate consumption with the absurd result that the optimum share of investment will be about 99·9 per cent if the maximisation of *ultimate* consumption is the sole aim of policy.

There is, however, an alternative approach to the problem which produces more manageable results, and this depends on the relationship between the private and social rates of return on capital. A private wealth owner obtains the private rate of return on capital from an incremental increase in investment, but with the model outlined in earlier chapters, the community gains more than this because extra investment will also raise the rate of technical progress and produce further possible external effects through the 'economies of scale multiplier'.[1] As the social rate of return on capital must exceed the private rate because of these external effects, it follows that optimum investment must exceed what will be invested in the absence of intervention if social preferences between the present and the future are the same as those of individual wealth owners. It is usually argued that societies discount the future less than individuals, but the excess of the social over the private rate of return that follows from endogenous technical progress and increasing returns to scale suggests that some public intervention to improve the investment opportunity function and to strengthen the investment function will be desirable, even if social and individual time preferences are the same. In the pages that follow, various ways in which these aims can be achieved will be outlined. How far the various policies should be pushed will clearly depend on assessments of external effects in particular cases, and no attempt will be made below to suggest general rules.

It is no accident that most of the policies for growth and redistribution that emerge relate to the tax system. A country's system of taxes and subsidies provides by far the widest range of available intervention points. There are obviously other points where governments can intervene, but there are a wide variety of methods of taxing and subsidising each economic activity with the result that

---

[1] Cf. Arrow's demonstration that the socially optimal ratio of gross investment to output is higher than the competitive level with his 'learning by doing' model in 'The economic implications of learning by doing', pp. 168-71.

fiscal policies provide a large number of policy tools in Tinbergen's sense. Monetary policy will obviously be used as well as fiscal policy, but this adds at most two further important policy tools. There is another consideration that is relevant to the importance of fiscal policy. All governments necessarily collect and administer taxes and subsidies, and they in any case employ civil servants, often a high proportion of the civil service, for this. Other policy tools as potentially selective as taxes and subsidies, such as direct intervention by the state in business decisions, involve the creation of a new civil service to perform any extra functions, and this is bound to add to the cost of such methods of intervention, and reduce the chances of their adoption.

It is therefore no accident that the bridge between theory and policy has generally been a fiscal one. Ricardo, who called his book *On the Principles of Political Economy and Taxation*, Marshall, Pigou, Keynes and Kaldor all saw that fiscal corollaries follow directly from the discovery of economic propositions capable of practical application. Fiscal policy is sometimes regarded as a separate branch of economics that can be studied in isolation. In fact, every useful economic proposition has its fiscal counterpart.

How far the analysis of this book has practical applications remains to be seen, but there is no particular difficulty about the derivation of policies where steady growth is assumed as it will be in the first part of this chapter. The real difficulties begin after this, when the applicability of the results to actual economies will be considered.

Policy and the Investment Opportunity Function

In this section the possible effects of policy on the investment opportunity function will be considered, and this is one of the two functions that determines the economy's equilibrium rate of growth. Policies will need to influence this function or the investment function favourably if they are to produce a higher equilibrium rate of growth.

The investment opportunity function is derived from the technical progress function, the production function, and a function determining n, the rate of growth of both population and the labour force (which will have the same *equilibrium* rate of growth). The factors that influence n have played no previous part in the analysis of this book, but policies to influence population growth are frequently used, and these include the obstruction and encouragement of immigration and emigration and the use of the tax system to discourage or encourage large families. It follows that n is very much subject to policy influences. The production function will not be directly influenced by policy, but the technical progress function will certainly be sensitive to this in so far as policy influences research and development expenditure. It follows that the two main ways in which policies can influence growth through the investment opportunity function are through policies to influence the rate of growth of the labour force, and research and development expenditure, and these will be considered in turn. The effect of a faster rate of growth of the labour force will be considered first.

Suppose that two economies are in equilibrium growth and that one has a higher n than the other because it has placed fewer barriers in the way of immigration, or because it maintains higher tax allowances for children which encourages larger families. Then the economy with the higher n must have a faster growth rate of aggregate output, for this will equal $A + n + B.S$ with constant returns to scale. The rate of growth of output per worker is $A + B.S$, and this means that the economy with faster labour growth will only have a higher rate of growth of output per worker and therefore (in equilibrium growth) a faster increase in living standards if it has a higher A, B or S. The argument of Part II of this book suggested that a higher n will be associated with both a higher B and a higher S, so faster population growth should have favourable effects on the standard of living. The first reason for this is derived from the argument of Chapter 6, where it was suggested that a *larger* labour force will raise the returns from successful research and development relatively to the costs of this, with the result that businesses will be induced to undertake more research and development which will have favourable effects on B and possibly on A also. It is, however, impossible to accommodate this line of argument within a steady growth framework, for a growing labour force will produce an *increasing* inducement to spend on research and development, and this is likely to produce a rising B which will place this effect outside the bounds of steady growth analysis. However, the other effect of n on the rate of growth of productivity, its effect on S, is perfectly compatible with steady growth. This effect works out in the following way. Where two economies have the same investment function and different rates of labour growth, the economy with a faster rate of growth of the labour force will have a higher rate of profit and this will lead to higher investment and, through the technical progress function, faster endogenous technical progress. This argument was developed in Chapter 10, where it was shown that for this reason economies with faster labour growth will enjoy a faster increase in output per worker and therefore in the standard of living, for these will increase at the same rate in steady growth.

The advantages of faster labour growth are still greater where there are increasing returns to scale. Unfortunately the effects of these on the economy's *equilibrium* growth rate can only be shown with Cobb–Douglas assumptions, when the equilibrium rate of growth of output is

$$(A+n+B.S). \left(\frac{z - \alpha.z}{1 - \alpha.z} \right) \quad \text{(from (11.3))},$$

where z is the returns to scale factor, and α is the Cobb–Douglas's capital exponent. The rate of growth of output per worker, $(g-n)$, will be:

$$(g-n) = (A+B.S). \left(\frac{z - \alpha.z}{1 - \alpha.z} \right) + n. \left(\frac{z - 1}{1 - \alpha.z} \right). \quad (14.1)$$

It is evident that $(g-n)$ will vary strongly with n where z exceeds 1.

There are then several reasons for supposing that faster growth of the labour force will be associated with a faster rate of growth of output per worker and a faster increase in living standards. There will be benefits from economies of scale and from the higher share of investment that should be associated with faster population growth which will produce more endogenously determined technical progress; and the benefits would be still greater if the effects of accelerating technical progress were not ruled out by the assumption of steady growth. The advantages from policies to achieve faster population growth therefore appear to be considerable where equilibrium growth is assumed. There is, however, an important qualification to this conclusion.

The principal objection to the very unclassical result that population growth is favourable to the standard of living is that it is based on the assumption that returns to scale are increasing, or at worst constant. The classical pessimism about population growth was based on a belief in the inevitability of eventual diminishing returns. Now it may be widely (though not universally) believed today that diminishing returns are avoidable in industry, and their relevance to agriculture may even be in doubt,[1] but there is another relationship that may matter just as much, namely the relationship between space and population. Many aspects of the standard of living depend on space or living room per head, and there is no doubt that there will be diminishing returns here as extra capital and population are added to a given geographical area, so the classical pessimism about population growth may turn out to be fundamentally right. It is certainly possible that economies with faster population growth will have living standards which move less satisfactorily through time, even though their output per head rises faster in both industry and agriculture. National accounts are constructed in a way which gives little weight to the true costs of space and living room, and this means that studies based on conventional statistics may well imply that $z \geqq 1$ with the result that faster population growth is apparently associated with faster increases in living standards. This may be a superficial result, for it may be due to weaknesses in the studies in question which measure output in ways which do not allow all the adverse effects of overcrowding to be shown. If space and the aspects of living standards that depend on this could be effectively measured, faster population growth might well turn out to be associated with a slower increase in the standard of living. The diminishing returns effects of the scarcity of space might well produce a z of less than 1, and with z less than 1 (in (14.1)) the classical result that faster population growth is associated with a slower rate of increase of the standard of living is very clearly arrived at.

There are fewer problems in the other area where policy may influence the investment opportunity function. Fig. 14.1, a diagram of the kind used in Chapter 6, shows the expected costs and returns from research and development expenditure. In the absence of government intervention, the expected returns from research and development are shown by DD, while the expected costs are shown by RR. The expected profits from research and development are maximised at E where DD and RR are parallel, and the rate of technical progress that results from this is OF. If firms prefer to push research and development spending to the limits that they can afford to minimise the risks of entry, or for other reasons, research and development expenditure will be pushed as far as H where the rate of technical progress achieved will be OJ. Suppose now that the

[1] See, for instance, Colin Clark, *Population Growth and Land Use* (Macmillan, 1967).

government subsidises research and development activity by paying a proportion G_r of the costs of research and development. Then the RR curve will be lowered $(1-G_r)$ times throughout its length, and the new curve which shows the costs of research and development, net of the government's subsidy (or research and development grants), is $R'R'$. The profit-maximising rate of technical progress will then be raised from OF to OF' (for DD and $R'R'$ are parallel at E' which is vertically above F'), and the maximum rate of technical

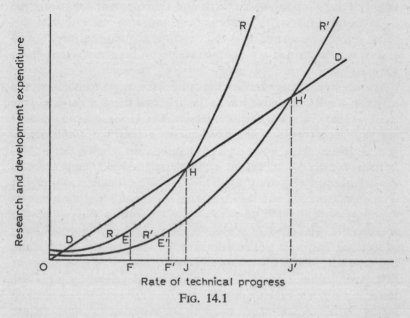

Fig. 14.1

progress that firms can afford will be raised from OJ to OJ'. To subsidise research and development will then apparently raise the rate of technical progress and therefore the economy's equilibrium rate of growth.

Research and development will be most easily subsidised through the tax system. Suppose that profits are taxed at rate T_p, and that research and development grants are G_r times total research and development expenditure, and that firms are allowed to write off the remainder of their research and development costs against their taxable profits immediately these are incurred. Suppose also that it is expected that these rates of taxes and grants will be maintained indefinitely. Then a research and development project with a gross cost of R will cost $R(1-G_r)$ net of research and development grants, and as this can be written off against taxable profits immediately, the net-of-tax cost of the project will be $R(1-G_r)(1-T_p)$. If the project is expected to produce future profits with a discounted present value of D before tax, the net-of-tax value of these expected profits will be $D(1-T_p)$. Then taxes and subsidies will reduce the costs of research and development $(1-G_r).(1-T_p)$ times, and expected profits $(1-T_p)$ times, with the result that the situation illustrated in Fig. 14.1 is produced by research and development grants at rate G_r at all rates of profits taxation. It is important to note that this result only holds if research and development expenditure (net of grants) can be written off against taxable profits immediately, as is assumed here.

The argument suggests that the crucial factor that influences the height of the RR line relatively to the height of the DD line is G_r, the rate of research and development grants. The U.S. Government does not pay formal research and development grants, but it contributes heavily to industrial research and development grants, but it contributes heavily to industrial research and development through the defence programme. In the U.K., the Government often pays a fraction of the costs of research and development, but it then expects to receive back an equivalent fraction of the returns where a project is successful. The effect of grants on these terms on the profitability of successful projects will be approximately neutral, for the RR and DD schedules will be influenced equally. It does not follow, however, that government support for research and development on these terms will provide no stimulus, for paying a fraction of the cost and taking nothing back where projects are unsuccessful must reduce the risks involved in research and development, and this will have a favourable effect in a two-dimensional analysis of the problem where both risk and expected returns are taken into account. Support on these terms will increase risk-taking and increase the proportion of unsuccessful projects to total projects – a very British result. It is obvious that the stimulus to research and development must be less than that illustrated in Fig. 14.1 if the government pays a proportion G_r of the costs and then takes G_r times any profits from successful projects. This amounts to research and development grants at a rate of G_r, and in addition a tax at rate G_r on successful projects, and this must be less useful than grants without the tax.

It is often thought that it must be wrong in principle that governments should contribute to the costs of research and development without sharing in the proceeds, but this may be a misconceived view of the problem. If firms typically push research and development to the limits that they can afford (and it was argued in Chapter 6 that this is more plausible than the assumption that they maximise the expected profits from research and development in a way that ignores the possible effects of these on the entry of new competitors), research and development grants will not produce abnormal profits. The grants will increase the research and development spending that firms can afford, and the outcome should be normal profits at a larger scale of research and development activity.[1] In Fig. 14.1, research and development expenditure is raised by research and development grants, and on the assumption that firms push research and development spending to the limits that they can afford, the rate of technical progress (in so far as this results from research and development spending) is raised from OJ to OJ'. At the same time, no firm obtains abnormal profits as a result of research and development grants. These simply raise the rate of technical progress with the result that the entire benefit goes to the users of the goods in question. This may be an overcorrection of the more common view that grants would primarily benefit those who receive them, but there will often be effects of this kind.

It then appears that the principal ways in which policies may influence the investment opportunity function are through the rate of population growth and research and development expenditure. Policies to raise the rate of population growth should be associated with faster growth of output per worker (as this is ordinarily measured), and policies to subsidise research and development should be associated with faster technical progress and therefore faster equilibrium growth.

Policy and the Investment Function

The equilibrium rate of growth will also be influenced by the investment function, and policies may influence this in several ways. Where

[1] A higher rate of technical progress and therefore a more favourable investment opportunity function will be associated with a higher equilibrium rate of profit, so the firms in receipt of research and development grants will earn a higher rate of profit because the rate of 'normal' profit will be higher, but all firms will receive this equally, so there will not be peculiar benefits to the firms that undertake research and development.

investment decisions are left in private hands, policies must act mainly through the tax system, and the impact of this can take several forms. It can be taken for granted that profits will be taxed in all countries where democratic pressures have some influence on policy, for it would appear intolerably inegalitarian if they were not. On the face of it, profits taxation can be expected to have adverse effects on the investment function, but it will turn out that these may be compensated or more than compensated by various investment incentives.

The best starting-point for an analysis of the influence of the tax system on investment is the simple impact of profits taxation without compensating incentives. It will be assumed initially that net profits are taxed at a rate of T_p, and that investment cannot be written off against tax at an accelerated rate. Then, if the rate of return on capital is r before tax, it will be $r(1-T_p)$ after tax if depreciation allowances correspond to the 'correct' rate of depreciation of plant. Similarly, if interest is tax-deductible, the net-of-tax cost of interest will be $i(1-T_p)$.

Taxation will not leave r unaltered, for taxes may be wholly or partly passed on, but this is not relevant to the present part of the argument which is solely concerned with the effect of taxation on investment at a particular rate of profit, which is all that is needed to show how taxation will influence the investment function. The full effects of profits taxation, whether this is passed on, and so on, will depend on both the investment function and the investment opportunity function, and this cannot be discussed until the effects of taxation on the investment function have been analysed.

In Chapter 8 a particular diagram was used to show how capital accumulation would be influenced by the rate of profit and wealth owners' preferences between consumable current income and growth, and this basic diagram can easily be adapted to show the influence of profits taxation and the various possible investment incentives. In Fig. 14.2, the line DG (where $r = OD = OG$) shows the various permutations of consumable current income and growth that are open to the owners of a firm that does not borrow. Profits taxation at a rate of T_p will move this wealth owners' opportunity line downwards at the particular rate of profit, r, to $D'G'$ where

$$OD' = OG' = (1-T_p).r.$$

If the tangency points between successively higher wealth owners' indifference curves and opportunity lines lie on a straight line passing

through the origin as was suggested in Chapter 8, profits taxation
will reduce both the rate of capital accumulation and the ratio
of consumable current income to capital $(1-T_p)$ times at each
rate of profit. Thus, in Fig. 14.2, the rate of growth of capital is
reduced from Og to Og', and Og' will equal $(1-T_p)$ times Og.
Then, where there is profits taxation without compensating incentives, the rate of growth of capital is likely to be reduced at each
rate of profit.

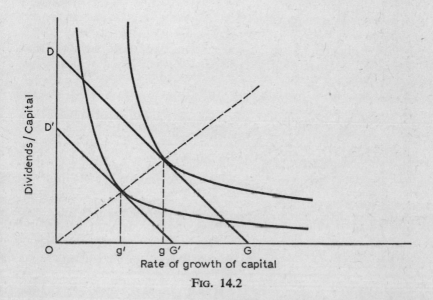

FIG. 14.2

A simple and much used method of compensating for this adverse
effect of taxation is accelerated depreciation, which allows businesses
to write off capital against tax more quickly than the true rate at
which capital depreciates, and 'free depreciation' is the extreme form
of this. With free depreciation, the incentive used in Britain in 1972
for investment in plant and machinery, firms can write off the entire
costs of investment against their taxable profits immediately. Then,
if a company always reinvests its entire profits, it will never pay tax
for it will always have £1 million of investment to offset against every
£1 million of taxable profits. In contrast, a company which invested
nothing would pay the full rate of profits taxation on its entire profits.
The diagrammatic effect of this is shown in Fig. 14.3, where profits

taxation at rate T_p moves the wealth owners' opportunity line downwards from DG to $D'G$. Taxation does not reduce the growth that
companies can finance (at each rate of profit) if they reinvest their
entire profits, so there is no inward movement of the opportunity
line at G where no dividends are paid. There is, however, a full
$(1-T_p)$ times downward movement of the opportunity line on the
vertical axis where profits are entirely distributed, with the result

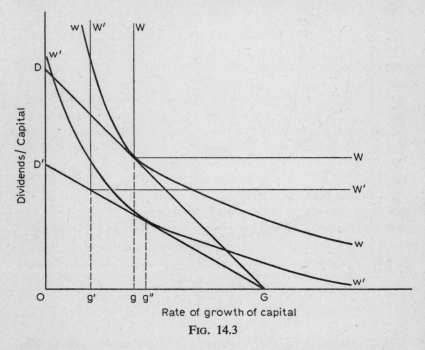

Fig. 14.3

that the maximum dividend that firms can pay is reduced $(1-T_p)$
times.

It will be evident from Fig. 14.3 that profits taxation together with
free depreciation may increase or reduce the rate of capital accumulation. If successive wealth owners' indifference curves take the
square-shaped form appropriate to perfect complementarity between
current consumption and growth, a shift in the wealth owners'
opportunity line from DG to $D'G$ will reduce the rate of growth of
capital from Og to Og'. If, however, the successive indifference curves
are w and w' which show high substitutability between currently
consumable income and growth, then the rate of growth of capital

will be increased from Og to Og''. Thus whether profits taxation (together with free depreciation) increases or reduces the rate of capital accumulation at each rate of profit will depend on the shape of wealth owners' indifference curves.

It is evident that profits taxation together with such incentives as are used will have an income effect and a substitution effect on wealth owners. The income effect of profits taxation must be unfavourable, for this must move wealth owners to a lower indifference curve than they would otherwise be on, but with investment incentives there will also be a favourable substitution effect, for these will reduce the cost of growth in terms of consumable current income. Thus, in the absence of taxation, wealth owners must forgo 1 per cent of dividend/capital to obtain an extra 1 per cent of investment/capital, but with taxation and free depreciation they will only need to forgo $(1 - T_p)$ per cent of dividend/capital to obtain an extra 1 per cent of accumulation, and this should lead to some substitution of accumulation for consumable current income. The net effect of taxation on accumulation will depend on the relative size of these income and substitution effects. With the square-shaped indifference curves W and W' there is no substitution effect, so the income effect must predominate with the result that higher taxation must reduce accumulation. With the indifference curves w and w' the substitution effect is stronger than the income effect, with the result that the combined effects of taxation and free depreciation increase capital accumulation.

Up to now accelerated depreciation is the only investment incentive that has been considered, and investment grants and tax credits are possible alternative or supplementary incentives. Investment grants have been used to stimulate investment in the U.K. where they are still available in development areas, while tax credits are the investment incentive that has been favoured in the U.S.A. Their effect on investment is almost identical. With investment grants at rate G_i, the government makes an outright grant to a business that invests I of $I.G_i$, while with tax credits at rate C_T, the tax bill of a business that invests I is reduced by $I.C_T$. It will be evident that these are of equal value to profitable companies where $C_T = G_i$. With these incentives, businesses can invest much more than their profits without borrowing if they are granted free depreciation in addition. For instance, with investment grants and free depreciation, a business which earns a rate of return on capital of r before tax can expand its capital at a rate of $r/(1 - G_i)$ without borrowing if it pays no dividends.

On the other hand, it will pay the full rate of tax on its entire profits
if it does not invest. Investment grants clearly increase the force of
the favourable substitution effect, for only $(1-G_i)(1-T_p)$ per cent
of consumable current income will need to be forgone to pay for
an extra 1 per cent of accumulation, and investment grants should
have a favourable income effect as well. In Fig. 14.4, investment
grants (and free depreciation) shift the wealth owners' opportunity
line from DG to $D'G'$ where OD' is $(1-T_p)$ times OD, and

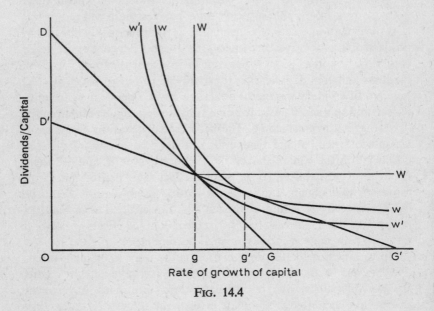

Fig. 14.4

OG' is $1/(1-G_i)$ times OG. It will be seen that the rate of grant
has been fixed just high enough to eliminate the adverse income
effects of taxation. Then there is no adverse effect on investment
where the indifference curves are WW, etc., and there is a strong
favourable effect where income and growth are substitutable as
with ww and $w'w'$, where the rate of growth of capital is raised from
Og to Og'.

The rate of investment grant that removes the adverse income
effect of profits taxation that is illustrated in Fig. 14.4 is

$$\left(\frac{1-b}{b}\right)\left(\frac{T_p}{1-T_p}\right)$$

where b is the ratio of gross investment to gross profits in the absence of taxation.[1] With a lower rate of investment grant than this (and

$$\left(\frac{1-b}{b}\right) \cdot \left(\frac{T_p}{1-T_p}\right)$$

is a very high rate of grant when free depreciation is allowed in addition), profits taxation and the compensating system of incentives may have net favourable or unfavourable effects on accumulation. Indeed, favourable or unfavourable effects are possible at any point between the two limiting cases where on the one hand there is no unfavourable income effect

$$\text{i.e.} \quad G_i = \left(\frac{1-b}{b}\right) \cdot \left(\frac{T_p}{1-T_p}\right)$$

and, on the other, no favourable substitution effect (i.e. $G_i = 0$ and accelerated depreciation is not allowed).

Profits taxation is the only form of taxation of wealth owners that has been considered so far, but others, for instance capital gains and wealth taxes, can easily be brought into the argument. The effect of a capital gains tax at a rate of T_g is illustrated in Fig. 14.5. This will shift the wealth owners' opportunity line from DG to DG' in steady growth where $OG' = (1-T_g) . OG$, i.e. it will reduce the maximum rate of growth of capital that wealth owners can enjoy, net of tax, without reducing their maximum ratio of consumption to capital. It follows that a capital gains tax will have both an unfavourable income effect and an unfavourable substitution effect, so it will have a particularly unfavourable effect on accumulation. It will obviously require exceptional compensation if it is not to have adverse effects on the investment function. A wealth tax, in contrast, will have an unfavourable income effect but no adverse substitution effect, so its unfavourable effects on accumulation will be less severe. Any other tax on wealth owners can obviously be analysed similarly, and its income and substitution effects shown.

---

[1] If gross profits are P, gross investment will be $b.P$, and investment grants will be worth $b.P.G_i$, and in addition, as a result of free depreciation, $b.P.(1-G_i)$ can be written off against tax at once so that taxable profits will be $P[1-b(1-G_i)]$ and tax payable $P.[1-b(1-G_i)].T_p$. The rate of grant that just compensates for taxation is where $b.P.G_i = P[1-b(1-G_i)].T_p$, i.e. where

$$G_i = \left(\frac{1-b}{b}\right)\left(\frac{T_p}{1-T_p}\right).$$

It is an obvious weakness in the argument so far that this is based on the assumption that firms do not borrow. However, it was argued in Chapter 8 that borrowing does not alter the fundamental nature of the problem, for firms will necessarily borrow from wealth owners who will have preferences between income and growth, and it can be assumed that these will resemble those in the diagrams. The

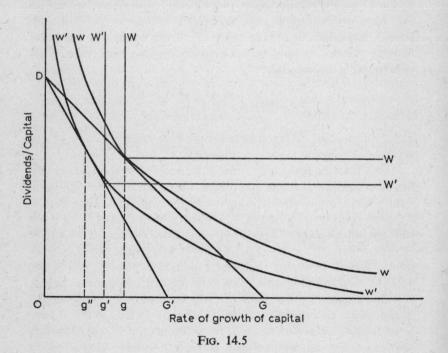

FIG. 14.5

main complication that is introduced by borrowing is the introduction of further types of asset, for wealth owners will hold both equity shares and fixed-interest-bearing bonds, and companies will finance investment through both equities and fixed-interest borrowing. It was argued in Chapter 8 that this complication will make accumulation a function of both the excess of the rate of profit over the rate of interest, and of r itself. Taxation together with free depreciation has an interesting effect on $(r-i)$, for with free depreciation the rate of return on any particular project (prior to the distribution of profits to shareholders) is the same after tax as it is before tax,[1] while interest is tax-deductible against profits taxation. Then profits taxation will not reduce r at all (prior to distribution), but i will be reduced $(1 - T_p)$ times with the result that there should be a substantial net favourable effect on capital accumulation in so far as this depends on the excess of the rate of profit over the rate of interest.[2]

It will be evident that the overall effect of company taxation and the various compensating incentives is bound to be unclear so long as nothing is known about the shape of wealth owners' indifference curves and therefore the relative size of the income and substitution effects. All that can be known is that company taxation without incentives of any kind must reduce the rate of capital accumulation at each rate of profit, while there must be a net favourable effect if investment grants are as high as something like

$$\left(\frac{1-b}{b}\right) \cdot \left(\frac{T_p}{1-T_p}\right)$$

and free depreciation on the remaining cost of investment is available in addition. In situations within these limits, and all actual situations are likely to lie within these limits, the important points are the *aggregate* effects of taxation and government grants on net company incomes which will influence the size of the unfavourable income effect; the net-of-tax cost of reinvestment in terms of distribution which will influence the size of the favourable substitution effect; and the sensitivity of investment to $(r - i)$ which will be relevant to the favourable effects of free depreciation. It is obviously only where all three of these effects are favourable that it will be clear that a country's system of taxes and grants will have net favourable effects on the investment function, and this is scarcely a possibility, for

---

[1] Suppose a company invests C in a project which is expected to yield gross profits of P_1 in its first year, P_2 in its second year, ..., and P_n in its nth year. With profits taxation and free depreciation, the investment would reduce the company's tax bill by $C.T_p$ in the year the investment was made, so the initial cost of the project (net of tax) would be $C(1-T_p)$. The expected profits net of tax would all be $(1-T_p)$ times the gross profits before tax (since no further depreciation allowances could be offset against them), so these would be $P_1(1-T_p)$, $P_2(1-T_p)$, ..., $P_n(1-T_p)$. Then profits taxation combined with free depreciation would reduce the cost of an investment and all gross profits earned with it in the same proportion, $(1-T_p)$: 1, so the expected rate of return would be unaffected by T_p.

[2] See W. A. Eltis, 'Taxation and investment', in Sir Robert Shone (ed.), *Problems of Investment* (Blackwell, 1971), for a fuller account of this line of argument.

political pressures in favour of the equal taxation of the various categories of income (and, *a fortiori*, pressures to redistribute) are bound by definition to produce an unfavourable income effect, i.e. to make wealth owners poorer as a result of taxation at all rates of profit. This unfavourable income effect may be compensated if the substitution effect or the sensitivity of investment to $(r-i)$ is strong enough, and taxation will not then have adverse overall effects on the investment function.

It is a reasonable presumption that if two otherwise similar economies have the same adverse income effect from the various taxes on profits and wealth, and one has a stronger substitution effect than the other, i.e. a lower cost of growth in terms of consumption, then the one with the stronger substitution effect will invest more at each rate of profit. Hence, if political factors determine the overall weight of taxation on profits and wealth, economic factors suggest that it will be favourable to growth if the tax system is so arranged that accumulation is as cheap as possible in terms of current consumption.

There is a further complication that needs to be taken into account here. An efficient system of company taxation should allow profits earned by companies with more finance than they need to be passed on costlessly to other companies with prospects for investment but insufficient finance. With steady growth assumptions, this is necessary to ensure adequate competition, and it is still more important in the real world.[1] Some of the devices which produce favourable substitution effects act as a tax on the passage of finance between companies by the traditional mechanism where dividends are paid by companies with more finance than they need to shareholders who use this money to subscribe to new issues made by other companies. The taxation of dividends at a higher rate than retentions in a corporation tax system will produce a favourable substitution effect,

---

[1] The minority report of the *Royal Commission on the Taxation of Profits and Incomes*, Cmd 9474 (HMSO, June 1955), which Kaldor signed, puts the case for the free movement of capital between companies most strongly: 'It can be argued also that the system of financing capital expenditure so largely out of the undistributed profits of companies does not ensure the best use of the community's savings. It makes it more difficult for fast-expanding firms to raise funds in the capital market; it strengthens the monopolistic tendencies in the economy, and it encourages wasteful expenditure on behalf of those firms who have more money than they can use and who are yet prevented (by custom and tradition as well as by the instruments of public control) from channelling those funds to their most profitable potential use.' (pp. 387-8).

but it will act as a tax on this traditional transfer mechanism. Investment grants, on the other hand, which also produce a favourable substitution effect, will not act as a tax on the passage of money from company to company, and the effect of free depreciation will also be neutral.[1] This suggests that where governments seek to correct for the unfavourable income effects of taxation with favourable substitution effects, the best methods to produce these will be investment grants and accelerated depreciation rather than the extra taxation of dividends in a corporation tax system of the kind used in the U.S.A. and, until recently, in the U.K. also.

If governments fail to correct for the adverse effects of profits taxation, the investment function will show a weaker relationship between the rate of profit and planned accumulation than that arrived at in Chapter 8. For instance, in the complete absence of compensating incentives, the investment function can be expected to become:

$$k = x_1^*(1-T_p)r + x_2^*(1-T_p).(r-i) \qquad (14.2)$$

where x_1^* and x_2^* are the proportions of net-of-tax profits devoted to accumulation. If x_1^* and x_2^* are independent of the rate of taxation as in Fig. 14.2, they will equal x_1 and x_2, and the rate of accumulation will then be reduced exactly $(1-T_p)$ times at each rate of profit. It is to be noted that this is the maximum adverse effect that taxation is likely to have on the investment function, for it allows for no favourable substitution effects from investment incentives. It should then show greater adverse effects in steady growth than any actual tax system would produce.

Up to now the analysis of the long-term effects of taxation and investment incentives has been confined to the effects of these on the investment function alone, which has greatly limited the scope of the analysis, for the ultimate effects of company taxation, the proportion that is passed on, and so on, cannot be derived from just the investment function. These will necessaily depend on both the investment function and the investment opportunity function.

[1] Suppose that there are cash grants and free depreciation on the remaining cost of investment, and that company A pays a dividend of $P(1-T_p)$ instead of investing $P/(1-G_i)$. Its shareholders can then subscribe $P(1-T_p)$ to a new issue by company B. Company B can then invest an extra $P/(1-G_i)$ and finance this through investment grants of $P.G_i/(1-G_i)$, leaving P to be otherwise financed. A tax saving of $P.T_p$ and the $P.(1-T_p)$ obtained from the new issue are just sufficient for this, so company B can invest just as much as company A. This would not be the case if company A's dividends were taxed at a higher rate than T_p.

The full effect of a $(1-T_p)$ times reduction in the rate of capital accumulation at each rate of profit is illustrated in Fig. 14.6, where KK and $K'K'$ are the economy's investment function before and after tax. $K'K'$ is $(1-T_p)$ times the distance from the vertical axis of KK at each rate of profit. It can be seen that on these assumptions profits taxation will raise the rate of profit from Or to Or', and reduce the rate of growth from Og to Og'. The fact that profits taxation is associated with a higher rate of profit means that it is at

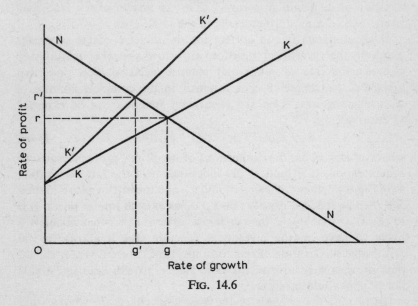

FIG. 14.6

least partly passed on. The precise proportion that is passed on can obviously only be estimated when various limiting assumptions are made. For instance, with CES assumptions, the proportion that is passed on is $1/(F+\sigma.E)$ (from Table 10.2) where $E = (B.S)/(A+n)$, and

$$F = 1 + \frac{x_2 \cdot i}{g} \, (1 - \text{Elasticity of } i \text{ with respect to } r),$$

and this will be two-thirds if $E = \frac{1}{2}$, $F = 1\frac{1}{6}$ and $\sigma = \frac{2}{3}$, and it will be one-half even if E is as high as 1 and F is as high as $1\frac{1}{2}$. Moreover, the above formula may understate the proportion of profits taxation that is passed on, for it rests on the assumption of perfect competition and Kaldor has argued that company tax systems are generally much more favourable to large firms than to small, with the result that profits taxation can be expected to raise the 'degree of monopoly' with favourable effects on the share of profits.[1] This would raise the *NN* function in Fig. 14.6 and so produce still further passing-on of profits taxation.

The fact that a considerable proportion of profits taxation will be passed on, even in conditions of perfect competition, will not remove its adverse effects on investment and growth. In perfect competition, a $(1-T_p)$ times reduction in the rate of accumulation at each rate of profit will reduce the share of investment something like

$$(1-T_p) \cdot \left(\frac{\sigma + \sigma.E}{F + \sigma.E} \right)$$

times (from Table 10.2), so investment will not be reduced very much less than $(1-T_p)$ times, which will obviously have substantial adverse effects on growth and output per worker. The adverse effects of taxation on investment and growth will be still greater in conditions of imperfect competition when a higher proportion of profits taxation will be passed on.

Of course, these are about the strongest adverse effects that the tax system can produce. With accelerated depreciation and investment grants, accumulation can be reduced much less than $(1-T_p)$ times at each rate of profit, so taxation will have a much smaller adverse effect on the investment function than in Fig. 14.6. There may in fact be no adverse effects at all; indeed, there may even be favourable effects if the substitutability of accumulation for consumable current income is great enough, and in this case there would be no passing-on of profits taxation (apart from the effects due to the influence of taxation on industrial concentration). It should certainly be found that a smaller proportion of profits taxation is passed on in countries with strong investment incentives than in countries where 'consumption from profits' and accumulation are taxed at much the same rate.

There must obviously be considerable doubts about the full effects of the tax system on investment while the extent to which wealth owners are prepared to substitute accumulation for consumable current income is unknown. The overall weight of taxation on wealth

---

[1] See N. Kaldor, *An Expenditure Tax* (Allen & Unwin, 1955), the chapter on Company Taxation'.

M

owners will be what matters most if accumulation and consumable current income are broadly regarded as complementary, and here more taxation will be damaging to growth, whatever the technical details of assessment. On the other hand, if wealth owners consider that faster accumulation provides adequate compensation for less present consumption, the tax system can be so arranged that its adverse effects on investment and growth are slight, or indeed so that the net effect of the various taxes and incentives is favourable.

That is all that will be said about the possible influence of policies on the equilibrium growth rate of economies. It is now time to turn to the relevance of the analysis to policies in the short period.

Policy and Actual Growth

It has been argued that certain policies will be associated with faster equilibrium growth, and the obvious question this raises is whether these are relevant to the growth of actual economies. Their relevance to this rests on the argument of Chapter 12 where the relationship between actual growth and equilibrium growth was discussed. It was argued there that over long periods, in all but one of the cases considered, economies will achieve growth rates, profit rates and investment shares at normal-capacity working that correspond quite closely to those produced by the fundamental equations. The investment function and the investment opportunity function determine the accumulation needed to keep economies on their EE lines, and mechanisms were outlined which suggest that there are strong reasons why periods when growth exceeds that needed for EE will alternate with periods where investment is insufficient for this. If this basic line of argument is correct, then the investment function and the investment opportunity function will really determine the rate of growth, the rate of profit at normal-capacity working, and the share of investment at normal-capacity working, about which economies fluctuate. It is to be expected that the investment functions and the investment opportunity functions of actual economies will change through time, so the rate of profit, the rate of growth and the share of investment that results from their intersection will not be constant, but fluctuations should still be around their changing values.

This means that the results that follow from the analysis of the earlier part of the chapter should be directly relevant to the growth of actual economies, for countries which so arrange their affairs that they have continuously stronger investment opportunity functions than others should have higher rates of profit and growth at normal-capacity working, while countries with stronger investment functions should have higher rates of growth and lower rates of profit.

There will obviously be fluctuations in all economies, so there may be considerable periods when actual trends in the values of the major variables differ from those that result from the fundamental equations. Governments can obviously do much to limit fluctuations, and it might be thought that they could eliminate these altogether with effective demand management policies. The argument of Chapter 12 ignored the possibility of intervention to manage effective demand, and even then wide fluctuations in demand were not inevitable, though they were certainly a distinct possibility. With demand management policies it should be possible to reduce the degree of fluctuation still further. It might be thought that governments could always so manage demand that the short-run savings function intersected the short-run investment function at normal-capacity working, thus maintaining continuous normal-capacity working and reducing fluctuations to the minimum possible. There are, however, difficulties with this *simpliste* view of demand management.

The first and most serious difficulty which this line of policy might encounter is illustrated in Fig. 14.7. Here, the short-run investment and savings functions intersect at X where EE intersects the normal-capacity working axis, and so it is possible for the economy to be in equilibrium at the ideal capacity working point, but the equilibrium at X is unstable because II is steeper than SS. The greater steepness of II is due to the greater sensitivity of investment to the degree of capacity working. II would be less steep if entrepreneurs were confident that an approximation to continuous normal-capacity working would be maintained, but faced by an investment function that is steeper than the saving function, government policy can hardly aim at continuous normal-capacity working. If SS cannot be made steeper than II (and it cannot if the acceleration principle is sufficiently strong), the economy will move rapidly away from X in an upward or downward direction, and if governments diagnose the situation correctly they will appreciate that they must choose between possible stable equilibrium points at very high or very low degrees of capacity working, for it is only there that II will be flat enough to make stable equilibrium possible. The government has the power to choose between equilibrium at high- and low-capacity working, but any attempt to achieve normal-capacity working will be futile. Once demand has been raised sufficiently to send the economy off the floor, output will shoot upwards towards Y'. Any attempt to arrest expansion near X will be useless because the investment function is inevitably steeper than the saving function near X, given the strength of the acceleration principle near X. Similarly, any attempt

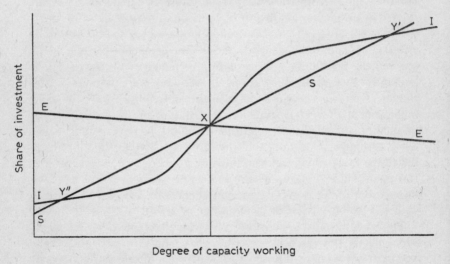

Degree of capacity working

FIG. 14.7

to limit a contraction in demand so that the economy corrects for overcapacity working by simply moving down to normal-capacity working will be equally futile. Any downward movement from Y' will be slight, or else the economy will move right down towards Y''.

Then, where II is steeper than SS at normal-capacity working, those responsible for demand management must choose between the inflationary and balance of payments difficulties associated with overcapacity working, and the unemployment that results from undercapacity working. It is not surprising that some economies fluctuate between points like these, even though governments seek to manage effective demand with the most sophisticated tools, for this cannot by itself cope with the problem of an unstable relationship between II and SS.

If, faced by this problem, governments prefer overcapacity working on welfare grounds – and the benefits will be particularly great if technical progress varies with the degree of capacity working[1] – they are likely to be faced with serious balance of payments difficulties because there will be shortages of capacity to produce whole ranges of capital and consumer goods. This may rule out continuous over-capacity working unless governments are very willing to devalue (or to impose effective import quotas) when the balance of payments moves into deficit, and the advantages of currency devaluation from the point of view of domestic economic performance have been widely discussed.[2] Obviously, all countries cannot simultaneously attain a competitive edge through devaluation, but those that can will be able to bear the costs of excessive imports during periods of overcapacity working because they will have an adequate basic surplus. Clearly, any attempt to maintain continuous working at the upper rather than the lower equilibrium point will require some measure of this kind. However, a continuous series of devaluations could produce intolerable cost inflation, so the choices open to governments are by no means straightforward.

It could in fact turn out that stop–go or an alternation between periods of high- and low-capacity working was impossible to avoid, for a falling rate of profit at the upper equilibrium point (and the argument of Chapter 12 suggests that this may or may not fall) would produce a falling investment function which would prevent the maintenance of continuous overcapacity working. A series of devaluations to make it possible to run an inflationary economy at full pressure might then achieve more in the short run than in the very long run.

There will be difficulties in demand management even where the relationship between II and SS is entirely stable, as in Fig. 14.8. Here, SS is steeper than II, but II intersects the normal-capacity working axis below X because entrepreneurs expect a lower rate of growth than the equilibrium rate. Here, if governments are content to maintain normal-capacity working at X', investment will be insufficient for the potential rate of growth. In time, the investment

[1] See p. 276 above.
[2] See, for instance, W. Beckerman, 'The determinants of economic growth', in P. D. Henderson (ed.), *Economic Growth in Britain* (Weidenfeld & Nicolson, 1966); N. Kaldor, 'Conflicts in national economic objectives', *Economic Journal*, vol. LXXXI (Mar 1971); and John Mills, *Growth and Welfare: A New Policy for Britain* (Martin Robertson, 1972).

M*

function will rise towards X because the rate of profit will be rising, but governments may not wish to wait until this has its full effect. If they so manage demand that the savings function falls to $S'S'$, investment will at once become sufficient for the potential rate of growth, but the economy will no longer be working at normal capacity. This will again have inflationary and balance of payments consequences, so governments may again only be able to achieve an economy's growth potential if they have adequate policies to deal with the balance of payments consequences of overcapacity working.

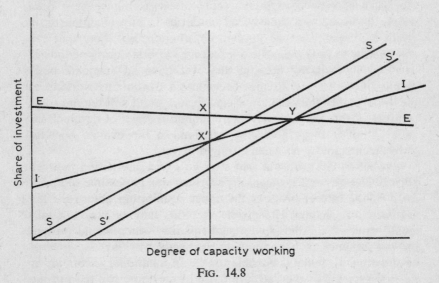

Fig. 14.8

It is then very far from clear that control over the level of effective demand gives governments the power to avoid fluctuations. These are inherent in a situation where the investment function is steeper than the saving function over part of its range, and it has been shown that there may even be difficulties where the relationship between these functions is an entirely stable one. However, if situations are correctly diagnosed, governments can at least make rational choices between the various possible policies. There are clearly situations where full employment, growth at the potential rate, stable exchange rates and the containment of inflationary pressure cannot all be achieved in the short run, and public policies should depend on conscious political choices between these objectives.

A Postscript on Equality

Much of this book has been concerned with the problem of distribution, so it is appropriate to conclude with a few words about the implications of the argument for policy to redistribute incomes and wealth. It was argued in Chapter 13 that the distribution of incomes between earned incomes and profits depends on three basic sets of factors. Income distribution at full employment will depend partly on the economy's fundamental equations, and partly on the market power of labour and capital. In addition, the share of profits will vary with the economy's actual degree of capacity working. Now the growth policies that have been outlined in this chapter will be favourable to profits through all three of these sets of considerations. The demand management policies which have just been discussed point to the desirability of high degrees of capacity working. The policies to produce faster equilibrium growth rates will, almost without exception, raise the share of profits, for faster equilibrium growth is almost inevitably associated with a higher share of profits. The chances that the market power of labour will be raised relatively to that of capital appear slight, for the various tax policies that favour investment and research and development are likely to favour large established firms more than they favour newcomers, so the degree of monopoly is likely, if anything, to be raised; though this line of argument is clearly weaker than the others. That faster growth will almost certainly be associated with a higher share of profits has serious social consequences.

It is widely believed that income and wealth should be distributed more equally than they are in most developed economies. Inequalities in earned income can be reduced to a considerable extent through the tax system if there is sufficient political support for this, but a major source of inequality in most countries is due to the unearned incomes and capital gains that accrue to those with great wealth. There are particular problems in redistributing incomes derived from profits because of the role these play in the growth process and, given this, those who wish to reduce inequality will find it disturbing that the policies which favour growth and efficiency are likely to produce a more unequal distribution of incomes and wealth. Some might consider this a high price to pay for growth.

It may be that there is no real cause for concern about the connection between faster growth and the share of profits in the National

Income, for there are two broad reasons why the share of profits may be expected to fall through time, and indeed it has fallen in the U.K. and the U.S.A. in the past century. It appeared in Chapter 11 that economies of scale may have unfavourable long-term effects on the share of profits, and it appeared in Chapter 13 that industry may need an increasing degree of monopoly to maintain profits in the face of growing ratios of salaried staff. Then the favourable effects for profits of faster growth may do no more than temporarily arrest declining trends. There is, however, no reason at all to expect historical trends towards a more equal distribution of wealth, and there is no evidence of any tendencies in this direction. Given this, it must disturb those who favour redistribution that faster growth will give much to the owners of industrial capital whose wealth will inevitably increase with the nation's capital stock.

One method of breaking the connection between growth and the dominant ownership of wealth by a few is believed to be the imposition of high and effective capital gains taxes, wealth taxes and death duties, but the argument of this book suggests that this approach to the problem is superficial. In the first place, a considerable proportion of capital gains and wealth taxes is likely to be passed on if the argument of the earlier part of this chapter is correct, with the result that they will reduce the rate of growth and output per worker, and only redistribute income in so far as there is less profit where there is less growth. Then they will not break the connection between growth and inequality. They will merely involve the choice of less of both. More fundamentally, it can be shown that capital gains taxes, wealth taxes and death duties will only redistribute wealth if workers' saving is substantial and runs far ahead of saving for house ownership. The importance of this line of argument follows directly from Pasinetti's theory of the determination of the rate of profit, where he points out the fundamental importance of the relationship between the ownership of wealth and the proportion of saving that is contributed by the various classes. In equilibrium, the proportion of total saving by each class must equal the proportion of wealth owned by each class. Then if manual workers save for nothing but house ownership, it follows that they cannot own any proportion of the nation's industrial wealth. No kind of profit or wealth taxation can alter this fact. Wealth can be taxed at any rate at all and the nation's industrial capital must still be owned by those who save.[1] In the absence of workers' saving, the sole effect of attempts to tax wealth owners more heavily will be to weaken the investment function which will raise the rate of profit (before tax) and reduce the rate of growth. The distribution of industrial wealth will remain untouched. The taxation of private wealth owners may of course permit the accumulation of public wealth, but if the bulk of industry is privately owned, the profit-earning part of the capital stock will remain in the same hands as before.

While this conclusion is discouraging to a particular line of social policy, there is an alternative approach to the problem through which much may be achieved. There are vast obstacles in the way of the direct redistribution of wealth, but the problems involved in changing the share of aggregate saving that is contributed by workers and property owners are much simpler to solve. If workers can be persuaded to contribute half a country's savings, they will come to own half of its wealth, and this process can be accelerated quite sharply. If a wealth tax is a tax on the accumulation of the rich, then the other half of redistributional policy is a subsidy on the accumulation of the poor, in other words the subsidisation of the interest paid to workers on such wealth as they possess. There is doubt about the effect of the interest rate on saving, so it may be questioned whether higher interest rates will produce more workers' saving. However, these doubts are largely due to the fact that higher interest rates produce a positive substitution effect in favour of saving and a negative income effect against saving, and the latter will not apply to most manual workers for they do not have significant expected future incomes from wealth. They are subject solely to the incentive to substitute future income for present incomes, so interest incentives should be favourable to workers' saving and particularly the interest rates of around 25 per cent that are paid on limited sums (mainly by making some saving tax-deductible) in countries that seek to encourage widespread property ownership. Such interest rates may not be so very much more than the marginal social return on investment when increasing returns and the external effects of investment on technical progress are allowed for. Moreover, the subsidisation of workers' interest would only require higher taxation elsewhere (to achieve a given degree of capacity working) if net workers' saving failed to rise, and an increase in aggregate saving would be

[1] My attention was drawn to this line of argument by a paper which R. Nowell-Smith read in Oxford in 1971.

compatible with a reduction in the interest rates paid by borrowers (of fixed-interest as against equity finance), and a reduction in the shadow interest rate used in the public sector.

In countries that have not specifically adopted policies to subsidise interest on small savings, workers are often exploited with interest rates that are kept down to provide cheap public sector finance, so that the poor receive lower yields on their saving than the rich. In the U.K., in particular, the interest rates paid by the Government for small savings are often particularly low, and the ratio of workers' saving in the National Income is also very low.[1] It is no accident that the distribution of wealth is highly unequal. To change this state of affairs by subsidising the interest on small saving presents a line of policy which stands a genuine chance of altering the distribution of wealth, and this follows directly from modern growth theory. With policies which are less deeply rooted in economic theory, causes and symptoms are easily confused.

It has been argued that some of the other theory outlined in this book is relevant to policy problems. The scope for more effective economic management and more effective policies for social change will obviously be great if the fundamental theory that underlies the working of economics can be understood. In modern economies there are important interconnections between the rate of profit, the share of profits, the share of investment, the rate of growth, technical progress functions, returns to scale, and so on. Such interconnections are bound to be exceedingly complex, but they are also of fundamental importance. In this book, an attempt has been made to clarify some of these interrelationships, and to suggest certain new ones.

[1] See, for instance, Sir John Hicks, 'Saving, investment and taxation: an international comparison', *Three Banks Review* (June 1968).

References

A. Ando and F. Modigliani, 'The "life cycle" hypothesis of saving: aggregate implications and tests', *American Economic Review*, vol. LIII (Mar 1963).

A. Ando (1960), *see* F. Modigliani.

K. J. Arrow, H. B. Chenery, B. Minhas and R. M. Solow, 'Capital–labour substitution and economic efficiency', *Review of Economics and Statistics*, vol. XLIII (Aug 1961).

K. J. Arrow, 'The economic implications of learning by doing', *Review of Economic Studies*, vol. XXIX (June 1962).

H. Asher, *Cost–Quantity Relationships in the Airframe Industry*, R-291 (Santa Monica, Calif.: RAND Corporation, 1956).

Pranab Bardhan, 'Equilibrium growth in a model with economic obsolescence of machines', *Quarterly Journal of Economics*, vol. LXXXIII (May 1969).

W. Beckerman and Associates, *The British Economy in 1975* (Cambridge U.P., 1965).

W. Beckerman, 'The determinants of economic growth', in P. D. Henderson (ed.), *Economic Growth in Britain* (London: Weidenfeld & Nicolson, 1966).

J. Black, 'The technical progress function and the production function', *Economica*, vol. XXIX (May 1962).

J. Black, 'Technical progress and optimum savings', *Review of Economic Studies*, vol. XXIX (June 1962).

C. J. Bliss, 'On putty-clay', *Review of Economic Studies*, vol. XXXV (Apr 1968).

Murray Brown and J. S. de Cani, 'Technological change and the distribution of income', *International Economic Review*, vol. IV (Sep 1963).

E. H. Phelps Brown and P. E. Hart, 'The share of wages in National Income', *Economic Journal*, vol. LXII (June 1952).

E. H. Phelps Brown and Margaret H. Browne, *A Century of Pay* (London: Macmillan, 1968).

M. Bruno, E. Burmeister and E. Sheshinski, 'Nature and implications of the reswitching of techniques', *Quarterly Journal of Economics*, vol. LXXX (Nov 1966).

E. Burmeister and A. R. Dobell, *Mathematical Theories of Economic Growth* (New York: Macmillan, 1970).

E. Burmeister (1966), *see* M. Bruno.

J. S. de Cani (1963), *see* Murray Brown.

D. G. Champernowne, 'Some implications of golden age conditions when savings equal profits', *Review of Economic Studies*, vol. XXIX (June 1962).

H. B. Chenery (1961), *see* K. J. Arrow.

Colin Clark, *Population Growth and Land Use* (London: Macmillan, 1967).

C. W. Cobb and Paul H. Douglas, 'A theory of production', *American Economic Review*, supplement, vol. XVIII (Mar 1928).

J. Conlisk, 'A neoclassical growth model with endogenously positioned technical change frontier', *Economic Journal*, vol. LXXIX (June 1969).

E. F. Denison, assisted by Jean-Pierre Poullier, *Why Growth Rates Differ: Postwar Experience in Nine Western Countries* (Washington, D.C.: Brookings Institution, 1967).

A. R. Dobell (1970), *see* E. Burmeister.

Paul H. Douglas (1928), *see* C. W. Cobb.

W. A. Eltis, 'Investment, technical progress, and economic growth', *Oxford Economic Papers*, vol. XV (Mar 1963).

W. A. Eltis, *Economic Growth: Analysis and Policy* (London: Hutchinson, 1966).

W. A. Eltis, 'Technical progress, profits, and growth', *Oxford Economic Papers*, vol. XX (July 1968).

W. A. Eltis, M. FG. Scott and J. N. Wolfe (eds.), *Induction, Growth and Trade: Essays in Honour of Sir Roy Harrod* (Oxford U.P., 1970).

W. A. Eltis, 'The determination of the rate of technical progress', *Economic Journal*, vol. LXXXI (Sep 1971).

W. A. Eltis, 'Taxation and investment', in Sir Robert Shone (ed.), *Problems of Investment* (Oxford: Basil Blackwell, 1971).

W. Fellner, 'Trends in the activities generating technical progress', *American Economic Review*, vol. LX (Mar 1970).

Milton Friedman, *Essays in Positive Economics* (Chicago U.P., 1953).

Milton Friedman, *A Theory of the Consumption Function* (Princeton U.P., 1957).

J. K. Galbraith, *The New Industrial State* (London: Hamish Hamilton, 1967).

H. A. J. Green, 'Growth models, capital and stability', *Economic Journal*, vol. LXX (Mar 1960).

Z. Griliches (1967), *see* D. W. Jorgensen.

F. H. Hahn and R. C. O. Matthews, 'The theory of economic growth: a survey', *Economic Journal*, vol. LXXIV (Dec 1964).

Bernard F. Haley, 'Distribution in the United States', in Jean Marchal and Bernard Ducros (eds.), *The Distribution of National Income* (London: Macmillan, 1968).

R. S. Hamada, 'Portfolio analysis, market equilibrium and corporation finance', *Journal of Finance*, vol. XXIV (Mar 1969).

G. C. Harcourt, *Some Cambridge Controversies in the Theory of Capital* (Cambridge U.P., 1972).

R. F. Harrod, 'An essay in dynamic theory', *Economic Journal*, vol. XLIX (Mar 1939).

R. F. Harrod, review of J. R. Hicks, *Value and Capital*, in *Economic Journal*, vol. XLIX (June 1939).

R. F. Harrod, *Towards a Dynamic Economics* (London: Macmillan, 1948).

R. F. Harrod, *Economic Essays* (London: Macmillan, 1952).

R. F. Harrod, 'Are monetary and fiscal policies enough?', *Economic Journal*, vol. LXXIV (Dec 1964).

P. E. Hart (1952), *see* E. H. Phelps Brown.

J. L. Harvey and A. Newgarden (eds.), *Management Guides to Mergers and Acquisitions* (New York: Wiley, 1969).

J. R. Hicks, *The Theory of Wages* (London: Macmillan, 1932).

J. R. Hicks, 'Thoughts on the theory of capital – the Corfu Conference', *Oxford Economic Papers*, vol. XII (June 1960).

J. R. Hicks, *Capital and Growth* (Oxford U.P., 1965).

J. R. Hicks, *Critical Essays in Monetary Theory* (Oxford U.P., 1967).

Sir John Hicks, 'Saving, investment and taxation: an international comparison', *Three Banks Review* (London), June 1968.

J. R. Hicks, 'A Neo-Austrian growth theory', *Economic Journal*, vol. LXXX (June 1970).

J. Hirshleifer, *Investment, Interest and Capital* (Englewood Cliffs, N.J.: Prentice-Hall, 1970).

M. Inagaki, review of R. M. Solow, *Growth Theory: An Exposition*, in *Journal of Economic Literature*, vol. x (June 1972).

H. G. Johnson, 'The neo-classical one-sector growth model: a geometrical exposition and extension to a monetary economy', *Economica*, vol. xxxiii (Aug 1966).

D. W. Jorgensen and Z. Griliches, 'The explanation of productivity change', *Review of Economic Studies*, vol. xxxiv (July 1967).

N. Kaldor, 'A model of the trade cycle', *Economic Journal*, vol. l (Mar 1940).

N. Kaldor, *An Expenditure Tax* (London: Allen & Unwin, 1955).

N. Kaldor, 'Alternative theories of distribution', *Review of Economic Studies*, vol. xxiii (1955-6).

N. Kaldor, 'A model of economic growth', *Economic Journal*, vol. lxvii (Dec 1957).

N. Kaldor, 'Capital accumulation and economic growth', in F. A. Lutz and D. C. Hague (eds.), *The Theory of Capital* (London: Macmillan, 1961).

N. Kaldor and J. A. Mirrlees, 'A new model of economic growth', *Review of Economic Studies*, vol. xxix (June 1962).

N. Kaldor, 'Marginal productivity and the macro-economic theories of distribution', *Review of Economic Studies*, vol. xxxiii (Oct 1966).

N. Kaldor, *Causes of the Slow Rate of Growth of the United Kingdom*, Inaugural Lecture (Cambridge U.P., 1966).

N. Kaldor, 'Conflicts in national economic objectives', *Economic Journal*, vol. lxxxi (Mar 1971).

M. Kalecki, 'The determinants of distribution of the National Income', *Econometrica*, vol. vi (Apr 1938).

M. Kalecki, *Essays in the Theory of Economic Fluctuations* (London: Allen & Unwin, 1939).

M. Kalecki, *Theory of Economic Dynamics* (London: Allen & Unwin, 1954).

M. Kalecki, *Studies in the Theory of Business Cycles 1933-9* (Oxford: Basil Blackwell, 1966).

J. W. Kendrick and R. Sato, 'Factor prices, productivity and economic growth', *American Economic Review*, vol. liii (Dec 1963).

C. M. Kennedy, 'Induced bias in innovation and the theory of distribution', *Economic Journal*, vol. lxxiv (Sep 1964).

Kieran A. Kennedy, *Productivity and Industrial Growth: The Irish Experience* (Oxford U.P., 1971).

J. M. Keynes, *A Treatise on Money* (London: Macmillan, 1930).

J. M. Keynes, *The General Theory of Employment, Interest and Money* (London: Macmillan, 1936).

L. R. Klein and R. F. Kosobud, 'Some econometrics of growth: great ratios of economics', *Quarterly Journal of Economics*, vol. LXXV (May 1961).

H. Leibenstein, 'Allocative efficiency versus X-efficiency', *American Economic Review*, vol. LVI (June 1966).

David Levhari and Paul A. Samuelson, 'The nonswitching theorem is false', *Quarterly Journal of Economics*, vol. LXXX (Nov 1966).

T. R. Malthus, *Essay on Population*, 3rd ed. (London, 1806).

T. R. Malthus, *Principles of Political Economy*, 1st ed. (London, 1820).

Edwin Mansfield, *The Economics of Technological Change* (London: Longmans, 1969).

Robin Marris, *The Economic Theory of 'Managerial' Capitalism* (London: Macmillan, 1964).

Alvin L. Marty, 'The neoclassical theorem', *American Economic Review*, vol. LIV (Dec 1964).

R. C. O. Matthews, 'The new view of investment: Comment', *Quarterly Journal of Economics*, vol. LXXVIII (Feb 1964).

R. C. O. Matthews (1964), *see* F. H. Hahn.

J. E. Meade, 'The effect of savings on consumption in a state of steady growth', *Review of Economic Studies*, vol. XXIX (June 1962).

Merton H. Miller (1958), *see* Franco Modigliani.

John Mills, *Growth and Welfare: A New Policy for Britain* (London: Martin Robertson, 1972).

B. Minhas (1961), *see* K. J. Arrow.

J. A. Mirrlees (1962), *see* N. Kaldor.

Franco Modigliani and Merton H. Miller, 'The cost of capital, corporation finance, and the theory of investment', *American Economic Review*, vol. XLVIII (June 1958).

Franco Modigliani and A. Ando, 'The permanent income and the life cycle hypothesis of saving behaviour: comparisons and tests', in *Proceedings of the Conference on Consumption and Saving*, vol. II (Philadelphia, 1960).

Franco Modigliani (1963), *see* A. Ando.

Franco Modigliani, 'The life cycle hypothesis of saving and inter-country differences in the saving ratio', in W. A. Eltis, M. FG. Scott and J. N. Wolfe (eds.), *Induction, Growth and Trade: Essays in Honour of Sir Roy Harrod* (Oxford U.P., 1970).

K. A. Naqvi (1967), *see* Joan Robinson.

William D. Nordhaus, *Invention, Growth and Welfare* (Cambridge, Mass.: MIT Press, 1969).

L. L. Pasinetti, 'Rate of profit and income distribution in relation to the rate of economic growth', *Review of Economic Studies*, vol. XXIX (Oct 1962).

L. L. Pasinetti, 'Changes in the rate of profit and switches of technique', *Quarterly Journal of Economics*, vol. LXXX (Nov 1966).

David Ricardo, *Works and Correspondence*, ed. P. Sraffa (Cambridge U.P., 1951).

Joan Robinson, *The Economics of Imperfect Competition* (London: Macmillan, 1933).

Joan Robinson, 'Euler's theorem and the problem of distribution', *Economic Journal*, vol. XLIV (Sep 1934).

Joan Robinson, 'The model of an expanding economy', *Economic Journal*, vol. LXII (Mar 1952).

Joan Robinson, 'The production function and the theory of capital', *Review of Economic Studies*, vol. XXI (1953-4).

Joan Robinson, *The Accumulation of Capital* (London: Macmillan, 1956).

Joan Robinson, 'A neo-classical theorem', *Review of Economic Studies*, vol. XXIX (June 1962).

Joan Robinson, *Essays in the Theory of Economic Growth* (London: Macmillan, 1962).

Joan Robinson, 'Solow on the rate of return', *Economic Journal*, vol. LXXIV (June 1964).

Joan Robinson and K. A. Naqvi, 'The badly behaved production function', *Quarterly Journal of Economics*, vol. LXXXI (Nov 1967).

Paul A. Samuelson (1966), *see* David Levhari.

R. Sato, 'The estimation of biased technical progress and the production function', *International Economic Review*, vol. XI (June 1970).

R. Sato (1963), *see* J. W. Kendrick,

Joseph A. Schumpeter, *The Theory of Economic Development* (Cambridge, Mass.: Harvard U.P., 1934).

M. FG. Scott, 'Supply and demand refurbished', *Oxford Economic Papers*, vol. XIX (July 1967).

E. Sheshinski (1966). *see* M. Bruno.

Sir Robert Shone, *Investment and Economic Growth*, Stamp Memorial Lecture (London: Athlone Press, 1966).

R. M. Solow, 'A contribution to the theory of economic growth', *Quarterly Journal of Economics*, vol. LXX (Feb 1956).

R. M. Solow, 'Technical change and the aggregate production function', *Review of Economics and Statistics*, vol. XXXIX (Aug 1957).

R. M. Solow, *Growth Theory: An Exposition* (Oxford U.P., 1970).

R. M. Solow (1961), *see* K. J. Arrow.

T. Sowell, 'The general glut controversy reconsidered', *Oxford Economic Papers*, vol. XV (Nov 1963).

P. Sraffa, *Production of Commodities by Means of Commodities* (Cambridge U.P., 1960).

J. Steindl, *Maturity and Stagnation in American Capitalism* (Oxford: Basil Blackwell, 1952).

P. J. Verdoorn, 'Fattori che regolano lo svillupo della produttività del lavoro', *L'Industria* (1947).

A. A. Walters, 'Production and cost functions', *Econometrica*, vol. XXXI (Jan–Apr 1963).

Knut Wicksell, *Lectures on Political Economy* (London: Routledge & Kegan Paul, 1934).

P. J. D. Wiles, *Price, Cost and Output*, 2nd ed. (Oxford: Basil Blackwell, 1961).

T. P. Wright, 'Factors affecting the cost of airplanes', *Journal of the Aeronautical Sciences*, III (1936).

Allyn Young, 'Increasing returns and economic progress', *Economic Journal*, vol. XXXVIII (Dec 1928).

Official

Monthly Bulletin of Statistics (United Nations, New York).

National Accounts of OECD Countries (OECD, Paris).

Royal Commission on the Taxation of Profits and Income, *Final Report*, Cmd 9474 (London: HMSO, June 1955).

Index